Handbook of Software Engineering

Volume II

Handbook of Software Engineering
Volume II

Edited by **Tom Halt**

CLANRYE INTERNATIONAL

New Jersey

Published by Clanrye International,
55 Van Reypen Street,
Jersey City, NJ 07306, USA
www.clanryeinternational.com

Handbook of Software Engineering: Volume II
Edited by Tom Halt

International Standard Book Number: 978-1-63240-294-3 (Hardback)

Printed in the United States of America.

Contents

Permissions

List of Contributors

Preface

Software engineering is an area of computer science engineering, which is related to designing, development, and maintenance of software. It wouldn't be wrong to say that Software Engineering is one of the youngest braches of engineering. In fact, it started only in the early 1940s and it was not before the year 1968 that the term itself was coined.

In today's world, this field has many applications in all branches of engineering. However, software engineering was initially introduced to address issues related to poor quality of software and ensure that software is built systematically and within the prescribed budget. Essentially, software engineering can be divided into ten sub-disciplines.

There are a limited set of activities involved in the production of a software development procedure. Software can never be manufactured; it is always developed with some parameters kept in mind. There is no single ideal approach to develop software. However, there are some procedural activities which are involved in the entire development process such as waterfall model, spiral model, agile model, etc. A software development process is never ending because iteration is always made to improve the quality of the product, even after it is delivered. These iterations are called updates. Software is a very essential part of computer science.

In this book, these aspects are discussed in chapters. I especially wish to acknowledge the contributing authors, without whom a work of this magnitude would clearly not have been realizable. I would also like to thank my publisher for giving me this unparalleled opportunity and my family for their continuous support.

Editor

A Simple Application Program Interface for Saving Java Program Data on a Wiki

Takashi Yamanoue, Kentaro Oda, and Koichi Shimozono

Computing and Communications Center, Kagoshima University, Korimoto, Kagoshima 890-0065, Japan

Correspondence should be addressed to Takashi Yamanoue, yamanoue@cc.kagoshima-u.ac.jp

Academic Editor: Andreas Menychtas

A simple application program interface (API) for Java programs running on a wiki is implemented experimentally. A Java program with the API can be running on a wiki, and the Java program can save its data on the wiki. The Java program consists of PukiWiki, which is a popular wiki in Japan, and a plug-in, which starts up Java programs and classes of Java. A Java applet with default access privilege cannot save its data at a local host. We have constructed an API of applets for easy and unified data input and output at a remote host. We also combined the proposed API and the wiki system by introducing a wiki tag for starting Java applets. It is easy to introduce new types of applications using the proposed API. We have embedded programs such as a simple text editor, a simple music editor, a simple drawing program, and programming environments in a PukiWiki system using this API.

1. Introduction

The Web is currently one of the most important infrastructures. However, managing a web site is not easy, and it is necessary to upload a file to a web server each time a new web page is created or an existing web page is modified. For example, teachers, including university instructors, often use web sites in class. However, preparing web-based learning materials is troublesome. In order to facilitate this task, we use a content management system (CMS), such as wiki software.

A wiki [1] is a web site that allows the easy creation and editing of any number of interlinked web pages via a web browser and can be used as a means of effective collaboration and information sharing. Wikipedia [2] is a well-known wiki site.

The Internet provides a large number of Java applets, through which multimedia data can be used. Such multimedia data can be used on wiki sites. As such, a number of wikis have extensions or plug-ins for embedding Java applets. Saving such Java applet data on a wiki site is advantageous, which makes the wiki more flexible and extensible. This allows more effective collaboration between users.

PukiWiki [3] software is commonly used in Japan. We have constructed an API for applets in order to allow easy and unified data input and output at a remote host. Moreover, we have combined the API and the PukiWiki system by introducing a wiki tag for starting Java applets. The proposed API, which can be used to make the wiki more flexible and extensible, is referred to as the *PukiWiki-Java Connector*.

The PukiWiki-Java Connector enables a number of Java programs to be easily embedded in PukiWiki. We have embedded programs such as a simple text editor, a simple music editor, a simple drawing program, a programming environment, and a voice recorder in PukiWiki. One to three days was required for embedding.

2. Pukiwiki-JAVA Connector

2.1. Outline of Usage. A wiki [1] is a web site whose users can add, modify, or delete its content via a web browser using a simplified markup language or a rich-text editor. Wikis are often used for collaboration. Users of a wiki create and edit each others content when they collaborate using the wiki. Users of a wiki often would like to use not only texts but also other rich media content such like figures or sounds for effective collaboration. Many of wikis can have such contents. However, it was hard to add and modify such contents via web browsers. PukiWiki-Java connector is a tool to solve such problem.

To implement our proposed connector to a wiki, we need a wiki platform, which is simple to extend and easy to deploy. We choose PukiWiki [4] as the platform. PukiWiki is simple to deploy than many other wikis because it needs minimized requirements; it even requires no data base engines such as MySQL. Installing Pukiwiki is just extracting PukiWiki tarball to the root directory of the web page. PukiWki also puts minimized requirements for its plugin specification [4]; it defines a relatively small set of rules to create plugins. So There are a lot of plug-ins for PukiWiki. PukiWiki supports not only Japanese language but also English, Chinese, and French.

The PukiWiki-Java Connector enables a Java program to input and output data on a remote host. A PukiWiki system is run at the host, and the system starts the Java program as a PukiWiki plug-in.

Figure 1 shows a use case diagram of the PukWiki-Java Connector and related items. A programmer creates the Java program for PukiWiki using the PukiWiki-Java Connector in a programming environment such as Eclipse. A web administrator uploads the Java program to a directory in the PukiWiki system. A user writes a PukiWiki web page that includes a Java program plug-in using a web browser on the user's side. A user uses the Java program by displaying the web page in a web browser. The user can save program data in the page. The data is loaded to the Java program when the user, or another user, next uses the program. Users can collaborate through Java programs using the PukiWiki-Java Connector.

It is easy to copy the saved data from the page to another page of the PukiWiki system that has the same Java program by coping and pasting the page.

Occasionally, we would like to use a wiki for a closed group. Basic authentication is an easy way to realize this task. The PukiWiki-Java Connector can also be used for a web site with basic authentication. When a Java program with the PukiWiki-Java Connector saves data to or loads data from a web page with basic authentication [5], a dialog box pops up, prompting the user to input an ID and corresponding password. Figure 2 shows an example of the dialog box.

Figure 3 shows an outline of the use of the PukiWiki-Java Connector. In this figure, Java program X is a program that uses PukiWiki-Java Connector. In addition, "#jcon(X)" is the plug-in for starting Java program X. Java program X is downloaded to a web browser at the user side when the wiki page with "#jcon(X)" is displayed by the web browser. The data of Java program X can be saved to or loaded from a page.

In order to save data to or load data from a web page, the PukiWiki-Java Connector provides an interface with the following methods. Java program X can implement the interface for saving and loading data:

public String getOutput();

public void setInput(String x);

public void setSaveButtonDebugFrame
(SaveButtonDebugFrame f);

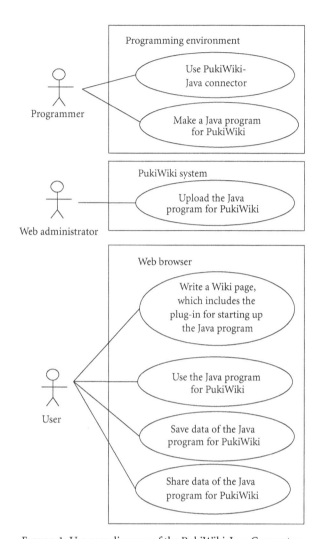

FIGURE 1: Use case diagram of the PukiWiki-Java Connector.

Here, get Output() is called from the PukiWiki-Java Connector when the data of Java program X is saved. The programmer of Java program X writes the code for returning the data to be saved as String type data in this override method. Moreover, setInput(String x) is called from the PukiWiki-Java Connector when data on the wiki page is loaded to this program. The programmer writes the code for inputting the data in this override method. Then, setSave-ButtonDebugFrame is used for debugging. *Factory method pattern* [6] is used to facilitate the embedding of several Java programs to PukiWiki. Figure 4 shows a class diagram of factory method pattern for the PukiWiki-Java Connector. In this figure, PukiWikiApplet is the abstract class that is started from the PukiWiki system. PukiWikiJavaApplication is the interface for a Java program that uses the PukiWiki-Java Connector. MyApplet is a concrete class for creating a Java program, and X is a concrete class of Java program X. MyApplet.class and X.class should be in the directory of *./javaApplications/bin/application/X/*.

2.2. Outline of Implementation. We assume that *wiki page X* contains the wiki tag, which starts the *Java program X* with

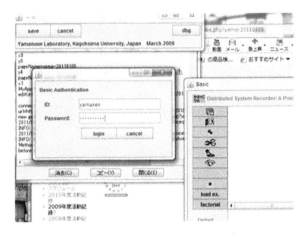

FIGURE 2: Basic authentication dialog box.

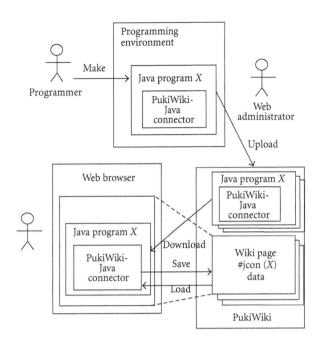

FIGURE 3: Outline of the use of the PukiWiki-Java Connector.

Pukiwiki-Java connector. *Data of X* is loaded from the page and it is saved to the page. Wiki page X has its *page name*.

Starting a Java Program. In order to start the Java program with the PukiWiki-Java Connector, the PukiWiki system must have the PHP code for the #jcon(X) plug-in. Algorithm 1 shows the PHP code. This code starts the applet at the path *./javaApplication/bin/applications/X/MyApplet*. Then, adding or modifying a PukiWiki system plug-in is not required for embedding a new Java application using the PukiWiki-Java Connector.

When the Java program X is started from the wiki page X, the URL of the page and the page name are acquired by the applet. The URL is used for loading data from the page. The URL and the page name are used for saving data to the page.

Loading Data. The source text of the wiki page X is acquired by *SaveButtonDegugFrame* class after the starting using the URL. The class looks for the saved data by parsing the page. The data is located in the page after the line of the wiki tag "#jcon(X)", and the data is enclosed by the tags "<pre>" and "</pre>". The tags show preformatted text in HTML. If the data was found out, the data is extracted from the wiki page, and it is sent to the Java program X using the set Input(x) method of the program. The *GetMethod* class of *Apache HttpClient* [7] is used for acquiring the page.

Saving Data. When the "save" button of the PukiWiki-Java connector is clicked, the source text of the wiki page X in the editing mode is acquired by the *SaveButtonDebugFrame* class using the URL for the editing mode and the *GetMethod* class. In the case of PukiWiki, the URL of a wiki page in the editing mode is represented by Algorithm 1.

The source text of the page for editing mode contains a pair of form tags <form ... > and </form>. The pair text area tags <textarea ... > and </textarea> is enclosed by the form tags. The text between the pair of text area tags shows the current source text of the wiki page in PukiWiki page syntax. So the text between the pair of text area tags has the

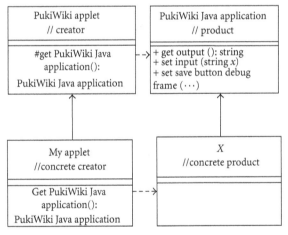

FIGURE 4: Factory method pattern for the PukiWiki-Java Connector.

#jcon(X) tag. In this mode, the data of X in normal mode wiki page is represented by the text in PukiWiki page syntax in instead of enclosed by the pair of <pre> and </pre> tags. Algorithm 2 shows an example of the source text of the page for editing mode.

The text after <textarea ... > tag until #jcon(X) tag is extracted and saved as the header text for saving.

After that, the getOutput() method of the Java program X is called from the *SaveButtonDebugFrame* class. This method returns the new text data for saving. The new text data is transformed into preformatted text in PukiWiki page format. The new page text for saving is created by concatenating the header text for saving and the new data in pre-formatted text. The new page text is saved to the PukiWiki site using the *Post Method* class of Apache Http Client.

```
[URL of the wiki page]?cmd=edit&page=[page name]
<?php
//PukiWiki - Yet another WikiWikiWeb clone
//
//jcon.inc.php
//     t.yamanoue, 2010
//...
function plugin_jcon_convert()
{
    if (PKWK_READONLY) return ";//Show nothing
    $args = func_get_args();//args
    if (count($args) >= 1) {$aw = array_shift($args);} else {$aw = 'draw';}
    $java_application_name = htmlspecialchars($aw,ENT_QUOTES);
        $ret = ";//return value
    $charset=CONTENT_CHARSET;
    $uri=get_script_uri();
$jcode="application.".$java_application_name.".MyApplet.class";
    $plginname="jcon(".$java_application_name.")";
        $ret = <<<EOD
<div>
<applet codebase= "./javaApplications/bin" code="$jcode"
    archive= "lib/commons-codec-1.3.jar,lib/commons-httpclient-3.1.jar,
        lib/commons-logging-1.1.1.jar"
    width="100" height="100">
<param name="action" value="$uri"/>
<param name="param1" value="plugin=$plginname"/>
<param name="charset" value="$charset"/>
</div>
EOD;
    return $ret;
}
?>
```

ALGORITHM 1: PHP code for starting the Java program with the PukiWiki-Java Connector.

```
....
<form .... >
<textarea ... >
...
#jcon (X)
Hello! (Data for X in pre-formatted syntax)
</textarea>
</form>
...
```

ALGORITHM 2: An example of the source text of the page in editing mode.

3. Using Sample Programs

We have created several sample Java programs using the PukiWiki-Java Connector. We also have created a PukiWiki system using these java programs and the plug-in PHP code of Figure 4 in order to allow users to easily try out a combination of Java programs with the PukiWiki-Java Connector and the PukiWiki system. The system can be downloaded at http://yama-linux.cc.kagoshima-u.ac.jp/pukiwiki-java/.

3.1. Simple Text Editor. Creating a simple text editor using the *JTextEditor* class in the swing package of Java is simple. We have embedded a text editor in the PukiWiki system using the PukiWiki-Java Connector. The user can use the text editor by writing the "#jcon(myEditor)" tag at the left side of a line in the editing page of PukiWiki (Figure 5). Then, when the user clicks the update button, the simple text editor and a small window for saving the test editor data will appear on the display (Figure 6). When the user clicks the "save" button in the small window after entering text, as shown in Figure 7, the written letters are saved on the wiki page, as shown in Figure 8.

3.2. Simple Music Editor. Another application is allowing several people to collaborate in creating music. In order to demonstrate this application, we have created a simple music editor for PukiWiki using Java codes on the Web. Figure 9 shows the GUI of the simple music editor. This music editor is started by the "#jcon(musicEditor2)" wiki tag. The user of this editor records a melody using the key board of the editor after clicking the "record" button. A vertical bar, which represents a note of the melody, appears in the editor when a key is pressed while recording. Recording will be ended

FIGURE 5: Tag that starts the simple text editor in the editing page of PukiWiki.

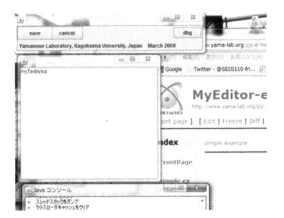

FIGURE 6: The simple text editor and the small window for saving data.

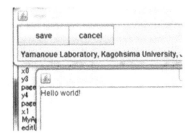

FIGURE 7: Close-up view of the simple text editor.

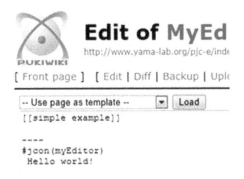

FIGURE 8: Saved text.

when the "stop" button is clicked. Notes can be added and edited after the recording using "new," "cut," "res" (reset), "mov" (move), "mod" (modify), and "clr" (clear) buttons, and when the "play" button is clicked, the melody is played. The melody is rewind by clicking the "—≪" button. When the "save" button is clicked, the notes are saved in the wiki page. One note of the melody is represented by the following line in the wiki page. *#t,[start time],n,[MIDI note number],l,[duration of the note].*

3.3. Draw. Another application is to share drawings among a group of people who are needed to collaborate frequently. The drawings should be modified by the group members as if the members were drawing on a white board during a meeting. In order to realize this capability, we embedded a drawing program into the PukiWiki system. We modified the drawing program of SOLAR-CATS [8, 9], which is a computer-assisted teaching system. This drawing program is started by the "#jcon(draw)" wiki tag. A drawing of this program is saved to wiki pages as a vector data text. Figure 10 shows an example of a drawing and its saved data. Figure 11 shows an example of using the drawing program to display a map of restaurants. The map was saved on a wiki page and can be modified when a new restaurant is opened or a restaurant closes. We also use this drawing program for in our own classes. Explanatory drawings can be improved during class and saved.

3.4. Programming Environment. Figure 12 shows an example of using a simple programming environment for a basic-like programming language that is embedded in the PukiWiki system. This environment is started by the "#jcon(basic)" wiki tag. The programming environment is also ported from SOLAR-CATS. The drawing program of the previous subsection is used for graphics output. This can be used for situations such like the following.

(1) A teacher of a class shows a program example in a wiki page to students.

(2) Students copy the program to their own wiki page and run the program in a web browser using this programming environment.

(3) The teacher tells students to make a specified program as an exercise of the class by modifying the original program.

(4) The teacher evaluates programs by running the programs at students' pages in the teacher's web browser.

We also have embedded PEN [10], a Japanese programming language's programming environment, into PukiWiki using this API.

Programs on a wiki make wiki pages rich and interactive.

3.5. Voice Recorder. Figure 13 shows an example of using a voice recorder. This is started by the "#jcon(voiceRecorder)" wiki tag. Voice is recorded when the "record" button is clicked. The recorded voice is played when the "play" button is clicked. Recording or playing will be stopped when the

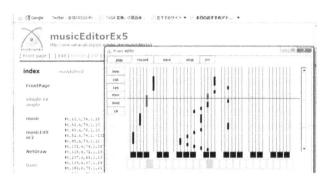

FIGURE 9: GUI of the simple music editor.

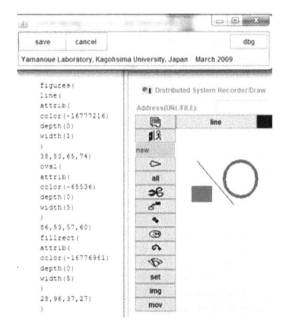

FIGURE 10: Drawing and its saved data.

"stop" button is clicked. The recorded voice is cleared when the "clear" button is clicked. Wave data of the recorded voice is encoded into a series of letters. A part of them is shown in the recorder's window, and they are stored in the page of PukiWiki when the "save" button is clicked. The saved voice is played again when the "play" button is clicked after the recorder window of the page is shown again.

It is not difficult to save many kinds of binary data to a page of PukiWiki using such encoding like this voice recorder.

4. Embedding Your Own Program

In this section, we demonstrate how to embed your own Java program using the PukiWiki-Java Connector in the PukiWiki system.

4.1. Downloading the API. First, an SDK of the PukiWiki-Java Connector, that is, *javaApplications.zip* or *javaApplications.jar*, should be downloaded to your Java programming environment. These SDKs can be downloaded from http://yama-linux.cc.kagoshima-u.ac.jp/pukiwiki-java/. After unzipping the file, the *javaApplications* directory will appear. In this section, the path of this directory is represented as <javaApplications>.

4.2. Creating the Source Directory. The new Java program is labeled *newAppli*. A new directory, named *newAppli*, should be created in the <javaApplications>/src/application directory. Then, *newAppli* will be the argument of the #jcon PukiWiki plug-in. newAppli is started by the #jcon(newAppli) tag at the left-most position of the editing page of PukiWiki.

4.3. Copying and Modifying MyApplet.Java. Next, MyApplet.java, in the *<javaApplications>/src/application/myEditro* directory, should be copied to the new <javaApplications>/src/application/newAppli directory.

For MyApplet.java in the new directory, the package declaration should be changed to application.new Appli, and the line "frame=new MyEditor();" should be changed to "frame=new New Appli();". Appropriate arguments are added to the constructor if needed. The method getPukiWikiJavaApplication is the factory method. The following is an example of the rewritten MyApplet.java:

```
package application.newAppli;
import connector.*;
public class MyApplet extends PukiWikiApplet{
    public PukiWikiJavaApplication getPukiWikiJava-
    Application(){
        System.out.println(
            "MyApplet.getPukiWikiJavaApplication");
        if(frame==null){
            frame=new MyEditor();
        }
        return this.frame;
    }
}.
```

The "connector" package in the above code includes, for example, a program for communicating with the PukiWiki

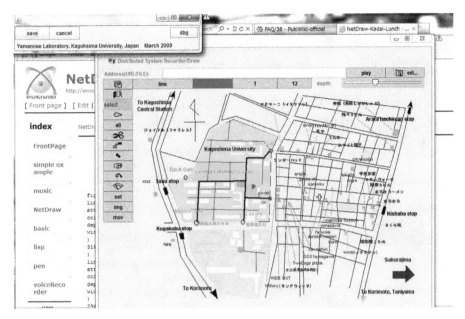

FIGURE 11: A map of restaurants displayed by the drawing program.

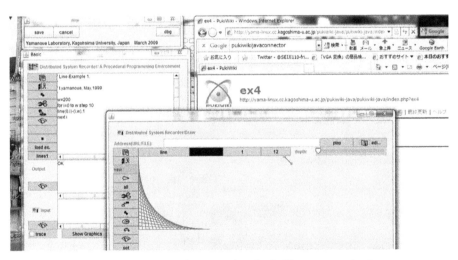

FIGURE 12: Programming environment for a basic-like programming language.

FIGURE 13: Voice recorder.

system, a wiki page syntax analyzer, and various translators for embedding data in the wiki page.

4.4. Copying the New Application Source Program. The source program of the new application should be copied into the newAppli source directory, that is, <javaApplications>/src/ application/newAppli. This application must have a subclass of the JFrame class. This subclass is started from the Puki-Wiki system. The name of this class is herein assumed to be NewAppli, and the source of this class is NewAppli.java. Other source programs are also copied into an appropriate directory if these programs are required by NewAppli.java.

4.5. Implementing the Interface. NewAppli.java must implement the PukiWikiJavaApplication interface, as shown in

Section 2. The connector package must also be imported, as exemplified by the following code:

```
package application.newAppli;

import connector.*;

…

public class NewAppli extends JFrame
    implements PukiWikiJavaApplication
{

    …

}.
```

The following three methods should be overridden in order to implement the PukiWikiJavaApplication interface, as shown in Section 2.

```
@Override
public String getOutput() {
    //TODO Auto-generated method stub
}
@Override
public void setInput(String x) {
    //TODO Auto-generated method stub
}
@Override
Public void setSaveButtonDebugFrame
    (SaveButtonDebugFrame f) {
    //TODO Auto-generated method stub
}.
```

The following code shows an example of an implementation of the overridden methods.

```
public String getOutput() {
    return this.myTextArea.getText(); //add
}
public void setInput(String x) {
    this.myTextArea.setText(x); //add
}
public void setSaveButtonDebugFrame
    (SaveButtonDebugFrame f) {
}.
```

4.6. Compiling and Uploading. The source codes in the newAppli directory should then be compiled. We assume that the compiled classes in the newAppli directory are in <javaApplications>/bin/application/newAppli directory and all other classes for running the NewAppli are in the <java-Applications>/bin directory. A local server program such as Xampp [11] can be used for debugging on the local host. If there are no errors, then all classes should be uploaded into the *./javaApplications/bin* directory of the PukiWiki system of the web server. The PukiWiki-Java Connector requires Apache httpclient. The jar files of httpclients must be in the *./javaApplications/bin/lib* directory. Finally, adding or modifying the PukiWiki system is not necessary.

5. Evaluation

5.1. Enriched Wiki Content. In Section 3, we demonstrated that a draw application, programming environments, and a music editor can be embedded into wiki content. Introducing new applications with the PukiWiki-Java connector is simple.

5.2. Minimized Porting Cost. The PukiWiki-Java Connector is already equipped with a wiki page syntax analyzer and various translators for embedding data into a wiki page. These components are easy to reuse by a programmer using the factory method pattern without thinking of such cumbersome things like a syntax analyzer and translators. Approximately three days were needed for one person to embed the drawing program of SOLAR-CATS into the Puki-Wiki system. Approximately three weeks were needed for one person to create a similar drawing program from scratch. Approximately two hours were needed for one person to embed the simple text editor into the PukiWiki system. Finally, approximately one day was needed for one person to embed the simple music editor and the programming environment for a basic-like programming language.

6. Related Research

There are many kinds of wiki software. Some of them are capable to have rich media content like PukiWiki with PukiWiki-Java connector. We compare such wikis and related work with PukiWiki with PukiWiki-Java connector in this section.

6.1. Java Applet Extensions and Plug-Ins. Some wikis, such as MediaWiki [12] and PukiWiki [3], have an extension or plug-in for starting a Java applet. However, these extensions do not have the ability to save the applet's data in a wiki page.

6.2. AnyWikiDraw. AnyWikiDraw [13] data can be saved on a wiki page. In addition, AnyWikiDraw can be used with various wikis, such as TWiki, PmWiki, and MediaWiki. However, AnyWikiDraw is a specialized system for drawing. On the other hand, Pukiwiki-Java connector is a general purpose API for embedding Java programs.

6.3. Galaxy Wiki. Galaxy Wiki [14] is a software development environment. Developers are able to experience "writing wiki page is wring source code" using this. Moreover, developers are able to compile, execute, and debug programs in wiki pages too. Galaxy Wiki is also a specialized system for software development.

6.4. AddesoWiki. Adessowiki [15] is a collaborative environment for development, documentation, teaching and knowledge repository of scientific computing algorithms. The system is composed of a collection of collaborative web pages in the form of a wiki. The articles of this wiki can embed programming code that will be executed on the server when the page is rendered, incorporating the results as figures, texts, and tables on the document. On the other hand, programs which use PukiWiki-Java connector are executed on local hosts. This makes the CPU load of hosts lighten.

6.5. Lively Wiki. Lively Wiki [16] is a development and collaboration environment based on the Lively Kernel, which enables users to create rich, interactive Web pages and applications. Lively Wiki can be used to expand itself. It is written entirely in JavaScript. Although our goals are similar to those of Lively Wiki, for conventional users, who cannot write JavaScript codes, using Lively Wiki is too complicated.

6.6. mbed. mbed [4] is a tool for rapid prototyping with microcontrollers. A web top programming environment can be used in the Web site of mbed such as Galaxy Wiki and AddesoWiki. The programming environment of mbed is also a specialized system for software development.

6.7. WIKIAPI. The WIKIAPI [2] provides a standard Java API to enable reading and writing to a wiki from within a Java Application. The Wiki API supports MediaWiki, MoinMoin Wiki, TWiki, and Confluence Wiki. WIKIAPI is used for accessing wiki pages from a Java application running on a local host. On the other hand, PukiWiki-Java connector is used for embedding Java applications and their data on wiki pages.

7. Concluding Remarks

We proposed the PukiWiki-Java Connecter, which is an API of applets for easy, unified data input and output at a remote host. The PukiWiki-Java Connecter is used to save Java program data in wiki pages. We also combined the proposed API and a wiki system by introducing a wiki tag for starting Java applets. A number of Java programs were demonstrated to embed into the wiki system in a short time. We intend to improve the proposed API by facilitating its use after obtaining feedback from users.

References

[1] W. Cunningham, "Wiki Wiki Web," 1995, http://c2.com/cgi/wiki?WikiWikiWeb.

[2] WIKIAPI, 2012, http://jwikiapi.sourceforge.net/.

[3] PukiWiki, 2001, http://pukiwiki.sourceforge.jp/.

[4] mbed, 2012, http://mbed.org.

[5] J. Franks, P. Hallam-Baker, J. Hostetler et al., "HTTP Authentication: Basic and Digest Access Authenti," RFC 2617, 1999.

[6] E. Gamma, R. Helman, R. Johnson, and J. Vlissides, *Design Patterns: Elements of Reusable Object-Oriented Software*, Addison-Wesley Longman, Boston, Mass, USA, 1995.

[7] HttpClient Home, 2010, http://hc.apache.org/httpcomponents-client-ga/.

[8] T. Yamanoue, "Sharing the same operation with a large number of users using P2P," in *3rd International Conference on Information Technology and Applications (ICITA '05)*, vol. 2, pp. 85–88, July 2005.

[9] T. Yamanoue, "A casual teaching tool for large size computer laboratories and small size seminar classes," in *Proceedings of the ACM SIGUCCS Fall Conference (SIGUCCS '09)*, pp. 211–216, October 2009.

[10] T. Nishida, A. Harada, R. Nakamura, Y. Miyamoto, and T. Matsuura, "Implementation and evaluation of PEN: the programming environment for novice," *IPSJ Journal*, vol. 47, no. 4, pp. 1063–1076, 2006 (Japanese).

[11] Wikipedia, 2011, http://www.wikipedia.org/.

[12] MediaWiki, 2007, http://www.mediawiki.org/wiki/MediaWiki.

[13] AnyWikiDraw, 2011, http://www.randelshofer.ch/anywikidraw/index.html.

[14] W. Xiao, C. Chi, and M. Yang, "On-line collaborative software development via wiki," in *International Conference on Object-Oriented Programming, Systems, Languages and Applications (OOPSLA '07)*, pp. 177–183, October 2007.

[15] R. A. Lotufo, R. C. Machado, A. Körbes, and R. G. Ramos, "Adessowiki on-line collaborative scientific programming platform," in *5th International Symposium on Wikis and Open Collaboration (WiKiSym '09)*, October 2009.

[16] R. Krahn, D. Ingalls, R. Hirschfeld, J. Lincke, and K. Palacz, "Lively wiki a development environment for creating and sharing active web content," in *5th International Symposium on Wikis and Open Collaboration (WiKiSym '09)*, Orland, Fla, USA, October 2009.

2

An Empirical Study on the Impact of Duplicate Code

Keisuke Hotta, Yui Sasaki, Yukiko Sano, Yoshiki Higo, and Shinji Kusumoto

Graduate School of Information Science and Technology, Osaka University, Osaka 565-0871, Japan

Correspondence should be addressed to Keisuke Hotta, k-hotta@ist.osaka-u.ac.jp

Academic Editor: Osamu Mizuno

It is said that the presence of duplicate code is one of the factors that make software maintenance more difficult. Many research efforts have been performed on detecting, removing, or managing duplicate code on this basis. However, some researchers doubt this basis in recent years and have conducted empirical studies to investigate the influence of the presence of duplicate code. In this study, we conduct an empirical study to investigate this matter from a different standpoint from previous studies. In this study, we define a new indicator "modification frequency" to measure the impact of duplicate code and compare the values between duplicate code and nonduplicate code. The features of this study are as follows the indicator used in this study is based on modification places instead of the ratio of modified lines; we use multiple duplicate code detection tools to reduce biases of detection tools; and we compare the result of the proposed method with other two investigation methods. The result shows that duplicate code tends to be less frequently modified than nonduplicate code, and we found some instances that the proposed method can evaluate the influence of duplicate code more accurately than the existing investigation methods.

1. Introduction

Recently, duplicate code has received much attention. Duplicate code is also called as "code clone." Duplicate code is defined as identical or similar code fragments to each other in the source code, and they are generated by various reasons such as copy-and-paste programming. It is said that the presence of duplicate code has negative impacts on software development and maintenance. For example, they increase bug occurrences: if an instance of duplicate code is changed for fixing bugs or adding new features, its correspondents have to be changed simultaneously; if the correspondents are not changed inadvertently, bugs are newly introduced to them.

Various kinds of research efforts have been performed for resolving or improving the problems caused by the presence of duplicate code. For example, there are currently a variety of techniques available to detect duplicate code [1]. In addition, there are many research efforts for merging duplicate code as a single module like function or method, or for preventing duplications from being overlooked in modification [2, 3]. However, there are precisely the opposite opinions that code cloning is a good choice for design of the source code [4].

In order to answer the question whether duplicate code is harmful or not, several efforts have proposed comparison methods between duplicate code and nonduplicate code. Each of them compares a characteristic of duplicate code and nonduplicate code instead of directly investigating their maintenance cost. This is because measuring the actual maintenance cost is quite difficult. However, there is no consensus on this matter.

In this paper, we conduct an empirical study that compares duplicate code to nonduplicate code from a different standpoint of previous research and reports the experimental result on open source software. The features of the investigation method in this paper are as follows:

(i) every line of code is investigated whether it is duplicate code or not; such a fine-grained investigation can accurately judge whether every modification conducted to duplicate code or to nonduplicate code;

(ii) maintenance cost consists of not only source code modification but also several phases prior to it; in order to more appropriately estimate maintenance cost, we define an indicator that is not based on modified lines of code but the number of modified places;

(iii) we evaluate and compare modifications of duplicate code and nonduplicate code on multiple open source software systems with multiple duplicate code detection tools, that is, because every detection tool detects different duplicate code from the same source code.

We also conducted a comparison experiment with two previous investigation methods. The purpose of this experiment is to reveal whether comparisons between duplicate code and nonduplicate code with different methods yield the same result or not. In addition, we carefully analyzed the results in the cases that the comparison results were different from each method to reveal the causes behind the differences.

The rest of this paper is organized as follows: Section 2 describes related works and our motivation of this study. Section 3 introduces the preliminaries. We situate our research questions and propose a new investigation method in Section 4. Section 5 describes the design of our experiments, then we report the results in Sections 6 and 7. Section 8 discusses threats to validity, and Section 9 presents the conclusion and future work of this study.

2. Motivation

2.1. Related Work. At present, there is a huge body of work on empirical evidence on duplicate code shown in Table 1. The pioneering report in this area is Kim et al.'s study on clone genealogies [5]. They have conducted an empirical study on two open source software systems and found 38% or 36% of groups of duplicate code were consistently changed at least one time. On the other hand, they observed that there were groups of duplicate code that existed only for a short period (5 or 10 revisions) because each instance of the groups was modified inconsistently. Their work is the first empirical evidence that a part of duplicate code increases the cost of source code modification.

However, Kapser and Godfrey have different opinions regarding duplicate code. They reported that duplicate code can be a reasonable design decision based on the empirical study on two large-scale open source systems [4]. They built several patterns of duplicate code in the target systems, and they discussed the pros and cons of duplicate code using the patterns. Bettenburg et al. also reported that duplicate code does not have much a negative impact on software quality [6]. They investigated inconsistent changes to duplicate code at release level on two open software systems, and they found that only 1.26% to 3.23% of inconsistent changes introduced software errors into the target systems.

Monden et al. investigated the relation between software quality and duplicate code on the file unit [7]. They use the number of revisions of every file as a barometer of quality: if the number of revisions of a file is great, its quality is low. Their experiment selected a large-scale legacy system, which was being operated in a public institution, as the target. The result showed that modules that included duplicate code were 40% lower quality than modules that did not include duplicate code. Moreover, they reported that the larger duplicate code a source file included, the lower quality it was.

Lozano et al. investigated whether the presence of duplicate code was harmful or not [8]. They developed a tool, CloneTracker, which traces which methods include duplicate code (in short, duplicate method) and which methods are modified in each revision. They conducted a pilot study, and found that: duplicate methods tend to be more frequently modified than nonduplicate methods; however, duplicate methods tend to be modified less simultaneously than nonduplicate methods. The fact implies that the presence of duplicate code increased cost for modification, and programmers were not aware of the duplication, so that they sometimes overlooked code fragments that had to be modified simultaneously.

Also, Lozano and Wermelinger investigated the impact of duplicate code on software maintenance [9]. Three barometers were used in the investigation. The first one is *likelihood*, which indicates the possibility that the method is modified in a revision. The second one is *impact*, which indicates the number of methods that are simultaneously modified with the method. The third one is *work*, which can be represented as a product of *likelihood* and *impact* ($work = likelihood \times impact$). They conducted a case study on 4 open source systems for comparing the three barometers of methods including and not including duplicate code. The result was that *likelihood* of methods including duplicate code was not so different from one of methods not including duplicate code; there were some instances that *impact* of methods including duplicate code were greater than one of methods not including duplicate code; if duplicate code existed in methods for a long time, their *work* tended to increase greatly.

Moreover, Lozano et al. investigated the relation between duplicate code, features of methods, and their changeability [10]. Changeability means the ease of modification. If changeability decreased, it will be a bottleneck of software maintenance. The result showed that the presence of duplicate code can decrease changeability. However, they found that changeability was more greatly affected by other properties such as length, fan-out, and complexity of methods. Consequently, they concluded that it was not necessary to consider duplicate code as a primary option.

Krinke hypothesized that if duplicate code is less stable than nonduplicate code, maintenance cost for duplicate code is greater than for nonduplicate code. He conducted a case study in order to investigate whether the hypothesis is true or not [11]. The targets are 200 revisions (a version per week) of source code of 5 large-scale open-source systems. He measured *added*, *deleted*, and *changed* LOCs on duplicate code and nonduplicate code and compared them. He reported that nonduplicate code was more *added*, *deleted*, and *changed* than duplicate code. Consequently, he concluded that the presence of duplicate code did not necessarily make it more difficult to maintain source code.

Göde and Harder replicated Krinke's experiment [12]. Krinke's original experiment detected line-based duplicate code meanwhile their experiment detected token-based duplicate code. The experimental result was the same as Krinke's one. Duplicate code is more stable than nonduplicate code in the viewpoint of added and changed. On

TABLE 1: Summarization of related work.

	How to investigate	Impact of duplicate code
Kim et al. [5]	Using clone linages and clone genealogies	A part of duplicate code is negative
Kapser and Godfrey [4]	Build several patterns of duplicate code and discuss about them	Nonnegative
Bettenburg et al. [6]	Investigate inconsistent changes to duplicate code at the release revel	Nonnegative
Monden et al. [7]	Calculate the number of revisions on every file	Negative
Lozano et al. [8]	Count the number of modifications on methods including duplicate code	Negative
Lozano and Wermelinger [9]	Using *work*	A part of duplicate code is negative
Lozano et al. [10]	Using changeability (the ease of modification)	Negative but not so high
Krinke [11]	Using stability (line level)	Nonnegative
Göde and Harder [12]	Using stability (token level)	Nonnegative
Krinke [13]	Using ages	Nonnegative
Rahman et al. [14]	Investigate the relationship between duplicate code and bugs	Nonnegative
Göde and Koschke [15]	Count the number of changes on clone genealogies	A part of duplicate code is negative

the other hand, from the deleted viewpoint, nonduplicate code is more stable than duplicate code.

Also, Krinke conducted an empirical study to investigate ages of duplicate code [13]. In this study, he calculated and compared average ages of duplicate lines and nonduplicate lines on 4 large-scale Java software systems. He found that the average age of duplicate code is older than nonduplicate code, which implies duplicate code is more stable than nonduplicate code.

Eick et al. investigated whether source code decays when it is operated and maintained for a long time [16]. They selected several metrics such as the amount of *added* and *deleted* code, the time required for modification, and the number of developers as indicators of code decay. The experimental result on a 15-year-operated large system showed that cost required for completing a single requirement tendS to increase.

Rahman et al. investigated the relationship between duplicate code and bugs [14]. They analyzed 4 software systems written in C language with bug information stored in Bugzilla. They use Deckard, which is an AST-based detection tool, to detect duplicate code. They reported that only a small part of the bugs located on duplicate code, and the presence of duplicate code did not dominate bug appearances.

Göde modeled how type-1 code clones are generated and how they evolved [17]. Type-1 code clone is a code clone that is exactly identical to its correspondents except white spaces and tabs. He applied the model to 9 open-source software systems and investigated how code clones in them evolved. The result showed that the ratio of code duplication was decreasing as time passed; the average life time of code clones was over 1 year; in the case that code clones were modified inconsistently, there were a few instances that additional modifications were performed to restore their consistency.

Also, Göde and Koschke conducted an empirical study on clone evolution and performed a detailed tracking to detect when and how clones had been changed [15]. In their study, they traced clone evolution and counted the number of changes on each clone genealogy. They manually inspected

the result in one of the target systems and categorized all the modifications on clones into consistent or inconsistent. In addition, they carefully categorized inconsistent changes into intentional or unintentional. They reported that almost all clones were never changed or only once during their lifetime, and only 3% of the modifications had high severity. Therefore, they concluded that many of clones do not cause additional change effort, and it is important to identify the clones with high threat potential to manage duplicate code effectively.

As described above, some empirical studies reported that duplicate code should have a negative impact on software evolution meanwhile the others reported the opposite result. At present, there is no consensus on the impact of the presence of duplicate code on software evolution. Consequently, this research is performed as a replication of the previous studies with solid settings.

2.2. Motivating Example. As described in Section 2.1, many research efforts have been performed on evaluating the influence of duplicate code. However, these investigation methods still have some points that they did not evaluate. We explain these points with the example shown in Figure 1. In this example, there are two similar methods and some places are modified. We classified these modifications into 4 parts, modification A, B, C, and D.

Investigated Units. In some studies, large units (e.g., files or methods) are used as their investigation units. In those investigation methods, it is assumed that duplicate code has a negative impact if files or methods having a certain amount of duplicate code are modified, which can cause a problem. The problem is the incorrectness of modifications count. For example, if modifications are performed on a method which has a certain amount of duplicate code, all the modifications are assumed as performed on the duplicate code even if they are actually performed on nonduplicate code of the method. Modification C in Figure 1 is an instance of this problem. This modification is performed on nonduplicate

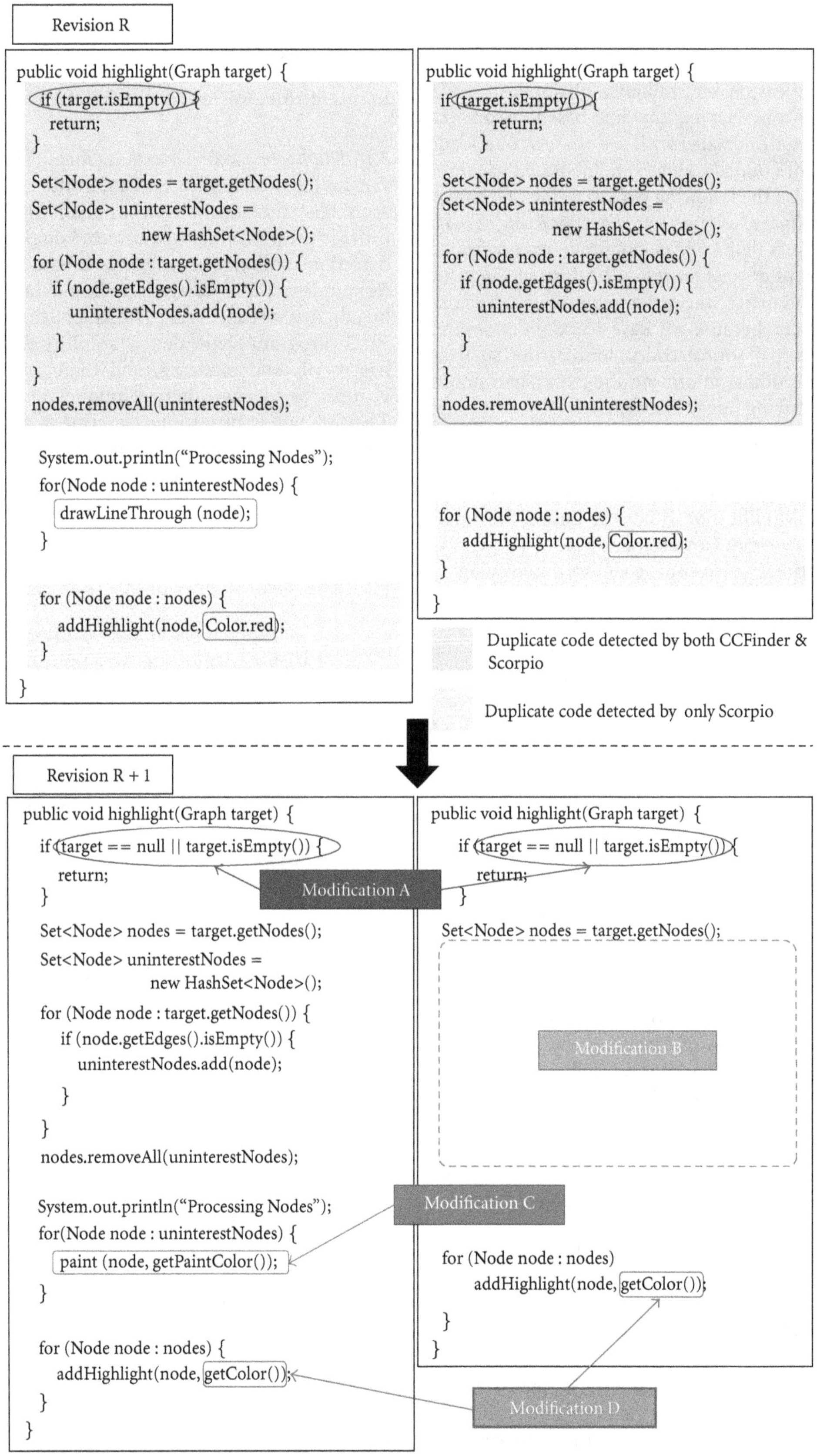

FIGURE 1: Motivating example.

code; nevertheless, it is regarded that this modification is performed on duplicate code if we use method as the investigation units.

Line-Based Barometers. In some studies, line-based barometers are used to measure the influence of duplicate code on software evolution. Herein, the line-based barometer indicates a barometer calculated with the amount of added/changed/deleted lines of code. However, line-based barometer cannot distinguish the following two cases: the first case is that *consecutive 10 lines of code were modified for fixing a single bug*; the second case is that *1 line modification was performed on different 10 places of code for fixing 10 different bugs*. In real software maintenance, the latter requires much more cost than the former because we have to conduct several steps before the actual source code modification such as identifying buggy module, informing the maintainer about the bugs, and identifying buggy instruction.

In Figure 1, Modification A is 1 line modification, and performed on 2 places, meanwhile Modification B is 7 lines modification on a single place. With line-based barometers, it is regarded that Modification B has the impact 3.5 times larger than Modification A. However, this is not true because we have to identify 2 places of code for modifying A meanwhile 1 place identification is required for B.

A Single Detection Tool. In the previous studies, a single detection tool was used to detect duplicate code. However, there is neither a generic nor strict definition of duplicate code. Each detection tool has its own unique definition of duplicate code, and it detects duplicate code based on the own definition. Consequently, different duplicate code is detected by different detection tools from the same source code. Therefore, the investigation result with one detector is different from the result from another detector. In Figure 1, a detector CCFinder detects lines highlighted with red as duplicate code, and another detector Scorpio detects not only lines highlighted with red but also lines highlighted with orange before modification. Therefore, if we use Scorpio, Modification D is regarded as being affected with duplicate code, nevertheless, it is regarded as not being affected with duplicate code if we use CCFinder. Consequently, the investigation with a single detector is not sufficient to get the generic result about the impact of duplicate code.

2.2.1. Objective of This Study. In this paper, we conducted an empirical study from a different standpoint of previous research. The features of this study are as follows.

Fine-Grained Investigation Units. In this study, every line of code is investigated whether it is duplicate code or not, which enables us to judge whether every modification is conducted on duplicate code or nonduplicate code.

Place-Based Indicator. We define a new indicator based on the number of modified places, not the number of modified lines. The purpose of place-based indicator is to evaluate the impact of the presence of duplicate code with different standpoints from the previous research.

Multiply Detector. In this study, we use 4 duplicate code detection tools to reduce biases of each detection method.

3. Preliminaries

In this section, we describe preliminaries used in this paper.

3.1. Duplicate Code Detection Tools. There are currently various kinds of duplicate code detection tools. The detection tools take the source code as their input data, and they provide the position of the detected duplicate code in it. The detection tools can be categorized based on their detection techniques. Major categories should be line based, token based, metrics based, AST (Abstract Syntax Tree) based, and PDG (Program Dependence Graph) based. Each technique has merits and demerits, and there is no technique that is superior to any other techniques in every way [1, 18]. The following subsections describe 4 detection tools that are used in this research. We use two token-based detection tools, which is for investigating whether both the token-based detection tools always introduce the same result or not.

3.1.1. CCFinder. CCFinder is a token-based detection tool [19]. The major features of CCFinder are as follows.

(i) CCFinder replaces user-defined identifiers such as variable names or function names with special tokens before the matching process. Consequently, CCFinder can identify code fragments that use different variables as duplicate code.

(ii) Detection speed is very fast. CCFinder can detects duplicate code from millions lines of code within an hour.

(iii) CCFinder can handle multiple popular programming languages such as C/C++, Java, and COBOL.

3.1.2. CCFinderX. CCFinderX is a major version up from CCFinder [20]. CCFinderX is a token-based detection tool as well as CCFinder, but the detection algorithm was changed to *bucket sort* to *suffix tree*. CCFinderX can handle more programming languages than CCFinder. Moreover, it can effectively use resources of multi core CPUs for faster detection.

3.1.3. Simian. Simian is a line-based detection tool [21]. As well as CCFinder family, Simian can handle multiple programming languages. Its line-based technique realizes duplicate code detection on small memory usage and short running time. Also, Simian allows fine-grained settings. For example, we can configure that duplicate code is not detected from *import* statements in the case of Java language.

3.1.4. Scorpio. Scorpio is a PDG-based detection tool [22, 23]. Scorpio builds a special PDG for duplicate code detection, not traditional one. In traditional PDGs, there are two types of edge representing data dependence and control dependence. The special PDG used in Scorpio has one

(a) *before modification*
  (1) A
  (2) B
  (3) line will be changed 1
  (4) line will be changed 2
  (5) C
  (6) D
  (7) line will be deleted 1
  (8) line will be deleted 2
  (9) E
  (10) F
  (11) G
  (12) H

(b) *after modification*
  (1) A
  (2) B
  (3) line changed 1
  (4) line changed 2
  (5) C
  (6) D
  (7) E
  (8) F
  (9) G
  (10) line added 1
  (11) line added 2
  (12) H

(c) *diff output*
3,4c3,4
<   line will be changed 1
<   line will be changed 2

>   line changed 1
>   line changed 2
7,8d6
<   line will be deleted 1
<   line will be deleted 2
11a10,11
>   line added 1
>   line added 2

ALGORITHM 1: A simple example of comparing two source files with `diff` (changed region is represented with identifier "c" like 3,4c3,4; deleted region is represented with identifier "d" like 7,8d6, added region is represented with identifier "a" like 11a10,11). The number before and after the identifier shows the correspond lines.

more edge, execution-next link, which allows detecting more duplicate code than traditional PDG. Also, `Scorpio` adopts some heuristics for filtering out false positives. Currently, `Scorpio` can handle only Java language.

3.2. Revision. In this paper, we analyze historical data managed by version control systems for investigation. Version control systems store information about changes to documents or programs. We can specify changes by using a number, *"revision"*. We can get source code in arbitrary revision, and we can also get modified files, change logs, and the name of developers who made changes in arbitrary two consecutive revisions with version control systems.

Due to the limit of implementation, we restrict the target version control system to Subversion. However, it is possible to use other version control systems such as CVS.

3.3. Target Revision. In this study, we are only interested in changes in source files. Therefore, we find out revisions that have some modifications in source files. We call such revisions as *target revisions*. We regard a revision R as the target revision, if at least one source file is modified from R to $R + 1$.

3.4. Modification Place. In this research, we use the number of places of modified code, instead lines of modified code. That is, even if multiple consecutive lines are modified, we regard it as a single modification. In order to identify the number of modifications, we use UNIX diff command. Algorithm 1 shows an example of diff output. In this example, we can find 3 modification places. One is a change in line 3 and 4, another is a deletion in line 7 and 8, and the other is an addition at line 11. As shown in the algorithm, it is very easy to identify multiple consecutive modified lines as a single modification; all we have to do is just parsing the output of diff so that the start line and end line of all the modifications are identified.

4. Proposed Method

This section describes our research questions and the investigation method.

4.1. Research Questions and Hypotheses. The purpose of this research is to reveal whether the presence of duplicate code really affects software evolution or not. We assume that *if duplicate code is more frequently modified than nonduplicate code, the presence of duplicate code has a negative impact on software evolution*. This is because if much duplicate code is included in source code though, it is never modified during its lifetime, the presence of duplicate code never causes inconsistent changes or additional modification efforts. Our research questions are as follows.

RQ1: Is duplicate code more frequently modified than non-duplicate code?

RQ2: Are the comparison results of stability between duplicate code and nonduplicate code different from multiple detection tools?

RQ3: Is duplicate code modified uniformly throughout its lifetime?

RQ4: Are there any differences in the comparison results on modification types?

To answer these research questions, we define an indicator, *modification frequency* (in short, MF). We measure and compare MF of duplicate code (in short, MF_d) and MF of nonduplicate code (in short, MF_n) for investigation.

4.2. Modification Frequency

4.2.1. Definition. As described above, we use MF to estimate the influence of duplicate code. MF is an indicator based on the number of modified code, not lines of modified code. This is because this research aims to investigate from a different standpoint from previous research.

We define MF_d in the formula:

$$MF_d = \frac{\sum_{r \in R} MC_d(r)}{|R|}, \tag{1}$$

where R is a set of target revisions, $MC_d(r)$ is the number of modifications on duplicate code between revision r and $r + 1$. We also define MF_n in the formula:

$$MF_n = \frac{\sum_{r \in R} MC_n(r)}{|R|}, \tag{2}$$

where $MC_n(r)$ is the number of modifications on nonduplicate code between revision r and $r + 1$.

These values mean the average number of modifications on duplicate code or nonduplicate code per revision. However, in these definitions, MF_d and MF_n are very affected by the amount of duplicate code included the source code. For example, if the amount of duplicate code is very small, it is quite natural that the number of modifications on duplicate code is much smaller than nonduplicate code. However, if a small amount of duplicate code is included but it is quite frequently modified, we need additional maintenance efforts to judge whether its correspondents need the same modifications or not. We cannot evaluate the influence of duplicate code in these situations in these definitions.

In order to eliminate the bias of the amount of duplicate code, we normalize the formulae (1) and (2) with the ratio of duplicate code. Here, we assume that

(i) $LOC_d(r)$ is the total lines of duplicate code in revision r,

(ii) $LOC_n(r)$ is the total lines of nonduplicate code on r,

(iii) $LOC(r)$ is the total lines of code on r, so that the following formula is satisfied:

$$LOC(r) = LOC_d(r) + LOC_n(r). \tag{3}$$

Under these assumptions, the normalized MF_d and MF_n are defined in the following formula:

$$
\begin{aligned}
\text{normalized } MF_d &= \frac{\sum_{r \in R} MC_d(r)}{|R|} \times \frac{\sum_{r \in R} LOC(r)}{\sum_{r \in R} LOC_d(r)}, \\
\text{normalized } MF_n &= \frac{\sum_{r \in R} MC_n(r)}{|R|} \times \frac{\sum_{r \in R} LOC(r)}{\sum_{r \in R} LOC_n(r)}.
\end{aligned} \tag{4}
$$

In the reminder of this paper, the normalized MF_d and MF_n are called as just MF_d and MF_n, respectively.

4.2.2. Measurement Steps. The MF_d and MF_n are measured with the following steps,

Step 1. It identifies target revisions from the repositories of target software systems. Then, all the target revisions are checked out into the local storage.

Step 2. It normalized all the source files in every target revision.

Step 3. It detects duplicate code within every target revision. Then, the detection result is analyzed in order to identify the file path, the lines of all the detected duplicate code.

Step 4. It identifies differences between two consecutive revisions. The start lines and the end lines of all the differences are stored.

Step 5. It counts the number of modifications on duplicate code and nonduplicate code.

Step 6. It calculates MF_d and MF_n.

In the reminder of this subsection, we explain each step of the measurement in detail.

Step 1. It obtains Target Revisions. In order to measure MF_d and MF_n, it is necessary to obtain the historical data of the source code. As described above, we used a version control system, Subversion, to obtain the historical data.

Firstly, we identify which files are modified, added, or deleted in each revision and find out target revisions. After identifying all the target revision from the historical data, they are checked out into the local storage.

Step 2. It normalizes Source Files. In the Step 2, every source file in all the target revisions is normalized with the following rules:

(i) deletes blank lines, code comments, and indents,

(ii) deletes lines that consist of only a single open/close brace, and the open/close brace is added to the end of the previous line.

The presence of code comments influences the measurement of MF_d and MF_n. If a code comment is located within a duplicate code, it is regarded as a part of duplicate code even if it is not a program instruction. Thus, the LOC of duplicate code is counted greater than it really is. Also, there is no common rule how code comments should be treated if they are located in the border of duplicate code and nonduplicate code, which can cause a problem that a certain detection tool regards such a code comment as duplicate code meanwhile another tool regards it as nonduplicate code.

As mentioned above, the presence of code comments makes it more difficult to identify the position of duplicate code accurately. Consequently, all the code comments are removed completely. As well as code comments, different detection tools handle blank lines, indents, lines including only a single open or close brace in different ways, which also influence the result of duplicate code detection. For this reason, blank lines and indents are removed, and lines that consist of only a single open or close brace are removed, and

TABLE 2: Target software systems—Experiment 1.

(a) Experiment 1.1

Name	Domain	Programming language	Number of Revisions	LOC (latest revision)
EclEmma	Testing	Java	788	15,328
FileZilla	FTP	C++	3,450	87,282
FreeCol	Game	Java	5,963	89,661
SQuirrel SQL Client	Database	Java	5,351	207,376
WinMerge	Text Processing	C++	7,082	130,283

(b) Experiment 1.2

Name	Domain	Programming language	Number of Revisions	LOC (latest revision)
ThreeCAM	3D Modeling	Java	14	3,854
DatabaseToUML	Database	Java	59	19,695
AdServerBeans	Web	Java	98	7,406
NatMonitor	Network (NAT)	Java	128	1,139
OpenYMSG	Messenger	Java	141	130,072
QMailAdmin	Mail	C	312	173,688
Tritonn	Database	C/C++	100	45,368
Newsstar	Network (NNTP)	C	165	192,716
Hamachi-GUI	GUI, Network (VPN)	C	190	65,790
GameScanner	Game	C/C++	420	1,214,570

TABLE 3: Overview of Investigation Methods.

Method	Krinke [11]	Lozano and Wermelinger [9]	Proposed method
Target Revisions	A revision per week	All	All
Investigation Unit	Line	Method	Place (consecutive lines)
Measure	ratio of Modified lines	*Work*	Modification frequency

the removed open or close brace is added to the end of the previous line.

Step 3. It detects Duplicate Code. In this step, duplicate code is detected from every target revision, and the detection results are stored into a database. Each detected duplicate code is identified by 3-tuple (v, f, l), where v is the revision number that a given duplicate code was detected; f is the absolute path to the source file where a given duplicate code exists; l is a set of line numbers where duplicate code exists. Note that storing only the start line and the end line of duplicate code is not feasible because a part of duplicate code is noncontiguous.

This step is very time consuming. If the history of the target software includes 1,000 revisions, duplicate code detection is performed 1,000 times. However, this step is fully automated, and no manual work is required.

Step 4. It identifies Differences between Two Consecutive Revisions. In Step 4, we find out modification places between two consecutive revisions with UNIX diff command. As described above, we can get this information by just parsing the output of diff.

Step 5. It Counts the Number of Modifications. In this step, we count the number of modifications of duplicate code and nonduplicate code with the results of the previous two steps. Here, we assume the variable for the number of modifications of duplicate code is MC_d, and the variable for nonduplicate code is MC_n. Firstly, MC_d and MC_n are initialized with 0, then they are increased as follows; if the range of specified modification is completely included in duplicate code, MC_d is incremented; if it is completely included in nonduplicate code, MC_n is incremented; if it is included in both of duplicate code and nonduplicate code, both MC_d and MC_n are incremented. All the modifications are processed with the above algorithm.

Step 6. It calculates MF_d and MF_n. Finally, MF_d and MF_n defined in the formula (4) are calculated with the result of the previous step.

5. Design of Experiment

In this paper, we conduct the following two experiments.

Experiment 1. Compare MF_d and MF_n on 15 open-source software systems.

Experiment 2. Compare the result of the proposed method with 2 previous investigation methods on 5 open-source software systems.

TABLE 4: Target software systems—Experiment 2.

Name	Domain	Programming language	Number of Revisions	LOC (latest revision)
OpenYMSG	Messenger	Java	194	14,111
EclEmma	Testing	Java	1,220	31,409
MASU	Source Code Analysis	Java	1,620	79,360
TVBrowser	Multimedia	Java	6,829	264,796
Ant	Build	Java	5,412	198,864

We describe these experiments in detail in the reminder of this section.

5.1. Experiment 1

5.1.1. Outline. The purpose of this experiment is to answer our research questions. This experiment consists of the following two subexperiments.

Experiment 1.1. We compare MF_d and MF_n on various size software systems with a scalable detection tool, CCFinder.

Experiment 1.2. We compare MF_d and MF_n on small size software systems with 4 detection tools, described in Section 3.1.

The reason why we choose only a single clone detector, CCFinder, on Experiment 1.1 is that the experiment took much time. For instance, we took a week to conduct the experiment on SQuirrel SQL Client.

The following items are investigated in each sub-experiment.

Item A. Investigate whether duplicate code is modified more frequently than nonduplicate code. In this investigation, we calculate MF_d and MF_n on the entire period.

Item B. Investigate whether MF tendencies differ according to the time.

To answer RQ1, we use the result of Item A of Experiments 1.1 and 1.2. For RQ2, we use the result of Item A of Experiment 1.1. For RQ3, we use Item B of Experiment 1.1 and Experiment 1.2. Finally, for RQ4, we use Item A of Experiment 1.1 and Experiment 1.2.

5.1.2. Target Software Systems. In Experiment 1, we select 15 open source software systems shown in Table 2 as investigation targets. 5 software systems are investigated in Experiment 1.1, and the other software systems are investigated in Experiment 1.2. The criteria for these target software systems are as follows:

(i) the source code is managed with Subversion;

(ii) the source code is written in C/C++ or Java;

(iii) we took care not to bias the domains of the targets.

TABLE 5: Ratio of duplicate code—Experiment 1.

(a) Experiment 1.1

Software Name	ccf	ccfx	sim	sco
EclEmma	13.1%	—	—	—
FileZilla	22.6%	—	—	—
FreeCol	23.1%	—	—	—
SQuirrel	29.0%	—	—	—
WinMerge	23.6%	—	—	—

(b) Experiment 1.2

Software Name	ccf	ccfx	sim	sco
ThreeCAM	29.8%	10.5%	4.1%	26.2%
DatabaseToUML	21.4%	25.1%	7.6%	11.8%
AdServerBeans	22.7%	18.2%	20.3%	15.9%
NatMonitor	9.0%	7.7%	0.7%	6.6%
OpenYMSG	17.4%	9.9%	5.8%	9.9%
QMailAdmin	34.3%	19.6%	8.8%	—
Tritonn	13.8%	7.5%	5.5%	—
Newsstar	7.9%	4.8%	1.5%	—
Hamachi-GUI	36.5%	23.1%	18.5%	—
GameScanner	23.1%	13.1%	6.6%	—

5.2. Experiment 2

5.2.1. Outline. In Experiment 2, we compare the results of the proposed method and two previously described investigation methods on the same targets. The purpose of this experiment is to reveal whether comparisons of duplicate code and nonduplicate code with different methods always introduce the same result. Also, we evaluate the efficacy of the proposed method comparing to the other methods.

5.2.2. Investigation Methods to Be Compared. Here, we describe 2 investigation methods used in Experiment 2. We choose investigation methods proposed by Krinke [11] (in short, Krinke's method) and proposed by Lozano and Wermelinger [9] (in short, Lozano's method). Table 3 shows the overview of these methods and the proposed method. The selection was performed based on the following criteria.

(i) The investigation is based on the comparison some characteristics between duplicate code and nonduplicate code.

(ii) The method has been published at the time when our research started (at 2010/9).

In the experiments of Krinke's and Lozano's papers, only a single detection tool `Simian` or `CCFinder` was selected. However, in this experiment, we selected 4 detection tools for bringing more valid results.

We developed software tools for Krinke's and Lozano's methods based on their papers. We describe Krinke's method and Lozano's method briefly.

Krinke's Method. Krinke's method compares stability of duplicate code and nonduplicate code [11]. Stability is calculated based on ratios of modified duplicate code and modified nonduplicate code. This method uses not all the revisions but a revision per week.

First of all, a revision is extracted from every week history. Then, duplicate code is detected from every of the extracted revisions. Next, every consecutive two revisions are compared for obtaining where added lines, deleted lines, and changed lines are. With this information, the ratios of added lines, deleted lines, and changed lines on duplicate and nonduplicate code are calculated and compared.

Lozano's Method. Lozano's method categorized Java methods, then compare distributions of maintenance cost based on the categories [9].

Firstly, Java methods are traced based on their owner class's full qualified name, start/end lines, and signatures. Methods are categorized as follows:

AC-Method. Methods that always had duplicate code during their lifetime;

NC-Method. Methods that never had duplicate code during their lifetime;

SC-Method. Methods that sometimes had duplicate code and sometimes did not.

Lozano's method defines the followings where m is a method, P is a period (a set of revisions), and r is a revision.

(i) *ChangedRevisions*(m, P): a set of revisions that method m is modified in period P,

(ii) *Methods*(r): a set of methods that exist in revision r,

(iii) *ChangedMethods*(r): a set of methods that were modified in revision r,

(iv) *CoChangedMethods*(m, r): a set of methods that were modified simultaneously with method m in revision r. If method m is not modified in revision r, it becomes 0. If modified, the following formula is satisfied:

$$ChangedMethod(r) = m \cup CoChangedMethod(m, r).$$
$$(5)$$

TABLE 6: Overall results—Experiment 1.

(a) Experiment 1.1

Software Name	ccf	ccfx	sim	sco
EclEmma	N	—	—	—
FileZilla	N	—	—	—
FreeCol	N	—	—	—
SQuirrel	N	—	—	—
WinMerge	N	—	—	—

(b) Experiment 1.2

Software Name	ccf	ccfx	sim	sco
ThreeCAM	N	C	N	N
DatabaseToUML	N	N	N	N
AdServerBeans	N	N	N	N
NatMonitor	C	C	N	C
OpenYMSG	C	C	C	N
QMailAdmin	C	C	C	—
Tritonn	N	C	N	—
Newsstar	N	N	N	—
Hamachi-GUI	N	N	N	—
GameScanner	C	C	N	—

Then, this method calculates the following formulae with the above definitions. Especially, *work* is an indicator of the maintenance cost:

$$likelihood(m, P) = \frac{ChangedRevisions(m, P)}{\sum_{r \in P} | ChangedMethods(r) |},$$

$$impact(m, P)$$
$$= \frac{\sum_{r \in P} | CoChangedMethods(m, r) | / | Methods(r) |}{| ChangedRevisions(m, P) |},$$

$$work(m, P) = likelihood(m, P) \times impact(m, P).$$
$$(6)$$

In this research, we compare *work* between AC-Method and NC-Method. In addition, we also compare SC-Methods' *work* on duplicate period and nonduplicate period.

5.2.3. Target Software Systems. We chose 5 open-source software systems in Experiment 2. Table 4 shows them. Two targets, OpenYMSG and EclEmma, are selected as well as Experiment 1. Note that the number of revisions and LOC of the latest revision of these two targets are different from Table 2. This is because they had been being in development between the time-lag in Experiments 1 and 2. Every source file is normalized with the rules described in Section 4.2.2 as well as Experiment 1. In addition, automatically generated code and testing code are removed from all the revisions before the investigation methods are applied.

6. Experiment 1—Result and Discussion

6.1. Overview. Table 5 shows the average ratio for each target of Experiment 1. Note that "ccf," "ccfx," "sim," and "sco" in

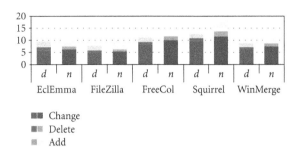

FIGURE 2: Result of Item A on Experiment 1.1.

TABLE 7: The average values of MF in Experiment 1.1.

Modification Type	MF	
	Duplicate code	Nonduplicate code
Change	7.0337	8.1039
Delete	1.0216	1.4847
Add	1.9539	3.7378
ALL	10.0092	13.3264

the table are the abbreviated form of CCFinder, CCFinderX, Simian, and Scorpio, respectively.

Table 6 shows the overall result of Experiment 1. In this table, "C" means $MF_d > MF_n$ in that case, and "N" means the opposing result. For example, the comparison result in ThreeCAM with CCFinder is $MF_d < MF_n$, which means duplicate code is not modified more frequently than nonduplicate code. Note that "—" means the cases that we do not consider because of the following reasons: (1) in Experiment 1.1, we use only CCFinder, so that the cases with other detectors are not considered; (2) Scorpio can handle only Java, so that the cases in software systems written in C/C++ with Scorpio are not considered.

We describe the results in detail in the following subsections.

6.2. Result of Experiment 1.1. Figure 2 shows all the results of Item A on Experiment 1.1. The labels "*d*" and "*n*" in *X*-axis means MF in duplicate code and nonduplicate code, respectively, and every bar consists of three parts, which means *change*, *delete*, and *add*. As shown in Figure 2, MF_d is lower than MF_n on all the target systems. Table 7 shows the average values of MF based on the modification types. The comparison results of MF_d and MF_n show that MF_d is less than MF_n in the cases of all the modification types. However, the degrees of differences between MF_d and MF_n are different for each modification type.

For Item B on Experiment 1.1, first, we divide the entire period into 10 sub-periods and calculate MF on every of the sub periods. Figure 3 shows the result. *X*-axis is the divided periods. Label "1" is the earliest period of the development, and label "10" is the most recent period. In the case of EclEmma, the number of periods that MF_d is greater than MF_n is the same as the number of periods that MF_n is greater than MF_d. In the case of FileZilla, FreeCol, and WinMerge, there is only a period that MF_d is greater than MF_n. In

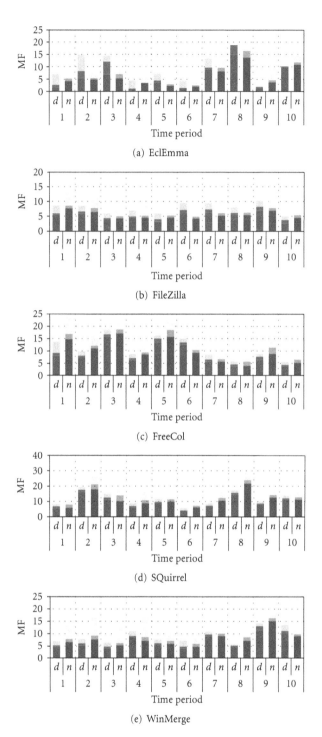

FIGURE 3: Result of Item B on Experiment 1.1 (divided into 10 periods).

the case of Squirrel SQL Client, MF_n is greater than MF_d in all the periods. This result implies that if the number of revisions becomes large, duplicate code tends to become more stable than nonduplicate code. However, the shapes of MF transitions are different from every software system.

For WinMerge, we investigated period "2," where MF_n is much greater than MF_d, and period "10," where is only the

TABLE 8: Comparing MFs based on programming language and detection tool.

(a) Comparison on programming language

Programming language	MF	
	Duplicate code	Nonduplicate code
Java	20.4370	24.1739
C/C++	49.4868	57.2246
ALL	32.8869	38.3384

(b) Comparison on detection tool

Detection tool	MF	
	Duplicate code	Nonduplicate code
CCFinder	38.2790	40.7211
CCFinderX	40.3541	40.0774
Simian	26.0084	42.1643
Scorpio	20.9254	24.1628
ALL	32.8869	38.3384

TABLE 9: The average values of MF in Experiment 1.2.

Modification type	MF	
	Duplicate code	Nonduplicate code
Change	26.8065	29.2549
Delete	3.8706	3.5228
Add	2.2098	5.5608
ALL	32.8869	38.3384

period that MF_d is greater than MF_n. In period "10," there are many modifications on test cases. The number of revisions that test cases are modified is 49, and the ratio of duplicate code in test cases is 88.3%. Almost all modifications for test cases are performed on duplicate code, so that MF_d is greater than MF_n. Omitting the modifications for test cases, MF_d and MF_n became inverted. However, there is no modification on test cases in period "2," so that MF_d is less than MF_n in this case.

Moreover, we divide the entire period by release dates and calculate MF on every period. Figure 4 shows the result. As the figure shows, MF_d is less than MF_n in all the cases for FileZilla, FreeCol, SQuirrel, and WinMerge. For EclEmma, there are some cases that $MF_d > MF_n$ at the release level. Especially, duplicate code is frequently modified in the early releases.

Although MF_d is greater than MF_n in the period "6" in Freecol and the period "10" in WinMerge, MF_d is less than MF_n in all cases at the release level. This indicates that duplicate code is sometimes modified intensively in a short period, nevertheless it is stable than nonduplicate code in a long term.

The summary of Experiment 1 is that duplicate code detected by CCFinder was modified less frequently than nonduplicate code. Consequently, we conclude that duplicate code detected by CCFinder does not have a negative impact on software evolution even if the target software is large and its period is long.

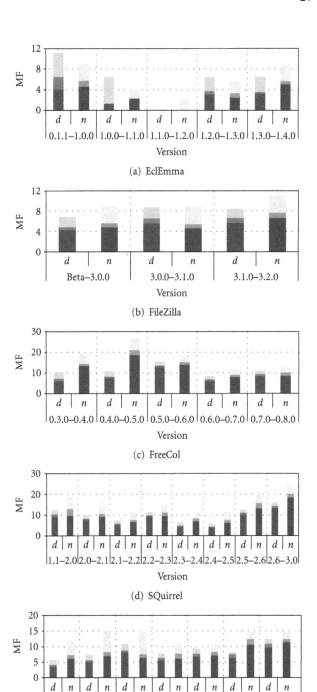

FIGURE 4: Result of Item B on Experiment 1.1 (divided by releases).

6.3. Result of Experiment 1.2. Figure 5 shows all the results of Item A on Experiment 1.2. In Figure 5, the detection tools are abbreviated as follows: CCFinder → C; CCFinderX → X; Simian → Si; Scorpio → Sc. There are the results of 3 detection tools except Scorpio on C/C++ systems, because Scorpio does not handle C/C++. MF_d is less than MF_n in the 22 comparison results out of 35. In the 4 target systems out of 10, duplicate code is modified less frequently than

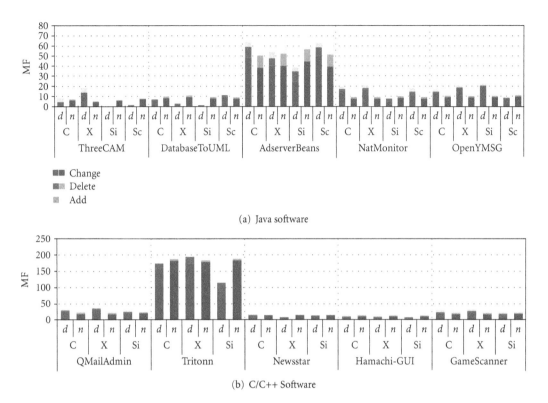

(a) Java software

(b) C/C++ Software

Figure 5: Result of Item A on Experiment 1.2.

nonduplicate code in the cases of all the detection tools. In the case of the other 1 target system, MF_d is greater than MF_n in the cases of all the detection tools. In the remaining systems, the comparison result is different for the detection tools. Also, we compared MF_d and MF_n based on programming language and detection tools. The comparison result is shown in Table 8. The result shows that MF_d is less than MF_n on all the programming language, and MF_d is less than MF_n on the 3 detectors, CCFinder, Simian, and Scorpio, meanwhile the opposing result is shown in the case of CCFinderX. We also compared MF_d and MF_n based on modification types. The result is shown in Table 9. As shown in Table 9, MF_d is less than MF_n in the cases of change and addition, meanwhile the opposing result is shown in the case of deletion.

We investigated whether there is a statistically significant difference between MF_d and MF_n by t-test. The result is that, there is no difference between them where the level of significance is 5%. Also, there is no significant difference in the comparison based on programming language and detection tool.

For Item B on Experiment 1.2, we divide the whole period into 10 subperiods likewise Experiment 1.1. Figure 6 shows the result. In this experiment, we observed that the tendencies of MF transitions loosely fall into three categories: (1) MF_d is lower than MF_n almost of all the divisions; (2) MF_d is greater than MF_n in the early divisions, meanwhile the opposite tendency is observed in the late divisions; (3) MF_d is less than MF_n in the early divisions, meanwhile the opposite

tendency is observed in the late divisions. Figure 6 shows the result of the 3 systems on which we observed remarkable tendencies of every category.

In Figure 6(a), period "4" shows that MF_n is greater than MF_d on all the detection tool meanwhile period "7" shows exactly the opposite result. Also, in period "5," there are hardly differences between duplicate code and nonduplicate code. We investigated the source code of period "4." In this period, many source files were created by copy-and-paste operations, and a large amount of duplicate code was detected by each detection tool. The code generated by copy-and-paste operations was very stable meanwhile the other source files were modified as usual. This is the reason why MF_n is much greater than MF_d in period "4."

Figure 6(b) shows that duplicate code tends to be modified more frequently than nonduplicate code in the anterior half of the period meanwhile the opposite occurred in the posterior half. We found that there was a large number of duplicate code that was repeatedly modified in the anterior half. On the other hand, there was rarely such duplicate code in the posterior half.

Figure 6(c) shows the opposite result of Figure 6(b). That is, duplicate code was modified more frequently in the posterior half of the period. In the anterior half, the amount of duplication was very small, and modifications were rarely performed on it. In the posterior half, amount of duplicate code became large, and modifications were performed on it repeatedly. In the case of Simian detection, no duplicate code was detected except period "5." This is because Simian

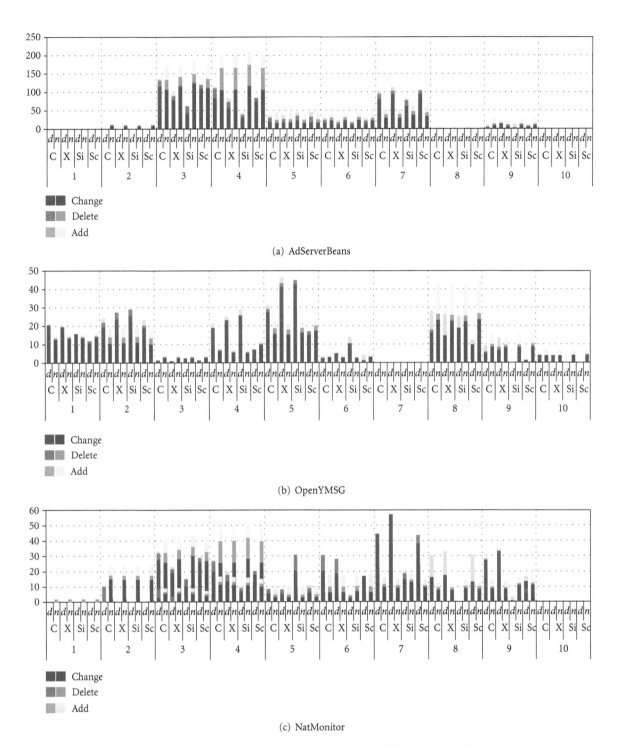

(a) AdServerBeans

(b) OpenYMSG

(c) NatMonitor

FIGURE 6: Result of Item B on Experiment 1.2 (divided into 10 periods).

detects only the exact-match duplicate code meanwhile the other tools detect exact match and renamed duplicate code in the default setting.

In Experiment 1.1, we investigate MF tendencies at the release level. However, we cannot apply the same investigation way to Experiment 1.2. This is because the target software systems in Experiment 1.2 is not enough mature to have multiple releases. Instead, we investigate MF tendencies at the most fine-grained level, at the revision level. Figure 7 shows the result of the investigation at the revision level for AdServerBeans, OpenYMSG, and NatMonitor. The X-axis of each graph indicates the value of $MF_d - MF_n$. Therefore, if the value is greater than 0, MF_d is greater than MF_n at the revision and vice versa. For AdServerBeans, MF tendencies are similar for every detection tool except revision 21 to 26. For other 2 software systems, MF comparison results differ

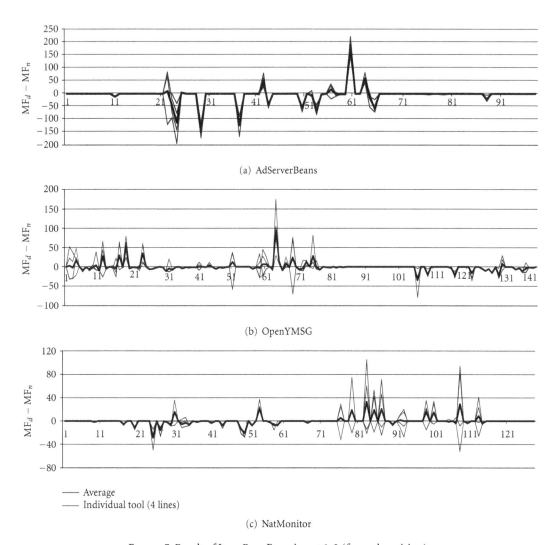

(a) AdServerBeans

(b) OpenYMSG

(c) NatMonitor

FIGURE 7: Result of Item B on Experiment 1-2 (for each revision).

from each detection tool in most of the revisions. As the figures show, tendencies of MF transition differ from clone detectors nevertheless there seems to be small differences between clone detectors in 10 sub-periods division. However, these graphs do not consider modification types. Therefore, we cannot judge what type of modification frequently occurred from the graphs.

The summary of Experiment 1.2 is as follows: we found some instances that duplicate code was modified more frequently than nonduplicate code in a short period on each detection tool; however, in the entire period, duplicate code was modified less frequently than nonduplicate code on every target software with all the detection tools. Consequently, we conclude that the presence of duplicate code does not have a seriously-negative impact on software evolution.

6.4. Answers for RQs

RQ1: Is duplicate code more frequently modified than nonduplicate code? The answer is *No*. In Experiment 1.1, we found that MF_d is lower than MF_n in all the target systems. Also,

we found a similar result in Experiment 1.2: 22 comparison results out of 35 show that MF_d is lower than MF_n, also MF_d is lower than MF_n in average. This result indicates that the presence of duplicate code does not seriously affect software evolution, which is different from the common belief.

RQ2: Are the comparison results of stability between duplicate code and nonduplicate code different from multiple detection tools? The answer is *Yes*. In Experiment 1.2, the comparison results with CCFinderX are different from the results with other 3 detectors. Moreover, MF_n is much greater than MF_d in the case of Simian. At present, we cannot find the causes of the difference of the comparison results. One of the causes may be the ratio of duplicate code. The ratio of duplicate code is quite different for each detection tool on the same software. However, we cannot see any relation between the ratio of duplicate code and MF.

RQ3: Is duplicate code modified uniformly throughout its lifetime? The answer is *No*. In Item B of Experiments 1.1

and 1.2, there are some instances that duplicate code was modified more frequently than nonduplicate code in a short period though MF_d is less than MF_n in the whole period. However, these MFs tendencies depend on target software systems, so that we cannot find characteristics of such variability.

RQ4: Are there any differences in the comparison results on modification types? The answer is *Yes*. In Experiment 1.1, MF_d is less than MF_n on all the modification types. However, there is a small difference between MF_d and MF_n in the case of deletion, meanwhile there is a large difference in the case of addition. In Experiment 1.2, MF_d is less than MF_n in the cases of change and addition. Especially, MF_n is more than twice as large as MF_d in the case of addition. However, MF_d is greater than MF_n in the case of deletion. These results show that deletion tends to be affected by duplicate code, meanwhile addition tends not to be affected by duplicate code.

6.5. Discussion. In Experiment 1, we found that duplicate code tends to be more stable than nonduplicate code, which indicates that the presence of duplicate code does not have a negative impact on software evolution. We investigated how the software evolved in the period, and we found that the following activities should be a part of factors that duplicate code is modified less frequently than nonduplicate code.

Reusing Stable Code. When implementing new functionalities, reusing stable code is a good way to reduce the number of introduced bugs. If most of duplicate code is reused stable code, MF_d becomes less than MF_n.

Using Generated Code. Automatically generated code is rarely modified manually. Also, the generated code tends to be duplicate code. Consequently, if the amount of generated code is high, MF_d will become less than MF_n.

On the other hand, there are some cases that duplicate code was more frequently modified than nonduplicate code in a short period. The period "7" on AdServerBeans (Experiment 1.2, Item B) is one of these instances. We analyzed the source code of this period to detect why MF_d was greater than MF_n in this period though the opposite results were shown in the other periods. Through the analysis, we found that there are some instances that the same modifications were applied to multiple places of code.

Algorithm 2 shows an example of unstable duplicate code. There are 5 code fragments that are similar to this fragment. Firstly, lines labeled with "%" (shown in Algorithm 2(b)) were modified to replace the getter methods into directly accesses to fields. In the next, a line labeled with "#" is removed (shown in Algorithm 2(c)). These two modifications were concentrically conducted in period "7." Reusing unstable code like this example can cause additional costs for software maintenance. Moreover, a code fragment was not simultaneously changed with its correspondents at the second modification. If this inconsistent change was introduced unintentionally, it might cause a bug. If so, this

TABLE 10: Ratio of duplicate code—Experiment 2.

Software Name	ccf	ccfx	sim	sco
OpenYMSG	12.4%	6.2%	2.7%	5.5%
EclEmma	6.9%	4.8%	2.0%	3.7%
MASU	25.6%	26.5%	11.3%	15.4%
TVBrowser	13.6%	10.9%	5.4%	19.0%
Ant	13.9%	12.1%	6.2%	15.6%

TABLE 11: Overall results—Experiment 2.

Software Name	Method	Tools			
		ccf	ccfx	sim	sco
OpenYMSG	Proposed	N	C	C	N
	Krinke	N	C	C	N
	Lozano	—	—	N	—
EclEmma	Proposed	N	N	N	N
	Krinke	N	N	N	C
	Lozano	N	N	—	—
MASU	Proposed	C	N	C	C
	Krinke	C	C	C	C
	Lozano	C	C	C	C
TVBrowser	Proposed	N	N	N	N
	Krinke	C	C	C	C
	Lozano	C	C	C	C
Ant	Proposed	N	N	N	N
	Krinke	C	C	C	C
	Lozano	C	C	C	C

is a typical situation that duplicate code affects software evolution.

7. Experiment 2—Result and Discussion

7.1. Overview. Table 10 shows the average ratios of duplicate code in each target, and Table 11 shows the comparison results of all the targets. In Table 11, "C" means that duplicate code requires more cost than nonduplicate code, and "N" means its opposite. The discriminant criteria of "C" and "N" are different in each investigation method.

In the proposed method, if MF_d is lower than MF_n, the column is labeled with "C," and the column is labeled with "N" in its opposite case.

In Krinke's method, if the ratio of *changed* and *deleted* lines of code on duplicate code is greater than *changed* and *deleted* lines on nonduplicate code, the column is labeled with "C," and in its opposite case the column is labeled with "N." Note that herein we do not consider *added* lines because the amount of *add* is the lines of code added in the next revision, not in the current target revision.

In Lozano's method, if *work* in AC-Method is statistically greater than one in NC-Method, the column is labeled with "C." On the other hand, if *work* in NC-Method is statistically greater than one in AC-Method, the column is labeled with "N." Here, we use Mann-Whitney's U test under setting

```
(a) Before Modification
    int offsetTmp = dataGridDisplayCriteria
        .getItemsPerPage() *
            (dataGridDisplayCriteria.getPage() -1);
    if (offsetTmp > 0) --offsetTmp;
    if (offsetTmp < 0) offsetTmp = 0;
  final int offset = offsetTmp;
    String sortColumn =
            dataGridDisplayCriteria.getSortColumn();
    Order orderTmp =
            dataGridDisplayCriteria.getOrder()
                .equals(AdServerBeansConstants.ASC) ?
                    Order.asc(sortColumn) :
                        Order.desc(sortColumn);


(b) After 1st Modification
    int offsetTmp = dataGridDisplayCriteria
        .getItemsPerPage() *
            (dataGridDisplayCriteria.getPage() -1);
    if (offsetTmp > 0) --offsetTmp;
    if (offsetTmp < 0) offsetTmp = 0;
    final int offset = offsetTmp;
    String sortColumn =
%           dataGridDisplayCriteria.sortColumn;
    Order orderTmp =
%           dataGridDisplayCriteria.order
                .equals(AdServerBeansConstants.ASC) ?
                    Order.asc(sortColumn) :
                        Order.desc(sortColumn);


(c) After 2nd Modification
    int offsetTmp = dataGridDisplayCriteria
        .getItemsPerPage() *
            (dataGridDisplayCriteria.getPage() -1);
#
    if (offsetTmp < 0) offsetTmp = 0;
    final int offset = offsetTmp;
    String sortColumn =
        dataGridDisplayCriteria.sortColumn;
    Order orderTmp =
        dataGridDisplayCriteria.order
                .equals(AdServerBeansConstants.ASC) ?
                    Order.asc(sortColumn) :
                        Order.desc(sortColumn);
```

ALGORITHM 2: An example of unstable duplicate code.

5% as the level of significance. If there is no statistically significant difference in AC- and NC-Method, we compare *work* in duplicate period and nonduplicate period in SC-Method with Wlcoxon's singed-rank test. We also set 5% as the level of significance. If there is no statistically significant difference, the column is labeled with "—."

As this table shows, different methods and different tools brought almost the same result in the case of EclEmma and MASU. On the other hand, in the case of other targets, we get different results with different methods or different tools. Especially, in the case of TVBrowser and Ant, the proposed method brought the opposite result to Lozano's and Krinke's method.

7.2. Result of MASU. Herein, we show comparison figures of MASU. Figure 8 shows the results of the proposed method. In this case, all the detection tools except CCFinderX brought the same result that duplicate code is more frequently modified than nonduplicate code. Figure 9 shows the results of Krinke's method on MASU. As this figure shows, the comparison of all the detection detectors brought the same result that duplicate code is less stable than nonduplicate code. Figure 10 shows the results of Lozano's method on MASU with Simian. Figure 10(a) compares AC-Method and NC-Method. X-axis indicates maintenance cost (*work*) and Y-axis indicates cumulated frequency of methods. For readability, we adopt logarithmic axis on X-axis. In this

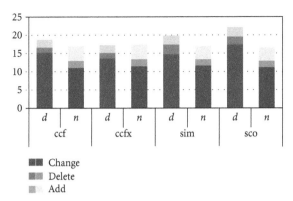

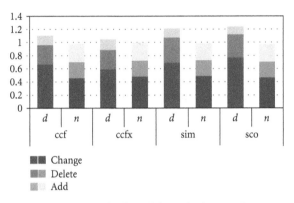

FIGURE 8: Result of the proposed method on MASU.

FIGURE 9: Result of Krinke's method on MASU.

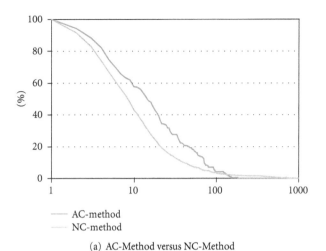

(a) AC-Method versus NC-Method

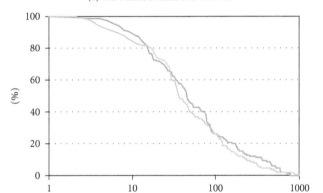

(b) SC-Method

FIGURE 10: Result of Lozano's Method on MASU with Simian.

case, AC-Method requires more maintenance cost than NC-Method. Also, Figure 10(b) compares duplicate period and nonduplicate period of SC-Method. In this case, the maintenance cost in duplicate period is greater than in nonduplicate period.

In the case of MASU, Krinke's method and Lozano's method regard duplicate code as requiring more cost than nonduplicate code in the cases of all the detection tools. The proposed method indicates that duplicate code is more frequently modified than nonduplicate code with CCFinder, Simian, and Scorpio. In addition, there is little differences between MF_d and MF_n in the result of the proposed method with CCFinderX, which is the only case that duplicate code is more stable than nonduplicate code. Considering all the results, we can say that duplicate code has a negative impact on software evolution on MASU. This result is reliable because all the investigation methods show such tendencies.

7.3. Result of OpenYMSG. Figures 11, 12, and 13 show the result of the proposed method, Krinke's method, and Lozano's method on OpenYMSG. In the cases of the proposed method and Krinke's method, duplicate code is regarded as having a negative impact with CCFinderX and Simian, meanwhile the opposing results are shown with CCFinder and Scorpio. In Lozano's method with Simian, duplicate code is regarded as not having a negative impact. Note that we omit the comparison figure on SC-Method

because there are only 3 methods that are categorized into SC-Method.

As these figures show, the comparison results are different for detection tools or investigation methods. Therefore, we cannot judge whether the presence of duplicate code has a negative impact or not on OpenYMSG.

7.4. Discussion. In the case of OpenYMSG, TVBrowser, and Ant, different investigation methods and different tools brought opposing results. Figure 14 shows an actual modification in Ant. Two methods were modified in this modification. The hatching parts are detected duplicate code and frames in them mean pairs of duplicate code between two methods. Vertical arrows show modified lines between this modification and the next (77 lines of code were modified).

This modification is a refactoring, which extracts the duplicate instructions from the two methods and merges them as a new method. In the proposed method, there are 2 modification places in duplicate code and 4 places in nonduplicate code, so that MF_d and MF_n become 51.13 and 18.13, respectively. In Krinke's method, DC + CC and

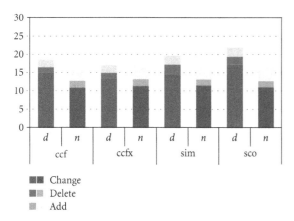

FIGURE 11: Result of the proposed method on OpenYMSG.

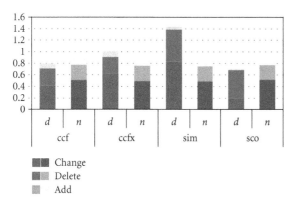

FIGURE 12: Result of Krinke's method on OpenYMSG.

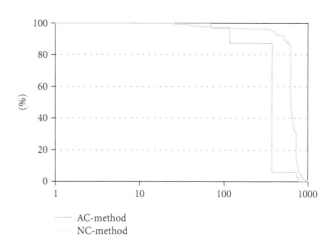

FIGURE 13: Result of Lozano's method on OpenYMSG with Simian.

DN + CN become 0.089 and 0.005, where DC, CC, DN, and CN indicate the ratio of deleted lines on duplicate code, changed lines on duplicate code, deleted lines on nonduplicate code, and deleted lines on nonduplicate code, respectively.

In this case, both the proposed method and Krinke's method regard duplicate code requiring more maintenance cost than nonduplicate code. However, there is a great difference in Krinke's method than the proposed method: in the proposed method, duplicate code is modified about 2.8 times as frequently as nonduplicate code; meanwhile, in Krinke's method, duplicate code is modified 17.8 times as frequently as nonduplicate code. This is caused by the difference of the barometers used in each method. In Krinke's method, the barometer depends on the amount of modified lines, meanwhile the barometer depends on the amount of modified places in the proposed method. This example is one of the refactorings on duplicate code. In Krinke's method, if removed duplicate code is large, duplicate code is regarded as having more influence. However, in the cases of duplicate code removal, we have to spend much effort if the number of duplicate fragments is high. Therefore, we can say that the proposed method can accurately measure the influence of duplicate code in this case.

This is an instance that is advantageous for the proposed method. However, we cannot investigate all the experimental data because the amount of the data is too vast to conduct manual checking for all the modifications. There is a possibility that the proposed method cannot accurately evaluate the influence of duplicate code in some situations.

In Experiment 2, we found that the different investigation methods or different detectors draw different results on the same target systems. In Experiment 1, we found that duplicate code is less frequently modified than nonduplicate code. However, the result of Experiment 2 shows that we cannot generalize the result of Experiment 1. We have to conduct more experiments and analyze the results of them in detail to gain more generic.

8. Threats to Validity

This section describes threats to validity of this study.

8.1. Features of Every Modification. In this study, we assume that cost required for every modification is equal to one another. However, the cost is different between every modification in the actual software evolution. Consequently, the comparison based on MF may not appropriately represent the cost required for modifying duplicate code and nonduplicate code.

Also, when we modify duplicate code, we have to consider maintaining the consistency between the modified duplicate code and its correspondents. If the modification lacks the consistency by error, we have to remodify them for repairing the consistency. The effort for consistency is not necessary for modifying nonduplicate code. Consequently, the average cost required for duplicate code may be different from the one required for nonduplicate code. In order to compare them more appropriately, we have to consider the cost for maintaining consistency.

Moreover, distribution of source code that should be modified are not considered. However, it differs from

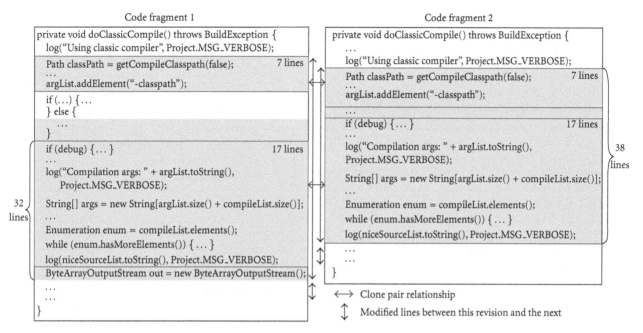

FIGURE 14: An Example of Modification.

every modification, thus we may get different results by considering the distribution of source code.

8.2. Identifying the Number of Modifications. In this study, modifying consecutive multiple lines are regarded as a single modification. However, it is possible that such an automatically processing identifies the incorrect number of modifications. If multiple lines that were not contiguous are modified for fixing a single bug, the proposed method presumes that multiple modifications were performed. Also, if multiple consecutive lines were modified for fixing two or more bugs by chance, the proposed method presumes that only a single modification was performed. Consequently, it is necessary to manually identify modifications if we have to use the exactly correct number of modifications.

Besides, we investigated how many the identified modifications occurred across the boundary of duplicate code and nonduplicate code. If this number is high, then the analysis suspects because such modifications increase both the counts at the same time. The investigation result is that, in the highest case, the ratio of such modifications is 4.8%. That means that almost all modifications occurred within either duplicate code or nonduplicate code.

8.3. Category of Modifications. In this study, we counted all the modifications, regardless of their categories. As a result, the number of modifications might be incorrectly increased by unimportant modifications such as format transformation. A part of unimportant modifications remained even if we had used the normalized source code described in Section 4.2.2. Consequently, manual categorization for the modifications is required for using the exactly correct number of modifications.

Also, the code normalization that we used in this study removed all the comments in the source files. If considerable cost was expended to make or change code comments on the development of the target systems, we incorrectly missed the cost.

8.4. Property of Target Software. In this study, we used only open-source software systems, so that different results may be shown with industrial software systems. Some researchers pointed out that industrial software systems include much duplicate code [24, 25]. Consequently, duplicate code may not be managed well in industrial software, which may increase MF_d. Also, properties of industrial software are quite different from ones of open source software. In order to investigate the impact of duplicate code on industrial software, we have to compare MF on industrial software itself.

8.5. Settings of Detection Tools. In this study, we used default settings for all the detection tools. If we change the settings, different results will be shown.

9. Conclusion

This paper presented an empirical study on the impact of the presence of duplicate code on software evolution. We assumed that if duplicate code is modified more frequently than nonduplicate code, the presence of duplicate code affects software evolution and compared the stability of duplicate code and nonduplicate code. To evaluate from a different standpoint from previous studies, we used a new indicator, modification frequency, which is calculated with the number of modified places of code. Also, we used 4 duplicate code detection tools to reduce the bias of duplicate code detectors. We conducted an experiment on 15 open-source software systems, and the result showed that duplicate code was less frequently modified than nonduplicate code. We also found some cases that duplicate code was intensively modified in a short period though duplicate code was stable than nonduplicate code in the whole development period.

Moreover, we compared the proposed method to other 2 investigation methods to evaluate the efficacy of the proposed method. We conducted an experiment on 5 open-source software systems, and in the cases of 2 targets, we got the opposing results to other 2 methods. We investigated the result in detail and found some instances that the proposed method could evaluate more accurately than other methods.

In this study, we found that duplicate code tends to be stable than nonduplicate code. However, more studies are required to generalize this result, because we found that different investigation methods may bring different results. As future work, we are going to conduct more studies with other settings to get the characteristics of harmful duplicate code.

Acknowledgments

This research is being conducted as a part of the Stage Project, the Development of Next Generation IT Infrastructure, supported by the Ministry of Education, Culture, Sports, Science, and Technology of Japan. This study has been supported in part by Grant-in-Aid for Scientific Research (A) (21240002) and Grant-in-Aid for Exploratory Research (23650014) from the Japan Society for the Promotion of Science, and Grant-in-Aid for Young Scientists (B) (22700031) from Ministry of Education, Science, Sports and Culture. This paper is an extended version of earlier conference papers [26, 27].

References

[1] S. Bellon, R. Koschke, G. Antoniol, J. Krinke, and E. Merlo, "Comparison and evaluation of clone detection tools," *IEEE Transactions on Software Engineering*, vol. 32, no. 10, pp. 804–818, 2007.

[2] M. D. Wit, A. Zaidman, and A. V. Deursen, "Managing code clones using dynamic change tracking and resolution?" in *Proceedings of the 25th IEEE International Conference on Software Maintenance (ICSM '09)*, pp. 169–178, September 2009.

[3] M. P. Robillard, W. Coelho, and G. C. Murphy, "How effective developers investigate source code: an exploratory study," *IEEE Transactions on Software Engineering*, vol. 30, no. 12, pp. 889–903, 2004.

[4] C. J. Kapser and M. W. Godfrey, "'cloning considered harmful' considered harmful: patterns of cloning in software," *Empirical Software Engineering*, vol. 13, no. 6, pp. 645–692, 2008.

[5] M. Kim, V. Sazawal, D. Notkin, and G. C. Murphy, "An empirical study of code clone genealogies," in *Proceedings of the 13th ACM SIGSOFT Symposium on the Foundations of Software Engineering*, pp. 187–196, September 2005.

[6] N. Bettenburg, W. Shang, W. M. Ibrahim, B. Adams, Y. Zou, and A. E. Hassan, "An empirical study on inconsistent changes to code clones at the release level," *Science of Computer Programming*, vol. 77, no. 6, pp. 760–776, 2012.

[7] A. Monden, D. Nakae, T. Kamiya, S. Sato, and K. Matsumoto, "Software quality analysis by code clones in industrial legacy software," in *Proceedings of the 8th IEEE International Software Metrics Symposium*, pp. 87–94, June 2002.

[8] A. Lozano, M. Wermelinger, and B. Nuseibeh, "Evaluating the harmfulness of cloning: a change based experiment," in *Proceedings of the 4th International Workshop on Mining Software Repositories (MSR '07)*, May 2007.

[9] A. Lozano and M. Wermelinger, "Assessing the effect of clones on changeability," in *Proceedings of the 24th International Conference on Software Maintenance*, pp. 227–236, September 2008.

[10] A. Lozano, M. Wermelinger, and B. Nuseibeh, "Evaluating the relation between changeability decay and the characteristics of clones and methods," in *Proceedings of the 23rd IEEE/ACM International Conference on Automated Software Engineering*, pp. 100–109, September 2008.

[11] J. Krinke, "Is cloned code more stable than non-cloned code?" in *Proceedings of the 8th IEEE International Working Conference on Source Code Analysis and Manipulation, SCAM 2008*, pp. 57–66, September 2008.

[12] N. Göde and J. Harder, "Clone stability," in *Proceedings of the 15th European Conference on Software Maintenance and Reengineering (CSMR '11)*, pp. 65–74, March 2011.

[13] J. Krinke, "Is cloned code older than non-cloned code?" in *Proceedings of the 5th International Workshop on Software Clones (IWSC '11)*, pp. 28–33, May 2011.

[14] F. Rahman, C. Bird, and P. Devanbu, "Clones: what is that smell?" in *Proceedings of the 7th IEEE Working Conference on Mining Software Repositories*, pp. 72–81, May 2010.

[15] N. Göde and R. Koschke, "Frequency and risks of changes to clones," in *33rd International Conference on Software Engineering (ICSE '11)*, pp. 311–320, May 2011.

[16] S. G. Eick, T. L. Graves, A. F. Karr, U. S. Marron, and A. Mockus, "Does code decay? Assessing the evidence from change management data," *IEEE Transactions on Software Engineering*, vol. 27, no. 1, pp. 1–12, 2001.

[17] N. Göde, "Evolution of type-1 clones," in *Proceedings of the 9th IEEE International Working Conference on Source Code Analysis and Manipulation (SCAM '09)*, pp. 77–86, September 2009.

[18] E. Burd and J. Bailey, "Evaluating clone detection tools for use during preventative maintenance," in *Proceedings of the 2nd IEEE International Workshop on Source Code Analysis and Manipulation*, pp. 36–43, October 2002.

[19] T. Kamiya, S. Kusumoto, and K. Inoue, "CCFinder: a multilinguistic token-based code clone detection system for large scale source code," *IEEE Transactions on Software Engineering*, vol. 28, no. 7, pp. 654–670, 2002.

[20] CCFinderX, http://www.ccfinder.net/ccfinderx.html/.

[21] Simian, http://www.harukizaemon.com/simian/.

[22] Y. Higo and S. Kusumoto, "Code clone detection on specialized PDGs with heuristics," in *Proceedings of the 15th European Conference on Software Maintenance and Reengineering (CSMR '11)*, pp. 75–84, March 2011.

[23] Scorpio, http://sdl.ist.osaka-u.ac.jp/~higo/cgi-bin/moin.cgi/Scorpio/.

[24] S. Ducasse, M. Rieger, and S. Demeyer, "Language independent approach for detecting duplicated code," in *Proceedings of the 15th IEEE International Conference on Software Maintenance (ICSM '99)*, pp. 109–118, September 1999.

[25] S. Uchida, A. Monden, N. Ohsugi, T. Kamiya, K. I. Matsumoto, and H. Kudo, "Software analysis by code clones in open source software," *Journal of Computer Information Systems*, vol. 45, no. 3, pp. 1–11, 2005.

[26] K. Hotta, Y. Sano, Y. Higo, and S. Kusumoto, "Is duplicate code more frequently modified than non-duplicate code in software evolution?: an empirical study on open source software," in *Proceedings of the 4th the International Joint ERCIM Workshop on Software Evolution and International Workshop on Principles of Software Evolution*, September 2010.

[27] Y. Sasaki, K. Hotta, Y. Higo, and S. Kusumoto, "Is duplicate code good or bad? an empirical study with multiple investigation methods and multiple detection tools," in *Proceedings of the 22nd International Symposium on Software Reliability Engineering (ISSRE '11)*, Hiroshima, Japan, November 2011.

3

Specifying Process Views for a Measurement, Evaluation, and Improvement Strategy

Pablo Becker,[1] Philip Lew,[2] and Luis Olsina[1]

[1] GIDIS_Web, Engineering School, Universidad Nacional de La Pampa, General Pico, Argentina
[2] School of Software, Beihang University, Beijing, China

Correspondence should be addressed to Luis Olsina, olsinal@ing.unlpam.edu.ar

Academic Editor: Osamu Mizuno

Any organization that develops software strives to improve the quality of its products. To do this first requires an understanding of the quality of the current product version. Then, by iteratively making changes, the software can be improved with subsequent versions. But this must be done in a systematic and methodical way, and, for this purpose, we have developed a specific strategy called SIQinU (*Strategy for understanding and Improving Quality in Use*). SIQinU recognizes problems of quality in use through evaluation of a real system-in-use situation and proposes product improvements by understanding and making changes to the product's attributes. Then, reevaluating quality in use of the new version, improvement gains can be gauged along with the changes that led to those improvements. SIQinU aligns with GOCAME (*Goal-Oriented Context-Aware Measurement and Evaluation*), a multipurpose generic strategy previously developed for measurement and evaluation, which utilizes a conceptual framework (with ontological base), a process, and methods and tools. Since defining SIQinU relies on numerous phase and activity definitions, in this paper, we model different process views, for example, taking into account activities, interdependencies, artifacts, and roles, while illustrating them with excerpts from a real-case study.

1. Introduction

Even though software product launches now may consist of "continuous beta," users expect more and better functionality, combined with increased quality from the user's perception. Methodically improving the perceived quality, that is, its quality in use (QinU) particularly for web applications (WebApps), is not an easy job. WebApps—a kind of software applications—are no longer simple websites conveying information. Rather, they have become fully functional software applications often with complex business logic and sometimes critical to operating the business. Users, in addition, are becoming more demanding and diverse in their requirements. Consequently, WebApp quality and especially the quality in use, namely, the perceived quality by the end user has taken on increased significance as web and now cloud deployment have become mainstream delivery methods. Systematic means for evaluating QinU is important because it enables understanding the quality satisfaction level achieved by the application and provides useful information for recommendation and improvement processes in a consistent manner over time. Coincident with consistent and systematic evaluation of WebApp quality, the main goal is to ultimately improve its QinU.

This leads to our strategy with the objectives of understanding and improving the QinU—as nonfunctional requirements—of WebApps. QinU is currently redefined in the ISO 25010 standard [1], which was reused and enlarged by the 2Q2U (*internal/external Quality, Quality in use, actual Usability, and User experience*) quality framework—see [2] for an in-depth discussion. QinU from the actual usability standpoint (that embraces performance or "do" goals in contrast to hedonic or "be" goals [3]) is defined as the degree to which specified users can achieve specified goals with effectiveness in use, efficiency in use, learnability in use, and accessibility in use in a specified context of use [2].

Utilizing 2Q2U quality models, we developed SIQinU as an integrated means to evaluate and find possible problems in QinU which are then related to external quality (EQ) characteristics and attributes (by doing a mapping between

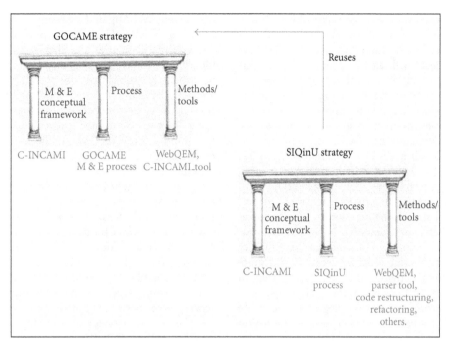

FIGURE 1: Allegory of the three GOCAME pillars, which are reused to a great extent by SIQinU.

QinU problems and EQ). This is followed by evaluating the application from the EQ standpoint and then making recommendations for improvements if necessary. The new version, based on recommended improvements, is reevaluated to gauge the improvement gain from both the EQ and QinU point of views. One aspect of SIQinU's uniqueness is that it collects user usage data from WebApps in a real context of use whereby code snippets are inserted (or using similar techniques) to gather data related to the task being executed by users at the subtask level enabling nonintrusive evaluations.

It is worth mentioning that SIQinU aligns with the GOCAME strategy [4]. GOCAME, a multipurpose goal-oriented strategy, was previously developed for supporting measurement and evaluation (M&E) programs and projects. Its rationale is based on three main pillars or principles, namely, (i) a conceptual framework utilizing an ontological base; (ii) a well-defined measurement and evaluation process; (iii) quality evaluation methods and tools instantiated from both the framework and process. This is allegorically depicted in Figure 1.

GOCAME's first principle is that designing and implementing a robust M&E program require a sound conceptual framework. Often times, organizations conduct start and stop measurement programs because they do not pay enough attention to the way nonfunctional requirements, contextual properties, metrics, and indicators should be designed, implemented, and analyzed. Any M&E effort requires an M&E framework built on a sound conceptual base, that is, on an ontological base, which explicitly and formally specifies the main agreed concepts, properties, relationships, and constraints for a given domain. To accomplish this, we utilize the C-INCAMI (*Contextual-Information Need,*

Concept model, Attribute, Metric, and Indicator) framework and its components [4, 5] based on our metrics and indicators ontology.

GOCAME's second principle requires a well-established M&E process in order to guarantee repeatability in performing activities and consistency of results. A process prescribes a set of phases, activities, inputs and outputs, interdependencies, sequences and parallelisms, check points, and so forth. Frequently, process specifications state what to do but do not mention the particular methods and tools to perform specific activity descriptions. Thus, to provide repeatability and replicability in performing activities, a process model for GOCAME was proposed in [6], which is also compliant with both the C-INCAMI conceptual base and components. Finally, methods and tools—the third pillar in the GOCAME strategy—can be instantiated from both the conceptual framework and process, for example, the WebQEM (*Web Quality Evaluation*) methodology [7] and its tool called C-INCAMI_tool [4].

SIQinU utilizes the above three GOCAME principles while also reusing the C-INCAMI conceptual base and process. However, since SIQinU is a specific-purpose goal-oriented strategy, it has specific processes, methods, and procedures that are not specified in GOCAME. Since the process aspect is critical in specifying SIQinU, given of its numerous interrelated phases and activities, this work defines its process model in detail through illustration with excerpts of a real case study. This case study was thoroughly illustrated in [8], and also aspects of its internal and external validity were considered in [9] as well.

Note that processes can be modeled taking into account different views [10] such as (i) functional that includes the activities' structure, inputs, and outputs; (ii) informational that includes the structure and interrelationships among artifacts produced or consumed by the activities; (iii) behavioral that models the dynamic view of processes; (iv) organizational that deals with agents, roles, and responsibilities. Additionally, a methodological view is described in [11], which is used to represent the process constructors (e.g., specific methods) that can be applied to different descriptions of activities. In order to specify all these views, different modeling languages can be used. However, no modeling language fits all needs and preferences. Each has its own strengths and weaknesses, which can make it more suitable for modeling certain views than others [12].

This paper using UML 2.0 activity diagrams [13] and the SPEM profile [14] stresses the functional, informational, organizational, and behavioral views for the SIQinU process. Modeling its process helps to (i) ease the repeatability and understandability among practitioners, (ii) integrate and formalize different activities that are interrelated in different phases, and (iii) promote the learnability and interoperability by reusing the same ontological base coming from the C-INCAMI framework. This paper is an extension of the work presented in [15] elaborating on new aspects and views (e.g., informational and organizational) for both GOCAME and SIQinU process, as we remark later on. Summarizing, the main contributions of this paper are

(i) a six-phased strategy (SIQinU) useful for understanding and improving the QinU for WebApps, which is specified and illustrated from the process viewpoint regarding activities (i.e., the functional view), interdependencies (behavioral view), artifacts (informational view), and roles (organizational view).

(ii) foundations for reusing a multipurpose goal-oriented strategy (i.e., GOCAME) to derive and integrate more specific-purpose strategies (e.g., SIQinU) regarding its conceptual M&E framework, methods, and process views.

The remainder of this paper is organized as follows. Section 2 gives an overview of the six-phased SIQinU strategy. Section 3 provides the GOCAME rationale considering its three pillars, which are to a great extent reused by SIQinU; particularly, in Section 3.4, we discuss why SIQinU is in alignment with GOCAME regarding its conceptual M&E framework (Section 3.1), its process views (Section 3.2), and its methods (Section 3.3). Section 4 models and illustrates the six-phased SIQinU process from the above-mentioned process views. Section 5 analyzes related work considering the two quoted contributions, and, finally, in Section 6, concluding remarks as well as future work are discussed.

2. Overview of the SIQinU Strategy

SIQinU is an evaluation-driven strategy to iteratively and incrementally improve a WebApp's QinU by means of mapping actual system-in-use problems—that happened while real users were performing common WebApp tasks—to measurable EQ product attributes and by then improving

the current WebApp and assessing the gain both at EQ and QinU levels. SIQinU can be implemented in an economic and systematic manner that alleviates most of the problems identified with typical usability testing studies which can be expensive, subjective, nonrepeatable, time consuming, and unreliable due to users being observed in an intrusive way. This is accomplished through utilizing server-side capabilities to collect user usage data from log files adding, for example, snippets of code in the application to specifically record data used to calculate measures and indicator values for QinU in a nonintrusive way.

Note that SIQinU can apply to systems in use other than WebApps if data can be collected for analysis regarding user activities. This may be possible in client-server network environments where the developer has control over the server code and the activities of users at their client workstations can be collected. Therefore, the major constraint is in collecting easily large amounts of data in a nonintrusive manner from which to measure and evaluate the QinU serving as the basis for improvement.

The SIQinU strategy uses quality models such as those specified in the ISO 25010 standard [1] and its enhancement, that is, the 2Q2U quality framework [2]. Once the QinU model has been established, the data collected, and metrics and indicators calculated, a preliminary analysis is made. If the agreed QinU level is not met, then EQ requirements are derived considering the application's QinU problems and its tasks, subtasks, and associated screens. In turn, taking into account the derived EQ requirements, an evaluation of the WebApp attributes is performed by inspection. Thus a product analysis regarding the EQ evaluation is performed, and changes for improvement are recommended. If the improvement actions have been implemented, then the new version is reevaluated to gauge the improvement gain both from the EQ and the QinU standpoint. Ultimately, SIQinU is a useful strategy not only for understanding but also—and most importantly—for improvement purposes.

SIQinU uses the concepts for nonfunctional requirements specification, measurement, and evaluation design, and so forth, established in the C-INCAMI framework as we will see in Section 3.1. Also, SIQinU has an integrated, well-defined, and repeatable M&E process, which follows to great extent the GOCAME process as we will discuss in Sections 3.2 and 3.3. Specifically, the SIQinU process embraces six phases as shown in Figure 2, which stresses the main phases and interdependencies.

Additionally, Table 1 provides, with Phase (Ph.) reference numbers as per Figure 2, a brief description of each phase, the involved activities, and main artifacts. Section 4 thoroughly illustrates phases, activities, interdependencies, artifacts, as well as roles taking into account aspects of the functional, behavioral, informational, and organizational views.

Lastly, in the Introduction, we stated as contribution that GOCAME—a previously developed strategy—can be reused to derive and integrate more specific-purpose strategies (as is the case of SIQinU) regarding its conceptual M&E framework, process, and methods. Therefore, in the following section, the GOCAME strategy regarding these principles is outlined.

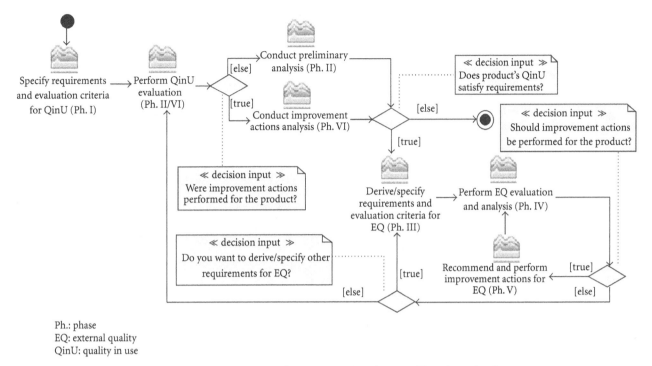

Ph.: phase
EQ: external quality
QinU: quality in use

FIGURE 2: Process overview of SIQinU stressing phases and interdependencies.

3. GOCAME Strategy

GOCAME is a multipurpose M&E strategy that follows a goal-oriented and context-sensitive approach in defining projects. It allows the definition of M&E projects including well-specified context descriptions, providing therefore more robust evaluation interpretations among different project results at intra- and interorganization levels.

GOCAME is based on the three above-mentioned pillars, namely, a conceptual framework (described in Section 3.1); a M&E process (Section 3.2); methods and tools (Section 3.3). Finally, in Section 3.4, we discuss why SIQinU is in alignment with GOCAME regarding these capabilities.

3.1. C-INCAMI Conceptual Framework. The C-INCAMI framework provides a domain (ontological) model defining all the concepts and relationships needed to design and implement M&E processes. It is an approach in which the requirements specification, M&E design, and analysis of results are designed to satisfy a specific information need in a given context. In C-INCAMI, concepts and relationships are meant to be used along all the M&E activities. This way, a common understanding of data and metadata is shared among the organization's projects lending to more consistent analysis and results across projects.

Following the main activities of the process (shown in Section 3.2), the framework—that is, the related concepts and relationships—is structured in six components or modules, namely,

(i) *measurement and evaluation project definition*;

(ii) *nonfunctional requirements specification*;

(iii) *context specification*;

(iv) *measurement design and implementation*;

(v) *evaluation design and implementation*;

(vi) *analysis and recommendation specification*.

For illustration purposes, Figure 3 shows the main concepts and relationships for four components (i.e., from (ii) to (v)), and Table 2 defines the used terms, stressed in *italic* in the following text. The entire modeling of components can be found in [4, 5].

Briefly outlined, the GOCAME strategy follows a goal-oriented approach in which all the activities are guided by agreed *Information Needs*; these are intended to satisfy particular nonfunctional requirements of some *Entity* for a particular purpose and stakeholder's viewpoint. The nonfunctional requirements are represented by *Concept Models* including high-level *Calculable Concepts*, as in ISO 25010's quality models [1], which, in turn, measurable *Attributes* of the entity under analysis are combined. The instantiated quality models are the backbone for measurement and evaluation. *Measurement* is specified and implemented by using *Metrics*, which define how to represent and collect attributes' values; *Evaluation* is specified and implemented by using *Indicators*, which define how to interpret attributes' values and calculate higher-level calculable concepts of the quality model.

Since each *MEProject* does not occur in isolation, we therefore say that measurement and evaluation should be supported by *Context*; thus, context specifications may be

TABLE 1: SIQinU phases, activities, and artifacts.

Phases (Ph.)	Phase description and activities involved	Artifacts (work products)
Ph. I Specify requirements and evaluation criteria for QinU	Taking into account the recorded data of the WebApp's usage, we reengineer QinU requirements. This embraces designing tasks, defining user type, specifying usage context and characteristics. Activities include (see Figure 8) (i) establish information need; (ii) specify project context; (iii) design tasks; (iv) select QinU concept model; (v) design QinU measurement and evaluation; (vi) design Preliminary Analysis	(1) Information Need specification (2) Context specification (3) Task/subtasks specification (4) QinU NFR tree (5) QinU metrics and indicators specification (6) Analysis design
Ph. II Perform QinU evaluation and conduct preliminary analysis	As per Ph. I, data is collected purposely targeting QinU attributes for improvement. Depending on the WebApp's data collection capabilities, we collect data such as the date/time, the data is gathered, errors, task, and subtask completion and accuracy, and so forth. It includes (see Figure 12) (i) collect and parse data pertaining to tasks with their subtasks; (ii) quantify QinU attributes; (iii) calculate QinU indicators; (iv) conduct preliminary analysis	(1) Parsed data file (2) Measure and indicator values for QinU (3) QinU preliminary analysis report
Ph. III Derive/Specify Requirements and Evaluation Criteria for EQ	Based on Ph. I and II, we derive EQ requirements, that is, characteristics and attributes, with their metrics and indicators in order to understand the current WebApp's quality. Activities include (see Figure 13) (i) select EQ concept model; (ii) design EQ measurement; (iii) design EQ evaluation	(1) EQ NFR tree (2) EQ metrics and indicators specification
Ph. IV Perform EQ evaluation and analysis	Activities include (see Figure 15) (i) quantify EQ attributes; (ii) calculate EQ indicators; (iii) conduct an EQ analysis and identify parts of the WebApp that need improvement	(1) Measure and indicator values for EQ (2) EQ analysis report (and new report after reevaluation)
Ph. V Recommend, perform improvement actions, and reevaluate EQ	Using the EQ attributes that require improvement, we make improvement recommendations for modifying the WebApp, that is, version 1 to 1.1. Activities include (see Table 9) (i) recommend improvement actions; (ii) design improvement actions; (iii) perform improvement actions; (iv) evaluate improvement gain to note improvement from benchmark in Ph. IV. Note that once changes were made on the WebApp (Phase V), evaluators could detect that other EQ attributes (from problems identified in QinU) should be derived—under the premise that if further EQ improvement in these new attributes will result in greater impact on the improvement gain in QinU. This concern is taken into account in the process as shown in Figure 2	(1) EQ recommendations report (2) Improvement plan (3) New application version
Ph. VI Reevaluate QinU and analyze improvement actions	Once the new version has been used by real users, we evaluate QinU again to determine the influence of what was improved for the WebApp's EQ on QinU. This provides insight to further develop the *depends-on* and *influences* relationships [8]. Activities include (i) evaluate QinU again to determine level of improvement from Ph. II; (ii) conduct improvement action analysis, which includes developing *depends-on* and *influences* relationships between EQ improvements and QinU	(1) New measure and indicator values for QinU (2) QinU improvement analysis report (3) EQ/QinU attribute relationship table (see Table 11)

provided in order to support sounder analysis, interpretations, and recommendations. A summarized description for each component is provided below.

3.1.1. M&E Project Definition Component. This component defines and relates a set of *Project* concepts needed to articulate M&E activities, roles, and artifacts.

A clear separation of concerns among *Nonfunctional Requirements Project, Measurement Project,* and *Evaluation Project* concepts is made for reuse purposes as well as for easing management's role. The main concept in this component is a measurement and evaluation project (*MEProject*), which allows defining a concrete requirement project with the information need and the rest of the nonfunctional requirements information. From this requirement project, one or more measurement projects can be defined and associated; in turn, for each measurement project, one or more evaluation projects could be defined. Hence, for each measurement and evaluation project we can manage associated subprojects accordingly. Each project also has information such as responsible person's name and contact

TABLE 2: Some M&E terms—see [4] for more details.

Concept	Definition
Project terms	
Evaluation project	A project that allows, starting from a measurement project and a concept model of a nonfunctional requirement project, assigning indicators, and performing the calculation in an evaluation process.
Measurement project	A project that allows, starting from a nonfunctional requirements project, assigning metrics to attributes, and recording the values in a measurement process.
MEProject (i.e., measurement and evaluation project)	A project that integrates related nonfunctional requirements, measurement and evaluation projects, and then allows managing and keeping track of all related metadata and data.
Project	Planned temporal effort, which embraces the specification of activities and resources constraints performed to reach a particular goal.
Nonfunctional requirements project	A project that allows specifying nonfunctional requirements for measurement and evaluation activities.
Nonfunctional requirements terms	
Attribute (synonyms: property, feature)	A measurable physical or abstract property of an entity category.
Calculable concept (synonym: characteristic, dimension)	Abstract relationship between attributes of entities and information needs.
Concept model (synonyms: factor, feature model)	The set of subconcepts and the relationships between them, which provide the basis for specifying the concept requirement and its further evaluation or estimation.
Entity	A concrete object that belongs to an entity category.
Entity category (synonym: object)	Object category that is to be characterized by measuring its attributes.
Information need	Insight necessary to manage objectives, goals, risks, and problems.
Requirement tree	A requirement tree is a constraint to the kind of relationships among the elements of the concept model, regarding the graph theory.
Context terms	
Context	A special kind of entity representing the state of the situation of an entity, which is relevant for a particular information need. The situation of an entity involves the task, the purpose of that task, and the interaction of the entity with other entities as for that task and purpose.
Context property (synonyms: context attribute, feature)	An attribute that describes the context of a given entity; it is associated to one of the entities that participates in the described context.
Measurement terms	
Calculation method	A particular logical sequence of operations specified for allowing the realization of a formula or indicator description by a calculation.
Direct metric (synonyms: base, single metric)	A metric of an attribute that does not depend upon a metric of any other attribute.
Indirect metric (synonyms: derived, hybrid metric)	A metric of an attribute that is derived from metrics of one or more other attributes.
Measure	The number or category assigned to an attribute of an entity by making a measurement.
Measurement	An activity that uses a metric definition in order to produce a measure's value.
Measurement method (synonyms: counting rule, protocol)	The particular logical sequence of operations and possible heuristics specified for allowing the realization of a direct metric description by a measurement.
Metric	The defined measurement or calculation method and the measurement scale.
Scale	A set of values with defined properties. *Note.* The scale type depends on the nature of the relationship between values of the scale. The scale types mostly used in software engineering are classified into nominal, ordinal, interval, ratio, and absolute.
Unit	A particular quantity defined and adopted by convention, with which other quantities of the same kind are compared in order to express their magnitude relative to that quantity.

TABLE 2: Continued.

Concept	Definition
Evaluation terms	
Decision criterion (synonym: acceptability level)	Thresholds, targets, or patterns used to determine the need for action or further investigation, or to describe the level of confidence in a given result.
Elementary indicator (synonyms: elementary preference, criterion)	An indicator that does not depend upon other indicators to evaluate or estimate a calculable concept.
Elementary model (synonym: elementary criterion function)	Algorithm or function with associated decision criteria that model an elementary indicator.
Evaluation (synonym: calculation)	Activity that uses an indicator definition in order to produce an indicator's value.
Global indicator (synonyms: global preference, criterion)	An indicator that is derived from other indicators to evaluate or estimate a calculable concept.
Global model (synonyms: scoring, aggregation model, or function)	Algorithm or function with associated decision criteria that model a global indicator.
Indicator (synonym: criterion)	The defined calculation method and scale in addition to the model and decision criteria in order to provide an estimate or evaluation of a calculable concept with respect to defined information needs.
Indicator value (synonym: preference value)	The number or category assigned to a calculable concept by making an evaluation.

information, starting and ending date, amongst other relevant information. Ultimately, this separation of concerns for each MEProject facilitates the traceability and consistency for intra- and interproject analysis.

3.1.2. Nonfunctional Requirements Specification Component.
This component includes concepts and relationships needed to define the nonfunctional requirements for measurement and evaluation. One key concept is the *Information Need*, which specifies (see Figure 3)

(i) the purpose for performing the evaluation (which can be for instance "understand," "predict," "improve," "control," etc.);

(ii) the focus concept (*CalculableConcept*) to be assessed (e.g., "operability," "quality in use," "actual usability," etc.);

(iii) the category of the entity (*EntityCategory*) that will be assessed, for example, a "Web application" (which its superCategory is a "product" or "information system") and the concrete *Entities* (such as "JIRA," "Mantis" WebApps, etc.). Other super categories for entities can be "resource," "process," "information system-in-use" (e.g., as a Web application-in-use), and "project"

(iv) the userViewpoint (i.e., the intended stakeholder as "developer," "final user," etc.) from which the focus concept (and model) will be evaluated;

(v) the *Context* that characterizes the situation defined by the previous items to a particular MEProject.

The focus concept constitutes the higher-level concept of the nonfunctional requirements; in turn, a calculable concept and its subconcepts are related by means of a *Concept Model*.

This model may be a tree-structured representation in terms of related mid-level calculable concepts and lower-level measurable *Attributes*, which are associated to the target entity. Predefined instances of metadata for information needs, entities, and entity categories, calculable concepts, attributes, and so forth, and its corresponding data can be obtained from an organizational repository to support reusability and consistency in the requirements specification along the organizational projects.

3.1.3. Context Specification Component. This component includes concepts and relationships dealing with the context information specification. The main concept is *Context*, which represents the relevant state of the situation of the entity to be assessed with regard to the stated information need. We consider Context as a special kind of *Entity* in which related relevant entities are involved. Consequently, the context can be quantified through its related entities. By relevant entities, we mean those that could affect how the focus concept of the assessed entity is interpreted (examples of relevant entities of the context may include resources as a network infrastructure, a working team, lifecycle types, the organization, or the project itself, among others).

In order to describe the situation, attributes of the relevant entities (involved in the context) are used. These are also Attributes called *Context Properties* and can be quantified to describe the relevant context of the entity under analysis. A context property inherits the metadata from the Attribute class such as name, definition, and objective, and also adds other information (see Figure 3). All these context properties' metadata are meant to be stored in the organizational repository, and, for each MEProject, the particular metadata and its values are stored as well. A detailed illustration of context and the relationship with other C-INCAMI components can be found in [5].

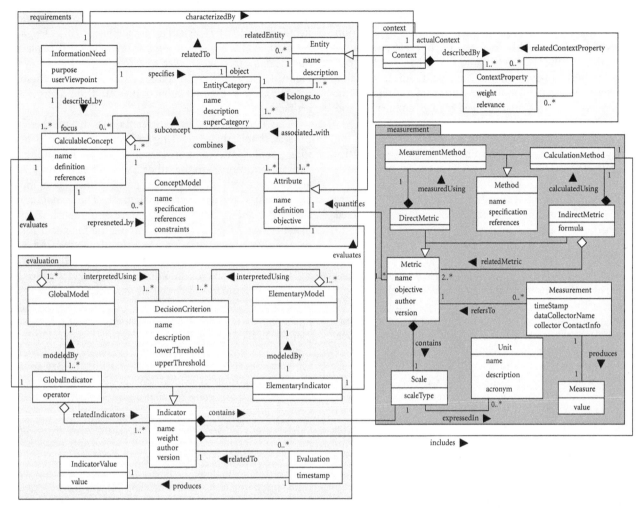

FIGURE 3: Main concepts and relationships of the C-INCAMI framework. Four out of six C-INCAMI components are depicted as packages, namely, nonfunctional requirements specification, context specification, measurement design and implementation, and evaluation design and implementation.

3.1.4. Measurement Design and Implementation Component. This module includes the concepts and relationships intended to specify the measurement design and implementation, for instance, the concrete Entities that will be measured, the selected *Metric* for each attribute, and so on.

Regarding measurement design, a metric provides a *Measurement* specification of how to quantify a particular attribute of an entity, using a particular *Method*, and how to represent its values, using a particular *Scale*. The properties of the measured values in the scale with regard to the allowed mathematical and statistical operations and analysis are given by the *scaleType* [16]. Two types of metrics are distinguished. *Direct Metrics* are those for which values are obtained directly from measuring the corresponding entity's attribute, by using a *Measurement Method*. On the other hand, *Indirect Metrics*' values are calculated from others direct metrics' values following a function specification and a particular *Calculation Method*.

For measurement implementation, a Measurement specifies the activity by using a particular metric description in

order to produce a *Measure* value. Other associated metadata is the data collector name and the timestamp in which the measurement was performed.

3.1.5. Evaluation Design and Implementation Component. This component includes the concepts and relationships intended to specify the evaluation design and implementation. Indicator is the main term, which allows specifying how to calculate and interpret the attributes and calculable concepts of nonfunctional requirement models.

Two types of indicators are distinguished. First, *Elementary Indicators* that evaluate lower-level requirements, namely, attributes combined in a concept model. Each elementary indicator has an *Elementary Model* that provides a mapping function from the metric's measures (the domain) to the indicator's scale (the range). The new scale is interpreted using agreed *Decision Criteria*, which help analyze the level of satisfaction reached by each elementary nonfunctional requirement, that is, by each attribute. Second, *Partial/Global Indicators*, which evaluate mid-level and higher-level requirements, that is, subcharacteristics and characteristics in a concept model. Different aggregation models (*GlobalModel*), like logic scoring of preference models, neuronal networks models, and fuzzy logic models, can be used to perform evaluations. The global indicator's value ultimately represents the global degree of satisfaction in meeting the stated information need for a given purpose and user viewpoint.

As for the implementation, an *Evaluation* represents the activity involving a single calculation, following a particular indicator specification—either elementary or global—producing an *Indicator Value*.

It is worthy to mention that the selected metrics are useful for a measurement process as long as the selected indicators are useful for an evaluation process in order to interpret the stated information need.

3.1.6. Analysis and Recommendation Specification Component. This component includes concepts and relationships dealing with analysis design and implementation as well as conclusion and recommendation. Analysis and recommendation component uses information coming from each MEProject (which includes requirements, context, measurement, and evaluation data and metadata). By storing all this information and by using different kinds of statistical techniques and visualization tools, stakeholders can analyze the assessed entities' strengths and weaknesses with regard to established information needs, and justify recommendations in a consistent way. Note this component is not shown in Figure 3. However, it is shown in Table 5 from the process specification standpoint.

3.2. GOCAME Measurement and Evaluation Process. When modeling a process, often engineers think more about what a process must do rather than how activities should be performed. In order to foster repeatability and reproducibility, a process specifies (i.e., prescribes or informs) a set of phases and activities, inputs and outputs, interdependencies, among other concerns. Also, to deal with the inherent complexity of processes, process views—also quoted in process modeling literature as perspectives—are used. A view is a particular model or approach to represent, specify, and communicate regarding the process. For instance, according to [10], a process can be modeled taking into account four views, namely, functional, behavioral, informational, and organizational.

Considering these process views, the functional perspective for GOCAME represents what activities and tasks (instead of the often-used term "task" in process modeling, which represents a fine grained or atomic activity, we will use the term "sub-activity" in the rest of the text, since, in Section 4, for QinU modeling, the term task has a very specific meaning) should be specified, what hierarchical activities structure (also known as task breakdown structure) there exists, what conditions (pre- and postconditions) should be accomplished, and what inputs and outputs (artifacts) will be required. Taking into account the terminology and components used in the C-INCAMI framework (Section 3.1), the integrated process of GOCAME embraces

the following core activities: (i) *Define Non-Functional Requirements*; (ii) *Design the Measurement*; (iii) *Design the Evaluation*; (iv) *Implement the Measurement*; (v) *Implement the Evaluation*; (vi) *Analyze and Recommend* as shown in Figure 4. In addition, in Table 3, we enumerate these six activities, their involved subactivities, and the main output artifacts.

The behavioral view represents the dynamics of the process, that is, the sequencing and synchronization of activities, parallelisms, iterations, feedback loops, beginning and ending conditions, among other issues. The core GOCAME activities as well as sequences, parallelisms, main inputs, and outputs are depicted in Figure 4. The ≪*datastore*≫ stereotype shown in the figure represents repositories; for instance, the *Metrics* repository stores the metadata for the previously designed metrics. More details for the GOCAME functional and behavioral process views can be found in [6].

On the other hand, the informational view is concerned with those artifacts produced or required (consumed) by activities, the artifact breakdown structure, strategies of configuration management, and traceability models. For example, for illustration purpose, in Figure 5, the structure for the *Non-Functional Requirements Specification,* and *Metrics Specification* documents, which are outputs of *A.1* and *A.2* activities (see Table 3) is modeled. As the reader can observe in Figure 5(a), the *Non-Functional Requirements Specification* artifact is composed of the *Information Need Specification*, the *Context Specification* and the *Non-Functional Requirements Tree* documents. Besides, the *Metrics Specification* artifact (Figure 5(b)) is composed of a set of one or more *Metric Specification*, which in turn is composed of a *Scale* and a *Calculation* or *Measurement Method* descriptions. Note that, aimed at easing the communication among stakeholders these models can complement the textual specification made in the third column of Table 3.

Finally, the organizational view deals with what agents and their associated resources participate-plan-execute-control what activities; which roles (in terms of responsibilities and skills) are assigned to agents; what groups' dynamic and communication strategies are used, among other aspects. To illustrate this, Figure 6 depicts the different roles and their associated GOCAME activities. In Table 4, each role definition and its involved activities are also listed. Note that we have used italics in the definition column (in Table 4) to show the terminological correspondence between the process role definition and the C-INCAMI conceptual framework. It is important to remark that a role can be assumed by a human or an automated agent. And a human agent can be embodied by one or more persons, that is, a team.

In order to combine the above views, Table 5 presents a template which specifies just the *Analyze and Recommend* activity. The template specifies the activity name, objective and description, the subactivities and involved roles, input and output artifacts, pre- and postconditions. Also a diagram representing the *Analyze and Recommend* activity is attached as well to enable understanding and communicability.

Summarizing, the GOCAME M&E process can be described as follows. Once the *nonfunctional requirements*

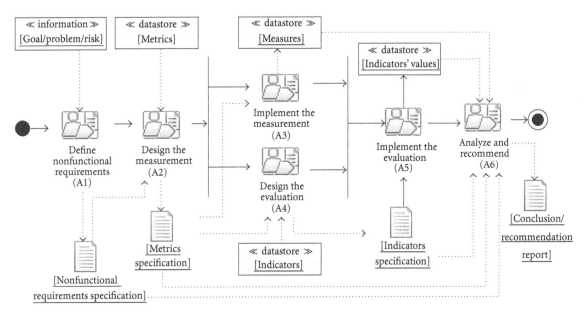

FIGURE 4: Overview of the GOCAME measurement and evaluation process.

TABLE 3: GOCAME core activities and main output artifacts.

Activities (A.)	Subactivities	Artifacts (Work Products)
A.1 Define Nonfunctional requirements	Subactivities include (i) establish information need; (ii) specify project context; (iii) select a concept model. Note that these (and below) subactivities can in turn be broken down in new ones—see [6] for more details.	Nonfunctional requirements specification (this artifact is composed of (i) information need specification; (ii) context specification; (iii) nonfunctional requirements tree)
A.2 Design the measurement	Subactivities include (i) establish entity (optional); (ii) assign one metric to each attribute.	Metrics specification
A.3 Implement the measurement	Subactivities include (i) establish entity; (ii) measure attributes	Measure values
A.4 Design the evaluation	Subactivities include (i) identify elementary indicators; (ii) identify partial and global indicators.	Indicators specification (this artifact is composed of (i) elementary indicators specification; (ii) partial/global indicators specification)
A.5 Implement the evaluation	Subactivities include (i) calculate elementary indicators; (ii) calculate partial and global indicators	Indicator values
A.6 Analyze and recommend	Subactivities include (i) design the analysis; (ii) implement the analysis; (iii) elaborate the conclusion report; (iv) perform recommendations.	Conclusion/recommendation report (this artifact is composed of (i) analysis specification; (ii) analysis report; (iii) conclusion report; (iv) recommendations report)

project has been created by the *nonfunctional requirements manager*, then, the *define non-functional requirements* activity has a specific *goal* or *problem* (agreed with the *evaluation requester*) as input and a *nonfunctional specification document* as output. Then, in the *design the measurement* activity, the *metrics expert* identifies the metrics to quantify attributes. The metrics are selected from a *metrics repository*, and the output is the *metric specification document*. Once the measurement was designed—taking into account raised issues for the evaluator requester, for example, the precision of metrics, and so forth—the *evaluation design* and the

measurement implementation activities can be performed in any order or in parallel as shown in Figure 4. Therefore, the *design the evaluation* activity is performed by the *indicators expert* who allows identifying elementary and global indicators and their acceptability levels (agreed also with the *evaluation requester*). Both the *measurement design* and the *evaluation design* are led by the *measurement and evaluation managers* accordingly. To the *implement the measurement* activity, the *data collector* uses the specified metrics to obtain the measures, which are stored in the *measures repository*. Next, the *implement the evaluation* activity can be

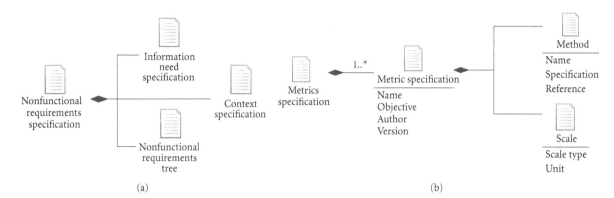

FIGURE 5: Excerpt of the informational view for A.1 and A.2 in Table 3, regarding artifact composition. (a) Nonfunctional requirements specification documents; (b) metrics specification document.

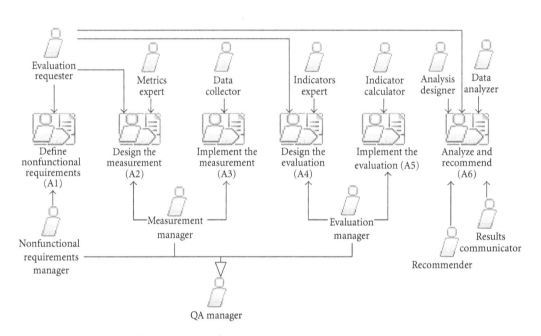

FIGURE 6: The organizational view: roles assigned to the GOCAME activities.

carried out by the *indicator calculator*—this role usually is enacted by a tool. Finally, *analyze and recommend* activity is performed by *analysis designer*, *data analyzer*, *recommender*, and *results communicator* roles. This activity has as inputs measures and indicators values (i.e., data), the requirements specification document, and the associated metrics and indicators specifications (i.e., metadata) in order to produce a *conclusion/recommendation report*.

3.3. GOCAME Methods and Tools: WebQEM and C-INCAMI_Tool.

While activities state "what" to do, methods describe "how" to perform these activities accomplished by agents and roles, which in turn can be automated by tools. In addition, a methodology is a set of related methods. Since the above M&E process includes activities such as specify the requirements tree and identify metrics, we have envisioned a methodology that integrates all these aspects and tools that automate them; that is, a set of well-defined

and cooperative methods, models, techniques, and tools that, applied consistently to the process activities, produces the different outcomes.

Particularly, the WebQEM and its associated tool the so-called C-INCAMI_Tool (see screenshots in Figure 7) were instantiated from the conceptual framework and process. The methodology supports an evaluation-driven approach, relying on experts and/or end users to evaluate and analyze different views of quality such as EQ and QinU for software and system-in-use applications. Note that GOCAME strategy and its methodology can be used to evaluate not only software/WebApps but also other entity categories, such as resources and processes.

In addition to the above-mentioned views, a method-ological view is presented in [11]. This represents the process constructors to be applied to the different descriptions of activities in a given process. Note that, for a specific activity description, we can have one or more methods that give

TABLE 4: GOCAME role definitions and involved activities.

Role name	Definition/comment	Activities (as per Figure 4)
Quality Assurance (QA) Manager	Responsible for leading a *measurement and evaluation project* (MEProject in Table 2) regarding the requester needs. Note this role is specified by three subroles as per Figure 5.	Note this role is responsible of the activities involved in three specific subroles as per Figure 5.
Nonfunctional requirements manager	Responsible for the *nonfunctional requirements project*. This role should be played by a nonfunctional requirement engineer.	(i) Define non-functional requirements
Measurement manager	Responsible for leading a *measurement project*.	(i) Design the measurement (ii) Implement the measurement
Evaluation manager	Responsible for leading an *evaluation project*.	(i) Design the evaluation (ii) Implement the evaluation
Evaluation requester	Responsible for requesting an evaluation. Note that this role can be accomplished by a human or an organization.	(i) Define nonfunctional requirements (ii) Design the measurement (iii) Design the evaluation
Metrics expert	Responsible for identifying the appropriate *metrics* from a catalogue for each *attribute* of the *requirements tree*, based on the established *information need*.	(i) Design the measurement
Data collector	Responsible for gathering *measures* of the *attributes* using the *metrics* specification. Note that the data collector role can be accomplished by either a human agent or an automatic agent.	(i) Implement the measurement
Indicators expert	Responsible for identifying the most appropriate *indicators* from a catalogue and to define *decision criteria* for each *attribute* and *calculable concept* of the *requirements tree* based on the established *information need*.	(i) Design the evaluation
Indicator calculator	Responsible for calculating the *indicators values* using the *indicators* specification. Note this role usually is accomplished by an automatic agent.	(i) Implement the evaluation
Analysis Designer	Responsible for identifying the appropriate data analysis methods and techniques to be used regarding scales, scale types, and the project/business commitment in addition to visualization and documentation techniques.	(i) Analyze and Recommend
Data analyzer	Responsible for conducting the data analysis based on the design of the analysis. Note this role can be accomplished by either a human agent or an automatic agent or both.	(i) Analyze and recommend
Recommender	Responsible for conducting the recommendations based on the conclusion report and taking into account the business commitment.	(i) Analyze and recommend
Results communicator	Responsible for communicating the evaluation results and recommendations to the evaluation requester.	(i) Analyze and recommend

support to the same activity, and, for a given method, we can have one or more tools that enact it. For instance, in Table 3, for the *A.5* activity, and particularly for the *calculate the partial/global indicators* subactivity, many methods can accomplish this such as "linear additive scoring method," "neural network method," among others.

3.4. Why Is SIQinU in Alignment with GOCAME? As we have indicated in the last paragraph of Section 2, SIQinU also relies on the three GOCAME principles above outlined and depicted in Figure 1. In fact, SIQinU utilizes the C-INCAMI conceptual base, underlying process and methods as we discuss in Section 4. However, since SIQinU is a specific-purpose goal-oriented strategy, it has specific activities, some particular methods, and procedures that are not taken into account in GOCAME. Moreover, while GOCAME is a multipurpose strategy regarding the strategy aim, SIQinU is a specific-purpose strategy. This is so, because in GOCAME the information need purpose can be "understand," "predict," "improve," "control"—as indicated in Section 3.1.2—while, in SiQinU, the purposes are just "understand" and ultimately "improve." In addition, GOCAME was designed to allow assessing different calculable concepts and entities such as the EQ or QinU of any product (including WebApps), the cost of a product, the capability quality of a resource, among others. Meanwhile, SIQinU was designed to evaluate specifically QinU of systems in-use (in a non-intrusive way) and EQ of systems, as for example, WebApps. Even more in SiQinU, from the nonfunctional requirements standpoint, QinU is evaluated from the "do goals" or pragmatic view, rather than from the "be goals" (subjective view), as thoroughly discussed in [2].

TABLE 5: Process template in which information and views are documented for the *Analyze and Recommend* activity.

Activity: analyze and recommend   *Code* (in Figure 4): A6

Objective: elaborate and communicate a conclusion report and (if necessary) a recommendation report for a decision-making process.

Description: identify and select procedures, techniques and tools to be used in order to analyze data, metadata, and information, coming from metrics and indicators, for a given information need. Based on the analysis results, a conclusion report is produced, and, a recommendations report, if necessary, is yielded as well. All these reports are communicated to the evaluation requester.

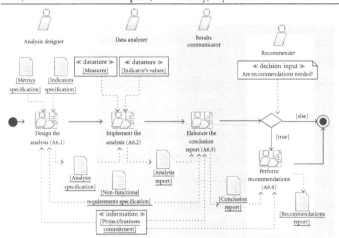

Subactivities:

(i) Design the analysis (A6.1)

(ii) Implement the analysis (A6.2)

(iii) Elaborate the conclusion report (A6.3)

(iv) Perform recommendations (A6.4)

Involved roles:

(i) Analysis designer

(ii) Data analyzer

(iii) Recommender

(iv) Results communicator

Input artifacts:

(i) Nonfunctional requirements specification

(ii) Metrics specification

(iii) Indicators specification

(iv) Measures

(v) Indicators values

(vi) Project/business commitment

Output Artifacts:

Conclusion/Recommendation report.

Note that this artifact is composed of

(i) Analysis specification;

(ii) Analysis report;

(iii) Conclusion Report; and

(iv) Recommendations report.

Preconditions: a MEProject must be implemented.

Postconditions: the MEProject finishes when the conclusion and/or recommendation report is communicated and agreed on between the QA manager and the requester of the evaluation.

Considering the process, SIQinU also reuses the GOCAME activities. For example, the GOCAME A1, A2, A4 activities, and, to some extent, the A6 activity (recall Figure 4) are included in SIQinU Ph. I and Ph. III (recall Figure 2). Likewise, the A3 and A5 activities are included in Ph. II and Ph. IV phases. However, there are particular activities in SIQinU that are not included into GOCAME. For example, in Phase V, we have activities devoted to produce WebApp improvements, as well as in Phase II, there exist activities for data filtering and collection, since SIQinU proposes utilizing server-side capabilities to gather, in a nonintrusive way, user usage data.

Considering the conceptual framework, SIQinU reuses totally C-INCAMI, that is, the ontological M&E conceptual base and its six components commented in Section 3.1. As above-mentioned SIQinU extends GOCAME activities, there are new activities (e.g., in Ph V for improvement techniques, and those related to nonintrusive data filtering in Ph. II), which lack the ontological root in C-INCAMI. Note that C-INCAMI concepts and components deal primarily with nonfunctional requirements, measurement, and evaluation

issues, rather than functional aspects for design refactoring, code programming or restructuring, and so forth, which implies other domain scope and model. Note that C-INCAMI is a flexible framework that can be extended and linked with other domain models and frameworks to deal, for example, with functional aspects.

Also measurement and evaluation methods as commented in Section 3.3 are reused. However, other methods and techniques that are not included in GOCAME such as those for changing the current WebApp version (in Phase V) are needed. Finally, all the roles defined in Table 4 are totally reused as well, adding new ones for the activities of Ph V as, for example, the "Maintenance Project Manager" role (i.e., the responsible for leading a maintenance project and identifying the appropriate methods, techniques, and tools to be used for change—improve—the application) and the "Developer" role (i.e., the responsible for conducting the software/web application changes).

Despite the mentioned similarities with GOCAME, the modeling of the functional and behavioral views in SIQinU is necessary given the amount of involved phases, activities,

FIGURE 7: Snapshots of the C-INCAMI tool.

subactivities, and their workflows. These issues will be highlighted in the next section.

4. A Process Model View for SIQinU

Process modeling is rather a complex endeavor. Given the inherent complexity of the process domain, a process can be modeled taking into account different views as analyzed in Section 3.2 for GOCAME. With the aim to model the SIQinU phases and activities, their inputs and outputs, sequences, parallelism, and iterations, we specify below using UML activity diagrams and the SPEM profile [14], the functional view taking into account behavioral concerns as well. Aspects of the organizational and informational views are to a lesser extent specified in the following diagrams, since as indicated in Section 3.4 many of the roles and artifacts are reused from the GOCAME strategy. Note that, in order to facilitate the communication, automation, and collaboration, different modeling languages and tools can be used to specify all the views. Each has its own strengths and weaknesses, which can make it more suitable for modeling certain views than others [12]. However, nowadays, SPEM is widely used and according to [17] can be adopted by researchers and practitioners for different disciplines, not just software engineering.

Also in Section 2 (Figure 2 and Table 1), we depicted the SIQinU phases, so below we concentrate on the specifications of activities and their descriptions. In order to illustrate the SIQinU process, excerpts of a case study conducted in mid-2010 are used (see details of the case study in [8]). This case study examined JIRA (http://www.atlassian.com/), a defect reporting WebApp in commercial use in over 24,000 organizations in 138 countries around the globe. JIRA's most common task, *Entering a new defect*, was evaluated in order to provide the most benefit, since entering a new defect represents a large percentage of the total usage of the application. We studied 50 beginner users in a real work environment in their daily routine of testing software and reporting defects in a software testing department of ABC, a company (with fictitious name but real one) specializing in software quality and testing. The beginner users were testers

which were the majority of users. Although there are other user categories such as test managers, QA managers, and administrators, testers are the predominant user type, so we chose beginner testers as our user viewpoint.

4.1. Phase I: Specify Requirements and Evaluation Criteria for QinU. Once the requirements project has been created, using the data of the WebApp's usage recorded in log files, we reengineer and establish QinU requirements, that is, characteristics with measurable attributes, with the objective of not only understanding but also improving the system-in-use with real users. From observations of the actual WebApp, this phase embraces defining user type, designing tasks, specifying usage context and dimensions for QinU (e.g., actual usability) and their attributes. Based on these specifications, metrics (for measurement) and indicators (for evaluation) are selected. Below we describe the seven core activities (see the flow in Figure 8) involved in Ph. I.

4.1.1. Establish Information Need. This activity, according to the C-INCAMI framework (recall requirements package in Figure 3), involves *Define the purpose* and *the user viewpoint*, *establish the object* and *the entity* under study, and *identify the focus* of the evaluation (see Figure 9). These activities are accomplished by the NFR manager role considering the evaluation requester's needs. In the case study, the purpose for performing the evaluation is to "understand" and "improve" the WebApp being used from the userViewpoint of a "beginner tester." The category of the entity (i.e., the object) assessed was a "defect tracking WebApp" while the entity being studied was "JIRA" (called in our study JIRA v.1). The focus (CalculableConcept) assessed is "actual usability" and its subcharacteristics, "effectiveness in use," "efficiency in use," and "learnability in use" [2].

4.1.2. Specify Project Context. Once the information need specification document is yielded, we optionally can *Specify Project Context* as shown in Figure 8. It involves the *Select relevant Context Properties* subactivity—from the organizational repository of context properties [5], and, for each

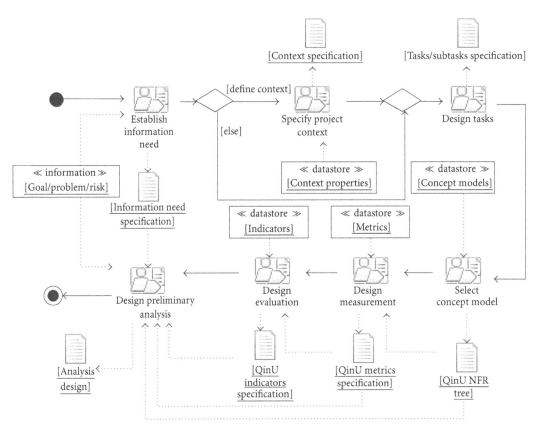

FIGURE 8: Overview for the specify requirements and evaluation criteria for QinU process (Ph. I).

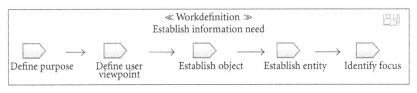

FIGURE 9: Activities for establish information need.

selected property, the *Quantify Context Property* activity must be performed—based on the associated metric. In the end, we get as output a context specification document for the specific project.

4.1.3. Design Tasks. In this activity, the most common and representative task or tasks should be designed. It is also important to choose a task that is performed for which sufficient data can be collected. In our case study, the selected task by the evaluation requester was "entering a new defect," as indicated above. This JIRA task included 5 subtasks specified by the task designer, namely: (i) Summary, steps, and results; (ii) Add Detail Info; (iii) Add Environment Info; (iv) Add Version Info; (v) Add Attachment (see details of tasks and screens in [8]).

4.1.4. Select QinU Concept Model. It involves both *Select a Model* and *Edit the Model* subactivities. Concept models are chosen from an organizational repository regarding the

quality focus. For example, in our case study, the NFR manager based on the previously stated information need and taking into account the concept focus to evaluate actual usability, he instantiated a concept model for the "do goals" of the user [2]. Then, if the selected model is not totally suitable, for example, some subcharacteristics or attributes are missing, it is necessary to *Edit the Model*, adding or removing subconcepts, and/or attributes accordingly.

Finally, a requirements tree where attributes are the leaves and the concept focus is the root is yielded. For the selected concept model and regarding the information need and task at hand, the NFR manager instantiated the model as shown in Table 6 (attributes are in italic). Basically, the NFR manager, in the end, needs to satisfy the objectives of the sponsoring organization, that is, the evaluation requester.

4.1.5. Design QinU Measurement. For each attribute of the requirements tree—highlighted in italic in Table 6—we *Identify a Metric* to quantify them. The appropriate metrics

TABLE 6: Instantiated QinU NFR tree for JIRA case study.

---

1. Actual usability
   1.1. Effectiveness in use
      1.1.1. *Subtask correctness*
      1.1.2. *Subtask completeness*
      1.1.3. *Task successfulness*
   1.2. Efficiency in use
      1.2.1. *Subtask correctness efficiency*
      1.2.2. *Subtask completeness efficiency*
      1.2.3. *Task successfulness efficiency*
   1.3. Learnability in use
      1.3.1. *Subtask correctness learnability*
      1.3.2. *Subtask completeness learnability*
      1.3.3. *Task successfulness learnability*

---

are selected from a repository. In the C-INCAMI framework, two types of metrics are specified, a direct metric which applies a measurement method, that is, our data collection procedures from log files, and an indirect metric which uses a formula (based on other direct and/or indirect metrics) and calculation method (recall measurement package in Figure 3). If the metric is indirect, it is necessary *identify related metrics* and *identify attributes quantified by related Metrics* (see Figure 10). These two subactivities allow identifying the extra attributes and metrics for the indirect metric so that data collector may later gather the data accordingly.

In the JIRA case study, the metrics used to measure attributes were selected by the metrics expert from a metric catalogue which contains over 30 indirect metrics and their associated direct metrics. Below we illustrate the selected indirect metric for the subtask completeness efficiency (coded 1.2.2 in Table 6) attribute:

> Metric: average ratio of subtasks that are completed incorrectly or correctly per unit of time to do it (AvgRCput).
>
> Interpretation: 0 <= AvgRCput, more is better.
>
> Objective: calculate the overall average proportion of the subtasks that are completed, whether correct or incorrect, per time unit (usually seconds or minutes).
>
> Calculation Method (Formula): AvgRCput = AvgRC/AvgTC
>
>> AvgRC = Average ratio of subtasks that are completed incorrectly or correctly
>> AvgTC = Average time for a complete subtask, correct or incorrect
>
> Scale: numeric
>
> Type of Scale: ratio
>
> Unit (type, description): subtasks effectiveness/time, subtask completeness effectiveness per time unit (usually seconds or minutes).

As final output of these activities, we get the QinU metrics specification document.

4.1.6. Design QinU Evaluation. Once the metric specifications have been completed, we can design an indicator for each attribute and calculable concept of the requirements tree. Taking into account the C-INCAMI framework (recall evaluation package in Figure 3), there are two indicator types: elementary and global indicators. The elementary Indicators evaluate attributes and map to a new scale based on the metric's measures. The new scale is interpreted to analyze the level of satisfaction reached by each attribute. On the other hand, the global indicators (also called partial indicator if it evaluates a subcharacteristic) evaluate characteristics in a concept model and serve to analyze the level of global (or partial) satisfaction achieved.

Following the activities flow depicted in Figure 11, for each attribute of the requirements tree, the indicators expert should specify an elementary indicator by means of the next iterative activities: *establish the elementary model, establish the calculation method* (optional), and *identify the scale.*

The first activity (*establish the elementary model*) involves establishing a function to map between measure and indicator values and define the associated decision criteria or acceptability levels (see Section 3.1.5). In our case, the indicators expert and the evaluation requester defined three acceptability ranges in the indicator percentage scale, namely, a value within 70–90 (a marginal—bold—range) indicates a need for improvement actions; a value within 0–70 (an unsatisfactory—italic—range) means changes must take place with high priority; a score within 90–100 indicates a satisfactory level—bold italic—for the analyzed attribute. The acceptance levels in this case study were the same for all indicators, both elementary and partial/global, but could be different depending on the needs of the evaluation requester.

Note that the *establish the calculation method* activity is not mandatory because usually the model used is an easily interpreted function. In other cases, the calculation method should be specified.

Regarding to the partial/global indicators, these are specified in a similar way to the elementary indicators, as we can see in Figure 11. For example, in the JIRA case study, a global (linear additive) aggregation model to calculate the requirements tree was selected, with equal weights for their elements. This approach was used given that it was an exploratory study. Different weights would be assigned based on the requester's objectives to reflect the different levels of importance relative to one another. For example, for effectiveness in use, some organizations may weigh mistakes or correctness more heavily than completeness depending on the domain. A pharmacy or accounting application, for example, may have a higher weighting for accuracy.

The final output for the QinU evaluation design is an indicators specification document for quality in use. An artifact hierarchy (i.e., the informational view) of the indicators specification document is shown in Figure 12.

4.1.7. Design Preliminary Analysis. Taking into account the underlying SIQinU improvement objective, the specific QinU requirements for the project, the task, the metrics and indicators specifications, as well as the data properties with

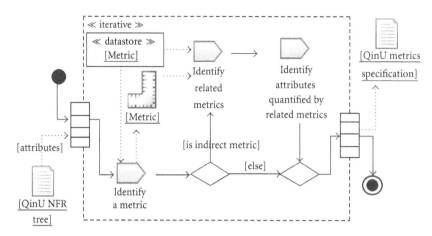

FIGURE 10: Design QinU Measurement activity.

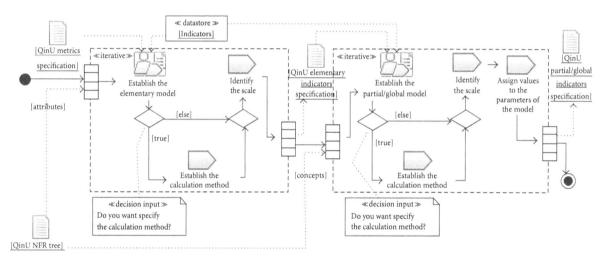

FIGURE 11: Design QinU evaluation activity.

regard to the scale, a preliminary analysis design should be drawn by the analysis designer role. This activity involves deciding on the allowable mathematical and statistical methods and techniques for analysis regarding the scale type, dataset properties, and so forth, the suitable tools for the kinds of analysis at hand, the presentation, and visualization mechanisms, and so forth.

4.2. Phase II: Perform QinU Evaluation and Analysis. This phase involves the basic activities to accomplish the first purpose of the SIQinU strategy, namely, understand the current QinU satisfaction level of the actual WebApp in use. To achieve this, the next four activities (see Figure 13) should be performed.

4.2.1. Collect Data. Taking into account the tasks specification, the log files with the user usage data are analyzed and the relevant data is filtered and organized to facilitate the measurement for each attribute in the next activity. Note that a tool can be used to process the log file for extracting the relevant data from user records.

4.2.2. Quantify Attributes. After collecting the data, we derive measurement values for each attribute in the QinU requirements tree. The values are obtained based on the measurement or calculation methods specified in QinU metrics specification according to the *design QinU measurement* activity (Figure 10).

4.2.3. Calculate Indicators. Taking into account the measures (values) and the indicators specification, the indicators values are calculated by the indicators calculator. The global indicator value ultimately represents the degree of satisfaction in meeting the stated information need for a concrete entity, for a given purpose, and user viewpoint. Within the *calculate indicators* activity, first, the *calculate elementary indicator* activity should be performed for each attribute of the requirements tree, and then, using these indicators' values and the specified partial or global model, the partial and global indicators are calculated by performing the *Calculate Partial/Global Indicator* activity for each calculable concept. Table 7, columns 2 and 3, shows each element of the QinU nonfunctional requirements tree evaluated at task level

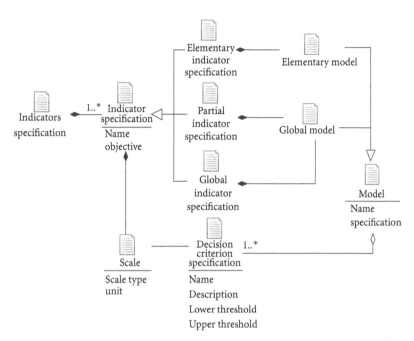

FIGURE 12: An informational view of the QinU indicators specification document.

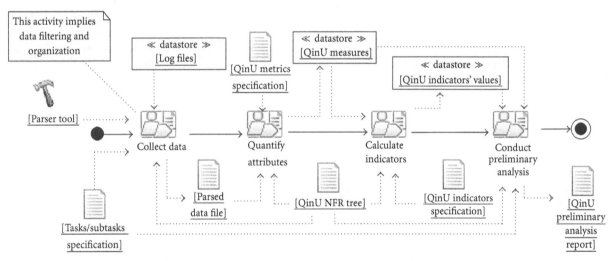

FIGURE 13: Overview for the perform QinU evaluation and analysis phase (Ph. II).

with elementary, partial and global indicators for the current version of JIRA (i.e., v.1).

4.2.4. Conduct Preliminary Analysis. After calculating indicators at all levels, that is, elementary, partial, and global, a preliminary analysis on the current JIRA WebApp task is conducted by the data analyzer role. Basically, it follows the analysis design (produced in the *design preliminary analysis* activity, in Ph. I), that is, implementing the designed procedures and planned tools, and storing results according to established formats in order to produce the preliminary analysis report. The analysis allows us to understand how the application performs overall (globally) and also with respect

to each particular attribute for each part of the task (i.e., at subtask levels) being executed by a given user group type.

In the case study, the preliminary analysis was conducted for the above-mentioned task, its five subtasks, and their associated screens in JIRA, for the beginner user type. This allows the recommender to gauge more specifically where users had difficulty, for example, low task successfulness, low completion rate in using the application, among others.

4.3. Phase III: Derive/Specify Requirements and Evaluation Criteria for EQ. Taking into account the preliminary analysis report yielded in Phase II for QinU and the requirements tree defined in Phase I, in Phase III, a requirements tree for

TABLE 7: QinU evaluation of JIRA, both before (v.1) and after implementing improvements (v.1.1). EI stands for elementary indicator; P/GI stands for partial/global indicator.

Characteristics and attributes	JIRA v.1		JIRA v.1.1	
	EI	P/G I	EI	P/G I
1. Actual Usability		53.3%		67.0%
1.1. Effectiveness in use		73.2%		86.7%
1.1.1. *Subtask correctness*	**86.4**%		**91.9**%	
1.1.2. *Subtask completeness*	**87.9**%		**95.5**%	
1.1.3. *Task successfulness*	45.5%		72.7%	
1.2. Efficiency in use		29.3%		42.8%
1.2.1. *Subtask correctness efficiency*	37.4%		44.3%	
1.2.2. *Subtask completeness efficiency*	37.5%		47.3%	
1.2.3. *Task successfulness efficiency*	13.1%		36.8%	
1.3. Learnability in use		57.3%		71.6%
1.3.1. *Subtask correctness learnability*	**78.8**%		75.1%	
1.3.2. *Subtask completeness learnability*	26.4%		77.3%	
1.3.3. *Task successfulness learnability*	66.7%		62.5%	

EQ is derived. This requirements tree is tailored considering those product features that would need improvement with potential positive impact in QinU, mainly for those problems found in Phase II. In this phase, metrics and indicators are specified in order to evaluate the WebApp through its inspection involving three main activities (see Figure 14), namely, *select EQ concept model, design EQ measurement,* and *design EQ evaluation.* Note that these activities are similar to Phase I activities (recall Figure 8), but now from the EQ viewpoint.

4.3.1. Select EQ Concept Model. Given the preliminary analysis report performed in Phase II which may have reported potential problems of the actual WebApp, EQ characteristics and attributes possibly related to those QinU dimensions are identified, resulting then in a new requirements tree. The activities to be performed by the NFR manager are *select a model* and *edit the model.*

In the case study, in this activity, the requirements tree for the EQ viewpoint was established using 2Q2U (as in Phase I), instantiating the characteristics operability and information quality to determine possible effects on effectiveness in use, efficiency in use, and learnability in use. Those EQ characteristics and attributes that are possibly related to those QinU dimensions with potential problems have been instantiated resulting in the requirements tree shown on the left side of Table 8.

4.3.2. Design EQ Measurement. Following Figure 14, once the EQ model was instantiated in a requirements tree, the measurement should be designed to produce the metric specifications to perform Phase IV. As can be seen in Figure 15, this activity is similar to designing the QinU measurement (recall Figure 10 in Phase I) and is performed by the metrics expert, but now the process is executed for EQ attributes. In addition, next to *identify a metric* for an attribute from the repository and its related metrics and

attributes (if the selected metric is an indirect metric), the *select a tool* activity can be performed to choose a tool that automates the metric method.

In the case study, for each attribute from the EQ requirements tree shown in Table 8, a metric was identified by the metrics expert. For instance, for the attribute navigability feedback completeness (coded 1.1.1.1), the metric is as follows.

Indirect Metric: task navigability feedback completeness (TNFC).

Objective: calculate the average of completeness considering the navigational feedback completeness level for all subtask screens for the given task.

Calculation method (formula):

$$\text{TNFC} = \sum_{j=1}^{j=n} \left(\sum_{i=1}^{i=m} \text{NFC}_{ij}/m \right)/n, \qquad (1)$$

for $j = 1$ to n, where n is the number of subtasks of the given task,

for $i = 1$ to m, where m is the number of screens for subtask j.

Interpretation: $0 <= \text{TNFC} <= 3$, more is better.

Scale: numeric.

Scale type: ratio.

Unit: completeness level (*Note*: this metric can be converted to percentage unit, i.e., TNFC/0.03).

As this is an indirect metric, related metric and attribute were identified:

Attribute: screen navigation feedback.

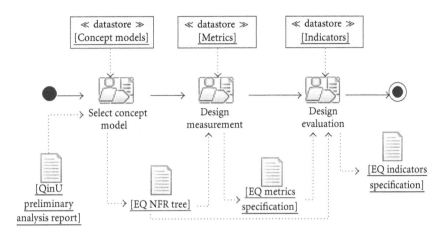

FIGURE 14: Overview for the derive/specify requirements and evaluation criteria for EQ process (Ph. III).

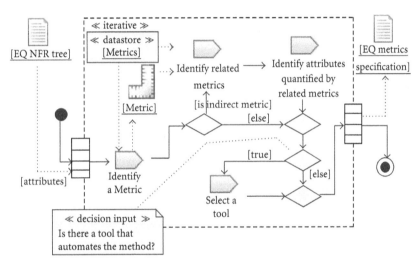

FIGURE 15: Activity flow involved in design external quality measurement activity.

Direct metric: navigation feedback completeness level (NFC).

Objective: determine the screen meets the criteria for navigation feedback completeness. *Note*: This metric is similar to the breadcrumb or path capability available in many WebApps.

Measurement method (type: objective): the screen is inspected to determine the rating (0–3), where evaluators through inspection observe the availability of the previous (backward), current, and next location (forward) mechanism. Screens should support the completeness of this navigation feedback.

Scale: numerical.

Scale type: ratio.

Allowed values: (0) has none; (1) has one of them; (2) has two of them; (3) has all of them.

Unit: completeness level.

4.3.3. Design EQ Evaluation. Similar to Phase I, one indicator per each attribute and concept of the EQ requirements

tree should be identified by the indicators expert. In our case, when elementary, partial, and global indicators were designed, new acceptability ranges (DecisionCriterion in Figure 3) were agreed between the evaluation requester and the indicators expert. The three acceptability ranges in the indicator percentage scale were as follows: a value within 60–80 (a marginal—bold—range) indicates a need for improvement actions; a value within 0–60 (an unsatisfactory—italic—range) means changes must take place with high priority; a score within 80–100 indicates a satisfactory level—bold italic—for the analyzed attribute. Note that this indicator mapping does not necessarily have to be the same as the QinU mapping (e.g., may have different range thresholds) but rather should meet the information need and goals of the evaluation requester.

4.4. Phase IV: Perform EQ Evaluation and Analysis. Based on metric and indicator specifications obtained in Phase III, the measurement and evaluation of the EQ requirements and the analysis of the current product situation are performed. This phase is similar to Phase II, but now for EQ. The involved activities are shown in Figure 16. Note the similarity with Phase II (recall Figure 13), but, for Phase IV, the *collect data* activity is not performed, that is, it is just carried out in Phase II to obtain user data usage from log files in a nonintrusive way. In this phase, the measurement and evaluation activities are done by inspection.

Once each attribute is measured by the data collector in *quantify attributes* activity, and all indicators are calculated in *calculate indicators* activity, the data analyzer role should *conduct EQ analysis*. The latter activity generates an EQ analysis report with information that allows us to identify, for instance, parts of the application that needs improvement from the EQ viewpoint. In Table 8 (columns 2 and 3), we can see the EQ evaluation results from JIRA (v.1) case study. Note, for example, that some attributes such as error prevention (coded 1.2.2.1.) and context-sensitive help availability (coded 1.1.2.1) need improvement with high priority. Also, we can observe that, for some elementary indicators (attributes), no improvement is needed, for example, stability of main control (coded 1.2.1.2).

4.5. Phase V: Recommend, Perform Improvement Actions, and Reevaluate EQ. Considering the previous EQ analysis report generated in *Conduct EQ Analysis* activity (Phase IV), we make recommendations to improve the application for those EQ attributes that needed improvement. After the recommended changes were completed in the current WebApp and a new version generated, we reevaluate the EQ to determine the improvement gain between both product versions. The activities for this phase are shown in Table 9 and described below.

4.5.1. Recommend Improvement Actions. Based on the EQ analysis report generated in Phase IV, the *recommend improvement actions* activity is carried out by the recommender in order to produce a recommendations report. This document has a set of recommendations for which attributes of the WebApp can be improved. For instance, a ranking of elementary indicators scored from weaker—that is, that fell in the unsatisfactory acceptability level—to stronger, but which did not fall in the satisfactory or bold italic levels can be listed.

Then, the evaluation requester can prioritize recommendations made for improvement action. Considering the case study, in this activity, some of the recommendations listed in the recommendations report were the following:

(i) for increasing the satisfaction level of defaults attribute (1.2.3.1) change fields to have default and make mandatory because they are critical defect description correctness and completeness;

(ii) for increasing the satisfaction level of Error Prevention attribute (1.2.2.1) add context sensitive help and eliminate nonvalid platform combinations.

4.5.2. Design Improvement Actions. Based on the previous recommendations report, the maintenance project manager

produces an improvement plan indicating how to actually change the application. This "how" implies planning methods and techniques to be used to actually accomplish the improvement actions in the next activity (*perform improvement actions*). Methods and techniques for changing the WebApp can range from parameterized reconfigurations, code restructuring, refactoring (as made in [18]) to architectural redesign. The eventual method employed depends on the scope of the improvement recommendation as well as the resources of the evaluation requester and the desired effect. The expected effect may include an application easier to operate and learn, faster to run, more secure, among many other aspects.

For example, taking into account the two improvement recommendations listed in the above activity, the improvement plan included the following.

(i) *Recommendation*: add context sensitive help to improve the error prevention (1.2.2.1) attribute. *Action taken*: defect steps moved to next screen on add detail info, with help, examples shown to aid user.

(ii) *Recommendation*: eliminate nonvalid platform combinations to improve error prevention (1.2.2.1). *Action taken*: help provided and invalid combinations not allowed.

(iii) *Recommendation*: change fields to have default and make mandatory because they are critical defect description correctness and completeness to improve the defaults (1.2.3.1) attribute. *Action taken*: done where possible.

4.5.3. Perform Improvement Actions. With the improvement plan, the developer of the WebApp performs changes accordingly, resulting in a new application version (see the activity flow in Table 9). The ABC developer of our JIRA case study made some of the recommended changes, including those shown above, resulting in a new product version termed JIRA v.1.1. This new JIRA version had many other improvements not shown, one of which was the reduction of workload through eliminating one subtask and moving more related items together to make the overall task design more efficient. Thus, JIRA v.1.1 only has 4 subtasks, instead of 5. Because JIRA does not give access to its source code, the developer could not enact all the changes that were recommended; so only some improvements were made. Rather, through changing its configuration, they were able to perform most of the changes. Note that some recommended changes that could not be made were due to the application under study, and not due to SIQinU.

4.5.4. Evaluate Improvement Gain. Once changes were made, the WebApp can be reevaluated by inspection to determine which attributes have been improved, which have not, and get a score which can be compared to the outcomes of Phase IV. The activities involved are *quantify attributes*, *calculate indicators*, and *conduct EQ analysis*. The output is a new EQ analysis report in which the changes made

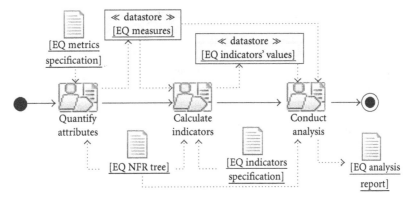

FIGURE 16: Overview for perform EQ evaluation and analysis phase (Ph. IV).

TABLE 8: EQ evaluation of JIRA, both before (v.1) and after (v.1.1) implementing improvements.

| | JIRA v.1 | | JIRA v.1.1 | |
Characteristics and attributes	EI	P/G I	EI	P/G I
External Quality		38%		**74%**
1. Operability		30%		**60%**
1.1. Learnability		26%		59%
1.1.1. Feedback suitability		38%		38%
1.1.1.1. Navigability feedback completeness	*33%*		*33%*	
1.1.1.2. Task progress feedback appropriateness	*30%*		*30%*	
1.1.1.3. Entry form feedback awareness	*50%*		*50%*	
1.1.2. Helpfulness		15%		**80%**
1.1.2.1. Context-sensitive help availability	*20%*		**80%**	
1.1.2.2. Help completeness	*10%*		**80%**	
1.2. Ease of use		34%		61%
1.2.1. Controllability		**80%**		**80%**
1.2.1.1. Permanence of main controls	**60%**		**60%**	
1.2.1.2. Stability of main controls	**100%**		**100%**	
1.2.2. Error management		0%		30%
1.2.2.1. Error prevention	*0%*		*30%*	
1.2.3. Data entry ease		23%		73%
1.2.3.1. Defaults	*10%*		*50%*	
1.2.3.2. Mandatory entry	*10%*		*80%*	
1.2.3.3. Control appropriateness	*50%*		*90%*	
2. Information quality		45%		**88%**
2.1. Information suitability		45%		**88%**
2.1.1. Consistency		40%		**90%**
2.1.2. Information coverage		50%		85%
2.1.2.1. Appropriateness	*50%*		*90%*	
2.1.2.2. Completeness	*50%*		*80%*	

between the WebApp versions are compared to determine the improvement gain.

In Table 8 (columns 4 and 5), we can see the results obtained when JIRA v.1.1 was evaluated from EQ viewpoint. As can be seen from comparing the 2 evaluations (columns 2 and 3 with 4 and 5), the overall partial indicator for ease of use improved significantly from 34% to 61% with improvements in many of the individual attributes and

an overall improvement in the global indicator from 38% to 74%. The next and final phase examines how these improvements in EQ affect QinU in a real context of use.

4.6. Phase VI: Reevaluate Quality in Use and Analyze Improvement Actions. Once the new application version (generated in Phase V, particularly in *perform improvement actions* activity) has been used by the same user group type in its

TABLE 9: Process template in which information and views are documented for the *recommend, perform improvement actions, and reevaluate EQ activities.*

Activity: recommend, perform improvement actions, and reevaluate EQ   *code* (in Figure 2): Ph. V

Objective: improve the current application version and determine the improvement gain from the EQ standpoint.

Description: Considering the EQ analysis report generated in conduct EQ analysis activity (Phase IV), the recommender makes recommendations to improve the current application, and the maintenance project manager produces an improvement plan to enhance the current WebApp. After the recommended changes were implemented by the developer and a new version generated, a reevaluation of the EQ is performed to determine the improvement gain between both application versions.

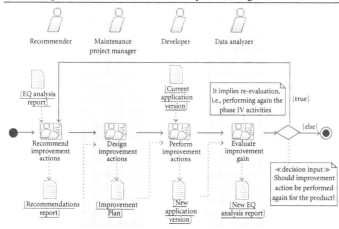

Subactivities:

(i) Recommend improvement actions

(ii) Design improvement actions

(iii) Perform improvement actions

(iv) Evaluate improvement gain (i.e., in Phase IV)

Involved roles:

(i) Recommender

(ii) Maintenance project manager

(iii) Developer

(iv) Data analyzer

Input artifacts:

(i) EQ analysis report

(ii) Current application version

Output artifacts:

(i) EQ recommendations report

(ii) Improvement plan

(iii) New application version

(iv) New EQ analysis report (from Phase IV)

Preconditions: there are EQ attributes with low level of satisfaction met, so improvement actions are needed to enhance the current software/web application version.

Postconditions: the Phase V finishes when the EQ attributes met the agreed satisfaction level.

same real context of use that the previous version, then, we are able to perform the QinU reevaluation (in a similar way to Phase II, recall Figure 13) to determine if what was improved from the EQ viewpoint had a positive quality-in-use effect using the identical tasks.

The activities involved are the same that in Phase II (see Figure 2), namely, *collect data, quantify attributes* and *calculate indicators*. Finally, *conduct improvement actions analysis* activity is performed to determine the improvement gain and also to hypothesize EQ/QinU relationships. These activities are described below according to the JIRA case study.

4.6.1. Collect Data, Quantify Attributes, and Calculate Indicators. When JIRA v.1.1 was evaluated from the EQ viewpoint, and its satisfaction level was achieved, then this new release was used by real users in the same real context of use as JIRA v.1. After 12 weeks (the same time period), we performed the QinU reevaluation (using the same nonfunctional requirements, metrics, and indicators designed in Phase I) to determine if what was improved from the EQ viewpoint had a positive quality-in-use effect with the same task (Entering a new defect). Following the SIQinU activities involved in Phase VI, we collect the data (i.e., the data collector using

the same parser tool), quantify the attributes, and calculate all the indicators in a similar way as in Phase II. In Table 7, columns 4 and 5, we show the evaluation results for JIRA v.1.1.

4.6.2. Conduct Improvement Actions Analysis. Once all indicators were calculated, data analyzer looks at each particular attribute's change for each part of the task being executed by the user group noting the difference to calculate quantified improvement between both WebApp versions from the QinU viewpoint. Table 10 shows the attributes and indicator values regarding the QinU requirements tree depicted in Table 6 for JIRA v.1 and JIRA v.1.1 with the right most columns showing the change.

As we can see from Table 10, all attributes noted improvement with the exception of task successfulness learnability and subtask correctness learnability. A possible explanation for this is that due to metric design with data collected over a 12-week period that the learning process did not improve as much as expected. Remembering our earlier comments that temporal analysis over time is important as user behavior can change over time, these beginning users possibly were not able to ramp up their learning during this time period. And, on the other hand, if the case study had been longer, we may have seen different behavior and hence measurements. However, their negative change was small compared to the positive changes in the other attributes resulting in an overall average change of attributes evaluation of 13.7%. While the indicators show that most of the attributes in JIRA v.1.1 still need some or significant improvement, there has been notable improvement from JIRA v.1. Again, as previously mentioned, due to the limitations in changing code in JIRA, configurations changes enabled many changes and improvements, but not all, it is possible that JIRA v.1.1 could be even better if more changes could be made. In other instances, depending on the software under evaluation, the tools/methods available to the maintenance project manager, and the time/resources available, more improvements could be made.

4.6.3. Develop "Depends-on" and "Influences" Relationships. A final action of Ph. VI (recall Table 1) is to develop *depends-on* and *influences* relationships between EQ improvements and QinU, which outputs the EQ/QinU attribute relationship table. These come also from the "influences" and "depends-on" relationships stated in the ISO 25010 standard. Table 11 summarizes the relationships found in this first case study. We discovered through our EQ evaluation, that some attributes could be improved and lead to specific improvements in QinU given the context of testers executing the specific task of entering a new defect in JIRA. In carrying out SIQinU, we were able to map EQ attributes to QinU attributes with the goal of ultimately achieving real improvement not only for JIRA but for WebApps and software design in general.

The weakness of our analysis is that we are only able to hypothesize the precise relationships between EQ and QinU attributes, but we cannot quantify the exact contribution from each because we made more than one change at a time. If we made only one change and then measured QinU for JIRA v.1.1, then we could make a more precise hypothesis for a one-to-one or one-to-many relationship. Most likely, those uncovered would be one-to-many, as one-to-one relationships probably are rare in this situation.

Regarding the hypothetical EQ/QinU relationships found in the JIRA case study, they can be further validated through additional case studies; case studies that can be carried out using our proposed SIQinU strategy grounded on a conceptual M&E framework (C-INCAMI), processes, and methods, which ensure repeatability and consistency of results. By doing this, we can generalize the conclusions of found relationships, that is, whether real improvements can be achieved not only for JIRA but for WebApps and software systems in general.

On the other hand, we are aware that this paper does not answer, from the experimental software engineering standpoint, the question of the effectiveness of the proposed strategy to accomplish similar or better objectives and results than using, for example, other strategies for improvement. The JIRA case study was made in a real context of a company, where beginner testers were performing their daily task and experts using SIQinU, as a first study. An experimental study to compare the effectiveness of SIQinU with another strategy

should be performed as future work. Nevertheless, we can state that SIQinU is quite scalable in terms of amount of tasks and users performing tasks, and amount of metrics and indicators as well. Once the nonfunctional requirements are developed and data collection procedure is set, that is, the parser tool that filter and organize data from log files which serve as input to get the metrics values, then any number of metrics (and indicators) can be determined across an unlimited number of users. That is the scalability power of this nonintrusive strategy versus using usability observation and heuristic techniques.

5. Related Work

In recent years, the ISO/IEC has worked on a new project, called SQuaRE (*Software product Quality Requirements and Evaluation*), that proposes integrating many ISO standards related to quality models, M&E processes, and so forth. Although ISO 25000 [19] has guidelines for the use of the new series of standards, the documents aimed at specifying M&E processes are not issued yet. So the standards for software measurement process (ISO 15939 [20]) and the process for evaluators (ISO 14598-5 [21]) are still in effect and considered the most recent. Taking into account these standards, the process for measurement has two core activities, namely, *plan the measurement process* and *perform the measurement process* [20].The evaluation process involves five activities: *establishment of evaluation requirements, specification of the evaluation, design of the evaluation, execution of the evaluation plan*, and *conclusion of the evaluation* [21]. We have observed that there is so far no single ISO standard that specifies in an integrated way the M&E process and approach as a whole.

Other work, worthy to mention, is the CMMI (capability maturity model integration) [22] de facto standard, which provides support for process areas such as *measurement and analysis*, among others. It aligns information needs and measurement objectives with a focus on goal-oriented measurement—following to some extent the GQM (*goal question metric*) [23] approach and the [20] measurement process. Although CMMI specifies (specific/generic) practices to accomplish the given process area goals, a process model itself is not defined. To a certain extent, it represents practices (i.e., actions/activities) without explicitly establishing sequences, parallelisms, control points, and so forth. Some specific practices for measurement and analysis are for example, *establish measurement objectives, specify measures, obtain measurement data*, and *analyze measurement data*. However, a clear distinction between M&E processes is missing in addition to lacking a robust conceptual base for its terms.

Regarding improvement strategies for evaluation of WebApps, we can consider the work in [18], where authors present an approach for incremental EQ improvement whereby the results from EQ evaluation were used to make changes and improvements in a WebApp through WMR (*web model refactoring*) in a systematic way. But although a set of activities is considered, the underlying process is

TABLE 10: QinU attributes satisfaction level for JIRA v.1 and JIRA v.1.1 with improvements.

Attributes	v.1	v.1.1	Change	
1.1.1. *Subtask correctness*	**86.4%**	**91.9%**	5.5%	↑
1.1.2. *Subtask completeness*	**87.9%**	**95.5%**	7.6%	↑
1.1.3. *Task successfulness*	45.5%	**72.7%**	27.2%	↑
1.2.1. *Subtask correctness efficiency*	37.4%	44.3%	6.9%	↑
1.2.2. *Subtask completeness efficiency*	37.5%	47.3%	9.8%	↑
1.2.3. *Task successfulness efficiency*	13.1%	36.8%	23.7%	↑
1.3.1. *Subtask correctness learnability*	**78.8%**	**75.1%**	−3.7%	↓
1.3.2. *Subtask completeness learnability*	26.4%	**77.3%**	50.9%	↑
1.3.3. *Task successfulness learnability*	66.7%	62.5%	−4.2%	↓
	Average change		13.7%	

TABLE 11: Summary of the influence relationships between EQ and QinU attributes.

EQ attribute	QinU attribute
1.1.2.2 Operability.Learnability.Helpfulness.HelpCompleteness	Learnability in Use. Subtask completeness learnability
2.1.1 Information Quality.InfoSuitability.Consistency	
1.2.1.2 Operability.EaseOfUse.Controllability.StabilityMainControls	Effectiveness in Use. Task Successfulness
1.1.1.2 Operability.Learnability.Feedback Suitability.TaskProgressFeedbackAppropriateness	
1.1.1.3 Operability.Learnability.Feedback Suitability.EntryFormFeedbackAwareness	Efficiency in Use. Subtask completeness efficiency
1.1.2.1 Operability.Learnability.Helpfulness.Context-sensitiveHelpAvailability	
1.2.3.1 Operability.EaseOfUse.DataEntryEase.Defaults	
1.2.3.2 Operability.EaseOfUse.DataEntryEase.MandatoryEntry	
1.2.3.3 Operability.EaseOfUse.DataEntryEase.ControlAppropriateness	
2.1.1 Information Quality.InfoSuitability.Consistency	Effectiveness in Use.Subtask completeness
1.1.2.2 Operability.Learnability.Helpfulness.HelpCompleteness	
1.2.2.1 Operability.EaseOfUse.Error Mgmt.Error Prevention	
1.2.3.1 Operability.EaseOfUse.DataEntryEase.Defaults	
1.2.3.3 Operability.EaseOfUse.DataEntryEase.ControlAppropriateness	Effectiveness in Use.Sub-task correctness
2.1.2.2 Information quality.InfoSuitability.InfoCoverage.Completeness	
2.1.2.2 Information quality.InfoSuitability.InfoCoverage.Appropriateness	

neither well defined nor modeled regarding process views. On the other hand, in [24], a systematic approach to specify, measure, and evaluate QinU was discussed. However, the process used is not explicitly shown, and the outcomes were used just for understanding the current situation of the QinU for an e-learning application, without proposing any improvement strategy.

With the aim of developing quality software, there are several works that focus on improving and controlling the development process and the intermediate products because the quality of the final product is strongly dependent on the qualities of intermediate products and their respective creation processes. For example [25], deal with the use of a software project control center (SPCC) as a means for on-line collecting, interpreting, and visualizing measurement data in order to provide purpose- and role-oriented information to all involved parties (e.g., project manager, quality assurance manager) during the execution of a development project. On the other hand, in [26], the authors considered introducing usability practices into the defined software development process. With this goal in mind, authors offer to software developers a selection of human-computer interface (HCI) techniques which are appropriate to be incorporated into a defined software process. The HCI techniques are integrated into a framework organized according to the kind of software engineering activities in an iterative development where their application yields a higher usability improvement. Also, in the usability field, in [27], authors explore how some open source projects address issues of usability and describe the mechanisms, techniques, and technology used by open source communities to design and refine the interfaces to their programs. In particular, they consider how these developers cope with their distributed community, lack of domain expertise, limited resources, and separation from their users. However, in SIQinU, we start identifying problems in systems in-use, that is, with running applications used by real users in a real context. Therefore, SIQinU is not focused on early stages of the development process but on how we can understand the current application-in-use's QinU and how we can change the attributes of a software system to improve its QinU.

Taking into account the complexity of processes, in [28], authors propose the use of an electronic process guide to provide a one-off improvement opportunity through the benefits of declaring a defined, systematic, and repeatable approach to software development. An electronic process guide offers several advantages over a printed process handbook, including easy access over the web for the most up-to-date version of the guide, electronic search facilities and hypernavigation to ease browsing information. In this work, authors combine the electronic process guide with the experience management, which refers to approaches to structure and store reusable experiences. It aims at reducing the overhead of information searching that can support software development activities. Experience management also appears to be more effective when it is process centric. Thus, the two concepts have a symbiotic relationship in that the process guide is more useful when supported by experiences and the experience base is more useful when it is process focused. The electronic process guide/experience repository (EPG/ER) is an implementation of this relationship and supports users through provision of guidance that is supplemented by task-specific experiences. However, our process specification is devoted specifically to represent the different views (as proposed in [10]) for measurement and evaluation activities rather than software development activities.

Regarding integrated strategies for M&E, it is worthy to mention the GQM$^+$ Strategies [29]—which are based on the GQM approach—as an approach that allows defining and assessing measurement goals at different organization levels, but it does not specify formal process views to conduct the evaluation and improvement lifecycle as we have shown as an integral component of SiQinU. Also, since issued, the GQM model was at different moments enlarged with proposals of processes and methods. However, [30] pointed out GQM is not intended to define metrics at a level of detail suitable to ensure that they are trustworthy, in particular, whether or not they are repeatable. Moreover, an interesting GQM enhancement, which considers indicators, has recently been issued as a technical report [31]. This approach uses both the balanced scorecard and the *goal-question-indicator-measurement* methods, in order to purposely derive the required enterprise goal-oriented indicators and metrics. It is a more robust approach for specifying enterprise-wide information needs and deriving goals and subgoals and then operationalizing questions with associated indicators and metrics. However, this approach is not based on a sound ontological conceptualization of metrics and indicators as in our research. Furthermore, the terms "measure" and "indicator" are sometimes used ambiguously, which inadvertently can result in datasets and metadata recorded inconsistently, and so it cannot assure that measurement values (and the associated metadata like metric version, scale, scale type, unit, measurement method, etc.) are trustworthy, consistent, and repeatable for further analysis among projects.

Finally, in [32], authors propose the CQA approach, consisting of a methodology (CQA-Meth) and a tool that implements it (CQA-Tool). They have applied this approach in the evaluation of the quality of UML models such as use cases, class, and statechart diagrams. Also authors have connected CQA-Tool to the different tools needed to assess the quality of models. CQA-Tool, apart from implementing the methodology, provides the capacity for building a catalogue of evaluation techniques that integrates the evaluation techniques (e.g., metrics, checklists, modeling conventions, guidelines, etc.), which are available for each software artifact. Compared with our strategies, the CQA approach lacks for instance an explicit conceptual framework from a terminological base. On the other hand, other related work in which authors try to integrate strategic management, process improvement, and quantitative measurement for managing the competitiveness of software engineering organizations is documented in [33]. In this work, a process template to specify activities from different views is considered. However, the integration of the three capabilities as made in GOCAME and SIQinU is not explicit and formalized.

6. Concluding Remarks

Ultimately, the main contribution of this paper is SIQinU, an integrated specific-purpose strategy—that is, for understanding and improving QinU—whose rationale is based on well-defined M&E processes, founded on a M&E conceptual framework backed up by an ontological base, and supported by methods and tools.

In this paper, we have specified the process of the SIQinU strategy modeled stressing the functional, informational, organizational, and behavioral views. Moreover, to illustrate the SIQinU process, excerpts from a JIRA case study were used where real users were employed to collect data and ultimately prove the usefulness of the strategy in improving the application in a process-oriented systematic means. We have also shown SIQinU, to be a derivation of GOCAME, based on three foundations, namely, the process, the conceptual framework, and methods/tools. Relying on the GOCAME foundation, SIQinU has been defined as a systematic approach with the appropriate recorded metadata of concrete projects' information needs, context properties, attributes, metrics, and indicators. This ensures that collected data are repeatable and comparable among the organization's projects. Otherwise, analysis, comparisons, and recommendations can be made in a less robust, nonconsistent, or even incorrect way.

SIQinU, although reusing the general principles of GOCAME, is a specific-purpose goal-oriented strategy with specific activities and methods that are not taken into account in GOCAME. Where GOCAME is a multipurpose strategy with general purposes such as "understand," "predict," "improve," and "control," SiQinU objectives are targeted to "understand" and ultimately "improve." In addition, as discussed in Section 3.4, SIQinU was specifically designed to evaluate QinU and EQ for WebApps, from the "do goals" perspective rather than from the "be goals."

As future work, we are planning to extend SIQinU to include processes and methods not only to gather data in a nonintrusive way (as currently it does) but also to gather data using more traditional intrusive methods such as video recording, observations, and questionnaires. This could not only help to add robustness to Phase III particularly in the derivation process from QinU problems to EQ attributes but also supplement the analysis in Phase II and VI.

Acknowledgment

This work and line of research is supported by the PAE 2007 PICT 2188 project at UNLPam, from the Science and Technology Agency, Argentina.

References

[1] ISO/IEC CD 25010.3. Systems and software engineering. Systems and software Quality Requirements and Evaluation (SQuaRE). System and software quality models, 2009.

[2] P. Lew, L. Olsina, and L. Zhang, "Quality, quality in use, actual usability and user experience as key drivers for web application evaluation," in *Proceedings of the 10th International Conference on Web Engineering (ICWE '10)*, vol. 6189 of *Lecture Notes in Computer Science*, pp. 218–232, Springer, Vienne, Austria, 2010.

[3] N. Bevan, "Extending quality in use to provide a framework for usability measurement," in *Proceedings of the 1st International Conference on Human Centered Design (HCD '09)*, vol. 5619 of *Lecture Notes in Computer Science*, pp. 13–22, Springer, San Diego, Calif, USA, 2009.

[4] L. Olsina, F. Papa, and H. Molina, "How to measure and evaluate web applications in a consistent way," in *Web Engineering: Modeling and Implementing Web Applications*, G. Rossi, O. Pastor, D. Schwabe, and L. Olsina, Eds., HCIS, chapter 13, pp. 385–420, Springer, London, UK, 2008.

[5] H. Molina and L. Olsina, "Assessing web applications consistently: a context information approach," in *Proceedings of the 8th International Conference on Web Engineering (ICWE '08)*, pp. 224–230, Yorktown Heights, NJ, USA, July 2008.

[6] P. Becker, H. Molina, and L. Olsina, "Measurement and evaluation as quality driver," *Journal ISI (Ingénierie des Systèmes d'Information)*, vol. 15, no. 6, pp. 33–62, 2010.

[7] L. Olsina and G. Rossi, "Measuring Web application quality with WebQEM," *IEEE Multimedia*, vol. 9, no. 4, pp. 20–29, 2002.

[8] P. Lew, L. Olsina, P. Becker, and L. Zhang, "An integrated strategy to understand and manage quality in use for web applications," *Requirements Engineering Journal*, vol. 16, no. 3, 2011.

[9] E. Mendes, "The need for empirical web engineering: an Introduction," in *Web Engineering: Modelling and Implementing Web Applications*, G. Rossi, O. Pastor, D. Schwabe, and L. Olsina, Eds., HCIS, chapter 14, pp. 421–447, Springer, London, UK, 2008.

[10] B. Curtis, M. Kellner, and J. Over, "Process modelling," *Communications of the ACM*, vol. 35, no. 9, pp. 75–90, 1992.

[11] L. Olsina, "Applying the flexible process model to build hypermedia products," in *Proceedings of the Hypertext and Hypermedia: Tools, Products, Methods (HHTPM '97)*, pp. 211–221, Hermes Ed., Paris, France, 1997.

[12] S. Acuña, N. Juristo, A. Merona, and A. Mon, *A Software Process Model Handbook for Incorporating People's Capabilities*, Springer, 1st edition, 2005.

[13] UML.Unified Modeling Language Specification, Version 2.0. Document/05-07-04, 2004.

[14] SPEM. Software Process Engineering Metamodel Specification. Doc./02-11-14., Ver.1.0, 2002.

[15] P. Becker, P. Lew, and L. Olsina, "Strategy to improve quality for software applications: a process view," in *Proceedings of the International Conference of Software and System Process (ICSSP '11)*, pp. 129–138, ACM, Honolulu, Hawaii, USA, 2011.

[16] N. E. Fenton and S. L. Pfleeger, *Software Metrics: a Rigorous and Practical Approach*, PWS Publishing Company, 2nd edition, 1997.

[17] F. García, A. Vizcaino, and C. Ebert, "Process management tools," *IEEE Software*, vol. 28, no. 2, pp. 15–18, 2011.

[18] L. Olsina, G. Rossi, A. Garrido, D. Distante, and G. Canfora, "Web applications refactoring and evaluation: a quality-oriented improvement approach," *Journal of Web Engineering, Rinton Press, US*, vol. 7, no. 4, pp. 258–280, 2008.

[19] ISO/IEC 25000. Software Engineering—Software product Quality Requirements and Evaluation (SQuaRE)—Guide to SQuaRE, 2005.

[20] ISO/IEC 15939. Software Engineering—Software Measurement Process, 2002.

[21] ISO/IEC 14598-5. International Standard, Information technology—Software product evaluation—Part 5: process for evaluators, 1999.

[22] CMMI Product Team. CMMI for Development Version 1.3 (CMMI-DEV, V.1.3) CMU/SEI-2010-TR-033, SEI Carnegie-Mellon University, 2010.

[23] R. Basili, G. Caldiera, and H. D. Rombach, "The goal question metric approach," in *Encyclopedia of Software Engineering*, J. J. Marciniak, Ed., vol. 1, pp. 528–532, John Wiley & Sons, 1994.

[24] G. Covella and L. Olsina, "Assessing quality in use in a consistent way," in *Proceedings of the International Conference on Web Engineering (ICWE '06)*, pp. 1–8, ACM, San Francisco, Calif, USA, July 2006.

[25] J. Munch and J. Heidrich, "Software project control centers: concepts and approaches," *Journal of Systems and Software*, vol. 70, no. 1-2, pp. 3–19, 2004.

[26] X. Ferre, N. Juriste, and A. M. Moreno, "Framework for integrating usability practices into the software process," in *Proceedings of the 6th International Conference on Product Focused Software Process Improvement (PROFES '05)*, vol. 3547 of *Lecture Notes in Computer Science*, pp. 202–215, Springer, 2005.

[27] D. M. Nichols and M. B. Twidale, "Usability processes in open source projects," *Software Process Improvement and Practice*, vol. 11, no. 2, pp. 149–162, 2006.

[28] F. Kurniawati and R. Jeffery, "The use and effects of an electronic process guide and experience repository: a longitudinal study," *Information and Software Technology*, vol. 48, no. 7, pp. 566–577, 2006.

[29] V. R. Basili, M. Lindvall, M. Regardie et al., "Linking software development and business strategy through measurement," *Computer*, vol. 43, no. 4, pp. 57–65, 2010.

[30] B. A. Kitchenham, R. T. Hughes, and S. G. Linkman, "Modeling software measurement data," *IEEE Transactions on Software Engineering*, vol. 27, no. 9, pp. 788–804, 2001.

[31] W. Goethert and M. Fisher, Deriving Enterprise-Based Measures Using the Balanced Scorecard and Goal-Driven Measurement Techniques. Software Engineering Measurement and Analysis Initiative, CMU/SEI-2003-TN-024, 2003.

[32] M. Rodrìguez, M. Genero, D. Torre, B. Blasco, and M. Piattini, "A methodology for continuos quality assessment of software artefacts," in *Proceedings of the 10th International Conference on Quality Software (QSIC '10)*, pp. 254–261, Zhangjiajie, China, July 2010.

[33] J. G. Guzmán, H. Mitre, A. Seco, and M. Velasco, "Integration of strategic management, process improvement and quantitative measurement for managing the competitiveness of software engineering organizations," *Software Quality Journal*, vol. 18, no. 3, pp. 341–359, 2010.

4

Evaluating the Effect of Control Flow on the Unit Testing Effort of Classes: An Empirical Analysis

Mourad Badri and Fadel Toure

Software Engineering Research Laboratory, Department of Mathematics and Computer Science, University of Quebec at Trois-Rivières, Trois-Rivières, QC, Canada G9A 5H7

Correspondence should be addressed to Mourad Badri, mourad.badri@uqtr.ca

Academic Editor: Filippo Lanubile

The aim of this paper is to evaluate empirically the relationship between a new metric (*Quality Assurance Indicator*—Qi) and testability of classes in object-oriented systems. The Qi metric captures the distribution of the control flow in a system. We addressed testability from the perspective of unit testing effort. We collected data from five open source Java software systems for which JUnit test cases exist. To capture the testing effort of classes, we used different metrics to quantify the corresponding JUnit test cases. Classes were classified, according to the required testing effort, in two categories: high and low. In order to evaluate the capability of the Qi metric to predict testability of classes, we used the univariate logistic regression method. The performance of the predicted model was evaluated using Receiver Operating Characteristic (ROC) analysis. The results indicate that the univariate model based on the Qi metric is able to accurately predict the unit testing effort of classes.

1. Introduction

Software testing plays a crucial role in software quality assurance. It has, indeed, an important effect on the overall quality of the final product. Software testing is, however, a time and resources consuming process. The overall effort spent on testing depends, in fact, on many different factors including [1–5] human factors, process issues, testing techniques, tools used, and characteristics of the software development artifacts.

Software testability is an important software quality attribute. IEEE [6] defines testability as the degree to which a system or component facilitates the establishment of test criteria and the performance of tests to determine whether those criteria have been met. ISO [7] defines testability (characteristic of maintainability) as attributes of software that bear on the effort needed to validate the software product. Dealing with software testability raises, in fact, several questions such as [8, 9]: Why is one class easier to test than another? What makes a class hard to test? What contributes to the testability of a class? How can we quantify this notion?

Metrics (or models based on metrics) can be used to predict (assess) software testability and better manage the testing effort. Having quantitative data on the testability of a software can, in fact, be used to guide the decision-making of software development managers seeking to produce high-quality software. Particularly, it can help software managers, developers, and testers to [8, 9] plan and monitor testing activities, determine the critical parts of the code on which they have to focus to ensure software quality, and in some cases use this data to review the code. One effective way to deal with this important issue is to develop prediction models that can be used to identify critical parts of the code requiring a (relative) high testing effort. Moreover, having quantitative data on the testing effort actually applied during the testing process (such as testing coverage measures) will also help to better identify, in an iterative and relative way, the critical parts of the code on which more testing effort is required to ensure software quality.

A large number of object-oriented (OO) metrics were proposed in the literature [10]. Some of these metrics, related to different OO attributes (such as size, complexity, coupling, and cohesion), were already used in recent years to assess testability of OO software systems (e.g., [4, 8, 9, 11–15]). According to Gupta et al. [9], none of the OO metrics is alone sufficient to give an overall estimation of software testability. Software testability is, in fact, affected by many different factors [1–3, 5]. Moreover, few empirical studies have been conducted to examine the effect of these metrics on testability of classes, particularly when taking into account the testing effort level. As far as we know, this issue has not been empirically investigated. In addition, as mentioned by Baudry et al. [2, 3], testability becomes crucial in the case of OO software systems where control flows are generally not hierarchical but diffuse and distributed over whole architecture.

We proposed in [16] a new metric, called *Quality Assurance Indicator* (Qi), capturing in an integrated way different attributes of OO software systems such as complexity (control flow paths) and coupling (interactions between classes). The metric captures the distribution of the control flow in a system. The *Quality Assurance Indicator* of a class is based on different intrinsic characteristics of the class, as well as on the *Quality Assurance Indicator* of its collaborating classes (invoked classes). The metric has, however, no ambition to capture the overall quality (or testability) of OO software systems. Moreover, the objective is not to evaluate a design by giving absolute values, but more relative values that may be used for identifying: (1) before the testing process begins, the critical classes that will require a (relative) high testing effort, and (2) during the testing process, the classes on which more testing effort is required to ensure software quality (iterative distribution of the testing effort). In this paper, we focus on the first objective. Applying equal testing effort to all classes of a software is, indeed, cost-prohibitive and not realistic, particularly in the case of large and complex software systems. Increasing size and complexity of software systems brings, in fact, new research challenges. One of the most important challenges is to make testing effective with reasonable consumption of resources. We compared in [16] the Qi metric using the Principal Components Analysis (PCA) method to some well-known OO metrics. The evaluated metrics were grouped in five categories: coupling, cohesion, inheritance, complexity, and size. The achieved results provide evidence that the Qi metric captures, overall, a large part of the information captured by most of the evaluated metrics. Recently, we explored the relationship between the Qi metric and testability of classes [15]. Testability was basically measured (inversely) by the number of lines of test code and the number of *assert* statements in the test code. The relationship between the Qi metric and testability of classes was explored using only correlation analysis. Moreover, we have not distinguished among classes according to the required testing effort.

The purpose of the present paper is to evaluate empirically the relationship between the Qi metric and testability of classes in terms of required unit testing effort. The question we attempt to answer is how accurately do the Qi metric predicts (high) testing effort of classes. We addressed testability from the perspective of unit testing. We performed an empirical analysis using data collected from five open

source Java software systems for which JUnit test cases exist. To capture testability of classes, we used different metrics to measure some characteristics of the corresponding JUnit test cases. Classes were classified, according to the required unit testing effort, in two categories: high and (relatively) low. In order to evaluate the relationship between the Qi metric and testability of classes, we performed a statistical analysis using correlation and logistic regression. We used particularly the univariate logistic regression analysis to evaluate the effect of the Qi metric on the unit testing effort of classes. The performance of the predicted model was evaluated using Receiver Operating Characteristic (ROC) analysis. We also include in our study the well-known SLOC metric as a "baseline" to compare against the Qi metric (We wish to thank an anonymous reviewer for making this suggestion.). This metric is, indeed, one of the most used predictors in source code analysis. In summary, the results indicate that the Qi metric is a significant predictor of the unit testing effort of classes.

The rest of this paper is organized as follows: Section 2 gives a survey on related work on software testability. The Qi metric is introduced in Section 3. Section 4 presents the selected systems, describes the data collection, introduces the test case metrics we used to quantify the JUnit test cases, and presents the empirical study we performed to evaluate the relationship between the Qi metric and testability of classes. Finally, Section 5 summarizes the contributions of this work and outlines directions for future work.

2. Software Testability

Fenton and Pfleeger [17] define software testability as an external attribute. According to Gao and Shih [18], software testability is related to testing effort reduction and software quality. For Sheppard and Kaufman [19], software testability impacts test costs and provides a means of making design decisions based on the impact on test costs. Zhao [5] argues that testability expresses the affect of software structural and semantic on the effectiveness of testing following certain criterion, which decides the quality of released software. According to Baudry et al. [2, 3], software testability is influenced by different factors including controllability, observability, and the global test cost. Yeh and Lin [1] argue also that diverse factors such as control flow, data flow, complexity, and size contribute to testability. Zhao [5] states that testability is an elusive concept, and it is difficult to get a clear view on all the potential factors that can affect it. Many testability analysis and measurement approaches have been proposed in the literature. These approaches were investigated within different application domains.

Freedman [20] introduces testability measures for software components based on two factors: observability and controllability. Observability is defined as the ease of determining if specific inputs affect the outputs of a component, and controllability is defined as the ease of producing specific outputs from specific inputs. Voas [21] defines testability as the probability that a test case will fail if a program has a fault. He considers testability as the combination of the probability that a location is executed, the probability of a fault at a location, and the probability that corrupted results will propagate to observable outputs. Voas and Miller [22] propose a testability metric based on inputs and outputs domains of a software component, and the PIE (Propagation, Infection and Execution) technique to analyze software testability [23].

Binder [24] defines testability as the relative ease and expense of revealing software faults. He argues that software testability is based on six factors: representation, implementation, built-in text, test suite, test support environment, and software process capability. Each factor is further refined to address special features of OO software systems, such as inheritance, encapsulation, and polymorphism. Khoshgoftaar et al. [25] address the relationship between static software product measures and testability. Software testability is considered as a probability predicting whether tests will detect a fault. Khoshgoftaar et al. [26] use neural networks to predict testability from static software metrics.

McGregor and Srinivas [27] investigate testability of OO software systems and introduce the visibility component measure (VC). Bertolino and Strigini [28] investigate testability and its use in dependability assessment. They adopt a definition of testability as a conditional probability, different from the one proposed by Voas et al. [21], and derive the probability of program correctness using a Bayesian inference procedure. Le Traon et al. [29–31] propose testability measures for data flow designs. Petrenko et al. [32] and Karoui and Dssouli [33] address testability in the context of communication software. Sheppard and Kaufman [19] focus on formal foundation of testability metrics. Jungmayr [34] investigates testability measurement based on static dependencies within OO systems by considering an integration testing point of view.

Gao et al. [35] consider testability from the perspective of component-based software development and address component testability issues by introducing a model for component testability analysis [18]. The definition of component testability is based on five factors: understandability, observability, controllability, traceability, and testing support capability. According to Gao and Shih [18], software testability is not only a measure of the effectiveness of a testing process, but also a measurable indicator of the quality of a software development process. Nguyen et al. [36] focus on testability analysis based on data flow designs in the context of embedded software.

Baudry et al. [2, 3, 37] address testability measurement (and improvement) of OO designs. They focus on design patterns as coherent subsets in the architecture, and explain how their use can provide a way for limiting the severity of testability weaknesses. The approach supports the detection of undesirable configurations in UML class diagrams. Chowdhary [38] focuses on why it is so difficult to practice testability in the real world and discusses the impact of testability on design. Khan and Mustafa [39] focus on testability at the design level and propose a model predicting testability of classes from UML class diagrams. Kout et al. [40] adapt this model to the code level and evaluate it using two case studies.

Bruntink and Van Deursen [4, 8] investigate factors of testability of OO software systems using an adapted version of the *fish bone* diagram developed by Binder [24]. They studied five open source Java systems, for which JUnit test cases exist, in order to explore the relationship between OO design metrics and some characteristics of JUnit test classes. Testability is measured (inversely) by the number of lines of test code and the number of *assert* statements in the test code. This paper explores the relationship between OO metrics and testability of classes using only correlation analysis and did not distinguish among classes according to the testing effort.

Singh et al. [11] use OO metrics and neural networks to predict the testing effort. The testing effort in this work is measured in terms of lines of code added or changed during the life cycle of a defect. Singh et al. conclude that the performance of the developed model is to a large degree dependent on the data used. In [41], Singh and Saha attempt to predict the testability of Eclipse at package level. This study was, however, limited to a correlation analysis between source code metrics and test metrics. Badri et al. [13] performed a similar study to that conducted by Bruntink and Van Deursen [4, 8] using two open source Java systems in order to explore the relationship between lack of cohesion metrics and testability characteristics. In [14], Badri et al. investigate the capability of lack of cohesion metrics to predict testability of classes using logistic regression methods.

3. Quality Assurance Indicator

In this section, we give a summary of the definition of the *Quality Assurance Indicator* (Qi) metric. The Qi metric is based on the concept of *Control Call Graphs*, which are a reduced form of traditional *Control Flow Graphs*. A control call graph is, in fact, a control flow graph from which the nodes representing instructions (or basic blocs of sequential instructions) not containing a call to a method are removed.

The Qi metric is normalized and gives values in the interval [0, 1]. A low value of the Qi of a class means that the class is a high-risk class and needs a (relative) high testing effort to ensure its quality. A high value of the Qi of a class indicates that the class is a low-risk class (having a relatively low complexity and/or the testing effort applied actually on the class is relatively high—proportional to its complexity).

3.1. Control Call Graphs. Let us consider the example of method M given in Figure 1(a). The S_i represent blocs of instructions that do not contain a call to a method. The code of method M reduced to control call flow is given in Figure 1(b). The instructions (blocs of instructions) not containing a call to a method are removed from the original code of method M. Figure 1(c) gives the corresponding control call graph. Unlike traditional call graphs, control call graphs are much more precise models. They capture the structure of calls and related control.

3.2. Quality Assurance Indicator. We define the Qi of a method M_i as a kind of estimation of the probability that the control flow will go through the method without any failure. It may be considered as an indicator of the risk associated with a method (and a class at a high level). The Qi of a method M_i is based, in fact, on intrinsic characteristics of

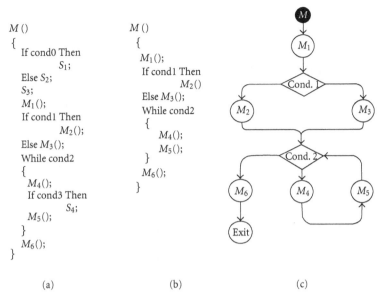

M ()
{
   If cond0 Then
        S_1;
   Else S_2;
   S_3;
   M_1();
   If cond1 Then
        M_2();
   Else M_3();
   While cond2
   {
     M_4();
     If cond3 Then
        S_4;
     M_5();
   }
   M_6();
}

M ()
{
   M_1();
   If cond1 Then
        M_2()
   Else M_3();
   While cond2
   {
     M_4();
     M_5();
   }
   M_6();
}

(a)   (b)   (c)

FIGURE 1: A method and its corresponding control call graph.

the method, such as its cyclomatic complexity and its unit testing coverage (testing effort applied actually on the method), as well as on the Qi of the methods invoked by the method M_i. We assume that the quality of a method, particularly in terms of reliability, depends also on the quality of the methods it collaborates with to perform its task. In OO software systems, objects collaborate to achieve their respective responsibilities. A method of poor quality can have (directly or indirectly) a negative impact on the methods that use it. There is here a kind of propagation, depending on the distribution of the control flow in a system that needs to be captured. It is not obvious, particularly in the case of large and complex OO software systems, to identify intuitively this type of interferences between classes. This type of information is not captured by traditional OO metrics. The Qi of a method M_i is given by:

$$\mathrm{Qi}_{M_i} = \mathrm{Qi}_{M_i}^* \cdot \sum_{j=1}^{n_i} \left[P\left(C_j^i\right) \cdot \prod_{M \in \sigma_j} \mathrm{Qi}_M \right] \qquad (1)$$

with Qi_{M_i}: quality assurance indicator of method M_i, $\mathrm{Qi}_{M_i}^*$: intrinsic quality assurance indicator of method M_i, C_j^i: jth path of method M_i, $P(C_j^i)$: probability of execution of path C_j^i of method M_i, Qi_M: quality assurance indicator of the method M included in the path C_j^i, n_i: number of linear paths of the control call graph of method M_i, and σ_j: set of the methods invoked in the path C_j^i.

By applying the previous formula (1) to each method, we obtain a system of N equations (N is the number of methods in the program). The obtained system is not linear and is composed of several multivariate polynomials. We use an iterative method (method of successive approximations) to solve it. The system is, in fact, reduced to a fixed point problem. In order to better understand our approach, we give

in what follows the Qi of the method M given in Figure 1 as a simple example of application:

$$\mathrm{Qi}_M = \mathrm{Qi}_M^* \left[\mathrm{Qi}_{M_1} \left(0.5\mathrm{Qi}_{M_2} + 0.5\mathrm{Qi}_{M_3} \right) \times \left(0.75\mathrm{Qi}_{M_4} \mathrm{Qi}_{M_5} \mathrm{Qi}_{M_6} + 0.25\mathrm{Qi}_{M_6} \right) \right]. \qquad (2)$$

Furthermore, we define the Qi of a class C (noted Qi_C) as the product of the Qi of its methods:

$$\mathrm{Qi}_C = \prod_{M \in \delta} \mathrm{Qi}_M, \qquad (3)$$

where δ is the set of methods of the class C. The calculation of the Qi metric is entirely automated by a tool that we developed for Java software systems.

3.3. Assigning Probabilities. The control call graph of a method can be seen as a set of paths that the control flow can pass through. Passing through a particular path depends, in fact, on the states of the conditions in the control structures. To capture this probabilistic characteristic of the control flow, we assign a probability to each path C of a control call graph as follows:

$$P(C) = \prod_{A \in \theta} P(A), \qquad (4)$$

where θ is the set of directed arcs composing the path C and $P(A)$ the probability of an arc to be crossed when exiting a control structure.

To facilitate our experiments (simplify analysis and calculations), we assigned probabilities to the different control structures of a Java program according to the rules given in Table 1. These values are assigned automatically during the static analysis of the source code of a program when generating the Qi models. As an alternative way, the probability values may also be assigned by programmers (knowing the code) or obtained by dynamic analysis. Dynamic analysis is out of the scope of this paper.

TABLE 1: Assignment rules of the probabilities.

Nodes	Probability assignment rule
(if, else)	0.5 for the exiting arc "condition = true" 0.5 for the exiting arc "condition = false"
while	0.75 for the exiting arc "condition = true" 0.25 for the exiting arc "condition = false"
(do, while)	1 for the arc: (the internal instructions are executed at least once)
(switch, case)	$1/n$ for each arc of the n cases
(?,:)	0.5 for the exiting arc "condition = true" 0.5 for the exiting arc "condition = false"
for	0.75 for entering the loop 0.25 for skipping the loop
(try, catch)	0.75 for the arc of the "try" bloc 0.25 for the arc of the "catch" bloc
Polymorphism	$1/n$ for each of the eventual n calls

3.4. Intrinsic Quality Assurance Indicator. The *Intrinsic Quality Assurance Indicator* of a method M_i, noted $\mathrm{Qi}^*_{M_i}$, is given by

$$\mathrm{Qi}^*_{M_i} = (1 - F_i) \qquad (5)$$

with

$$F_i = \frac{(1 - \mathrm{tc}_i)\mathrm{CC}_i}{\mathrm{CC}_{\max}}, \qquad (6)$$

where CC_i: cyclomatic complexity of method M_i,

$$\mathrm{CC}_{\max} = \max_{1 \le i \le N} (\mathrm{CC}_i) \qquad (7)$$

tc_i: unit testing coverage of the method M_i, $\mathrm{tc}_i \in [0, 1]$.

Studies provided empirical evidence that there is a significant relationship between cyclomatic complexity and fault proneness (e.g., [42–44]). Testing activities will reduce the risk of a complex program and achieve its quality. Moreover, testing coverage provide objective measures on the effectiveness of a testing process.

4. Empirical Analysis

The goal of this study is to evaluate empirically the relationship between the Qi metric and testability of classes in terms of required testing effort. We selected from each of the investigated systems only the classes for which JUnit test cases exist. We noticed that developers usually name the JUnit test case classes by adding the prefix (suffix) "Test" ("TestCase") into the name of the classes for which JUnit test cases were developed. Only classes that have such name-matching mechanism with the test case class name are included in the analysis. This approach has already been adopted in other studies [45].

JUnit (http://www.junit.org/) is, in fact, a simple Framework for writing and running automated unit tests for Java classes. Test cases in JUnit are written by testers in Java. JUnit gives testers some support so that they can write those test cases more conveniently. A typical usage of JUnit is to test each class C_s of the program by means of a dedicated test case class C_t. To actually test a class C_s, we need to execute its test class C_t. This is done by calling JUnit's test runner tool. JUnit will report how many of the test methods in C_t succeed, and how many fail. However, we noticed by analyzing the JUnit test case classes of the subject systems that in some cases there is no one-to-one relationship between JUnit classes and tested classes. This has also been noted in other previous studies (e.g., [46, 47]). In these cases, several JUnit test cases have been related to a same tested class. The matching procedure has been performed on the subject systems by two research assistants separately (a Ph.D. student (second author of this paper) and a Master student, both in computer science). We compared the obtained results and noticed only a few differences. We rechecked the few results in which we observed differences and chose the correct ones based on our experience and a deep analysis of the code.

For each software class C_s selected, we calculated the value of the Qi metric. We also used the suite of test case metrics (Section 4.2) to quantify the corresponding JUnit test class (classes) C_t. The Qi metric has been computed using the tool we developed, and the test case metrics have been computed using the Borland (http://www.borland.com/) Together tool. For our experiments, knowing that the purpose of this study is to evaluate the relationship between the Qi metric and testability of classes, and that one of the main interests of such a work is to be able to predict the testing effort of classes using the Qi metric before the testing process begins, the testing coverage (tc_i, Section 3.4) is set to zero for all methods. As mentioned previously, we also include in our experiments the well-known SLOC (Source Lines Of Code) metric. The value of the SLOC metric has been computed, for each software class selected, using the Borland Together tool.

In this section, we present the systems we selected, discuss some of their characteristics, introduce the test case metrics we used to quantify the JUnit test cases, and present the empirical study we conducted to evaluate the relationship between the Qi metric and testability of classes in two steps: (1) analyzing correlations between the Qi metric and test case metrics and (2) evaluating the effect of the Qi metric on testability of classes, using univariate logistic regression, when the testing effort level is taken into account.

4.1. Selected Systems. Five open source Java software systems from different domains were selected for the study: ANT, JFREECHART (JFC), JODA-Time (JODA), Apache Commons IO (IO), and Apache Lucene Core (LUCENE). Table 2 summarizes some of their characteristics. It gives, for each system, the number of software classes, the number of attributes, the number of methods, the total number of lines of code, the number of selected software classes for which JUnit test cases were developed, and the total number of lines of code of selected software classes for which JUnit test cases were developed.

ANT (http://www.apache.org/) is a Java library and command-line tool whose mission is to drive processes described in build files as targets and extension points dependent upon each other. This system consists of 713 classes that are

TABLE 2: Some characteristics of the used systems.

	No. classes	No. attributes	No. methods	No. LOC	No. TClasses	No. TLOC
ANT	713	2491	5365	64062	111 (15.6%)	17609 (27.5%)
JFC	496	1550	5763	68312	226 (45.6%)	53115 (77.8%)
JODA	225	872	3605	31591	76 (33.8%)	17624 (55.8%)
IO	104	278	793	7631	66 (63.5%)	6326 (82.9%)
LUCENE	659	1793	4397	56902	114 (17.3%)	22098 (38.8%)

comprised of 2491 attributes and 5365 methods, with a total of roughly 64000 lines of code. JFC (http://www.jfree.org/jfreechart/) is a free chart library for Java platform. This system consists of 496 classes that are comprised of 1550 attributes and 5763 methods, with a total of roughly 68000 lines of code. JODA-Time (Java date and time API) (http://joda-time.sourceforge.net/) is the de facto standard library for advanced date and time in Java. Joda-Time provides a quality replacement for the Java date and time classes. The design allows for multiple calendar systems, while still providing a simple API. This system consists of 225 classes that are comprised of 872 attributes and 3605 methods, with a total of roughly 31000 lines of code. Apache Commons IO (IO) (http://commons.apache.org/io/) is a library of utilities to assist with developing Input-Output functionality. This system consists of 104 classes that are comprised of 278 attributes and 793 methods, with a total of roughly 7600 lines of code. LUCENE (Apache Lucene Core) (http://lucene.apache.org/) is a high-performance, full-featured text search engine library written entirely in Java. It is a technology suitable for nearly any application that requires full-text search, especially cross-platform. This system consists of 659 classes that are comprised of 1793 attributes and 4397 methods, with a total of roughly 56900 lines of code.

We can also observe from Table 2, for each system, that JUnit test cases were not developed for all classes. The percentage of selected software classes for which JUnit test cases were developed varies from one system to another: (1) ANT: 111 classes, which represents 15.6% of the classes in the system. The total number of lines of code of these classes is 17609, which represents 27.5% of the total number of lines of code of ANT. (2) JFC: 226 classes, which represents 45.6% of the classes in the system. The total number of lines of code of these classes is 53115, which represents 77.8% of the total number of lines of code of JFC. (3) JODA: 76 classes, which represents 33.8% of the classes in the system. The total number of lines of code of these classes is 17624, which represents 55.8% of the total number of lines of code of JODA. (4) IO: 66 classes, which represents 63.5% of the classes in the system. The total number of lines of code of these classes is 6326, which represents 82.9% of the total number of lines of code of IO. (5) Finally, LUCENE: 114 classes, which represents 17.3% of the classes in the system. The total number of lines of code of these classes is 22098, which represents 38.8% of the total number of lines of code of LUCENE. So, in total, our experiments will be performed on 593 classes and corresponding JUnit test cases.

Moreover, the software classes for which JUnit test cases were developed, in the five subject systems, are relatively large and complex.

(i) For ANT, the mean values of their *lines of code* and *cyclomatic complexity* (resp., 158.64 and 31.31—Standard deviation (σ): 154.2 and 31.1) are greater than the mean values of the same measures for all classes (resp., 89.85 and 17.10—σ: 130.15 and 23.66). The same trend is observed for other systems.

(ii) For JFC, the mean values of their *lines of code* and *cyclomatic complexity* are, respectively, 235.02 and 46.89 (σ: 273.12 and 57.17) and the mean values of the same measures for all classes are, respectively, 137.73 and 28.10 (σ: 216.12 and 44.51).

(iii) For JODA, the mean values of their *lines of code* and *cyclomatic complexity* are, respectively, 231.90 and 44.75 (σ: 277.81 and 39.72) and the mean values of the same measures for all classes are, respectively, 140.40 and 28.74 (σ: 204.41 and 29.85).

(iv) For IO, the mean values of their *lines of code* and *cyclomatic complexity* are, respectively, 95.85 and 22.46 (σ: 143.25 and 37.53) and the mean values of the same measures for all classes are, respectively, 73.38 and 17.65 (σ: 119.95 and 31.24).

(v) Finally, for LUCENE, the mean values of their *lines of code* and *cyclomatic complexity* are, respectively, 193.84 and 35.89 (σ: 339.15 and 60.91) and the mean values of the same measures for all classes are, respectively, 86.35 and 16.64 (σ: 187.45 and 34.69).

4.2. Test Case Metrics. In order to indicate the testability of a software class (noted C_s), we used the following suite of test case metrics to quantify the corresponding JUnit test class (noted C_t).

(i) *TLoc.* This metric gives the number of lines of code of a test class C_t. It is used to indicate the size of the test suite corresponding to a software class C_s.

(ii) *TAss.* This metric gives the number of invocations of JUnit *assert* methods that occur in the code of a test class C_t. JUnit *assert* methods are, in fact, used by the testers to compare the expected behavior of the class under test to its current behavior. This metric is used to indicate another perspective of the size of a test suite. It is directly related to the construction of the test cases.

We used in our study the selected software classes and the corresponding JUnit test cases. The objective was to use these classes to evaluate the relationship between the Qi metric, which captures in an integrated way different characteristics of a software class C_s, and the measured characteristics of the corresponding JUnit test case (s). The approach used in this paper is, in fact, based on the work of Bruntink and Van Deursen [4, 8]. The test case metrics TLoc and TAss have been introduced by Bruntink and Van Deursen in [4, 8] to indicate the size of a test suite. Bruntink and Van Deursen based the definition of these metrics on the work of Binder [24]. They used, particularly, an adapted version of the *fish bone* diagram developed by Binder [24] to identify factors of testability. These metrics reflect different source code factors [4, 8]: factors that influence the *number of test cases* required to test the classes of a system, and factors that influence the *effort required* to develop each individual test case. These two categories have been referred as *test case generation* and *test case construction* factors.

However, by analyzing the source code of the JUnit test classes of the systems we selected for our study, we found that some characteristics of the test classes (which are also related to the factors mentioned above) are not captured by these two metrics (like the set of local variables or invoked methods). This is why we decided to extend these metrics. In [15], we used the *THEff* metric, which is one of the Halstead Software Science metrics [48]. The *THEff* metric gives the effort necessary to implement or understand a test class C_t. It is calculated as "Halstead Difficulty" $*$ "Halstead Program Volume." Halsteasd Program Volume is defined as: $N \log_2 n$, where N = Total Number of Operators + Total Number of Operands and n = Number of Distinct Operators + Number of Distinct Operands. In this work, we wanted to explore the *THDiff* metric. This metric is also one of the Halstead Software Science metrics [48]. It gives the difficulty level of a test class C_t. It is calculated as ("Number of Distinct Operators"/2) $*$ ("Total Number of Operands"/"Number of Distinct Operands"). We assume that this will reflect also the difficulty of the class under test and the global effort required to construct the corresponding test class.

In order to understand the underlying orthogonal dimensions captured by the test case metrics, we performed a Principal Component Analysis (PCA) using the four test case metrics (TLoc, TAss, THEff, and THDiff). PCA is a technique that has been widely used in software engineering to identify important underlying dimensions captured by a set of metrics. We used this technique to find whether the test case metrics are independent or are capturing the same underlying dimension (property) of the object being measured. The PCA was performed on the data set consisting of test case metrics values from JFC system. As it can be seen from Table 2, JFC is the system that has the most JUnit test cases.

The PCA identified two Principal Components (PCs), which capture more than 90% of the data set variance (Table 3). Based on the analysis of the coefficients associated with each metric within each of the components, the PCs are interpreted as follows: (1) PC$_1$: TLoc and TAss. These metrics are, in fact, size-related metrics. (2) PC$_2$: THDiff. This is the

TABLE 3: Results of PCA analysis.

	PC$_1$	PC$_2$	PC$_3$
Prop (%)	79.974	12.136	5.554
Cumul (%)	79.974	92.111	97.665
TAss	**26.168**	23.958	0.001
THDiff	23.51	**29.656**	46.749
THEff	24.112	22.848	**52.964**
TLoc	**26.209**	23.538	0,287

Halstead Difficulty measure. It captures more data variance than the THEff (Halstead Effort) measure. The results of the PCA analysis suggest that (1) the information provided by the metric THEff is captured by the (size related) test case metrics TLoc and TAss, and (2) the metric THDiff is rather complementary to the test case metrics TLoc and TAss. So, we used in this work the suite of metrics (TLoc, TAss, and THDiff) to quantify the JUnit test cases. We assume that the effort necessary to write a test class C_t corresponding to a software class C_s is proportional to the characteristics measured by the used suite of test case metrics.

4.3. Correlation Analysis. In this section, we present the first step of the empirical study we performed to explore the relationship between the Qi metric and test case metrics. We performed statistical tests using correlation. We used a nonparametric measure of correlation. We used the Spearman's correlation coefficient. This technique, based on ranks of the observations, is widely used for measuring the degree of linear relationship between two variables (two sets of ranked data). It measures how tightly the ranked data clusters around a straight line. Spearman's correlation coefficient will take a value between -1 and $+1$. A positive correlation is one in which the ranks of both variables increase together. A negative correlation is one in which the ranks of one variable increase as the ranks of the other variable decrease. A correlation of $+1$ or -1 will arise if the relationship between the ranks is exactly linear. A correlation close to zero means that there is no linear relationship between the ranks. We used the XLSTAT (http://www.xlstat.com/) tool to perform the statistical analysis.

As mentioned previously, we also include the SLOC metric in our experiments. So, we analyzed the collected data set by calculating the Spearman's correlation coefficient r_s for each pair of metrics (source code metric (Qi, SLOC) and test case metric). Table 4 summarizes the results of the correlation analysis. It shows, for each of the selected systems and between each distinct pair of metrics, the obtained values for the Spearman's correlation coefficient. The Spearman's correlation coefficients are all significant. The chosen significance level is $\alpha = 0.05$. In summary, as it can be seen from Table 4, the results confirm that there is a significant relationship (at the 95% confidence level) between the Qi and SLOC metrics and the used test case metrics for all the subject systems. Moreover, the observed correlation values between the source code metrics (Qi and SLOC) and the test case metrics are generally comparable.

TABLE 4: Correlation values between Qi and SLOC metrics and test case metrics.

	ANT			JFC			JODA			IO			LUCENE		
	TAss	THDiff	TLoc	TAss	THDiff	TLoc	TAss	THDiff	TLoc	TAss	THDiff	TLoc	TAss	THDiff	TLoc
Qi	−0.361	−0.331	−0.553	−0.341	−0.209	−0.415	−0.762	−0.698	−0.805	−0.574	−0.550	−0.772	−0.467	−0.306	−0.457
SLOC	0.391	0.387	0.582	0.414	0.261	0.437	0.726	0.630	0.764	0.641	0.585	0.827	0.495	0.316	0.470

TABLE 5: Correlation values between test case metrics.

	ANT			JFC			JODA			IO			LUCENE		
	TAss	THDiff	TLoc	TAss	THDiff	TLoc	TAss	THDiff	TLoc	TAss	THDiff	TLoc	TAss	THDiff	TLoc
TAss	1	0,73	0,77	1	0,83	0,84	1	0,90	0,95	1	0,60	0,79	1	0,59	0,77
THDiff		1	0,79		1	0,76		1	0,91		1	0,74		1	0,85
TLoc			1			1			1			1			1

The measures of correlations between the Qi metric and the test case metrics are negative. As mentioned previously, a negative correlation indicates that the ranks of one variable (Qi metric) decrease as the ranks of the other variable (test case metric) increase. These results are plausible and not surprising. Indeed, as mentioned in Section 3, a low value of the Qi of a class indicates that the class is a high-risk class and needs a high testing effort to ensure its quality. A high value of the Qi of a class indicates that the class is a low-risk class and needs a relatively low testing effort. The measures of correlations between the size-related SLOC metric and the test case metrics are positive. These results are, in fact, plausible. A large class, containing a large number of methods in particular, will require a high testing effort.

We also calculated the Spearman's correlation coefficient r_s for each pair of test case metrics (Table 5). The global observation that we can make is that the test case metrics are significantly correlated between themselves. The chosen significance level here also is $\alpha = 0.05$.

4.4. Evaluating the Effect of the Qi Metric on Testability Using Logistic Regression Analysis. In this section, we present the empirical study we conducted in order to evaluate the effect of the Qi metric on testability of classes in terms of testing effort. We used the univariate logistic regression analysis.

4.4.1. Dependent and Independent Variables. The binary dependent variable in our study is testability of classes. We consider testability from the perspective of unit testing effort. The goal is to evaluate empirically, using logistic regression analysis, the relationship between the Qi metric (independent variable in our study) and testability of classes. Here also, we used the SLOC metric as a "baseline" to compare against the Qi metric. We used the test case metrics (TLoc, TAss, and THDiff) to identify the classes which required a (relative) high testing effort (in terms of size and difficulty). As mentioned earlier, the metrics TLoc and TAss have been introduced by Bruntink and Van Deursen [4, 8] to indicate the size of a test suite. These metrics reflect, in fact, different source code factors [4, 8]: factors that influence the *number of test cases* required to test the classes of a system, and factors that influence the *effort required* to develop each

TABLE 6: Distribution of classes.

	1	0
ANT	33.3%	66.7%
JFC	31.4%	68.6%
JODA	32.9%	67.1%
IO	30.3%	69.7%
LUCENE	29%	71%

individual test case. In order to simplify the process of testing effort categorization, and as a first attempt, we provide in this study only two categorizations: classes which required a high testing effort and classes which required a (relative) low testing effort. In a first step, we used the three test case metrics to divide the test classes into four groups as follows.

Group 4. This group includes the JUnit test cases for which the three following conditions are satisfied: (1) large number of lines of code (corresponding TLoc ≥ mean value of TLoc), (2) large number of invocations of JUnit *assert* methods (corresponding TAss ≥ mean value of TAss), and (3) high difficulty level (corresponding THDiff ≥ mean value of THDiff).

Group 3. This group includes the JUnit test cases for which only two of the conditions mentioned above are satisfied.

Group 2. This group includes the JUnit test cases for which only one of the conditions mentioned above is satisfied.

Group 1. This group includes the JUnit test cases for which none of the conditions mentioned above is satisfied.

In a second step, we merged these four groups in two categories according to the testing effort as follows: high (groups 4 and 3) and low (groups 2 and 1). We affected the value 1 to the first category and the value 0 to the second one. Table 6 summarizes the distribution of classes according to the adopted categorization. From Table 6, it can be seen that for (1) ANT, 33.3% of the selected classes for which JUnit test cases were developed have been categorized as classes having required a high testing effort. (2) JFC, 31.4% of the selected classes for which JUnit test cases were developed have been categorized as classes having required a high testing effort. (3) JODA, 32.9% of the selected classes for which JUnit test cases were developed have been categorized as classes having required a high testing effort. (4) IO, 30.3% of the selected classes for which JUnit test cases were developed have been categorized as classes having required a high testing effort. (5) Finally, for LUCENE, 29% of the selected classes for which JUnit test cases were developed have been categorized as classes having required a high testing effort. As it can be seen from Table 6, overall, one third of the classes (of each system) were categorized as classes having required a high testing effort.

4.4.2. Hypothesis. In order to evaluate the relationship between the Qi metric (and SLOC) and testability of classes, and particularly to find the effect of the Qi metric (and SLOC) on the testing effort, the study tested the following hypothesis.

Hypothesis 1 (Qi). A class with a low Qi value is more likely to require a high testing effort than a class with a high Qi value.

The Null Hypothesis. A class with a low Qi value is no more likely to require a high testing effort than a class with a high Qi value.

Hypothesis 2 (SLOC). A class with a high SLOC value is more likely to require a high testing effort than a class with a low SLOC value.

The Null Hypothesis. A class with a high SLOC value is no more likely to require a high testing effort than a class with a low SLOC value.

4.4.3. Logistic Regression Analysis: Research Methodology. Logistic Regression (LR) is a standard statistical modeling method in which the dependent variable can take on only one of two different values. It is suitable for building software quality classification models. It is used to predict the dependent variable from a set of independent variables and to determine the percent of variance in the dependent variable explained by the independent variables [42–44]. This technique has been widely applied to the prediction of fault-prone classes (e.g., [12, 43, 49–52]). LR is of two types: Univariate LR and Multivariate LR. A multivariate LR model is based on the following equation:

$$P(X_1, \ldots, X_n) = \frac{e^{(a + \sum_{i=1}^{i=n} b_i X_i)}}{1 + e^{(a + \sum_{i=1}^{i=n} b_i X_i)}}. \tag{8}$$

The X_is are the independent variables and the b_is are the estimated regression coefficients (approximated contribution) corresponding to the independent variables X_is. The larger the (normalized) absolute value of the coefficient, the stronger the impact of the independent variable on the probability of detecting a high testing effort. P is the probability of detecting a class with a high testing effort. The univariate regression analysis is a special case of the multivariate regression analysis, where there is only one independent variable (Qi or SLOC in our study).

The regression analysis here is not intended to be used to build a prediction model combining the two source code metrics (Qi and SLOC). Such models, and multivariate LR analysis, are out of the scope of this paper. Instead, our analysis intends to investigate the effect of the Qi metric on the testing effort and to compare it to the effect of the SLOC metric (taken as a well-known and proper baseline), in order to evaluate the actual benefits (ability) of the Qi metric when used to predict testability.

4.4.4. Model Evaluation. Precision and recall are traditional evaluation criteria that are used to evaluate the prediction accuracy of logistic regression models. Because precision and recall are subject to change as the selected threshold changes, we used the ROC (*Receiver Operating Characteristics*) analysis to evaluate the performance of the predicted model. The ROC curve, which is defined as a plot of sensitivity on the y-coordinate versus its 1-specificity on the x-coordinate, is an effective method of evaluating the quality (performance) of prediction models [53].

The ROC curve allows also obtaining a balance between the number of classes that the model predicts as requiring a high testing effort, and the number of classes that the model predicts as requiring a low testing effort. The optimal choice of the cut-off point that maximizes both sensitivity and specificity can be selected from the ROC curve. This will allow avoiding an arbitrary selection of the cut-off. In order to evaluate the performance of the prediction model, we used the AUC (Area Under the Curve) measure. It allows appreciating the model without subjective selection of the cutoff value. It is a combined measure of sensitivity and specificity. The lager the AUC measure, the better the model is at classifying classes. A perfect model that correctly classifies all classes has an AUC measure of 1. An AUC value close to 0.5 corresponds to a poor model. An AUC value greater than 0.7 corresponds to a good model [54].

Moreover, the issue of training and testing data sets is very important during the construction and evaluation of prediction models. If a prediction model is built on one data set (used as training set) and evaluated on the same data set (used as testing set), then the accuracy of the model will be artificially inflated [55]. A common way to obtain a more realistic assessment of the predictive ability of the model is to use cross validation (k-fold cross-validation), which is a procedure in which the data set is partitioned in k subsamples (groups of observation). The regression model is built using $k-1$ groups and its predictions evaluated on the last group. This process is repeated k times. Each time, a different subsample is used to evaluate the model, and the remaining subsamples are used as training data to build the model. We performed, in our study, a 10-fold cross-validation. We used the XLSTAT and R (http://www.r-project.org/) tools.

4.4.5. Univariate LR Analysis: Results and Discussion. Table 7 summarizes the results of the univariate LR analysis. The (normalized) *b-coefficient* is the estimated regression coefficient. The larger the absolute value of the coefficient, the stronger the impact of the Qi (SLOC) on the probability of detecting a high testing effort. The *P-value* (related to

TABLE 7: Results for univariate LR analysis.

		ANT	JFC	JODA	IO	LUCENE
Qi	R^2	0.365	0.160	0.214	0.488	0.177
	2Log	<0.0001	<0.0001	0.000	<0.0001	0.000
	b	−0.787	−0.478	−0.838	−1.066	−0.431
	P-value	<0.0001	<0.0001	0.022	<0.0001	0.000
	AUC	**0.81**	**0.72**	**0.85**	**0.89**	**0.70**
SLOC	R^2	0.255	0.194%	0.192	0.593	0.152
	2Log	<0.0001	<0.0001	0.001	<0.0001	0.000
	b	0.589	0.545	0.562	3.022	0.605
	P-value	<0.0001	<0.0001	0.006	0.000	0.011
	AUC	**0.80**	**0.75**	**0.80**	**0.91**	0.67

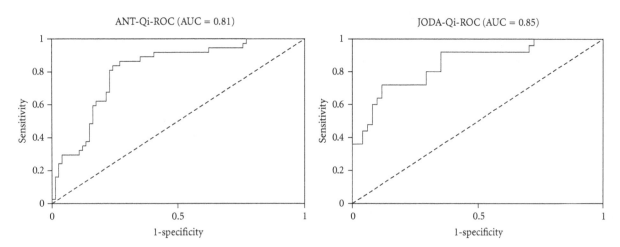

FIGURE 2: Univariate LR ROC curves for ANT and JODA systems.

the statistical hypothesis) is the probability of the coefficient being different from zero by chance and is also an indicator of the accuracy of the coefficient estimate. To decide whether the Qi and SLOC metrics are statistically significant predictors of testing effort, we used the $\alpha = 0.05$ significance level to assess the P-value. R^2 (Nagelkerke) is defined as the proportion of the total variance in the dependent variable (testing effort) that is explained by the model. The higher R^2 is, the higher is the effect of the Qi metric (and SLOC metric), and the more accurate is the model. In summary, the results show that, for the five investigated systems, the b-coefficient and the R^2 values of the Qi and SLOC metrics are significant. According to these results, we can conclude that the Qi and SLOC metrics are significantly related to the testing effort. The AUC values confirm that the univariate LR models based on the metrics Qi and SLOC are able to accurately predict the unit testing effort of classes.

The results show, for system ANT, for example, that the normalized b-coefficients of the metrics Qi and SLOC (resp., 0.787 and 0.589) are significantly different from zero according to their P-values. The used significance level is 0.05. The metric Qi has the highest R^2 value (0.365). According to the obtained results, the metrics Qi and SLOC are significantly related to the testing effort. The AUC values

confirm that univariate LR models based on the metrics Qi and SLOC are able to accurately predict the unit testing effort of classes. However, we can see from Table 7 that the univariate LR model based on the metric Qi is slightly more predictive of testing effort than the one based on the metric SLOC (R^2 and b-coefficient values). Overall, the accuracies of both models are comparable, depending upon systems, except may be for system LUCENE where the model based on the SLOC metric has an AUC score of 0.67. For system LUCENE, the model based on the Qi metric has an AUC score of 0.7. Figure 2 gives the univariate LR ROC curves of the Qi metric for ANT and JODA systems.

4.5. Threats to Validity. The study performed in this paper should be replicated using many other systems in order to draw more general conclusions about the relationship between the Qi metric and testability of classes. In fact, there are a number of limitations that may affect the results of the study or limit their interpretation and generalization.

The achieved results are based on the data set we collected from the investigated systems. As mentioned earlier (Section 4.1), we analyzed 593 Java classes and corresponding JUnit test cases. Even if we believe that the analyzed data set is large enough to allow obtaining significant results, we do not claim that our results can be generalized to all systems. The study should be replicated on a large number of OO software systems to increase the generality of our findings.

Moreover, the classes for which JUnit test cases were developed, and this in all the investigated systems, are relatively large and complex. It would be interesting to replicate this study using systems for which JUnit test cases have been developed for a maximum number of classes. This will allow observing the performance of the prediction models with data collected from classes of varying sizes (small, medium, and large).

It is also possible that facts such as the development style used by the developers for writing test cases and the criteria they used while selecting the software classes for which they developed test classes (randomly or depending on their size or complexity e.g., or on other criteria) may affect the results or produce different results for specific applications. We observed, in fact, that in some cases the developed JUnit classes do not cover all the methods of the corresponding software classes. This may be due to the style adopted by the developers while writing the test cases (or other considerations). As the source code metrics (Qi and SLOC) are computed using the complete code of the classes, this may affect (bias) the results.

Finally, another important threat to validity is from the identification of the relationship between the JUnit test cases and tested classes. As mentioned in Section 4, we noticed by analyzing the code of the JUnit test cases of the investigated systems that, in some cases, there is no one-to-one relationship between JUnit test cases and tested classes. In these cases, several JUnit test cases have been related to a same tested class. Even if we followed a systematic approach for associating the JUnit test cases to the corresponding tested classes, which was not an easy task, unfortunately we have not been able to do that for all classes. This may also affect the results of our study or produce different results from one system to another.

5. Conclusions and Future Work

The paper investigated empirically the relationship between a metric (Quality Assurance Indicator—Qi) that we proposed in a previous work and testability of classes in terms of required testing effort. The Qi metric captures, in an integrated way, different OO software attributes. Testability has been investigated from the perspective of unit testing. We performed an empirical analysis using data collected from five open source Java software systems for which JUnit test cases exist. To capture testability of classes, we used different metrics to measure some characteristics of the corresponding JUnit test cases. Classes were classified according to the required testing effort in two categories: high and low. In order to evaluate the relationship between the Qi metric and testability of classes, we used the univariate logistic regression method. The performance of the predicted model was evaluated using Receiver Operating Characteristic (ROC) analysis. We also include in our study the well-known SLOC metric as a "baseline."

The results indicate that (1) the Qi metric is statistically related to the test case metrics and (2) the univariate regression model based on the Qi metric is able to accurately predict the unit testing effort of classes. Overall, the accuracies of the model based on the Qi metric and the one based on the SLOC metric are comparable. Based on these results, we can reasonably claim that the Qi metric is a significant predictor of the unit testing effort of classes. We hope these findings will help to a better understanding of what contributes to testability of classes in OO systems, and particularly the effect of control flow on the testing effort.

The performed study should, however, be replicated using many other OO software systems in order to draw more general conclusions. The findings in this paper should be viewed as exploratory and indicative rather than conclusive. Moreover, knowing that software testability is affected by many different factors, it would be interesting to extend the used suite of test case metrics to better reflect the testing effort.

As future work, we plan to extend the used test case metrics to better reflect the testing effort, include some well-known OO metrics in our study, explore the use of the Qi metric during the testing process in order to better guide the distribution of the testing effort, and finally replicate the study on various OO software systems to be able to give generalized results.

Acknowledgments

The authors would like to acknowledge the support of this paper by NSERC (National Sciences and Engineering Research Council of Canada) Grant. The authors would also like to thank the editor and anonymous reviewers for their very helpful comments and suggestions.

References

[1] P. L. Yeh and J. C. Lin, "Software testability measurement derived from data flow analysis," in *Proceedings of the 2nd Euromicro Conference on Software Maintenance and Reengineering*, Florence, Italy, 1998.

[2] B. Baudry, B. Le Traon, and G. Sunyé, "Testability analysis of a UML class diagram," in *Proceedings of the 9th International Software Metrics Symposium (METRICS '03)*, IEEE CS, 2003.

[3] B. Baudry, Y. Le Traon, G. Sunyé, and J. M. Jézéquel, "Measuring and improving design patterns testability," in *Proceedings of the 9th International Software Metrics Symposium (METRICS '03)*, IEEE Computer Society, 2003.

[4] M. Bruntink and A. van Deursen, "An empirical study into class testability," *Journal of Systems and Software*, vol. 79, no. 9, pp. 1219–1232, 2006.

[5] L. Zhao, "A new approach for software testability analysis," in *Proceedings of the 28th International Conference on Software Engineering (ICSE '06)*, pp. 985–988, May 2006.

[6] IEEE, *IEEE Standard Glossary of Software Engineering Terminology*, IEEE Computer Society Press, 1990.

[7] ISO/IEC 9126: Software Engineering Product Quality, 1991.

[8] M. Bruntink and A. Van Deursen, "Predicting class testability using object-oriented metrics," in *Proceedings of the 4th IEEE International Workshop on Source Code Analysis and Manipulation (SCAM '04)*, pp. 136–145, September 2004.

[9] V. Gupta, K. K. Aggarwal, and Y. Singh, "A Fuzzy Approach for Integrated Measure of Object-Oriented Software Testability," *Journal of Computer Science*, vol. 1, no. 2, pp. 276–282, 2005.

[10] B. Henderson-Sellers, *Object-Oriented Metrics Measures of Complexity*, Prentice-Hall, 1996.

[11] Y. Singh, A. Kaur, and R. Malhota, "Predicting testability effort using artificial neural network," in *Proceedings of the World Congress on Engineering and Computer Science*, San Francisco, Calif, USA, 2008.

[12] Y. Singh, A. Kaur, and R. Malhotra, "Empirical validation of object-oriented metrics for predicting fault proneness models," *Software Quality Journal*, vol. 18, no. 1, pp. 3–35, 2009.

[13] L. Badri, M. Badri, and F. Touré, "Exploring empirically the relationship between lack of cohesion and testability in object-oriented systems," in *Advances in Software Engineering*, T.-h. Kim, H.-K. Kim, M. K. Khan et al., Eds., vol. 117 of *Communications in Computer and Information Science*, Springer, Berlin, Germany, 2010.

[14] L. Badri, M. Badri, and F. Touré, "An empirical analysis of lack of cohesion metrics for predicting testability of classes," *International Journal of Software Engineering and Its Applications*, vol. 5, no. 2, 2011.

[15] M. Badri and F. Touré, "Empirical analysis for investigating the effect of control flow dependencies on testability of classes," in *Proceedings of the 23rd International Conference on Software Engineering and Knowledge Engineering (SEKE '11)*, 2011.

[16] M. Badri, L. Badri, and F. Touré, "Empirical analysis of object-oriented design metrics: towards a new metric using control flow paths and probabilities," *Journal of Object Technology*, vol. 8, no. 6, pp. 123–142, 2009.

[17] N. Fenton and S. L. Pfleeger, *Software Metrics: A Rigorous and Practical Approach*, PWS Publishing Company, 1997.

[18] J. Gao and M. C. Shih, "A component testability model for verification and measurement," in *Proceedings of the 29th Annual International Computer Software and Applications Conference (COMPSAC '05)*, pp. 211–218, July 2005.

[19] J. W. Sheppard and M. Kaufman, "Formal specification of testability metrics in IEEE P1522," in *Proceedings of the IEEE Systems Readiness Technology Conference Autotestcom (AUTOTESTCON '01)*, pp. 71–82, Valley Forge, Pa, USA, August 2001.

[20] R. S. Freedman, "Testability of software components," *IEEE Transactions on Software Engineering*, vol. 17, no. 6, pp. 553–564, 1991.

[21] J. M. Voas, "PIE: a dynamic failure-based technique," *IEEE Transactions on Software Engineering*, vol. 18, no. 8, pp. 717–727, 1992.

[22] J. M. Voas and K. W. Miller, "Semantic metrics for software testability," *The Journal of Systems and Software*, vol. 20, no. 3, pp. 207–216, 1993.

[23] J. M. Voas and K. W. Miller, "Software testability: the new verification," *IEEE Software*, vol. 12, no. 3, pp. 17–28, 1995.

[24] R. V. Binder, "Design for testability in object-oriented systems," *Communications of the ACM*, vol. 37, no. 9, 1994.

[25] T. M. Khoshgoftaar, R. M. Szabo, and J. M. Voas, "Detecting program modules with low testability," in *Proceedings of the 11th IEEE International Conference on Software Maintenance*, pp. 242–250, October 1995.

[26] T. M. Khoshgoftaar, E. B. Allen, and Z. Xu, "Predicting testability of program modules using a neural network," in *Proceedings of the 3rd IEEE Symposium on Application-Specific Systems and SE Technology*, 2000.

[27] J. McGregor and S. Srinivas, "A measure of testing effort," in *Proceedings of the Conference on Object-Oriented Technologies*, pp. 129–142, USENIX Association, June1996.

[28] A. Bertolino and L. Strigini, "On the use of testability measures for dependability assessment," *IEEE Transactions on Software Engineering*, vol. 22, no. 2, pp. 97–108, 1996.

[29] Y. Le Traon and C. Robach, "Testability analysis of co-designed systems," in *Proceedings of the 4th Asian Test Symposium (ATS '95)*, IEEE Computer Society, Washington, DC, USA, 1995.

[30] Y. Le Traon and C. Robach, "Testability measurements for data flow designs," in *Proceedings of the 4th International Software Metrics Symposium*, pp. 91–98, Albuquerque, NM, USA, November 1997.

[31] Y. Le Traon, F. Ouabdesselam, and C. Robach, "Analyzing testability on data flow designs," in *Proceedings of the 11th International Symposium on Software Reliability Engineering (ISSRE '00)*, pp. 162–173, October 2000.

[32] A. Petrenko, R. Dssouli, and H. Koenig, "On evaluation of testability of protocol structures," in *Proceedings of the International Workshop on Protocol Test Systems (IFIP '93)*, Pau, France, 1993.

[33] K. Karoui and R. Dssouli, "Specification transformations and design for testability," in *Proceedings of the IEEE Global Elecommunications Conference (GLOBECOM '96)*, 1996.

[34] S. Jungmayr, "Testability measurement and software dependencies," in *Proceedings of the 12th International Workshop on Software Measurement*, October 2002.

[35] J. Gao, J. Tsao, and Y. Wu, *Testing and Quality Assurance for Component-Based Software*, Artech House, 2003.

[36] T. B. Nguyen, M. Delaunay, and C. Robach, "Testability analysis applied to embedded data-flow software," in *Proceedings of the 3rd International Conference on Quality Software (QSIC '03)*, 2003.

[37] B. Baudry, Y. Le Traon, and G. Sunyé, "Improving the testability of UML class diagrams," in *Proceedings of the International Workshop on Testability Analysis (IWoTA '04)*, Rennes, France, 2004.

[38] V. Chowdhary, "Practicing testability in the real world," in *Proceedings of the International Conference on Software Testing, Verification and Validation*, IEEE Computer Society Press, 2009.

[39] R. A. Khan and K. Mustafa, "Metric based testability model for object-oriented design (MTMOOD)," *ACM SIGSOFT Software Engineering Notes*, vol. 34, no. 2, 2009.

[40] A. Kout, F. Touré, and M. Badri, "An empirical analysis of a testability model for object-oriented programs," *ACM SIGSOFT Software Engineering Notes*, vol. 36, no. 4, 2011.

[41] Y. Singh and A. Saha, "Predicting testability of eclipse: a case study," *Journal of Software Engineering*, vol. 4, no. 2, 2010.

[42] V. R. Basili, L. C. Briand, and W. L. Melo, "A validation of object-oriented design metrics as quality indicators," *IEEE Transactions on Software Engineering*, vol. 22, no. 10, pp. 751–761, 1996.

[43] Y. Zhou and H. Leung, "Empirical analysis of object-oriented design metrics for predicting high and low severity faults," *IEEE Transactions on Software Engineering*, vol. 32, no. 10, pp. 771–789, 2006.

[44] K. K. Aggarwal, Y. Singh, A. Kaur, and R. Malhotra, "Empirical analysis for investigating the effect of object-oriented metrics on fault proneness: a replicated case study," *Software Process Improvement and Practice*, vol. 14, no. 1, pp. 39–62, 2009.

[45] A. Mockus, N. Nagappan, and T. T. Dinh-Trong, "Test coverage and post-verification defects: a multiple case study," in

Proceedings of the 3rd International Symposium on Empirical Software Engineering and Measurement (ESEM '09), pp. 291–301, October 2009.

[46] B. V. Rompaey and S. Demeyer, "Establishing traceability links between unit test cases and units under test," in *Proceedings of the 13th European Conference on Software Maintenance and Reengineering (CSMR '09)*, pp. 209–218, March 2009.

[47] A. Qusef, G. Bavota, R. Oliveto, A. De Lucia, and D. Binkley, "SCOTCH: test-to-code traceability using slicing and conceptual coupling," in *Proceedings of the International Conference on Software Maintenance (ICSM '11)*, 2011.

[48] M. H. Halstead, *Elements of Software Science*, Elsevier/North-Holland, New York, NY, USA, 1977.

[49] L. C. Briand, J. W. Daly, and J. Wüst, "A unified framework for cohesion measurement in object-oriented systems," *Empirical Software Engineering*, vol. 3, no. 1, pp. 65–117, 1998.

[50] L. C. Briand, J. Wüst, J. W. Daly, and D. Victor Porter, "Exploring the relationships between design measures and software quality in object-oriented systems," *Journal of Systems and Software*, vol. 51, no. 3, pp. 245–273, 2000.

[51] T. Gyimóthy, R. Ferenc, and I. Siket, "Empirical validation of object-oriented metrics on open source software for fault prediction," *IEEE Transactions on Software Engineering*, vol. 31, no. 10, pp. 897–910, 2005.

[52] A. Marcus, D. Poshyvanyk, and R. Ferenc, "Using the conceptual cohesion of classes for fault prediction in object-oriented systems," *IEEE Transactions on Software Engineering*, vol. 34, no. 2, pp. 287–300, 2008.

[53] K. El Emam and W. Melo, "The prediction of faulty classes using object-oriented design metrics," National Research Council of Canada NRC/ERB 1064, 1999.

[54] D. Hosmer and S. Lemeshow, *Applied Logistic Regression*, Wiley-Interscience, 2nd edition, 2000.

[55] K. El Emam, "A Methodology for validating software product metrics," National Research Council of Canada NRC/ERB 1076, 2000.

5

A Multi-Layered Control Approach for Self-Adaptation in Automotive Embedded Systems

Marc Zeller and Christian Prehofer

Fraunhofer Institute for Communication Systems ESK, Hansastraße 32, 80686 Munich, Germany

Correspondence should be addressed to Marc Zeller, marc.zeller@esk.fraunhofer.de

Academic Editor: Phillip A. Laplante

We present an approach for self-adaptation in automotive embedded systems using a hierarchical, multi-layered control approach. We model automotive systems as a set of constraints and define a hierarchy of control loops based on different criteria. Adaptations are performed at first locally on a lower layer of the architecture. If this fails due to the restricted scope of the control cycle, the next higher layer is in charge of finding a suitable adaptation. We compare different options regarding responsibility split in multi-layered control in a self-healing scenario with a setup adopted from automotive in-vehicle networks. We show that a multi-layer control approach has clear performance benefits over a central control, even though all layers work on the same set of constraints. Furthermore, we show that a responsibility split with respect to network topology is preferable over a functional split.

1. Introduction

There has been considerable work on self-adaptive systems which can reconfigure their software configuration at runtime [1–3]. However, applying these techniques to networked, embedded systems poses several new problems due to limitations and reliability requirements of embedded systems [4]. In particular, we focus on automotive embedded systems, where the main constraints are

  (i) limited memory resources,

  (ii) heterogeneous hardware platforms,

  (iii) different subnetworks connected by a gateway,

  (iv) various requirements of different functionalities, and

  (v) high demand on safety and reliability.

The focus of this paper is on self-adaptation in automotive embedded systems using a hierarchical, multi-layered control approach implemented by concrete instances of a control architecture.

Today's automobiles consist of an increasing number of interconnected electronic devices—so-called electronic control units (ECUs)—which realize most functionalities of the car by software. This networked embedded system keeps the vehicle running by controlling the engine and the breaks, provides active safety features (e.g., antilock breaking system), makes driving more convenient, and entertains the passengers with a large number of information and comfort services (e.g., air conditioning, audio player). Especially modern driver assistance systems, which distribute their functionality over several components, increase the complexity of today's vehicular embedded systems enormously. Managing nowadays vehicle software systems means managing over 2,000 software components, running on up to 100 ECUs [5].

Enhancing automotive embedded systems with self-adaptation provides a promising solution for the current challenges in automotive embedded systems [6]. So-called self-* properties, like self-configuration, self-healing, self-optimization or self-protection [7] improve the scalability, robustness, and flexibility of the system [8]. With the size of automotive systems, it becomes difficult to calculate all configurations and all failure cases in advance. Hence, the adaptation of the system may have to be calculated during runtime. In this work, we focus on the adaptation control of the system after the breakdown of a hardware platform. The actual reconfiguration of the system itself is not the focus here and can, for instance, be performed during a (partial) restart of the system.

For realizing systems with these self-managing capabilities, a control component is needed [9]. This external component supervises the system and initiates the adaptation during runtime using closed feedback-loops (so-called control loops) [10]. In the autonomic computing *(AC)* paradigm, the elements of the system are managed by control loops based on the so-called *MAPE-K cycle* [11] which optimizes the operation of the supervised elements and enables the realization of self-* properties. Such a control loop continuously monitors and analyzes the system and its environment. Based on this information it plans the next steps and executes the planned actions. The different phases have access to a common knowledge base which provides information about the supervised elements or system.

Especially for automotive systems with various requirements and constraints, enabling self-adaptation and building a control architecture are a challenging task. Different aspects of the automotive system like safety issues must be considered by the control components appropriately. Furthermore, the control architecture has to react quickly to changing conditions, either from inside the system (e.g., hardware or software failures) or from outside the system (e.g., changing environmental conditions).

The control component of a self-adaptive system can be realized in different ways. Either a single-centralized control entity may realize the adaptation of a software system, or multiple control components may realize the adaptation of composite of software systems in a decentralized manner [12]. While centralized control may not be efficient for realizing adaptation in large, complex, and heterogeneous systems (e.g., automotive embedded systems), fully decentralized approaches may lead to a coordination overhead within the system.

An alternative is hierarchical multi-layered control architectures, as discussed in [11], where multiple control loops cooperate to achieve adaptation. In this work, we model such automotive systems using a set of constraints as introduced in [13]. Based on this, we can define the operation and responsibility of each local control cycle in the hierarchy based on different functional criteria. Thus, resulting in a control architecture with a certain number of control loops arranged in a specific way using multiple layers. Even though all control cycles work on the same set of constrains, local responsibility means that only some variables can be controlled and the others are fixed. This also means that some constraints are out of scope for some local control cycles. We compare different options, regarding different splits of responsibility as well as multi-layered control versus centralized control.

In summary, the main contributions of this paper are as follows.

(i) We introduce different instances of the multi-layered control approach for automotive embedded systems which hierarchically enforce system requirements on several layers. Therefore, the software components of the system are clustered based on different functional criteria realizing a control architecture with different numbers of layers.

(ii) We compare these concrete instances of the multi-layered approach in a self-healing scenario with realistic setups of up to 100 ECUs. It is shown that local repair based on a layered control approach in such a system is more efficient than a pure central approach. Secondly, it shows that a responsibility split based on locality w.r.t. network topology performs better than a split regarding functional areas.

The structure of this paper is as follows. In Section 2 a brief introduction to automotive embedded systems is given. Section 3 describes our approach for hierarchical, multi-layered control. Afterwards, we propose concrete instances of our multi-layered control approach for self-adaptive automotive software system. In Section 5, we outline how to realize self-adaptation during runtime using our multi-layered control approach. Moreover, we introduce a coordination mechanism for the different control loops within the multi-layered control architecture. Section 6 presents the results of the experiments which we performed to compare our concrete instances of the multi-layered approach with a centralized control approach. Section 7 discusses related work.

2. Automotive Embedded Systems

An automotive embedded system is a distributed real-time system with heterogeneous hardware platforms (ECUs) interconnected by different network buses [5]. Moreover, the automotive embedded system consists of various functionalities which are implemented in software and which must satisfy different requirements.

Thereby, an automotive embedded system A consists of a set of inputs I (sensors), a set of functionalities $F = \{f_1, \ldots, f_n\}$ (features), and a set of outputs O (actuators). The set of functionalities is realized by a set of software components SW, where each feature f_i is implemented by a set of software components SW_{f_i} with $\text{SW}_{f_i} \subset \text{SW}$. Software components, sensors, and actuators are connected to each other in a specified way. This so-called function network can be represented by a directed graph $G_f(V_f, E_f)$. The vertices V_f represent software components, actuators, or sensors. The directed edges E_f indicate a data flow from one vertex to another by sending messages. Each vertex may have multiple incoming edges and multiple outgoing edges.

The so-called system configuration c describes the allocation of the software components ($\text{SW} = \{s_1, \ldots, s_n\}$) to the available ECUs ($P = \{p_1, \ldots, p_m\}$) at time t

$$c(t) : \text{SW} \longrightarrow P = \{0, 1\}^{n \times m} \qquad (1)$$

with $n \cdot m$ variables $x_{i,j}$. If the software component s_i is assigned to ECU p_j, then $x_{i,j} = 1$, else it is 0. The allocation

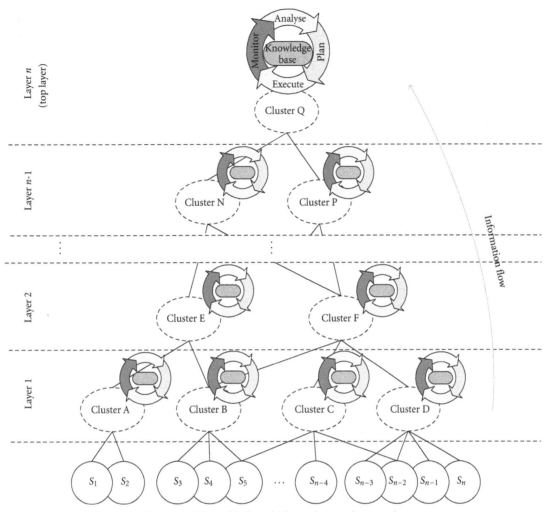

FIGURE 1: Hierarchical, multi-layered control approach.

of a specific software component $s_i \in$ SW is represented by φ:

$$\varphi(s_i) = p_j, \quad p_j \in P. \tag{2}$$

Moreover, A consists of a set of constraints $\Psi = \{\psi_1, \ldots, \psi_p\}$ which represent the requirements of the system during runtime and enable the definition of valid allocations. Abstractly, a linear constraint $\psi_k \in \Psi$ is defined as a Boolean formula:

$$\psi_k = \left(\sum_{i=1}^{n} \sum_{j=1}^{m} a_{i,j} x_{i,j} \right) \circ b \longrightarrow \{\text{true}, \text{false}\} \tag{3}$$

with the Boolean literals $x_{i,j} \in \{0, 1\}$ which represent the allocation of the software component s_i to the ECU p_j, the coefficients $a_{i,j}, b \in \mathbb{R}$, and the operator $\circ \in \{<, \leq, =, \geq, >\}$.

Typical constraints in terms of automotive systems concern hardware platform resources (e.g., volatile, non-volatile memory), network resources (e.g., bandwidth), task dependencies, task schedulability, timing, or the network topology. A detailed description of these equations, called system constraints, which define valid system configurations under real-time constraints, can be found in [13]. This set

of equations is optimized to be solved efficiently during runtime in order to enable the computation of valid system configurations in an adaptive system in reasonable time.

3. Hierarchical, Multi-Layered Control Approach

To cope with the complexity of modern automotive embedded systems, we propose a hierarchical, multi-layered control approach (see Figure 1). Resources for enforcing adaptations at runtime are scarce but absolutely inevitable for realizing self-* properties. Therefore, a divide-and-conquer strategy can be applied during design which partitions the automotive embedded system into smaller entities—so-called clusters.

A cluster cl is defined by a set of r software components $\{s_1, \ldots, s_r\} = \text{SW}_{\text{cl}} \subseteq \text{SW}$. The current cluster configuration $c_{\text{cl}}(t)$ describes the current allocation φ_{cl} of the software components SW_{cl} to the available ECUs at the time t according to (1).

Repeated partitioning of the automotive embedded system results in a hierarchy of clusters, representing the entire system. Thereby, each cluster has at least one parent cluster and any number of child clusters. The top level of this hierarchy consists of exactly one cluster. Each cluster within the hierarchy is controlled by its own control loop, thus building a multi-layered control architecture. A control loop is an external component which is not included within the cluster itself. It is supervising and controlling (adapting) the clustered elements during runtime, so that the constraints Ψ are satisfied during runtime (see Section 5).

Due to the repeated segmentation of the automotive embedded system, the clusters on the lowest layers in this control architecture are relatively small. They consist of only a few software components. Due to the individual implementation of the control loops at the lowest layers, this hierarchical, multi-layered control approach can be tailored individually for the needs of specific functionalities or subsystems of the automotive embedded system (e.g., safety-critical X-by-wire systems). As a drawback, the clusters on the lower layers have a restricted local scope and are not always capable of determining a new, valid cluster configuration which satisfies all given requirements.

At the higher layers, the number of software components included in a cluster, which must be controlled, is growing. Thus, the possibilities of determining a valid cluster configuration increase but also the complexity of determining a valid configuration is rising with the number of software components which are considered.

At the top layer, a single root cluster represents the top element in the hierarchy. It has a global view of the system and supervises the entire automotive embedded system during runtime with all its predefined requirements.

During runtime, the automotive embedded system is supervised by a hierarchy of multiple MAPE-K cycles which adapt the system in response to changes within the system or in the system's environment. Based on an individual knowledge base, each MAPE-K cycle manages its cluster in four stages.

Monitor. Each control component within the control architecture collects, aggregates, and filters specific parameters of their managed elements (software components within the cluster). The parameters which need to be monitored are given by the requirements which can be supervised by the scope of the control loop.

Analysis. During this stage the monitored data are analyzed and compared to the available data in the knowledge base of the control loop. Each control instance evaluates if the predefined requirements, which it supervises, are currently satisfied.

Plan. The plan stage provides mechanisms that create or compose a set of actions to adapt the supervised part of the system. In the context of automotive embedded systems, the planning stage determines a new cluster configuration which fulfills all predefined requirements.

Execute. During this stage the planned actions are executed. In our case, each control loop adapts the allocation of the

software components which are included in its cluster in the planned way.

Based on the hierarchy of MAPE-K cycles within our multi-layered control approach, it is possible to enhance the automotive embedded system by adaptation and self-* properties.

For building concrete instances of the hierarchical, multi-layered control approach to realize self-adaption within automotive embedded systems, different design options need to be addressed:

(i) number of layers within the control architecture,

(ii) number and scope of the different clusters within the hierarchy (resulting from the segmentation of the system),

(iii) realization of the coordination between multiple control loops.

In the next section, we address these issues and provide three different instances of the hierarchical, multi-layered control approach to realize self-adaptation in automotive embedded systems.

4. Instances of the Multi-Layered Control Approach for Automotive Embedded Systems

In this section, we present three concrete instances of the hierarchical, multi-layered control approach for automotive embedded systems.

The most intuitive approach is a topology-oriented structuring according to the network topology of today's in-vehicle networks (see Figure 2). For this purpose, the automotive embedded system—vehicle cluster on the top layer of the hierarchy—is divided into different clusters according to the physical sub-networks within the in-vehicle network which result from the segmentation of the car's functionalities into functional domains (e.g., power train, infotainment, chassis, comfort etc.). Thereby, five so-called Network Clusters are created which include all software components defined for a specific sub-network (domain). At the next layer of the hierarchy, each network cluster is split up according to the physical hardware platforms connected to the subnetwork. The resulting platform clusters represent the software components which are initially allocated to a specific ECU and control them by its own MAPE-K cycle. Since this control loop must be able to detect if the specific ECU is faulty and must adapt the allocation of the ECU's software components, it is implemented on one of the other ECUs within the sub-network.

Due to the increasing interconnection of the different vehicle domains (e.g., by advanced driver assistance systems), this kind of partitioning of automotive embedded systems may become less suitable for the realization of a multi-layered control architecture for automotive embedded systems. In other words, a local control loop responsible for a sub-network may not be able to find a local solution due to dependencies with other domains.

Another approach for a control architecture for automotive embedded systems is based on a function-oriented

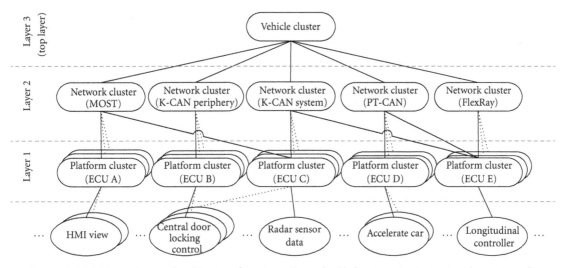

FIGURE 2: Multi-layered control architecture for automotive embedded systems (variant 1, topology oriented).

structuring of the in-vehicle network (cf. [14]). Thereby, the automotive embedded system is divided into five so-called safety clusters according to the safety integrity levels *(SIL) 0–4* defined by [15] or by the automotive safety integrity levels *(ASIL) A–D* as well as quality management *(QM)* defined by [16] which are used to classify the safety requirements of the car's functionalities (see Figure 3). Thus, functionalities with different safety requirements are monitored and controlled by specifically adjusted mechanisms. Safety-critical functionalities are reconfigured using adequate techniques which consider the functions' safety requirements, while other functionalities are adapted during runtime by other, more appropriate techniques. At the next layer of the hierarchy, each safety cluster is split up according to the functionalities included into the vehicle's domain. Each of the resulting feature clusters represents a functionality of the automobile which is realized by software and controls the functionalities' software components by its own MAPE-K cycle. This represents the logical structure of the automotive embedded system. Hence, interdependencies between different clusters due to interconnected sub-networks may be avoided.

A more fine-granular segmentation of the system is achieved by combing the two previous approaches (topology oriented and function oriented) for the realization of a concrete instance of the multi-layered control approach for automotive embedded systems (see Figure 4). Therefore, the automotive embedded system is firstly decomposed according to the different safety requirements of the car's functionalities. Hence, functionalities which are not safety-critical may be deactivated easily in certain situations (e.g., in case failures within the system during runtime). At the next layer, the system is partitioned according to the physical sub-networks within the in-vehicle network. Thereby, adaptations within a specific sub-network are realized by one specific MAPE-K cycle. The next layer is formed by feature clusters which represent each of the car's software-based functionalities. Since many functionalities of today's automobiles, like advanced driver assistance systems, realize their functionality using the same sensor input data or the same actuators, certain software functions which are used by different functionalities are clustered as so-called services (cf. [14]). Thus, in this variant of a multi-layered control architecture each functionality is decomposed into one or more services which are organized in so-called service clusters. The lowest layer of the hierarchy is composed of these clusters. Since these services are used by more than one of the car's functionalities, a service can be part of more than one Feature Cluster. For instance, the adaptive cruise control *(ACC)* feature, which can automatically adjust the car's speed to maintain a safe distance to the vehicle in front, can be decomposed into the radar sensor service, the longitudinal controller service, the engine service to accelerate, and the braking system service to decelerate.

In all these approaches, the so-called vehicle cluster forms the top layer of the hierarchical, multi-layered control architecture. This cluster includes all software components of the automotive embedded system and its MAPE-K cycle has a global view of the supervised system.

By using one of these instances of the hierarchical, multi-layered control approach, self-adaptation and different self-* properties can be realized while considering the specific nature of today's automotive embedded systems. Thereby, the various requirements of these systems are monitored by several control components (MAPE-K cycles) which are organized hierarchically. Each MAPE-K cycle adapts the specific part of the networked embedded system which it supervises.

In the following section, we describe how self-adaptation is realized in automotive embedded systems using the multi-layered control approach.

5. Self-Adaptation with Multi-Layered Control

In the following, we discuss the operation of multi-layered control for our setting with a global set of system constraints. The aim of our hierarchical, multi-layered control approach is to preserve all predefined requirements of the automotive embedded system during runtime. Thereby, the proper

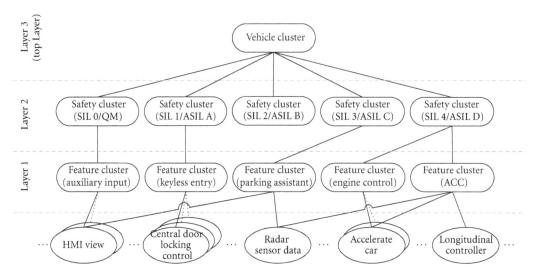

FIGURE 3: Multi-layered control architecture for automotive embedded systems (variant 2, function oriented).

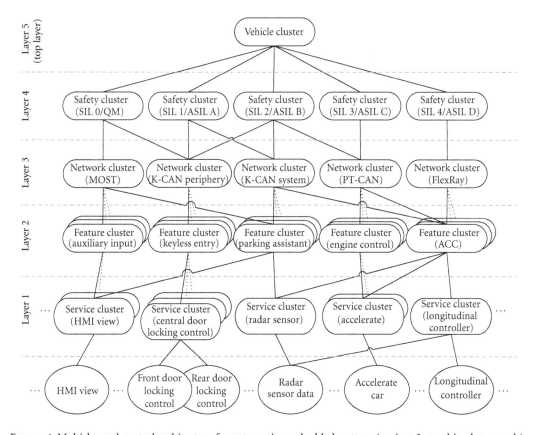

FIGURE 4: Multi-layered control architecture for automotive embedded systems (variant 3, combined approach).

system behavior of the automotive embedded system is guaranteed (see [4]). In our approach, each MAPE-K cycle within the hierarchy enforces all the requirements specified in the design, which are represented in form of linear, Boolean (in-) equations. If any of the predefined requirements are not satisfied anymore during runtime (e.g., caused by the breakdown of a hardware platform), the configuration of the system c is adapted to meet these constraints, if possible.

To enable a fast adaptation of the system during runtime, adaptations are performed on the lowest layer of the hierarchy by the cluster which detects the cause for the adaptation. Since all system constraints are considered by each control loop within the hierarchical, multi-layered control architecture, each MAPE-K cycle—even on the lowest layer of the hierarchy—is able to determine a new, valid system configuration. However, the different control cycles have different scope—hence the set of free variables is restricted to the local scope. In other words, the local control cycles are in charge of the placement of the software components of their cluster.

Only if a cluster was not able to reach a new valid cluster configuration, its parent cluster takes over the adaptation process. The root cluster (Vehicle Cluster in Section 4) is only involved in the adaptation process as the last instance. Since the root cluster has the global view and knowledge of the entire system, it is always capable of reaching a new valid system configuration—if one exits.

In the best case, the adaptation of the system is performed by the control loop of one single cluster. In the worst case, up to n control loops are involved in the process of adaptation within an n-layered control architecture. Thereby, constraint checks may be performed multiple times until a new, valid system configuration is found. This results in unnecessary computation overhead—unless a solution is found on the lower layers. On the other hand, on the top level, new placements for all components are to be determined, which is much more complex than solving equations on a lower layer of the hierarchy. For the local scope, only a limited, local number of placements are to be determined. Furthermore, on the local scope, equations may be trivially true for a specific configuration, if they are not affected by the free variables of this control cycle.

In the following, we aim to compare the different instances of the hierarchical control approach with a central control solution. Thus, we have a tradeoff between finding solutions locally with lower cost, but possibly with repeated attempts on different layers, versus a single control loop with a higher cost. Clearly, if the hierarchical solution has to resort to the top layer frequently, the centralized solution will be more efficient.

Control loops at the same layer of the control architecture shall not interfere with each other in order to avoid oscillation during adaptation—hence only one of them can be active at a time. In other words, they must be coordinated by a dedicated mechanism to avoid that several control components adapt the same part of the system simultaneously (see [17]). This needs to be ensured, typically by the next layer (see Section 5.1).

5.1. Coordination within Multi-Layered Control. The coordination of different control loops within our approach is based on the design pattern "hierarchical control" described in [17, 18], which is adopted for our specific application scenario.

To avoid that multiple control loops adapt the system simultaneously, an MAPE-K cycle notifies the control component of its parent cluster that it will adapt the system. If none of the other control loops in the same scope of the cluster is already adapting the automotive embedded systems, the request is permitted (see Figure 5). Otherwise the request is rejected. While the system is reconfigured, further requests for adaption are declined by the control component which executes the adaption or by the control components which has allowed the adaptation. Therefore, it is guaranteed that the system configuration of the

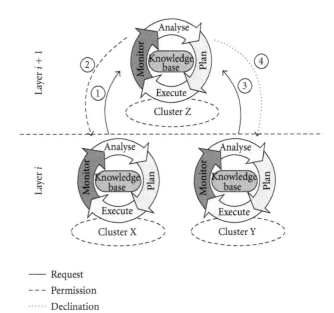

— Request
--- Permission
...... Declination

FIGURE 5: Coordination of control loops within the hierarchical, multi-layered control approach.

automotive embedded systems (or a specific subsystem) is not adapted simultaneously by multiple control components within the control architecture. Hence, oscillations during adaptation are avoided by this coordination approach. Nevertheless, different subsystems can be adapted in parallel (e.g., adaptations within different physical sub-networks of the networked embedded system).

This approach allows the coordination of multiple MAPE-K cycles within the hierarchical, multi-layered control architecture during runtime adaption with minimal communication overhead. Only two messages are exchanged to coordinate two control loops in case of runtime adaptation. During the "normal" operation of the system (monitoring and analysis of the correctly working networked embedded system), no coordination is required and hence no additional communication between different control loops within the multi-layered control architecture is performed.

6. Evaluation

In this section, we illustrate the potential benefits of our approach of hierarchical, multi-layered control for realizing self-adaptation in automotive embedded systems (see Section 4) w.r.t. efficiency of determining a new, valid system configuration in case of an ECU breakdown (self-healing scenario). At first, an initial assignment of software components to hardware is determined. After this, the adaptation of the system is triggered by simulating the breakdown of a randomly selected ECU. Moreover, we simulate the simultaneous breakdown of two randomly selected ECUs in a second self-healing scenario.

6.1. Evaluation Setup. In our experiments, we simulate the typical embedded systems of modern automobiles (see [5]). Therefore, we use various setups representing different sizes

TABLE 1: Experimental setups.

Setup	ECUs	Functions	Sensors/actuators	Subnetworks
1.1	20	500	40/40	4
1.2	30	750	50/50	4
1.3	40	1000	60/60	5
1.4	50	1250	70/70	5
1.5	60	1500	80/80	8
1.6	70	1750	90/90	8
1.7	80	2000	100/100	8
1.8	90	2250	110/110	8
1.9	100	2500	120/120	8
2.1	40	200	60/60	5
2.2	40	400	60/60	5
2.3	40	600	60/60	5
2.4	40	800	60/60	5
2.5	40	1000	60/60	5
2.6	40	1200	60/60	5
2.7	40	1400	60/60	5
2.8	40	1600	60/60	5
2.9	40	1800	60/60	5
2.10	40	2000	60/60	5

TABLE 2: Composition of network buses for different setups of automotive in-vehicle networks.

Number of networks	Composition
4	2x low speed CAN, 2x high speed CAN
5	3x low speed CAN, 2x high speed CAN
8	3x low speed CAN, 3x high speed CAN, 1x MOST, 1x FlexRay

and variants of automotive in-vehicle networks (see Table 1). While the ratio between the number of software components and the number of ECUs are fixed in the first setups (setup 1.1–1.9), we also perform experiments with setups where this ratio is variable (setup 2.1–2.10).

In all our experiments, the in-vehicle network consists of a central gateway (maximum throughput = 250 Kbyte/s, maximum delay = 100 ms) which interconnects all network buses. The network buses are either low speed or high speed CAN, MOST, or FlexRay systems. The parameters of these networks (bandwidth, maximum transmission delay, maximum message size) are introduced in [19]. The different configurations of the network buses in our experiments are listed in Table 2. An ECU is always connected to exactly one network bus. The number of ECUs is equally spread over the available network buses. Moreover, sensors and actuators are also directly connected to one of the network buses (cf. [20]). The connection of an ECU, a sensor, or an actuator to a certain network bus is done for each setup randomly.

An ECU is defined by volatile memory (RAM) with 32, 64, 128, 256, or 512 Kbyte as well as nonvolatile memory (ROM, Flash) of 64, 128, 256, 512, or 1024 Kbyte. Moreover, a certain CPU frequency is assigned to each ECU, which is between 50 MHz and 1 GHz (in steps of 50 MHz). The

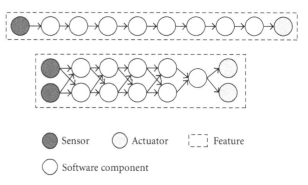

FIGURE 6: Example of a feature which is generated for our experiments.

value Δ is used to specify the ratio of the CPU frequency to a reference frequency of 100 MHz (Δ = reference frequency/CPU frequency).

The sensors in our generated in-vehicle networks provide data always periodically. These periods can vary for each sensor in a range between 20 ms and 200 ms (in steps of 5 ms). Actuators react directly on incoming events or messages and hence are aperiodic.

All parameters of the physical resources of the automotive in-vehicle network for our experiments are generated randomly and are equally distributed in the given ranges.

The function network $G_f(V_f, E_f)$ of the generated automotive embedded systems consists of a certain number of features. In all setups listed in Table 1, we assume that each feature of the vehicle consists of 8-9 software functions, as well as one or two sensors and actuators. Each of the software functions interacts with either one or two of the other functions which implement the same feature. We assume that there are no cycles within the function network. Figure 6 illustrates how a generated feature may look alike. Between a sensor and a software function as well as between a software function and an actuator, data in a range between 1 and 10 Bit are exchanged. Between different software functions, which implement a certain feature of the automotive system, data in a range between 2 and 20 Bit are exchanged each. Thereby, software functions, sensors, and actuators can be part of any number of features, but are at least part of one feature. All features are generated automatically in our evaluations, where all parameters are chosen randomly and equally distributed.

Each software function needs a certain amount of volatile and nonvolatile memory in order to be executed on a hardware platform. These values are in a range between total amount of the available memory of all ECUs/ (number of software functions * 2) and total amount of the available memory of all ECUs/number of software functions in all experiments. All software functions are periodic tasks. The period of a software function is between 20 ms and 200 ms (in steps of 5 ms). The deadline of a function is equal to its period. Furthermore, the worst case execution time (WCET) of a software function is calculated according to the *UUniFast algorithm* [21]. The value of the WCET refers to an ECU with the reference frequency of 100 MHz. Moreover, a priority is defined for each software function, which is

TABLE 3: Size of the set of system constraints.

Setup	No. of constraints	No. of literals
1.1	7,599	60,877
1.2	20,047	197,385
1.3	33,040	397,584
1.4	52,658	781,281
1.5	65,773	1,154,150
1.6	85,081	1,689,251
1.7	126,877	2,771,502
1.8	138,641	3,393,508
1.9	174,434	4,580,388
2.1	6,746	77,396
2.2	12,801	156,798
2.3	17,220	217,867
2.4	27,899	338,935
2.5	33,040	397,584
2.6	35,516	435,196
2.7	45,021	539,373
2.8	54,239	659,452
2.9	60,376	770,882
2.10	69,218	877,051

between 1 and number of software functions/number of ECUs. The parameters of each software function are also generated randomly and equally distributed in the given range of values.

Moreover, timing requirements in form of an end-to-end timing chain are defined consisting of one sensor input, a sequence of software functions, which are part of a certain feature, and one actuator. In the following, we assume that half of the features have a timing chain defined.

In all our experiments, the automotive embedded system consists of three different kinds of hardware platforms (ECUs). Each software function can only be executed on one kind of the hardware platforms. The definition on which kind of hardware platform a certain software function can be executed is done randomly. Thus, the allocation set for each software function/ECU contains about 33% of the vehicles' ECUs/software functions in all our evaluation setups. Other limitations of the automotive in-vehicle network, which must be considered during runtime, are expressed by the system constraints, as introduced in [13].

For reference, we list the number of these constraints and literals needed to solve the SAT problem for the given setups in Table 3.

For our experiments, the concrete control architecture variants for automotive embedded systems outlined in Section 4 are implemented. Furthermore, a centralized control architecture (similar to [22]) is implemented to compare our hierarchical, multi-layered approach with this state-of-the-art approach. According to [13] the SAT-solver SAT4J Version 2.2 [23] is used in all our experiments to determine a valid allocation of software components to ECUs within each MAPE-K cycle.

For each setup in Table 1, we perform tests with each variant for the control architecture 10 times and calculate the average values as well as the 95% confidence interval of the average values. All experiments are performed on an embedded platform with an Intel Atom Processor at 1.6 GHz and 1.5 Gbyte RAM (reference platform for the next generation in-vehicle infotainment systems).

6.2. Breakdown of an ECU. Figures 7(a) and 7(b) show the results of the experiments which are performed with the previously described variants of automotive embedded systems (see Table 1). In all experiments, we have measured the time needed to determine a new, valid allocation of software components after the breakdown of a randomly selected ECU occurred (self-healing scenario).

This result shows that when using one of the instances of the hierarchical, multi-layered control approach described in Section 4, less computation time is needed until a new valid system configuration is found, than using a centralized control approach with one single control loop. For the setups 1.x, the difference between the centralized approach and the variant 2 (function oriented) of our approach (see Figure 3) is quite small, especially for larger automotive in-vehicle networks. But using the variant 1 (topology oriented) of the hierarchical, multi-layered control architecture (see Figure 2), a significant performance optimization is reached. Moreover, using the combination of variant 2 and 3 (variant 3, see Figure 4), a new valid system configurations can be determined for small automotive embedded systems (setup 1.1–1.4) in less time than using a centralized control approach. However, with the growing size of the allocation problem which needs to be solved (size of the automotive embedded system), this variant of a hierarchical, multi-layered control architecture needs approximately the same time to determine a new valid system configuration. For large automotive embedded systems (setup 1.7–1.9) this variant needs even more time. For the setups 2.x, significant optimization of the time needed to determine a new, valid system configuration is reached by using our hierarchical, multi-layered approach for controlling the automotive embedded systems. The difference between the three instances of the multi-layered control approach is quite small. Yet the topology-oriented variant is performing better in all our experiments, although adaptation is performed for setup 2.x on the lowest layer of the hierarchy in all different instances of our multi-layered control approach.

The results of our experiments clearly show that the complexity of realizing self-adaptation in automotive embedded systems can be reduced significantly by using our hierarchical, multi-layered control approach. Furthermore, we also see that the topology-oriented variant is significantly better in most cases than variant 2, which clusters along the functional entities, or variant 3. This means in case of an ECU failure, the variant which considers solutions based on the local network has better chances to determine a new allocation on the lowest layer of the hierarchy than the second variant, which considers solutions based on functionality. While solutions based on functionality are more natural regarding the functional dependencies, there is the risk that a CPU

TABLE 4: Successful determination of valid configurations within the multi-layered control architectures (in %).

Setup	Variant 1			Variant 2			Variant 3				
	Layer 1	Layer 2	Layer 3	Layer 1	Layer 2	Layer 3	Layer 1	Layer 2	Layer 3	Layer 4	Layer 5
1.1	100	0	0	100	0	0	100	0	0	0	0
1.2	100	0	0	100	0	0	100	0	0	0	0
1.3	100	0	0	100	0	0	100	0	0	0	0
1.4	100	0	0	100	0	0	100	0	0	0	0
1.5	0	100	0	0	100	0	10	0	90	0	0
1.6	0	88.9	11.1	10	90	0	0	0	100	0	0
1.7	0	30	70	0	100	0	0	0	100	0	0
1.8	0	28.6	71.4	0	100	0	0	0	90	10	0
1.9	0	0	100	0	100	0	0	0	100	0	0

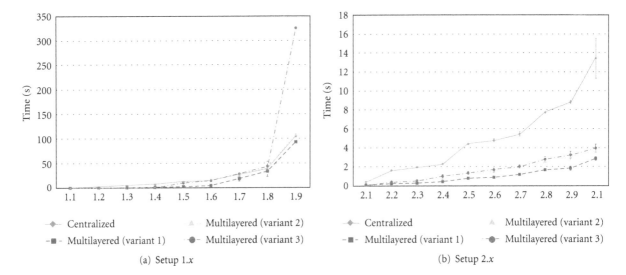

(a) Setup 1.x   (b) Setup 2.x

FIGURE 7: Time needed to determine a new, valid system configuration.

failure may affect several functional categories—hence a local repair by one control cycle is not possible (cf. Table 4).

This is also supported by the different results for the setup 1.x and 2.x. Here the topology-oriented variant of the multi-layered control architecture is significantly better compared to function-oriented variant or the combination of variant 1 and 2 for setups 2.x, while all three are closer in most experiments in setup 1.x (except 1.5–1.7). Furthermore, all instances of our hierarchical, multi-layered control approach are significantly better than the centralized approach for setup 2.x. Our multi-layered approach performs also much better than the centralized one for smaller automotive embedded systems (setup 1.1–1.4). In case of larger and more complex allocation problems (setup 1.5–1.9), only variant 1 of a hierarchical, multi-layered control architecture enables the calculation of a valid allocation in shorter time. Variant 2 (function-oriented) as well as variant 3 (combination of variant 1 and 2) of the layered control approach do not perform better in average than the central control architecture for these setups. This is because, for large allocation problems with many constraints (cf. Table 3), it is very difficult to find a new valid allocation with the local

scope of the control loops on the lower layer of a multi-layered control architecture (cf. Table 4). The chance to find a new, valid system configuration locally on the lowest layer of the hierarchically does not depend on the number of software components with are supervised by control loop (cf. results for setup 2.x in Figure 7(b)).

Furthermore, we measured the distance between the current and the newly determined system configuration (lower bound on the number of software component migrations needed to adapt the automotive embedded system) for rating the quality of the solutions. The results (Figures 8(a) and 8(b)) clearly show that using a hierarchical, multi-layered control architecture leads to solutions with a shorter distance to the current allocation when determining a new, valid allocation of software functions to ECUs using a SAT-solver-based approach. Especially, if it is possible to find a new, valid system configuration by a control loop on the lowest layer of the hierarchy (in our experiments for setup 1.1–1.4 and 2.x), a significant reduction of necessary migrations can be achieved. For larger automotive embedded systems (setup 1.5–1.9 in our experiments), a valid allocation of software functions to ECUs must often be determined by a control

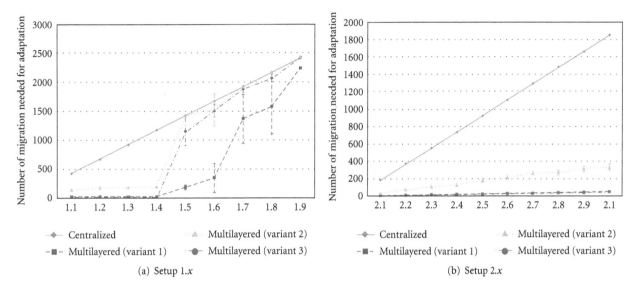

(a) Setup 1.x

(b) Setup 2.x

FIGURE 8: Distance between the current and the new system configuration.

loop on a higher layer of the hierarchy, because it is not possible to find a valid solution for the allocation problem within the local scope of one of the control instances at the lowest layer (cf. Table 4). In these tests, variant 1 of our hierarchical, multi-layered control approach performs much better than the other two variants described in Section 4 (see Figure 8(a)). Moreover, our experiments for setup 2.x show no significant difference in the results using variant 1 and variant 3 of our hierarchical, multi-layered control approach with respect to the quality of the newly determined system configuration. However, these two variants result in much better solutions for setup 2.x than the function-oriented variant of a hierarchical, multi-layered control architecture.

Thus, not only the needed time to determine a new, valid system configuration during the planning stage, but also time needed to execute the newly planned configuration is reduced significantly when using the hierarchical, multi-layered control approach in this self-healing scenario.

6.3. Simultaneous Breakdown of Two ECUs.
In additional tests, we evaluate the different instances of the hierarchical, multi-layered control approach for self-adaptation in automotive embedded systems using a self-healing scenario, in which two ECUs break down simultaneously. Thereby, all experiments are performed with the previously described variants of automotive embedded systems (see Table 1). Again we measured the time needed to determine a new, valid allocation of software components after the breakdown occurred. The results of these experiments are presented in Figures 9(a) and 9(b).

The results of these tests for setup 1.x show, that only using the topology-oriented variant of our hierarchical multi-layered control approach (variant 1) leads to a better performance for the self-adaptation in all experiments than the central control approach. Both the function-oriented approach and the combined approach based on variant 1 and

variant 2 are able to determine a new valid system configuration for small automotive embedded systems (setup 1.1–1.5) more quickly than the centralized control approach, but in case of larger allocation problems (setup 1.7–1.9) these approaches need more time to determine a valid allocation of software components than the central control architecture. Reason for this is that several different functionalities are affected by the breakdown of two ECU when using the variant 2 or 3 of a multi-layered control architecture (cf. Section 4). In these cases a valid system configuration is normally found by one of the control loops on the higher layers of the hierarchy (cf. Table 5). Thereby, multiple MAPE-K cycles are involved in the adaptation process which includes the repeated execution of the necessary calculations (e.g., for determining a new, valid system configuration). Hence, using a hierarchical, multi-layered control architecture results in a more complex adaptation process compared to the centralized control approach, if multiple control loops on different layers of the multi-layered control architecture are triggered during the adaptation process. When using the topology-oriented approach of the hierarchical, multi-layered control approach, the top layer of the hierarchy is only involved in the adaptation process, if more than one subnetwork is affected by the breakdown of the two ECUs, which is not always the case in our experiments. Thus, the adaptation can be planned more quickly using the topology-oriented variant of our hierarchical, multi-layered control approach than using one of the other variants evaluated in our experiments (see Figure 9(a)). The results for setup 2.x show, that a significant optimization of the time needed to determine a new, valid system configuration is achieved by using our hierarchical, multi-layered control approach compared to a central control architecture (see Figure 9(b)). Moreover, these results illustrat, that variant 1 and variant 3 of a hierarchical, multi-layered control architecture for self-adaptation in automotive embedded systems (presented in Section 4) are more suitable than variant 2 in case that

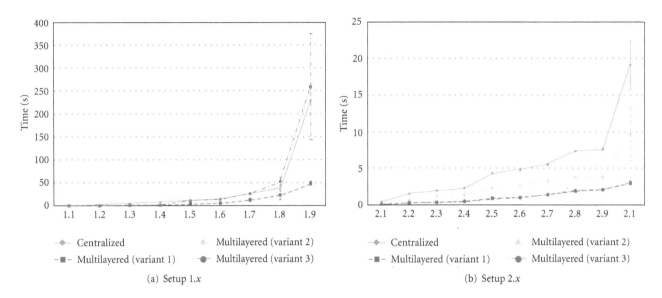

(a) Setup 1.x   (b) Setup 2.x

FIGURE 9: Time needed to determine a new, valid system configuration.

TABLE 5: Successful determination of valid configurations within the multi-layered control architectures (in %).

Setup	Variant 1			Variant 2			Variant 3				
	Layer 1	Layer 2	Layer 3	Layer 1	Layer 2	Layer 3	Layer 1	Layer 2	Layer 3	Layer 4	Layer 5
1.1	100	0	0	100	0	0	100	0	0	0	0
1.2	100	0	0	100	0	0	100	0	0	0	0
1.3	100	0	0	100	0	0	100	0	0	0	0
1.4	100	0	0	100	0	0	100	0	0	0	0
1.5	10	80	10	20	80	0	0	20	80	0	0
1.6	20	70	10	30	70	0	10	0	90	0	0
1.7	0	70	30	0	100	0	0	0	100	0	0
1.8	0	66.6	33.3	0	100	0	0	0	100	0	0
1.9	0	80	20	0	100	0	0	0	100	0	0

two control units break down simultaneously and all repair actions are performed locally on the lowest layer of the hierarchy.

Furthermore, the comparison of the quality of the solutions (see Figures 10(a) and 10(b)) shows that using our hierarchical, multi-layered control approach leads to solutions with a shorter distance to the current allocation when determining a new valid allocation of software functions to ECUs. Variant 2 and variant 3 of a hierarchical, multi-layered control architecture (presented in Section 4) lead to significant improvements w.r.t. the quality of the solution only for small automotive embedded systems (setup 1.1–1.7). However, the topology-oriented variant (variant 1) results in better solutions w.r.t. the distance between the current and the newly determined system configuration even for very large automotive embedded systems (see Figure 10(a)). Our experiments for setup 2.x also show, that the concrete instances of the hierarchical, multi-layered control approach in combination with a SAT-solver-based approach for the determination of a valid allocation for the systems' software

components results in much better solutions compared to the centralized control approach with one single MAPE-K cycle. The best results for this scenario (in which two ECUs breakdown simultaneously) are achieved when using either variant 1 or variant 3 of a hierarchical, multi-layered control architecture (see Figure 10(b)).

7. Related Work

In the past, various approaches for realization of a multi-layered control architecture have been presented.

Kramer and Magee outline a three-layered architecture for self-managed systems in [24]. On the lowest layer (component layer), a control loop provides self-optimization algorithms as well as mechanisms for event and status reporting to higher layers and operations to support the modification of supervised components. On the next layer (change management layer), a set of predefined configurations is activated in response to state changes of the system below. Finally, on the goal management layer, time

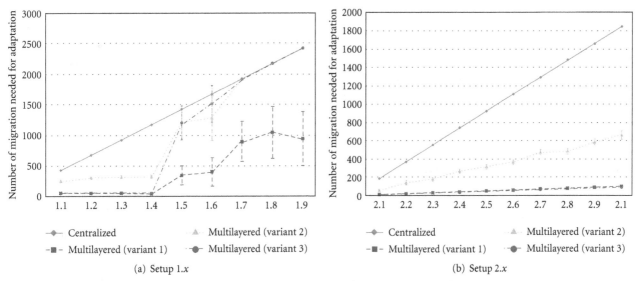

(a) Setup 1.x

(b) Setup 2.x

FIGURE 10: Distance between the current and the new system configuration.

consuming computations such as planning are performed to achieve the defined system goals. This three-layered control approach poses a generic reference architecture. The level of abstraction proposed by [24] reduces the complexity of self-management during runtime, but does not address the various functional and nonfunctional requirements of automotive embedded systems. To address this issue, we propose a divide-and-conquer strategy to split up the technical system into clusters according to different criteria.

In [25] a control architecture for embedded real-time systems is outlined. Simple module managers are running on each processing node of the system and one single global manager controls the whole system. The module managers collect information about the current condition of the system from their local point of view and transfer it to the global manager. The global manager analyzes the available information and decides which actions should be executed next. In this approach, the Module Managers do not need to implement the complete MAPE-K cycle and thus can run even on small processing nodes. The complex analysis and planning actions are performed by the Global Manager. Although this approach is well suited for the use within embedded systems, it consists of a relatively complex Global Manager component which still poses a single point of failure. Since the Global Manager is the only component to make decisions, its failure cannot be compensated. Within our hierarchical, multi-layered control approach, adaptations are performed by the control component which detects the cause for the adaptation. Only if it is not possible to determine a new, valid system configuration locally, a control loop at the next higher layer is involved in the adaptation process. Moreover, the multiple layers of our approach are able to consider the different aspects of automotive embedded system in contrast to the two-layered approach.

A first approach towards a control architecture for the realization of self-management in automotive embedded systems is presented in [22]. He describes a central control architecture for enabling autonomous management. The so-called system manager provides management functionalities on a system-wide basis. The Self-configurator uses these management functionalities to implement a control loop with a global knowledge base. The central control approach is not able to manage the growing complexity of today's automotive software systems in an adequate way. Our experiments show that our multi-layered approach is performing significantly better in determining a new, valid allocation of software components to ECUs (in case of a self-healing scenario) compared to the central approach (cf. Section 6). Moreover, the central control architecture results in a single point of failure which cannot be tolerated in safety-relevant systems like automobiles.

The concept of multiple control loops which cooperate to achieve a goal was already introduced by IBM [11]. To reduce the complexity of self-adaptation or self-management, multiple control loops must be decoupled with respect to time or respect to space and may be hierarchically organized [10], thereby, distinguishing between different time scales and different controlled variables (e.g., [26, 27]). Our hierarchical, multi-layered control approach is also based on the concepts of decoupling control loops by different controlled variables (software components) and organizing these control loops hierarchically. Thereby, it is possible to handle the complexity of self-adaptation in a networked embedded system which must fulfill various requirements with different scopes (e.g., an automotive in-vehicle network). Such a multi-layered control architecture for automotive embedded systems, where each control loop is responsible to supervise certain requirements and to adapt a certain part of the system, is introduced in [28]. Thereby, adaptation is performed locally on a lower layer first. If this fails, the next higher layer is in charge of finding a suitable adaptation. Yet in this approach no realistic set of system constraints, as done here, is used which enables the hierarchical enforcement of system requirements on several layers.

8. Conclusion

In this work, we have presented a hierarchical, multi-layered control approach for self-adaptation in automotive systems. We have introduced a multi-layer control approach which aims to cope with the rising complexity of today's automotive embedded systems by splitting up the system into a set of different clusters. By the segmentation of the system according to different aspects of the automotive system (locality or functionality), a hierarchy of these clusters is built. Based on such a hierarchical, multi-layered control architecture including multiple MAPE-K cycles, self-adaptation is realized during runtime by enforcing the systems' requirements.

We have compared different concrete instances of our hierarchical, multi-layered control approach in a self-healing scenario with realistic setups of up to 100 ECUs. This comparison shows that local repair based on a layered control architecture in such a system is more efficient than a pure centralized control approach. Not only w.r.t. the time needed to determine a new, valid system configuration after the breakdown of one or two ECUs, but also w.r.t. the quality of the newly determined solutions (the distance between the current and the newly determined system configuration). Moreover, it shows that a responsibility split based on locality with respect to network topology performs better than a split regarding functional areas in our self-healing scenario.

Thus, not only the needed time to determine a new, valid system configuration during the planning stage, but also the time needed to execute the newly planned configuration is reduced significantly when using our hierarchical, multi-layered control approach for self-adaptation in automotive embedded system in a self-healing scenario.

Furthermore, the multi-layered control approach presented in this work is adaptable to enhance other complex and networked embedded systems with real-time requirements (e.g., industrial plants, aircrafts or railways) with self-adaptation and self-* properties. Therefore, such networked embedded system must be split up into a set of different clusters based on aspects which are specific to the respective application domain. Moreover, realizing other self-* properties apart from self-healing (e.g., self-optimization) will be addressed in future work. In this context, a fully detailed discussion of local and global optima which are reached by using different control approaches for planning new system configurations in networked embedded systems as well as a comprehensive mathematical representation of the allocation problem, which needs to be solved to determine a new allocation of software components to hardware platforms, must be presented.

References

[1] J. Kramer and J. Magee, "Dynamic configuration for distributed systems," *IEEE Transactions on Software Engineering*, vol. 11, no. 4, pp. 424–436, 1985.

[2] P. Oreizy, N. Medvidovic, and R. N. Taylor, "Architecture-based runtime software evolution," in *Proceedings of the International Conference on Software Engineering*, pp. 177–186, April 1998.

[3] I. Georgiadis, J. Magee, and J. Kramer, "Self-Organising Software Architectures for Distributed Systems," in *Proceedings of the 1st Workshop on Self-Healing Systems (WOSS '02)*, pp. 33–38, November 2002.

[4] M. Zeller, G. Weiss, D. Eilers, and R. Knorr, "An approach for providing dependable self-adaptation in distributed embedded systems," in *Proceedings of the 26th Annual ACM Symposium on Applied Computing (SAC '11)*, pp. 236–237, March 2011.

[5] K. V. Prasad, M. Broy, and I. Krüger, "Scanning advances in aerospace automobile software technology," *Proceedings of the IEEE*, vol. 98, no. 4, pp. 510–514, 2010.

[6] G. Weiss, M. Zeller, D. Eilers, and R. Knorr, "Towards self-organization in automotive embedded systems," in *Proceedings of the 6th International Conference on Autonomic and Trusted Computing*, pp. 32–46, 2009.

[7] J. O. Kephart and D. M. Chess, "The vision of autonomic computing," *Computer*, vol. 36, no. 1, pp. 41–50, 2003.

[8] G. Weiss, M. Zeller, and D. Eilers, "Towards automotive embedded systems with self-x properties," in *New Trends and Developments in Automotive System Engineering*, InTech, 2011.

[9] G. Mühl, M. Werner, M. A. Jaeger, K. Herrmann, and H. Parzyjegla, "On the definitions of self-managing and self-organizing systems," in *Proceedings of the KiVS Workshopon Selbstorganisierende, Adaptive, Kontextsensitive verteilte Systeme*, 2007.

[10] Y. Brun, G. Di Marzo Serugendo, C. Gacek et al., "Engineering self-adaptive systems through feedback loops," *Software Engineering for Self-Adaptive*, pp. 48–70, 2009.

[11] P. Horn, "Autonomic Computing: IBM's Perspective on the State of Information Technology," 2001.

[12] B. H. Cheng, R. Lemos, H. Giese et al., "Software engineering for self-adaptive systems: a research roadmap," in *Software Engineering for Self-Adaptive Systems*, B. H. Cheng, R. Lemos, h. Giese, P. Inverardi, and J. Magee, Eds., pp. 1–26, Springer, Berlin, Heidelberg, 2009.

[13] M. Zeller, C. Prehofer, G. Weiss, D. Eilers, and R. Knorr, "Towards self-adaptation in real-time, networked systems: efficient solving of system constraints for automotive embedded systems," in *Proceedings of the 5th IEEE Int. Conference on Self-Adaptive and Self-Organizing Systems*, pp. 79–88, 2011.

[14] M. Broy, G. Reichart, and L. Rothhardt, "Architekturen softwarebasierter Funktionen im Fahrzeug: von den Anforderungen zur Umsetzung," *Informatik- Spektrum*, vol. 34, pp. 42–59, 2011.

[15] ICE, "IEC/DIN EN 61508: Functional safety of Electrical/Electronic/Programmable Electronic (E/E/PE) safety related systems: overview," International Electrotechnical Commission (IEC), 1998.

[16] ISO, "ISO/WD 26262: Road Vehicles—Functional Safety," International Organization for Standardization (ISO), 2005.

[17] R. de Lemos, H. Giese, H. Müller et al., "Software engineering for self-adpaptive systems: a second research roadmap," in *Software Engineering for Self-Adaptive Systems*, vol. 10431 of *Dagstuhl Seminar Proceedings*, 2011.

[18] D. Weyns, B. Schmerl, V. Grassi et al., "On patterns for decentralized control in self-adaptive systems," in *Software Engineering for Self-Adaptive Systems 2*, Springer, Berlin, Heidelberg, 2012.

[19] B. Hardung, *Optimisation of the allocation of functions in vehicle networks [Ph.D. thesis]*, Universität Erlangen-Nürnberg, 2006.

[20] K. Klobedanz, G. B. Defo, W. Mueller, and T. Kerstan, "Distributed coordination of task migration for fault-tolerant

FlexRay networks," in *Proceedings of the 5th International Symposium on Industrial Embedded Systems (SIES '10)*, pp. 79–87, July 2010.

[21] E. Bini and G. C. Buttazzo, "Measuring the performance of schedulability tests," *Real-Time Systems*, vol. 30, no. 1-2, pp. 129–154, 2005.

[22] M. Dinkel and U. Baumgarten, "Self-configuration of vehicle systems—algorithms and Simulation," in *Proceedings of the 4th International Workshop on Intelligent Transportation*, pp. 85–91, 2007.

[23] SAT4J, "A satisfiability library for Java," Version 2.2, 2009, http://www.sat4j.org/.

[24] J. Kramer and J. Magee, "Self-managed systems: an architectural challenge," in *Proceedings of the Future of Software Engineering*, pp. 259–268, May 2007.

[25] F. Kluge, S. Uhrig, J. Mische, and T. Ungerer, "A two-layered management architecture for building adaptive real-time systems," in *Proceedings of the 6th IFIP International Workshop on Software Technologies for Embedded and Ubiquitous Systems*, pp. 126–137, 2008.

[26] M. Litoiu, M. Woodside, and T. Zheng, "Hierarchical model-based autonomic control of software systems," *SIGSOFT Software Engineering Notes*, vol. 30, no. 4, pp. 1–7, 2005.

[27] A. Lapouchnian, S. Liaskos, J. Mylopoulos, and Y. Yu, "Towards requirements-driven autonomic systems design," in *Proceedings of the Workshop on Design and Evolution of Autonomic Application Software*, pp. 1–8, 2005.

[28] M. Zeller, G. Weiss, D. Eilers, and R. Knorr, "A multi-layered control architecture for self-management in adaptive automotive systems," in *Proceedings of the International Conference on Adaptive and Intelligent Systems (ICAIS '09)*, pp. 63–68, September 2009.

6

Can Faulty Modules Be Predicted by Warning Messages of Static Code Analyzer?

Osamu Mizuno and Michi Nakai

Kyoto Institute of Technology, Matsugasaki Goshokaido-cho, Sakyo-ku, Kyoto 606-8585, Japan

Correspondence should be addressed to Osamu Mizuno, o-mizuno@kit.ac.jp

Academic Editor: Chin-Yu Huang

We have proposed a detection method of fault-prone modules based on the spam filtering technique, "Fault-prone filtering." Fault-prone filtering is a method which uses the text classifier (spam filter) to classify source code modules in software. In this study, we propose an extension to use warning messages of a static code analyzer instead of raw source code. Since such warnings include useful information to detect faults, it is expected to improve the accuracy of fault-prone module prediction. From the result of experiment, it is found that warning messages of a static code analyzer are a good source of fault-prone filtering as the original source code. Moreover, it is discovered that it is more effective than the conventional method (that is, without static code analyzer) to raise the coverage rate of actual faulty modules.

1. Introduction

Recently, machine learning approaches have been widely used for fault-proneness detection [1]. We have introduced a text feature-based approach to detect fault-prone modules [2]. In this approach, we extract text features from the frequency information of words in source code modules. In other words, we construct a large metrics set representing the frequency of words in source code modules. Once the text features are obtained, the Bayesian classifier is constructed from text features. In the fault-prone module detection of new modules, we also extract text features from source code modules, and Bayesian model classifies modules into either fault-prone or nonfault-prone. Since less effort or cost needed to collect text feature metrics than other software metrics, it may be applied to software development projects easily.

On the other hand, since this approach accepts any input with text files, the accuracy of prediction could be improved by selecting appropriate input other than raw source code. We then try to find another input but source code. In this study, we use warning messages of a static code analyzer. Among many static code analyzers, we used PMD in this study. By replacing the input of fault-prone filtering from raw source code to warning messages of PMD, we can get the results of prediction by PMD and fault-prone filtering.

The rest of this paper is organized as follows. Section 2 describes the objective of this research. Section 3 shows a brief summary of the fault-prone filtering technique with PMD. In Section 4, the experiments conducted in this study are described. Section 5 discusses the result of the experiments. Finally, Section 6 concludes this study.

2. Objective

2.1. Fault-Prone Module Filtering. The basic idea of fault-prone filtering is inspired by the spam mail filtering. In the spam e-mail filtering, a spam filter first trains both spam and ham e-mail messages from the training data set. Then, an incoming e-mail is classified into either ham or spam by the spam filter.

This framework is based on the fact that spam e-mail usually includes particular patterns of words or sentences. From the viewpoint of source code, a similar situation usually occurs in faulty software modules. That is similar faults may occur in similar contexts. We thus guessed that similar to spam e-mail messages, faulty software modules have similar patterns of words or sentences. To obtain such features, we adopted a spam filter in fault-prone module prediction.

In other words, we try to introduce a new metric as a fault-prone predictor. The metric is "frequency of particular words." In detail, we do not treat a single word, but use combinations of words for the prediction. Thus, the frequency of a certain length of words is the only metric used in our approach.

From a viewpoint of effort, conventional fault-prone detection techniques require relatively much effort for application because they have to measure various metrics. Of course, metrics are useful for understanding the property of source code quantitatively. However, measuring metrics usually needs extra effort and translating the values of metrics into meaningful result also needs additional effort. Thus, easy-to-use technique that does not require much effort will be useful in software development.

We then try to apply a spam filter to identification of fault-prone modules. We named this approach as "fault-prone filtering." That is, a learner first trains both faulty and nonfaulty modules. Then, a new module can be classified into fault-prone or notfault-prone using a classifier. In this study, we define a software module as a Java class file.

Essentially, the fault-prone filtering does the text classification on the source codes. Of course, the text classification can be applied to the text information other than the source codes. We guessed that there is the other input for the text classification to achieve higher prediction accuracy. We then started seeking such information.

2.2. Static Code Analysis. The static code analysis is a method of analyzing without actually running software and finding the problem and faults in a software. By analyzing a source code structurally, we can find potential faults, violation of coding conventions, and so on. The static code analysis thus can assure the safety of software, reliability, and quality. It also reduces the cost of maintenance. In recent years, the importance of static code analysis has been emerging since finding potential faults or security hole is required at an early stage of the development. There are many kinds of tools for the static code analysis available [3]. Among them, we used the PMD (the meaning of PMD is not determined. "We have been trying to find the meaning of the letters PMD—because frankly, we do not really know. We just think the letters sound good together" [4]), since it can be applicable to the source code directly.

The PMD is one of static code analysis tools [5]. It is an open-source software and written in Java, and it is used for analyzing programs written in Java. PMD can find the code pieces that may cause the potential faults such as an unused variable and an empty catch block by analyzing the source code of Java. To do so, PMD has a variety of rule sets. According to the rule sets to be used, a broad range of purposes from the inspection of coding conventions to find potential faults can be used.

2.3. Characteristics of the Warning Messages of the Static Code Analyzer. Warning messages of a static code analyzer include rich information about potential faults in source codes. Figure 1 shows an example of warning messages. Usually, the number of warning messages generated by the static code analyzer becomes large in proportion to the length of source code. Since most of the messages are not harmful or trivial, warning messages are often ignored. It can be considered that these warning messages are quality aspects of the source code. Thus, we consider that the warning messages have less noise for fault-prone module prediction.

As mentioned in Section 2.1, applying the text information to the text classifier is an easy task. We thus implement the fault-prone filtering technique to use the warning messages of the static code analyzer. We then conduct experiments to confirm the effects of the warning messages to the performance of the fault-prone filtering approach.

2.4. Research Questions. In this study, we aim at answering the following research questions:

> RQ1: "can fault-prone modules be predicted by applying a text filter to the warning messages of a static code analyzer?"

> RQ2: "if RQ1 is true, is the performance of the fault-prone filtering becomes better with the warning messages of a static code analyzer?"

RQ1 tries to find a possibility to apply the warning messages to the fault-prone filtering technique. RQ2 investigates the prediction performance.

3. Fault-Prone Filtering with PMD

3.1. Applying PMD to Source Code. We used 10 rule sets of PMD in a standard rule sets: Basic, Braces, Code Size, Coupling, Design, Naming, Optimizations, Strict Exception, Strings, and Unused Code. These rule sets are frequently used for investigation of the quality of software. We apply PMD with 10 rule sets to all source code modules and get warning messages of PMD.

3.2. Classification Techniques. In this study, we used CRM114 (the controllable regex mutilator) spam filtering software [6] for its versatility and accuracy. Since CRM114 is implemented as a language to classify text files for general purpose, applying source code modules is easy. Furthermore, the classification techniques implemented in CRM114 are based mainly on Markov random field model instead of the naive Bayesian classifier.

In this experiment, we used the orthogonal sparse bigrams Markov model built in CRM114.

Orthogonal Sparse Bigrams Markov model (OSB)

Basically, CRM114 uses sparse binary polynomial Hash Markov model (SBPH). It is an extension of the Bayesian classification, and it maps features in the input text into a markov random field [7]. In this model, tokens are constructed from combinations of n words (n-grams) in a text file. Tokens are then

The class "ISynchronizerTest" has a Cyclomatic Complexity of 8 (Highest = 32).
This class has too many methods, consider refactoring it.
Avoid excessively long variable names like NUMBER_OF_PARTNERS
The field name indicates a constant but its modifiers do not
Variables should start with a lowercase character
Variables that are not final should not contain underscores (except for underscores in standard prefix/suffix).
Document empty constructor
Parameter "name" is not assigned and could be declared final
Avoid variables with short names like b1
Avoid variables with short names like b2
Parameter "b1" is not assigned and could be declared final
Parameter "b2" is not assigned and could be declared final
Parameter "message" is not assigned and could be declared final
Avoid using for statements without curly braces
Local variable "body" could be declared final
Parameter "monitor" is not assigned and could be declared final
Parameter "resource" is not assigned and could be declared final
Avoid using for statements without curly braces
. . .

FIGURE 1: A part of warning messages by PMD from a source code module of Eclipse.

mapped into a Markov random field to calculate the probability.

OSB is a simplified version of SBPH. It considers tokens as combinations of exactly 2 words created in the SBPH model. This simplification decreases both memory consumption of learning and time of classification. Furthermore, it is reported that OSB usually achieves higher accuracy than a simple word tokenization [8].

3.3. Tokenization of Inputs.

In order to perform fault-prone filtering approach, inputs of fault-prone filter must be tokenized. In this study, in order to use the warning messages of PMD as input of filtering, the messages need to be tokenized. Warning messages of PMD contains English text in natural language and a part of Java code. In order to separate them, we classified them into the following kind of strings:

(i) strings that consist of alphabets and numbers;

(ii) all kinds of brackets, semicolons, commas;

(iii) operators of Java and dot;

(iv) other strings (natural language message).

Furthermore, warning messages of PMD have file names and line numbers on the top of each line. In usual, they provide useful information for debug, but for learning and classification, they may mislead the learning of faulty modules. For example, once we learn a line number of a faulty module, the same line number of the other file is wrongly considered as faulty token.

3.4. Example of Filtering.

Here, we explain briefly how these classifiers work. We will show how to tokenize and classify the faulty modules in our filtering approach.

```
1:  if   x
2:  if          ==
3:  if               1
4:  if                    return
```

FIGURE 2: Example of tokens for OSB using the source code.

```
1:  underscores  in
2:  underscores       standard
3:  underscores            prefix/suffix)
```

FIGURE 3: Example of tokens for OSB using the warning messages.

3.4.1. Tokenization.

In OSB, tokens are generated so that these tokens include exactly 2 words. For example, a sentence "if (x == 1) return;" is tokenized as shown in Figure 2 By definition, the number of tokens drastically decreases compared to SBPH. As for the warning messages, an example of a sentence "underscores in standard prefix/suffix)." is shown in Figure 3

3.4.2. Classification.

Let T_{FP} and T_{NFP} be sets of tokens included in the fault-prone (FP) and the nonfault-prone (NFP) corpuses, respectively. The probability of fault-proneness is equivalent to the probability that a given set of tokens T_x is included in either T_{FP} or T_{NFP}. In OSB, the probability that a new module m_{new} is faulty, $P(T_{FP}|T_{m_{new}})$, with a given set of token $T_{m_{new}}$ from a new source code module m_{new} is calculated by the following Bayesian formula:

$$\frac{P(T_{m_{new}} T_{FP})P(T_{FP})}{P(T_{m_{new}} T_{FP})P(T_{FP}) + P(T_{m_{new}} T_{NFP})P(T_{NFP})}. \quad (1)$$

TABLE 1: Target project: Eclipse BIRT plugin.

Name	Eclipse BIRT plugin
Language	Java
Revision control	cvs
Type of faults	Bugs
Status of faults	Resolved; Verified; closed
Resolution of faults	Fixed
Severity	Blocker; critical; major; normal
Priority of faults	All
Total number of faults	4708

TABLE 2: The number of modules in Eclipse BIRT.

	Number of modules (files)
Nonfaulty	42,503
Faulty	27,641
Total	70,144

Intuitively speaking, this probability denotes that the new code is classified into FP. According to $P(T_{FP} \mid T_{m_{new}})$ and predefined threshold t_{FP}, classification is performed.

4. Experiment

4.1. The Outline of the Experiment. In this experiment, warning messages of PMD are used for fault-prone filtering as an input instead of a source code module, and Fault-prone module is predicted. And it is the purpose to evaluate the predictive accuracy of the proposed method. Therefore, two experiments using raw source code modules and the warning messages by the PMD as inputs are conducted. We then compare these results to each other.

4.2. Target Project. In this experiment, we use the source code module of an open source project, Eclipse BIRT (business intelligence and reporting tools). The source code module is obtained from this project by the SZZ (Śliwerski et al.) algorithm [9]. The summary of Eclipse BIRT project is shown in Table 1. All software modules in this project are used for both learning and classification by the procedure called training only errors (TOE). The number of modules is shown in Table 2.

4.3. Procedure of Filtering (Training on Errors). Experiment 1 performs the original fault-prone module prediction using the raw source code and OSB classifier by the following procedures:

(1) apply the FP classifier to a newly created software module (say, method in Java, function in C, and so on), M_i, and obtain the probability to be fault-prone;

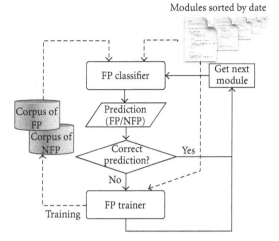

FIGURE 4: Outline of fault-prone filtering by training on errors.

(2) by the predetermined threshold t_{FP} ($0 < t_{FP} < 1$), classify the module M_i into FP or NFP;

(3) when the actual fault-proneness of M_i is revealed by fault report, investigate whether the predicted result for M_i was correct or not;

(4) if the predicted result was correct, go to step 1; otherwise, apply FP trainer to M_i to learn actual fault-proneness and go to step 1.

This procedure is called "training on errors (TOE)" procedure because training process is invoked only when classification errors happen. The TOE procedure is quite similar to actual classification procedure in practice. For example, in actual e-mail filtering, e-mail messages are classified when they arrive. If some of them are misclassified, actual results (spam or nonspam) should be trained.

Figure 4 shows an outline of this approach. At this point, we consider that the fault-prone filtering can be applied to the sets of software modules which are developed in the same (or similar) project.

Experiment 2 is an extension of Experiment 1 by appending additional steps as the first step as follows:

(1) obtain warning messages W_i of PMD by applying PMD to a newly created software module M_i;

(2) apply the FP classifier to the warning messages, W_i, and obtain the probability to be fault-prone;

(3) by the predetermined threshold t_{FP} ($0 < t_{FP} < 1$), classify the warning messages W_i into FP or NFP;

(4) when the actual fault-proneness of M_i is revealed by fault report, investigate whether the predicted result for W_i was correct or not;

(5) if the predicted result was correct, go to step (1); otherwise, apply FP trainer to W_i to learn actual fault-proneness and go to step (1).

TABLE 3: Classification result matrix.

		Prediction	
		Nonfault-prone	Fault-prone
Actual	Nonfaulty	True negative (tn)	False positive (fp)
	Faulty	False negative (fn)	True positive (tp)

4.4. Procedure of TOE Experiment. In the experiment, we have to simulate actual TOE procedure in the experimental environment. To do so, we first prepare a list of all modules found in Section 4.2. The list is sorted by the last modified date (d_i) of each module so that the first element of the list is the oldest module. We then start simulated experiment in the procedure shown in Algorithm 1. During the simulation, modules are classified by the order of date. If the predicted result s_i^p differs from actual status s_i^a, the training procedure is invoked.

4.5. Evaluation Measures. Table 3 shows a classification result matrix. True negative (tn) shows the number of modules that are classified as nonfault-prone, and are actually nonfaulty. False positive (fp) shows the number of modules that are classified as fault-prone, but are actually nonfaulty. On the contrary, false negative shows the number of modules that are classified as nonfault-prone, but are actually faulty. Finally, true positive shows the number of modules that are classified as fault-prone which are actually faulty.

In order to evaluate the results, we prepare two measures: recall and precision. Recall is the ratio of modules correctly classified as fault-prone to the number of entire faulty modules Recall is defined as $tp/(tp + fn)$. Precision is the ratio of modules correctly classified as fault-prone to the number of entire modules classified fault-prone. Precision is defined as $tp/(tp+fp)$. Accuracy is the ratio of correctly classified modules to the entire modules. Accuracy is defined as $(tp + tn)/(tn + tp + fp + fn)$. Since recall and precision are in the trade-off, F_1-measure is used to combine recall and precision [10]. F_1-measure is defined as $(2 \times recall \times precision)/(recall + precision)$. In this definition, recall and precision are evenly weighed.

From the viewpoint of the quality assurance, it is recommended to achieve higher recall, since the coverage of actual faults is of importance. On the other hand, from the viewpoint of the project management, it is recommended to focus on the precision, since the cost of the software unit test is deeply related to the number of modules to be tested. In this study, we mainly focus on the recall from the viewpoint of the quality assurance.

4.6. Result of Experiments. Tables 4 and 5 show the result of experiment using the original approach without PMD and the approach with PMD, respectively. Table 6 summarizes the evaluation measures for these experiments.

From Table 6, we can see that the approach with PMD has almost the same capability to predict fault-prone modules as the approach without PMD. For example, F_1 for the approach without PMD is 0.779, and for the approach with

TABLE 4: Result of prediction in Experiment 1 (without PMD).

		Prediction	
		Nonfault-prone	Fault-prone
Actual	Nonfaulty	30,521	11,982
	Faulty	2,360	25,281
	Total	32,821	37,263

TABLE 5: Result of prediction in Experiment 2 (with PMD).

		Prediction	
		Nonfault-prone	Fault-prone
Actual	Nonfaulty	22,982	19,521
	Faulty	1,674	25,967
	Total	24,656	45,488

TABLE 6: Evaluation measures of the results of experiments.

	Precision	Recall	Accuracy	F_1
Experiment 1 (without PMD)	0.678	0.915	0.796	0.779
Experiment 2 (with PMD)	0.571	0.939	0.698	0.710

PMD is 0.710. The result shows that the original approach without PMD is relatively better than the approach with PMD in precision, accuracy, and F_1 measures. The recall of the approach with PMD is better than the approach without PMD.

Figures 5 and 6 show the result of TOE history for the approaches without and with PMD, respectively. From this graph, we can see that evaluation measures first to decrease at the beginning of TOE procedure, then increase and become stable after learning and classification of 15,000 modules.

5. Discussions

At first, we discuss the advantage of the approach with PMD. From Table 6, we can see that the result of Experiment 2 has higher recall and lower precision than that of Experiment 1. Generally speaking, the recall is an important measure for the fault-prone module prediction because it implies how many actual faults can be detected by the prediction. Therefore, higher recall can be an advantage of the approach with PMD. However, the difference of the recalls between two experiments is rather small.

When we focus on the graphs of TOE histories shown in Figures 5 and 6, the difference between two experiments can be seen clearly. The transition of recall in Experiment 2 keeps higher than that of Experiment 1 from an early stage of the experiment. That is the recall of Experiment 2 reaches 0.90 at 10,000 modules learning. From this fact, we can say that the approach with PMD is efficient especially at an early stage of development. It can be considered as another advantage of the approach with PMD.

We discuss the reasons of the result that the approach with PMD does not shows a good evaluation measures at

t_{FP} : Threshold of probability to determine FP and NFP
s_i^p : Predicted fault status (FP or NFP) of M_i
for each M_i in list of modules sorted by d_i's
    $prob$ = fpclassify(M_i)
    if $prob > t_{\text{FP}}$ then s_i^p = FP
              else s_i^p = NFP
    endif
    if $s_i^a \neq s_i^p$ then fptrain(M_i, s_i^a)
    endif
endfor
fpclassify(M) :
    if Experiment 1 then
        Generate a set of tokens T_M from source code M.
        Calculate probability $P(T_{\text{FP}} \mid T_M)$
            using corpuses T_{FP} and T_{NFP}.
        Return $P(T_{\text{FP}} \mid T_M)$.
    if Experiment 2 then
        Generate a set of tokens T_W
            from warning messages W
            by applying PMD to the source code M.
        Calculate probability $P(T_{\text{FP}} \mid T_W)$
            using corpuses T_{FP} and T_{NFP}.
        Return $P(T_{\text{FP}} \mid T_W)$
fptrain(M, s^a) :
    if Experiment 1 then
        Generate a set of tokens T_M from M.
        Store tokens T_M to the corpus Ts^a.
    if Experiment 2 then
        Generate a set of tokens T_W from W
            by applying PMD to M.
        Store tokens T_W to the corpus Ts^a.

ALGORITHM 1: Procedure of TOE experiment.

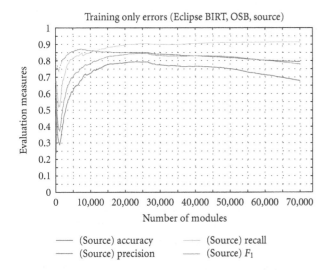

FIGURE 5: History of training on errors procedure in Experiment 1 (without PMD).

the end of the experiment. First, the selection of rule sets used in PMD may affect the result of experiment. Although we used 10 rule sets according to the past study, the selection of rule sets should be considered more carefully. For future research, we will investigate the effects of rule set selection to the accuracy of fault-prone filtering. Second, we need to apply this approach to more projects. We have conducted experiments on Eclipse BIRT.

Here, we investigate the details of our prediction. Table 7 shows a part of the probabilities for each token in the corpus for faulty modules. This table shows tokens with highest probabilities. The probability $P(T_x | T_{\text{FP}})$ shows the conditional probability that a token T_x exists in the faulty corpus. Although these probabilities do not mean immediately that these tokens make a module fault-prone, we guess that the investigation of these probabilities helps improving accuracy.

We can see that specific identifier such as "copyInstance" and specific literals such as "994," "654," and "715" appear frequently. It can be guessed that these literals denote line number in a particular source code. These literals are effective to predict the fault-proneness of the specific source code modules, but it can be a noise for the most other modules. In order to improve the overall accuracy of the classifier, eliminating literals that describe a specific source code should be taken into account.

Finally, we answer the research questions here. We have the following research questions in Section 2.4.

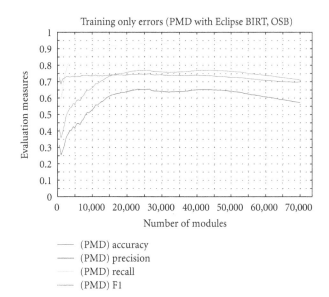

Training only errors (PMD with Eclipse BIRT, OSB)

—— (PMD) accuracy
—— (PMD) precision
—— (PMD) recall
—— (PMD) F1

FIGURE 6: History of training on errors procedure in Experiment 2 (with PMD).

TABLE 7: Probabilities for each token in the corpus for faulty modules. The "□" denotes any words.

$P\,(T_x \mid T_{\mathrm{FP}})$	T_x
0.56229	line 654
0.56229	715 Local
0.56229	"copyInstance" has
0.56229	654 Local
0.56229	instanceof The
0.56229	method copyInstance ()
0.56229	255 Parameter
0.56229	method "copyInstance"
0.56229	489 Avoid
0.56229	line 715
0.56229	copyInstance () has
0.56229	line 994
0.56229	line 474
0.56229	994 The
0.56215	715 □ variable
0.56215	blocks □ "pageNumber"
0.56215	on □ 994
0.56215	bb □ instantiating
0.56215	on □ 654
0.56215	The □ "copyInstance"
0.56215	654 □ variable
0.56215	994 □ String
0.56215	The □ copyInstance ()
0.56215	"copyInstance" □ a
0.56215	on □ 715
0.56215	on □ 474
0.56215	300 □ variables
0.56215	copyInstance () □ an

RQ1: "can fault-prone modules be predicted by applying a text filter to the warning messages of a static code analyzer?"

For this question, we can answer "yes" from the results in Table 5 and Table 6. It is obvious that the approach with PMD has prediction capability of the fault-prone modules at a certain degree.

RQ2: "if RQ1 is true, is the performance of the fault-prone filtering becomes better with the warning messages of a static code analyzer?"

For this question, we can say that the recall of the approach with PMD becomes higher and more stable during the development than the approach without PMD as shown in Table 6 and Figures 5 and 6. From the viewpoint of the quality assurance, it is a preferred property. We then conclude that the proposed approach has better performance to assure the software quality.

6. Conclusion

In this paper, we proposed an approach to predict fault-prone modules using warning messages of PMD and a text filtering technique. For the analysis, we stated two research questions: "can fault-prone modules be predicted by applying a text filter to the warning messages of static code analyzer?" and "is the performance of the fault-prone filtering becomes better with the warning messages of a static code analyzer?" We tried to answer this question by conducting experiments on the open source software. The results of experiments show that the answer to the first question is "yes." As for the second question, we can find that the recall becomes better than the original approach.

Future work includes investigating which parts of warning messages are really effective for fault-prone module prediction. Selection of rule sets of PMD is an interesting future research.

References

[1] C. Catal and B. Diri, "A systematic review of software fault prediction studies," *Expert Systems with Applications*, vol. 36, no. 4, pp. 7346–7354, 2009.

[2] O. Mizuno and T. Kikuno, "Training on errors experiment to detect fault-prone software modules by spam filter," in *Proceedings of the 6th Joint Meeting of the European Software Engineering Conference and the ACM SIGSOFT Symposium on the Foundations of Software Engineering*, pp. 405–414, 2007.

[3] N. Rutar, C. B. Almazan, and J. S. Foster, "A comparison of bug finding tools for java," in *Proceedings of the 15th International Symposium on Software Reliability Engineering*, pp. 245–256, IEEE Computer Society, Washington, DC, USA, 2004.

[4] T. Copeland, PMD—What does "PMD" mean?, http://pmd.sourceforge.net/meaning.html .

[5] T. Copeland, *PMD Applied*, Centennial Books, Arexandria, Va, USA, 2005.

[6] W. S. Yerazunis, *CRM114—the Controllable Regex Mutilator*, http://crm114.sourceforge.net/.

[7] S. Chhabra, W. S. Yerazunis, and C. Siefkes, "Spam filtering using a markov random field model with variable weighting schemas," in *Proceedings of the 4th IEEE International Conference on Data Mining, (ICDM '04)*, pp. 347–350, Riverside, Calif, USA, November 2004.

[8] C. Siefkes, F. Assis, S. Chhabra, and W. S. Yerazunis, "Combining winnow and orthogonal sparse bigrams for incremental spam filtering," in *Proceedings of the Conference on Machine Learning/European Conference on Principles and Practice of Knowledge Discovery in Databases (ECML PKDD '04)*, 2004.

[9] J. Śliwerski, T. Zimmermann, and A. Zeller, "When do changes induce fixes? (on Fridays)," in *Proceedings of the 2nd International Workshop on Mining Software Repositories*, pp. 24–28, St. Louis, Mo, USA, May 2005.

[10] C. J. van Rijsbergen, *Information Retrieval*, Butterworth, Boston, Mass, USA, 2nd edition, 1979.

7

Genetic Programming for Automating the Development of Data Management Algorithms in Information Technology Systems

Gabriel A. Archanjo and Fernando J. Von Zuben

Laboratory of Bioinformatics and Bioinspired Computing, School of Electrical and Computer Engineering,
University of Campinas (Unicamp), 13083-970 Campinas, SP, Brazil

Correspondence should be addressed to Gabriel A. Archanjo, archanjo@dca.fee.unicamp.br

Academic Editor: Phillip Laplante

Information technology (IT) systems are present in almost all fields of human activity, with emphasis on processing, storage, and handling of datasets. Automated methods to provide access to data stored in databases have been proposed mainly for tasks related to knowledge discovery and data mining (KDD). However, for this purpose, the database is used only to query data in order to find relevant patterns associated with the records. Processes modelled on IT systems should manipulate the records to modify the state of the system. Linear genetic programming for databases (LGPDB) is a tool proposed here for automatic generation of programs that can query, delete, insert, and update records on databases. The obtained results indicate that the LGPDB approach is able to generate programs for effectively modelling processes of IT systems, opening the possibility of automating relevant stages of data manipulation, and thus allowing human programmers to focus on more complex tasks.

1. Introduction

Information technology (IT) systems have become the basis of process management of today's successful enterprises. We can find this kind of system in virtually all fields of activities and inside corporations of any size. The intensive adoption of IT systems has promoted the emergence of an entire ensemble of technologies and services to supply a wide range of demands.

Similar to what happens in other areas of product development, methodologies, processes, and tools have been enhanced over the years in order to improve the development of software products, which are going to promote increasing productivity and reduced costs. The first methodologies were inspired by principles found in other areas of product development, like manufacturing. However, the dynamic environment involved in software development is fostering a continuous improvement and customization of methodologies to embrace inevitable uncertainties and necessary redefinition of the product specification, resulting in an iterative and evolutionary process [1].

The need for more agile methodologies is promoting the development of enhanced tools and techniques, more notably in the field of code and design reuse. Approaches to automate entire modules of the software development or to support decision on software engineering have been explored. However, the automated generation of computer algorithms still remains restricted to the scientific field. Knowledge discovery and data mining (KDD) applications are associated with many different approaches to extract relevant patterns from datasets, including solutions based on programs generated automatically. However, since the most common representation of data in the academic field is the linear dataset, due to its simplicity, the majority of works have been focusing on this representation. Using this type of data organization, genetic programming was employed to a wide range of applications, for instance, financial market analysis [2], cancer molecular classification [3], and bankruptcy prediction [4]. Nevertheless, large databases normally used on IT systems do not store records linearly. A more sophisticated framework is necessary to organize records in advanced structural configurations, as found on relational or object-oriented databases. Freitas [5] has proposed a framework for applying GP for classification and rule induction using relational databases. Ryu and Eick

[6] have used MASSON to induce programs that show commonalities between objects stored in an object-oriented database, and to derive queries with the purpose of extracting intentional information [7].

These works on KDD and query generation use the database only to organize and retrieve information, so that the programs do not modify the records. This limitation is not a problem since the objective is to find patterns in static data. On the other hand, aiming at modelling processes of IT systems, the capability to modify records is mandatory for the generated programs, since most processes are inherently conceived to change the state of a set of entities in the system. In the case of a library management system, for instance, the process of borrowing a book change the state of the system, associating a user and a book with a loan. By the same reasoning, in the case of a financial IT system, a process devoted to money transferring modifies the records related to the accounts involved. The modelling of these two examples are considered as case studies in this work.

To implement these kinds of processes, programs have to be able to find the proper associations among information stored in distinct data structures (tables or objects) and manipulate them in a correct manner. This work proposes linear genetic programming for databases (LGPDB), a tool for automatic generation of programs that can query, delete, insert, and update records in relational databases, and shows experiments that illustrate the feasibility of the proposed approach for automating the development of data management algorithms in IT systems. A preliminary version of LGPDB was presented in Archanjo and Von Zuben [8].

The paper is organized as follows. Section 2 presents an overview of the evolution of software development, covering three fields: methodologies, tools, and search-based software engineering. linear genetic programming for databases (LGPDB), a tool for automatic generation of data management algorithms for IT systems, is described in Section 3. An experiment for generating computer programs to provide features for a simple library system is described in Section 4. Section 5 introduces new instructions and a method for inducing more complex programs. The influence of records without consistent relationship on the evolutionary process is addressed in Section 6. Finally, in Section 7, concluding remarks and future prospects are outlined.

2. Evolution of Software Development

Just like the development of any other product, many methodologies, tools, and principles for software development have been created over the years, aiming at cost reduction, quality improvement, and increasing productivity.

2.1. Methodologies. When a product is under development, the sequence of steps from conception to the final product should be carefully conceived, focusing on high levels of productivity and quality, as long as low levels of cost and risk. In the 1970s, the first methodology for software development was denoted the Waterfall model [9], which specifies a sequence of phases, from requirements to operations, to deliver a software product.

Some mistakes in the first version of the project requirements is probably associated with misleading decision making. In the earlier stages of a project, it is common that even customers or the product managers do not know every specific detail of the project. Therefore, software prototyping was proposed to address this problem. Using this methodology, a software prototype is developed to answer open questions in the requirements that could only be managed by means of some experimentation. In this case, the client or any other person responsible for the software specification can interact with the prototype to check whether or not the most influential aspects of the project were properly addressed. This process can be repeated, producing multiple prototypes, until starting the product engineering.

Following the same idea of reducing risks and increasing interaction with experts who have the final assessment of the project, Boehm [10] has proposed the spiral model. In that model, phases like risk analysis, prototype development, and requirements are distributed over multiple cycles and, at the end of each one, the result is validated by people responsible for outlining the project. Extending these ideas, in the last decade, a new software development paradigm has gained attention, the agile software development (ASD) [11], in which iterative and evolutionary processes are the core idea. ASD breaks the project into multiple small cycles with constant analysis and customer feedback to reduce uncertainties surrounding the development of the product, decreasing costs, improving quality, and delivering products in the desired time range.

2.2. Tools and Techniques. Continuous software development and improvement, a core principle embraced by modern and more agile methodologies, require initiatives to increase productivity and to minimize the impact caused by frequent revisions in the software product, prevalent during the development phase. Although some tools presented in this section were proposed before the last revolution in the software development methodologies, they have gained more importance in software projects after the adoption of more agile methods.

Considering the high demand for IT systems, it is inevitable that multiple systems share similar features. Software engineers and programmers involved in system development across different project domains solve the same or similar problems during the development. These scenarios naturally promote the emergence of techniques to reuse software solutions. The most well-known strategies include the identification of high demanded features and the creation of a set of customizable software components, known as frameworks [12]. Currently, there are frameworks for almost everything, from user authentication to optical character recognition. Since frameworks add significant value to software development products, their creation is commercially exploited. Consequently, there are software companies that focus solely on developing frameworks. Software algorithms are not the only element that can be reused. Taking into account the importance of software architectural design, it was proposed the concept of design pattern [13] which is a catalogue of designs matured and validated in real-world applications, organized to be reused. Other notable strategy for software reuse has emerged with the success of the Internet. Instead of providing features via frameworks that have to be tightly coupled to applications, the features are provided as web services [14]. The rise of hardware and software services for broad integration of tools, features, and purposes, available on the web, has created a new computational concept, known as cloud computing [15].

Nowadays, in order to store and manage information about its processes, IT systems use a relational database which represents the information in a scalar and structured fashion. On the other hand, this kind of system is usually developed using object-oriented (OO) programming languages or similar programming paradigms that manage information in a nonscalar fashion, using composite variables like arrays and lists, hash maps, records, and objects. Therefore, both the database format and the algorithm that load and store information from the database should obey some consistency rules, so that changes promoted in one of them will be followed by corresponding changes in the other. Since this requisite must be handled by most IT systems, a technique called object-relational mapping (ORM) [16, 17] was proposed to minimize the amount of effort allocated to this task. In one instance of these approaches, instead of promoting pairwise changes in format and algorithm for each situation, an XML file is used to store the mapping between objects and database tables. A generic purpose framework does the conversion using that XML file. Thus, to change the mapping, it is only necessary to change the XML file.

Other issue that impacts productivity and costs in software development involves quality assurance processes. Methods to automate parts of the software test were proposed to improve testing procedures. One of the most-well known techniques is the automated unit testing that uses assertions to test if a source unit (i.e., the smallest testable part of the software) is working properly. For each unit, it is created a test case. A tool for this purpose, like JUnit [18], is used to run all tests and generate a report automatically. This testing strategy is receiving more and more attention, being employed as the core concept of a software development methodology called test-driven development [19].

2.3. Search-Based Software Engineering. In virtually all human activities, there are problems in which the objective is to find out the best decision, given different choices and problem restrictions. This kind of situation can be modelled mathematically and solved applying mathematical optimization techniques, like classical optimization methods or metaheuristics. Search-based software engineering (SBSE) is a research field that embodies optimization methods in software engineering tasks [20]. For example, in the case of software effort estimation, a dataset containing attributes of finished software projects (e.g., number of transactions and entities, complexity, team experience) and the necessary effort was used in [21] to provide estimations for new projects. Neural networks, k-nearest neighbor, and genetic programming were employed to map the relationship between those attributes and the necessary effort. Moreover,

SBSE has been applied to many other problems in software engineering, for instance, software testing [22], requirements [23], automated maintenance [24], and quality assurance [25]. The SBSE is a growing research field with a clear tendency of being incorporated into the next generation of real-world commercial software.

3. Linear Genetic Programming for Databases (LGPDB)

Section 2 has shown the evolution of software development, mainly by means of reusing solutions and automating processes. However, the task of transforming ideas, architecture designs, and processes into algorithms are predominantly being made by human programmers. Thus, an automatic method to generate this kind of algorithms is desired to improve the software development process and also to alleviate the burden usually assigned to human programmers.

The field of automated generation of computer programs is not new. In 1975, Holland [26] suggested the possibility of evolving genetic algorithm representations more similar to computer programs. In 1985, Cramer [27] evolved programs by means of genetic operators and natural selection. Finally, at the beginning of the 1990s, Koza [28] formalized the genetic programming (GP) as an extension of genetic algorithms designed specifically for program evolution. GP has been used for generating computer programs devoted to a wide range of applications, from robotics [29] to electrical circuit synthesis [30]. GP is an effective method to generate computer programs automatically. However, even with the extensive list of applications of GP, the usage of this approach on the IT environment is narrow and practically devoted exclusively to SBSE and KDD. It is important to mention the existence of other approaches for the automatic generation of computer programs with some restrictions. In the case of automatic programming [31], the objective is the generation of computer programs from a high level representation, specified by a human engineer, which models the solution. There are also many approaches for evolutionary programming where only the program parameters are optimized and not its structure. Finally, there are approaches that model solutions by combining automatically selected and parameterized algorithms [32]. However, in the case of this work, the capability of optimizing the parameters and the program structure in the level of instructions, using genetic programming, seems more appropriate for providing a general purpose tool for data manipulation.

Another relevant issue is the data representation since most works do not use a structured method. Generally, the datasets are composed of a sequence of attribute vectors. Nevertheless, IT systems usually have to organize information in more complex structures, involving multiple entities or objects. IT systems generally use a relational database to organize information. In [5], it was proposed a method for query generation, using a fixed query structure combined with a genetic program, to model relationships present in a relational database. However, in that work, the correct association among tables is fixed and it is informed *a priori*. Thus, the genetic program does not need to model the correct path associating records stored in distinct tables, as it will be implemented in this work. Instead of using a relational database, Ryu and Eick [6, 7] have used an object-oriented database and a domain knowledge base to generate queries using MASSON. The relationship and interactions among objects in the database are also defined *a priori*. The use of an object-oriented database is also a barrier since it is not a common approach for IT system development.

This work proposes a method to automate the development of algorithms capable of manipulating records for information technology systems. A commonly used architectural approach for this type of systems is the MVC (model-view-controller) [33] in which the application is divided into three layers. The model layer is responsible for data representation and management, for instance, creating methods to store and request information from the database and to convert database representations into programming language representations. The controller is responsible for modelling processes that manipulate data, sometimes called "business logic." Finally, the view creates an interface from user interaction to the controller layer. Regarding this architectural approach, the LGPDB programs implement the layers, controller, and model.

In order to induce computer programs to manipulate entities stored in a database, LGPDB is composed of a simple relational database management system (DBMS) and a programming induction module based on linear genetic programming (LGP). The LGPDB architecture is illustrated in Figure 1. The program induction module (PIM) is the core of the system. It is responsible for evolving the candidate solutions. For each candidate program in the population at the current generation, it is executed fitness cases, scripts with the desired outcome for the target algorithm. The program execution environment is used by PIM to execute candidate solutions, operating on the database. PIM compares the outcome provided by the candidate program with the outcome provided by the scripts in the fitness cases. Thus, it is possible to measure the quality of a candidate solution, a necessary step in the evolutionary process. In the case of inducing programs that modify records, the solutions have to address three issues: (i) relate multiple tables on the database in order to associate the input attributes with the target records, (ii) filter the target records using the input attributes, (iii) modify the target records using the input attributes. In the case of programs for querying, only the first two issues have to be addressed. The entire process, from modelling a system to generating computer programs automatically, is addressed in detail in the next sections.

3.1. Database Management System. This module provides, for users and programs, interface to set up the database and manage the records stored on it. In comparison with traditional DBMS like PostgresSQL or MySQL, this module provides a smaller set of features. On the other hand, it was developed exclusively for program induction. Therefore, it combines some features for this purpose.

(i) *In-memory database:* since the induction process may involve thousands of candidate programs running

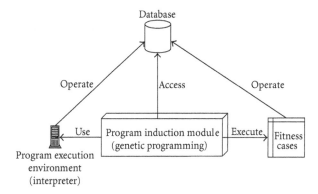

Figure 1: LGPDB architecture.

at each generation, each one performing multiple operations on the database, it is important to make the operations as simple as possible. In this case, features for recovering from adverse situations are unnecessary since the induction process can be repeated after such situation. Most importantly, the database operates entirely on the RAM memory, reducing the access time for the records on the database [34].

(ii) *Database comparison:* when evaluating candidate solutions, it is important to know if the correct records were manipulated and the desired state of the database was achieved. Therefore, this module provides a feature for database comparison, returning the set of different records between the outcome provided by the candidate programs and the outcome provided by the validation scripts (fitness cases).

(iii) *Weakly typed:* to reduce the amount of concepts that candidate programs have to capture from data to model an information manipulation process, the database fields and program variables are weakly typed. Thus, numerical, categorical, and textual data are stored in a generic representation that can be accessed and modified by programs through a unique interface.

Another important feature provided by the DBMS is the concept of transaction, in which multiple operations can be executed atomically and reversed if desired, or in the case of errors [35], using the command *rollback*(). This command is extensively used in the induction process to restore the state of the database. After the evaluation of each candidate solution, the command *rollback*() is executed, then all candidate programs start operating the database at the same state.

3.2. Software Induction Environment. This module is devoted to generating computer algorithms automatically by employing an inductive learning approach with genetic programming. Having the database configured and the desired features modelled, it is specified a set of input variables and the desired outcome for each feature. In the induction process, programs compete with each other to solve the problem. Mapping the relationship between the input and the outcome, genetic programs can model processes for information management.

3.3. Program Representation.

Computer program can be interpreted as a set of instructions that tell a computer how to perform a task. Instructions can access and operate upon information stored in memories. Loops and conditional branches can be created using conditional and jump functions. These elements, present on low-level machine program representations like assembly, are also present in some sense in the majority of other representations, from C language to the ones used in GP. In the case of LGPDB, the program representation was adapted for information management tasks. Therefore, the first notable difference is on the instruction set, defined exclusively to manipulate information in a relational database, as listed below.

(i) Select(Table tb, ResultSet rs). Select all records in tb and put them in rs. Before this process, the result set is cleared, therefore, any existent information stored before is deleted.

(ii) Filter(ResultSet rs, Attribute attr, Rule r, InputValue v). Filter the result set rs using the rule r and the input value v for the attribute attr.

(iii) Related(ResultSet rs1, ResultSet rs2). For each record in rs1, if there is no foreign key associating it with a record in rs2, remove it.

(iv) UnRelated(ResultSet rs1, ResultSet rs2). For each record in rs1, if there is a foreign key associating it with a record in rs2, remove it.

(v) Delete(Table tb, ResultSet rs). Delete all records in tb with the same id of the records in rs. By definition for our problem, every entity has an attribute id.

(vi) CreateRelation(Table tb, ResultSet rs1, ResultSet rs2). If there is a foreign key associating records in rs2 with table tb, insert records in table tb associating them with the records in rs2 and store these records in rs1.

(vii) SetRelation(ResultSet rs1, ResultSet rs2). If there is a foreign key associating records in rs2 with records in rs1, set the association in the records in rs1 using the id's of the records in rs2, and update the records in rs1 on the database.

As can be seen, the LGPDB instructions do not operate using memory addresses or a generic type of variable. The LGPDB uses a strongly typed genetic programming representation [36] in which instruction parameters have a specific type and all programs in the population have instructions well parameterized, consequently reducing the search space. Each type of parameter has a specific purpose. Table represents the database tables. ResultSet is a data structure for database record management. Attribute is the possible attributes of a given ResultSet considering its table. Rule is used to compare two variables, given a comparison criteria such as "equal," "not equal," "greater," and "less." InputValue is any information specified by the user.

There are different program structures that might be used for GP programs such as tree, graph, and linear array. The program structure affects execution order, use and locality of memory, and the application of genetic operators [37]. In the case of LGPDB, instructions have many parameters and the data manipulated by programs are in the database or in global variables. The linear structure representation [38] has been chosen because of the use of memory and the similarity with imperative programming languages. Therefore, LGPDB programs can be interpreted by human programmers easily. Conditions and loops are implicitly available by means of the instruction Filter. Depending on the rule and the input value, it is determined whether a set of records should be kept or not inside the data structure ResultSet. Every instruction that manipulates a ResultSet also implements a loop to access each record inside that data structure. Compared with the program representation used by programming languages for general purpose, LGPDB representation is more restrictive. However, since LGPDB programs are generated automatically, the expressiveness of the language affects the size of the search space of solutions. In order to reach feasibility for the target problems, it was necessary to create a representation with restrictions and highly specific functions.

3.4. Evolutionary Process.

As in any type of genetic algorithm, candidate solutions are evolved by means of natural selection. Candidate solutions compete, in an iterative process, generation after generation, to solve a problem. At each generation, solutions more adapted to solve the problem, given an evaluation criterion, are selected with more probability, to produce offspring to the next generation. Using this strategy, programs evolve along the generations until possibly reaching the desired solution. The first step in this process is the generation of the initial random population, given the maximum initial program size and the initial population size. The size of the program determines its complexity and the computational cost of its execution. The maximum size of a program can be increased along the generations, thus allowing more complex candidate solutions to be proposed in advanced stages of the evolutionary process. After the initialization, the iterative process that selects and creates a new population of candidate solution begins.

A selection strategy is necessary to implement the concept of survival of the fittest, so that individuals with the better fitness have a higher probability of being selected. LGPDB only selects the best individuals to generate offspring for the next generation, known as elitist strategy. The degree of adaptation of an individual for a given problem (fitness) is used to measure how far individuals are from the best solution. Since LGPDB employs a supervised and inductive learning strategy, the fitness of an individual is estimated based upon a set of examples containing input variables and the expected outcome, or simply *fitness cases*. In the induction database, the fitness cases are executed and the desired outcome is recorded. Candidate programs operate the induction database aiming at finding the correct sequence of instructions that changes the state of the database in order to arrive at the same state of the database obtained with the fitness cases. Comparing the desired outcome, provided by the fitness cases, and the outcome provided by each candidate program, it is possible to determine how distant the candidate program is from achieving the correct solution.

In LGPDB, the fitness function $F(p)$, for a given distance $D(p)$ and a program p, returns 1 if the individual has solved the problem completely or a positive value smaller than 1 for partial solutions, as shown in:

$$F(p) = \frac{1}{1 + D(p)}. \tag{1}$$

LGPDB programs can manipulate records by means of four basic database operations: query, deletion, insertion, and updating. The desired outcome presented by the fitness cases determines which type of operations candidate solutions can perform and the distance measure used by the fitness function, since distinct distance measures are used depending on the type of manipulation. For querying, it is provided a set of examples E containing input information and the expected result. In the evaluation, it is considered the distance between the result provided by this set and the result provided by the program, stored in the ResultSet rs0 by default. As shown in (2), for querying, the number of false negatives FN between the expected result set and the result set provided by a candidate solution is more penalized, using a constant $\alpha > 1$, than the number of false positives FP. At the beginning, it is better to query all the data than to query a subset possibly missing the desired information. Thus, the solution is improved by filtering the entire dataset along the generations. This strategy is also used in [6, 7] and has the objective of stimulating the evolution of filtering techniques:

$$D_{\text{query}}(p) = \sum_{i=0}^{E}(\text{FN}_i * \alpha + \text{FP}_i). \tag{2}$$

Instruction Delete() deletes records passed in a ResultSet as a parameter, therefore, the problem of inducting a program to delete records can be seen as a querying problem. If the desired records to be deleted are in the parameter ResultSet, like the correct records in rs0 for querying problems, the deletion operation is performed correctly. However, by this reasoning, the distance estimation must prioritize the false negatives. At the beginning, solutions tend to delete all records. The correct set of records to be deleted emerges adding filtering instructions throughout the evolution of the programs. The distance estimation for deletion is presented, as follows:

$$D_{\text{delete}}(p) = \sum_{i=0}^{T}(\text{FN}_i + \text{FP}_i * \alpha). \tag{3}$$

Querying and deletion operations manipulate entire records. All attributes of the target records are necessarily involved in the operation, hence, it is only necessary to check whether or not a record is presented in the result for comparison. In the case of insertion and updating, records are not totally inserted or updated in a single operation. In the case of insertion, for instance, one instruction creates an initial record (CreateRelation) and another set the value of individual attributes (SetRelation), one at a time. Therefore, in order to determine a distance for two database states with inserted or updated records, it is necessary to compare them in the level of attributes. Before the induction process, the database states are compared, then inserted or modified records are listed. Therefore, when comparing the program outcome and the desired one, two elements are considered: if the program has manipulated the correct records, in the case of updating, and the Hamming distance (HD) between the two results. The HD is calculated using attributes of records to be compared. If all attributes are equal in the two records, the distance is zero, otherwise, it is given by the number of different attributes. The total distance between the two results is the sum of the HD between each compared pair of records. In the case of updating, records listed to be altered have their HD multiplied by α, penalizing programs that have not manipulated them.

After selecting interesting candidate solutions, based on the evaluation method, the next step is the creation of a new population of solutions. For this purpose, conventional genetic operators for mutation and crossover are applied. Given an individual, the reproduction operator generates x new individuals with the same genome. In the case of this work, it generates new programs with the same instructions and parameters. Then, given a probability for each operator, crossover and mutation take place to promote variation in the individuals. The crossover operation is used to combine blocks or sections of good solutions to generate new ones. LGPDB uses linear crossover in which, given two individuals, a segment is randomly selected in each individual and then exchanged. Mutation simply promotes a small variation in an individual. In the case of LGPDB, one of the following mutation operations is selected given a probability: (1) change instruction type, (2) change instruction parameter, (3) add an instruction in a random position, (4) change the instruction position, and (5) remove an instruction from a random position.

The steps above are combined to form the evolutionary process, shown in the flowchart presented in Figure 2. In the first step, a copy of the original database is created to be used in the induction process. Then, the initial random population is generated. In the next step, the iterative process is started and each individual is evaluated. Since all individuals start operating the database in the same state, after the evaluation of an individual, a *rollback*() operation is performed to recover the state of the database for the next individual. After the evaluation of all individuals, the selection process takes place. If the problem has not yet been solved by any individual in the population at the current generation or the maximum number of generations has not been achieved, the genetic operators are employed to generate a new population of individuals from the selected individuals and the process proceeds to the evaluation step. This iterative process is repeated until the satisfaction of the stopping criteria. When a candidate program succeeds in solving the problem, a final step removes unnecessary

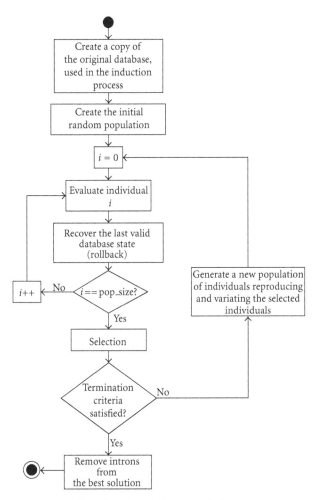

FIGURE 2: Flowchart of the LGPDB evolutionary process.

TABLE 1: A subset of the database tables for a library system. The attributes in italic are primary or foreign keys.

Table	Fields
user	*id*, name, email, user, password
author	*id*, name
book	*id*, *publisher_id*, title, pages, isbn
paper	*id*, title
periodical	*id*, *publisher_id*, year, volume, issue, isbn
publisher	*id*, name
tag	*id*, value
message	*id*, message
bookLoan	*id*, *book_id*, *user_id*
periodicalLoan	*id*, *periodical_id*, *user_id*
authorBookRel	*author_id*, *book_id*
authorPaperRel	*id*, *author_id*, *paper_id*
tagRel	*id*, *book_id*, *paper_id*, *tag_id*
messageRel	*id*, message

borrows books and periodicals that have authors and publishers. The entity-relationship diagram (ERD) [39] showing entities, attributes, and the relationships is presented in Figure 3.

The next step was to set up the relational database using the previously presented ERD to define the tables, attributes, and keys, as shown in Table 1. The database is composed of 14 tables, one for each entity and others to map many-to-many relationships among entities, like book and author, so that a book can be associated with multiple authors and vice versa.

After the initial setup, the database was populated with records, part of them is real data obtained on the Internet and others are hypothetical, used to simulate interesting relationships. Moreover, a few records without consistent relationships such as a book without author or a periodical without paper were inserted to promote the exploration of entity relationships by candidate solutions.

Finally, having defined and configured the database, the next step was the definition of which features have to be provided by the system, listed in Table 2.

As mentioned in Section 3.4, the LGPDB programs are evaluated under a set of fitness cases containing the input attributes and desired outcome for a given problem. Therefore, for each feature in Table 2, it is created a set of fitness cases. Table 3 shows an example of fitness case for the querying task Q4. The input is a tag previously inserted on the database, and the outcome is a set of books associated with that tag. Table 4 shows a fitness case for the deletion task D3. The input is the name of an author and the outcome is the deletion of books and papers. Table 5 shows an example for the insertion task I1. The input is the name of a book and a previously inserted message, and the outcome is the insertion of the records. Finally, for the updating task U1, Table 6 shows an example of fitness case. The input is the name of two publishers, the current and the new one. The outcome is the updating of the correct records.

instructions, called introns. The presence of introns does not affect the outcome of the program. However, it might consume significant computational resources. Aiming at removing introns, it is verified whether or not the execution of each instruction of a program affects the program outcome. Instructions that overwrites unused variables or manipulates variables not associated with the program outcome should be discarded. Moreover, programs without introns are more parsimonious and easier to be interpreted by humans. The interpretability is relevant in scenarios in which human programmers interact with the tool to validate the automatically generated programs or even to adapt them so that they become capable of performing similar tasks.

4. Experiment with a Library System

The induction of features for a library system was the first application of LGPDB [8]. It was used to validate the main concepts and to identify weak points for improvements.

In this experiment, it was modelled a simple library management system containing the entities User, Author, Book, Periodical, Paper, Publisher, Tag, and Message. The relationship between these entities is intuitive, like user

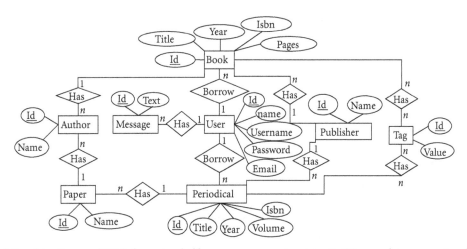

FIGURE 3: Entity-relationship diagram (ERD) for a simple library management system. Entities are drawn as rectangles, relationships as diamonds, and attributes as ovals.

TABLE 2: Features for the target system.

ID	Description
Q1	List books written by an author named X.
Q2	List users who borrowed books written by an author named X.
Q3	List users who borrowed a periodical containing a paper written by an author named X.
Q4	List books available for loan, having the tag X.
D1	Remove books published before the year X.
D2	Remove loan of a book titled X by the user Y.
D3	Remove books and papers authored by an author named X.
I1	Send the message Y to every user who borrowed a book titled X.
I2	Add a new tag Y for a book titled X.
U1	Update book publisher from X to Y.

TABLE 3: Example of a fitness case for the querying task Q4.

Feature	Q4
Description	List books available for loan, having the tag X.
Input	"Artificial Intelligence"
Type	Querying
Outcome	{"0," "Artificial intelligence: a modern approach," "0," "1132," "2009," "0137903952"}, {"1," "AI Programming Paradigms," "1," "946," "1991," "1558601910"}, {"2," "Machine Learning," "2," "432," "1997," "0070428077"}, {"3," "Genetic Programming," "3," "840," "1992," "0262111705"}

TABLE 4: Example of a fitness case for the deletion task D3.

Feature	D3
description	Remove books and papers authored by an author named X.
Input	"Peter Norvig"
Type	Deletion
Outcome	delete(book, 0) delete(book, 1) delete(paper, 142)

TABLE 5: Example of a fitness case for the insertion task I1.

Feature	I1
Description	Send the message Y to every user who borrowed a book titled X.
Input	"Machine Learning," "A new book is available with similar subject"
Type	Insertion
Outcome	Insert(messageRel, "2," "7") Insert(messageRel, "3," "8") Insert(messageRel, "4," "9")

TABLE 6: Example of a fitness case for the updating task U1.

Feature	U1
Description	Update book publisher from X to Y.
Input	"Springer," "Springer-Verlag"
Type	Updating
Outcome	Update(book, 13, "publihser_id," "10") Update(book, 14, "publisher_id," "10") Update(book, 15, "publisher_id," "10")

For each task, multiple fitness cases are used. The database instructions used as outcome manipulate the correct records, but without any association with the input information. The desired solution has to find the association between the input data and the records manipulated by the fitness cases, and the correct manipulations.

TABLE 7: Programs induced to provide the selected features for a library system.

ID	Program	Gen$_{avg}$	Gen$_{std}$	Gen$_{median}$	NC
Q1	select(author,rs3) select(authorBookRel,rs2) filter(name,equals,x,rs3) related(rs2,rs3) select(book,rs1) related(rs1,rs2)	75	34	79	0
Q2	select(author,rs2) filter(name,equals,x,rs2) select(authorBookRel,rs1) related(rs1,rs2) select(book,rs3) select(bookLoan,rs2) related(rs3,rs1) related(rs2,rs3) select(user,rs1) related(rs1,rs2)	283	161	265	0
Q3	select(author,rs3) select(paper,rs1) filter(name,equals,x,rs3) select(authorPaperRel,rs2) related(rs2,rs3) related(rs1,rs2) select(periodicalLoan,rs2) select(periodical,rs3) related(rs3,rs1) related(rs2,rs3) select(user,rs1) related(rs1,rs2)	430	205	365	0
Q4	select(tag,rs4) filter(value,equals,x,rs4) select(book,rs1) select(tagRel,rs2) related(rs2,rs4) related(rs1,rs2) select(bookLoan,rs3) unrelated(rs1,rs3)	216	134	198	0
D1	select(book,rs2) filter(date,less,x,rs2) delete(book,rs2)	28	31	14	0
D2	select(bookLoan,rs2) select(book,rs3) filter(title,equals,x,rs3) related(rs2,rs3) select(user,rs3) filter(name,equals,y,rs3) related(rs2,rs3) delete(bookLoan,rs2)	715	495	746	6
D3	select(paper,rs3) select(author,rs4) filter(name,equals,x,rs4) select(authorBookRel,rs1) select(book,rs2) relate(rs1,rs4) relate(rs2,rs1) select(authorPapelRel,rs4) select(author,rs1) delete(book,rs2) filter(name,equals,x,rs1) relate(rs4,rs1) relate(rs3,rs4) delete(paper,rs3)	402	374	279	3
I1	select(book,rs2) filter(title,equals,x,rs2) select(bookLoan,rs3) related(rs3,rs2) select(user,rs2) related(rs2,rs3) select(message,rs1) createRelation(messageRel,rs3,rs2) filter(text,equals,y,rs1) setRelation(rs3,rs1)	709	391	662	1
I2	select(tag,rs2) filter(value,equals,y,rs2) createRelation(tagRel,rs3,rs2) select(book,rs4) filter(name,equals,x,rs4) setRelation(rs3,rs4)	80	49	69	0
U1	select(publisher,rs2) filter(name,equals,x,rs2) select(book,rs4) select(publisher,rs3) filter(name,equals,y,rs3) related(rs4,rs3) setRelation(rs4,rs2)	209	201	151	0

Before the induction process, the following parameters have to be defined: number of available ResultSets nrs for manipulation, population size pop$_{size}$, maximum number of instructions in a program max$_{size}$, probability of crossover pcros, and probability of mutation pmut. Using the features Q1, I1, D1, and U1, empirical trials were performed looking for the configuration with the faster convergence to the correct solution, given by nrs = 4, pop$_{size}$ = 1000, max$_{size}$ = 20, pcros = 0.3, and pmut = 0.9. In fact, the convergence was not affected significantly by the crossover operator. A lower probability has been chosen in order to improve performance.

Finally, individual programs were induced to provide the features listed on Table 2. In Table 7, for each feature, it is shown one of the obtained induced programs and the average (Gen$_{avg}$), standard deviation (Gen$_{std}$), median (Gen$_{median}$) number of generations, and the number of attempts without convergence (NC) to the correct solution in 20 executions within the maximum of 2000 generations. The results indicate that LGPDB can induce very interpretable programs to query, delete, insert, and update records in relational databases. The induction of a program to perform the task D3 indicates that LGPDB can induce programs that alter multiple tables. Regarding the column "no convergence" (NC), only three tasks (D2, D3, I1), the evolutionary process

has not obtained the correct solution in all 20 executions. In 6 cases for the D2 task, 3 cases for the D3 task, and 1 case for the I1 task, the population converged to a local optimal candidate solution, and the genetic operators were not capable of conducting the population to more promising regions in the search space, even increasing the maximum number of generations of the evolutionary process. Nevertheless, for practical applications, multiple executions, characterized by a distinct set of randomly initialized individuals at the first generation, can be made until the convergence to the correct solution is reached. In the case of the applications tackled in this work, it is important to note that partial solutions are not acceptable. Therefore, programs have to reach the correct solution to be useful. Usually, processes devoted to manage information on IT systems have to achieve all goals, otherwise, they will accumulate errors not tolerated in this kind of application.

On the other hand, the results highlight some limitations of LGPDB. Although it is not an objective of LGPDB to be a high-performance classifier, given its purpose, more powerful filtering rules are desired. The restriction of not generating single programs that can alter information in multiple ways, for instance, inserting and deleting, has also to be addressed. The next section describes initial efforts to overcome these limitations.

5. Adding New Instructions and Inducing More Complex Programs

The previous experiment has shown that LGPDB can induce programs to query, delete, insert and update records in a relational database. However, this experiment has raised some shortcomings of the first version of LGPDB, such as its limitation as a classifier and the impossibility to generate programs that operate multiple tables using different operations. In order to overcome or at least alleviate these limitations, some improvements were made.

The list below shows three new instructions added to the LGPDB instruction set. The first two are used to combine filtering rules, using the operators *AND* and *OR*, in order to model associations involving more input values or attributes. The third instruction is used to set attributes in ResultSets using input values, passed as parameters.

(i) addRule(Operator op, Attribute attr, Rule r, Input-Value v, RuleObject ro). Add rule r, associated with the attribute attr and the input value v, to RuleObject ro with the operator op.

(ii) Filter_2(ResultSet rs, RuleObject ro). Filter the ResultSet rs using the combination of rules in the RuleObject ro.

(iii) setValue(Attribute attr, InputValue v, Operation o, ResultSet rs). Set the value of the attribute attr, for the records in rs, using the operation o and the input value v.

In fact, even without these new instructions, LGPDB can combine filtering rules using multiple Filter instructions, for instance, as shown in the induction of task D2. However, using multiple dissociated Filter instructions, LGPDB cannot model the *OR* operator. In order to demonstrate the combination of filtering rules using the *OR* operator, a new feature for the library system is proposed "List users who borrowed a book written by the authors X or Y." Fitness cases were created and a program was induced to model this feature, as shown in what follows:

```
select(author,rs3)
addRule(_,name,equals,X,rule1)
select(authorBookRel,rs2)
addRule(or,name,equals,Y,rule1)
filter_2(rs3,rule1)
select(user,rs1)
relate(rs2,rs3)
select(book,rs3)
relate(rs3,rs2)
select(bookLoan,rs4)
relate(rs4,rs3)
relate(rs1,rs4)
```

Beside the addition of new instructions, another improvement allows the induction of more complex processes, involving more tables and different operations. If

TABLE 8: A subset of the database tables for a financial system. The attributes in italic are primary or foreign keys.

Table	Fields
Client	*id*, name, ssn, address, phone
Account	*id*, number, branch, *client_id*, balance
Saving	*id*, number, branch, *client_id*, balance
Transaction	*id*, operation, *account_id*, value, code

TABLE 9: Example of a fitness case for the feature F1.

Feature	F1
Input	999-1, 111-1, 999-2, 111-2, 500
Outcome	database.update(account, 3002, "balance", "1800"); database.update(account, 3001, "balance," "1500"); database.insert(transaction, 4001, "send," "3002," "500," "t01"); database.insert(transaction, 4001, "recv," "3001," "500," "t01");

a process has multiple steps that are only dependent on the input values, these distinct steps can be tackled by distinct programs, induced separately. The final solution is the concatenation of the programs. Following the same procedures as in the experiment presented in Section 4, an experiment is proposed here to induce a program to update and insert records in a hypothetical financial system. The first step was the creation of the database with tables and fields presented in Table 8.

After setting up the database, the next step was the insertion of hypothetical records, part of them without consistent associations. In order to demonstrate how LGPDB can model a more complex process combining programs, the following task was chosen "Given the accounts A1 in the branch B1 and A2 in the branch B2, transfer the value V, from A1 to A2." For this task, multiple fitness cases similar to the one presented in Table 9 were created.

As can be seen, the outcome of the feature involves four database operations associated with the input information, two account updates and two transaction insertions. The first update adds the value 500 to the balance of the account 999-2, 111-2. On the other hand, the second update removes 500 from the balance of the account 999-1, 111-1. Finally, the other two subprograms insert logs to the transaction. This process is automatically divided into four induction process, one for each step. The final program that models the entire process is the concatenation of four LGPDB subprograms, induced separately, as shown in Algorithm 1.

6. Influence of Records without Consistent Relationships

Programs have to explore the relationships among different entities in the database to filter records and access new discriminant attributes. In order to list users who borrowed a book, for instance, it is necessary to relate tables user and bookLoan, thus filtering any user not associated with a loan.

```
//SubProg1
01: addRule(_,number,equals,B2,rule2)
02: select(branch,rs1)
03: filter_2(rs1,rule2)
04: Select(account,rs2)
05: addRule(_,number,equals,A2,rule1)
06: filter_2(rs2,rule1)
07: relate(rs2,rs1)
08: setValue(balance,V,+,rs2)
//SubProg3
09: clearEnvironment()
10: addRule(_,number,equals,B1,rule2)
11: addRule(_,number,equals,A1,rule1)
12: select(branch,rs4)
13: filter_2(rs4,rule2)
14: select(account,rs3)
15: relate(rs3,rs4)
16: filter_2(rs3,rule1)
17: setValue(balance,V,-,rs3)
//SubProg2
18: clearEnvironment()
19: addRule(_,number,equals,B1,rule1)
20: addRule(_,number,equals,A1,rule2)
21: select(account,rs4)
22: select(branch,rs2)
23: filter_2(rs4,rule2)
24: filter_2(rs2,rule1)
25: relate(rs4,rs2)
26: createRelation(transaction,rs2,rs4)
27: setValue(operation,send,=,rs2)
29: setValue(value,V,=,rs2)
30: setValue(id,transID,=,rs2)
31: //SubProg4
32: clearEnvironment()
33: addRule(_,number,equals,A2,rule1)
34: addRule(_,number,equals,B2,rule2)
35: select(branch,rs3)
36: select(account,rs4)
37: filter_2(rs4,rule1)
38: filter_2(rs3,rule2)
39: relate(rs4,rs3)
40: createRelation(transaction,rs1,rs4)
41: setValue(operation,recv,=,rs1)
42: setValue(id,transID,=,rs1)
43: setValue(value,V,=,rs1)
```

ALGORITHM 1: Final program that model the task F1. The four subprograms were induced separately and them concatenated.

This type of dissociation among entities is fully acceptable considering the system modelling.

However, other types of dissociation between entities are not expected like a book without author or a periodical without papers. If the database does not have dissociation of entities like that, programs are not rewarded to exploring these relationships, since relating authors with books does not filter any record, supposing that all authors are related with a book. Inserting hypothetical registers without consistent relationships, like a periodical without paper, programs are rewarded to explore this relationship, hence having

access to higher levels of relationship and more discriminant attributes.

If a program needs to find users who borrowed a periodical containing a paper written by a specific author, the program has to relate each entity, from user to author, before filtering the author with the name passed as the input, as shown in Figure 5. It is important to note that these hypothetical registers are used only in the induction database. The solutions obtained using this technique works straightforwardly on databases without this kind of record since real records are not associated with hypothetical ones, as show in Figure 4. The nodes are records in the database. The acronym of a node is the table of the record, as follows: *user* (US), *author* (AU), *book* (BO), *paper* (PA), *periodical* (PE), *tag* (TA), *message* (ME), *bookLoan* (BL), *periodicalLoan* (PL), *authorBookRel* (AB), *authorPaperRel* (AP), *tagRel* (TR), and *messageRel* (MR). The edges represent associations among records by means of *foreign keys*. At the left are the real records and at the right are the hypothetical ones. As can be seen, there is no link between real records (green) and hypothetical records (red).

7. Conclusion and Future Work

This paper presented linear genetic programming for databases (LGPDB), a tool devoted to induce programs capable of manipulating records stored in a relational database. LGPDB combines a linear genetic programming (LGP) induction environment and a simple database management system (DBMS). Generally, previous works on induction of programs that manipulate databases have focused exclusively on the use of databases as a method to organize and query information, mainly for knowledge discovery and data mining (KDD). This limitation is not a problem when the objective is to find patterns in static scenarios. However, to model processes of information technology (IT) systems, the capability of modifying records is mandatory for the generated programs, since most processes change the state of the entities in the system. The experiments performed and reported in this paper indicate that genetic programming can be used to generate programs for record querying, deletion, insertion, and updating.

The software engineer can select features for which he or she knows the exact outcome a program has to produce, given input information. For each feature of this type, evaluation cases are created. Using these cases and a program induction environment, LGPDB can generate programs to provide the target features. The proposed approach is a first step toward automating relevant and basic stages of IT system development, which may give the opportunity for human programmers to concentrate their efforts on more complex tasks. To pursue this goal, a method to integrate or convert programs in the LGPDB format into standard technologies (programming or database languages) is desired and will be addressed in a future work.

This work provides an initial effort on this issue and additional efforts are required. Section 5 has shown some improvements that have to be explored in more detail. The

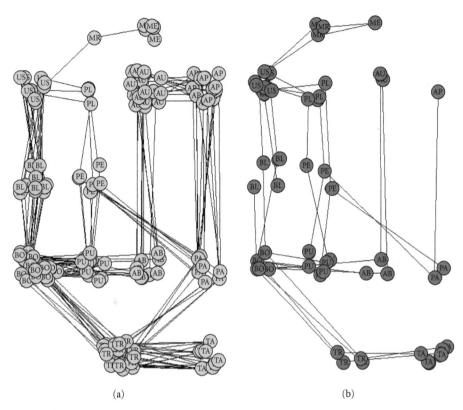

FIGURE 4: Association among real and hypothetical records. The nodes represent records and the edges the relationships between them by means of *foreign keys*. At the left are the real records and at the right are the hypothetical ones.

---

generation: 1, standardized fitness: 270.0
//select all users
select(user,rs1)
generation: 15, standardized fitness: 90.0
//select all users associated with a periodical loan
select(periodicalLoan,rs2) select(user,rs1) related(rs1,rs2)
generation: 62, standardized fitness: 75.0
//select all users associated with a periodical loan—disconsider loan without an existent Periodical
select(periodicalLoan,rs2) select(periodical,rs3) related(rs2,rs3) select(user,rs1) related(rs1,rs2)
generation: 148, standardized fitness: 60.0
//select all users associated with a periodical loan—disconsider periodical without paper
select(paper,rs1) select(periodicalLoan,rs2) select(periodical,rs3) related(rs3,rs1) related(rs2,rs3)
select(user,rs1) related(rs1,rs2)
generation: 364, standardized fitness: 45.0
//select all users associated with a periodical loan—disconsider paper without author
select(paper,rs1) select(authorPaperRel,rs2) related(rs1,rs2) select(periodicalLoan,rs2)
select(periodical,rs3) related(rs3,rs1) related(rs2,rs3) select(user,rs1) related(rs1,rs2)
generation: 401, standardized fitness: 0.0
//select all users associated with a periodical loan that has a paper from author X
select(author,rs3) select(paper,rs1) filter(name,equals,x,rs3) select(authorPaperRel,rs2)
related(rs2,rs3) related(rs1,rs2) select(periodicalLoan,rs2) select(periodical,rs3)
related(rs3,rs1) related(rs2,rs3) select(user,rs1) related(rs1,rs2)

FIGURE 5: The impact in the evolutionary process caused by registers without consistent relationships inserted in the database.

capability to break down a process into multiple simpler processes seems to be promising in the sense of expanding the methodology to deal with interrelated processes. In a future work, we will also consider experiments to evaluate the scalability of LGPDB, for instance, attacking problems with more tables and deeper associations among records in the database. In this context, local search operators may be required to improve the search capability of the evolutionary process.

Acknowledgment

The authors would like to thank CAPES and CNPq for the financial support.

References

[1] C. Larman, *Agile and Iterative Development: A Manager's Guide*, Addison-Wesley Professional, 2004.

[2] G. Wilson and W. Banzhaf, "Fast and effective predictability filters for stock price series using linear genetic programming," in *Proceedings of the IEEE Congress on Evolutionary Computation (CEC '10)*, pp. 1–8, Barcelona, Spain, July 2010.

[3] J. Yu, J. Yu, A. A. Almal et al., "Feature selection and molecular classification of cancer using genetic programming," *Neoplasia*, vol. 9, no. 4, pp. 292–303, 2007.

[4] T. Lensberg, A. Eilifsen, and T. E. McKee, "Bankruptcy theory development and classification via genetic programming," *European Journal of Operational Research*, vol. 169, no. 2, pp. 677–697, 2006.

[5] A. A. Freitas, "A genetic programming framework for two data mining tasks: classification and generalized rule induction," *Genetic Programming*, pp. 96–101, 1997.

[6] T. W. Ryu and C. F. Eick, "MASSON: discovering commonalities in collection of objects using genetic programming," in *Proceedings of the 1st Annual Conference on Genetic Programming*, pp. 200–208, MIT Press, 1996.

[7] T. W. Ryu and C. F. Eick, "Deriving queries from examples using genetic programming," in *Proceedings of the 2nd International Conference on Knowledge Discovery and Data Mining (KDD '96)*, pp. 303–306, August 1996.

[8] G. A. Archanjo and F. J. von Zuben, "Induction of linear genetic programs for relational database manipulation," in *Proceedings of the IEEE International Conference on Information Reuse and Integration (IRI '11)*, pp. 347–352, August 2011.

[9] W. W. Royce, "Managing the development of large software systems," in *Proceedings of the IEEE WESCON*, vol. 26, Los Angeles, Calif, USA, 1970.

[10] B. W. Boehm, "A spiral model of software development and enhancement," *Computer*, vol. 21, no. 5, pp. 61–72, 1988.

[11] A. Manifesto, "Manifesto for agile software development," *Retrieved November*, 29: 2006, 2001.

[12] M. E. Fayad, R. E. Johnson, and D. C. Schmidt, *Building Application Frameworks: Object-oriented Foundations of Framework Design*, 1999.

[13] E. Gamma, R. Helm, R. Johnson, and J. Vlissides, *Design Patterns: Elements of Reusable Object-oriented Software*, Addison-Wesley Longman, 1995.

[14] M. Bichier and K. J. Lin, "Service-oriented computing," *Computer*, vol. 39, no. 3, pp. 99–101, 2006.

[15] M. Armbrust, A. Fox, R. Griffith et al., "Above the clouds: a berkeley view of cloud computing," Tech. Rep. UCB/EECS-2009-28, EECS Department, University of California, Berkeley, Calif, USA, 2009.

[16] S. W. Ambler, *Mapping Objects to Relational Databases: What You Need to Know and Why*, IBM DeveloperWorks, 2000.

[17] S. W. Ambler, *Mapping Objects to Relational Databases: O/R Mapping in Detail*, Ambysoft, 2006.

[18] E. Gamma and K. Beck, Junit, 2005, http://www.junit.org/.

[19] K. Beck, *Test Driven Development: By Example*, Addison-Wesley Professional, 2003.

[20] M. Harman and B. F. Jones, "Search-based software engineering," *Information and Software Technology*, vol. 43, no. 14, pp. 833–839, 2001.

[21] C. J. Burgess and M. Lefley, "Can genetic programming improve software effort estimation? a comparative evaluation," *Information and Software Technology*, vol. 43, no. 14, pp. 863–873, 2001.

[22] E. B. Boden and G. F. Martino, "Testing software using order-based genetic algorithms," in *Proceedings of the 1st Annual Conference on Genetic Programming*, pp. 461–466, MIT Press, 1996.

[23] A. J. Bagnall, V. J. Rayward-Smith, and I. M. Whittley, "The next release problem," *Information and Software Technology*, vol. 43, no. 14, pp. 883–890, 2001.

[24] M. Harman, R. Hierons, and M. Proctor, "A new representation and crossover operator for search-based optimization of software modularization," in *Proceedings of the Genetic and Evolutionary Computation Conference (GECCO '02)*, pp. 1351–1358, 2002.

[25] T. M. Khoshgoftaar, Y. Liu, and N. Seliya, "A multiobjective module-order model for software quality enhancement," *IEEE Transactions on Evolutionary Computation*, vol. 8, no. 6, pp. 593–608, 2004.

[26] J. H. Holland, *Adaptation in Natural and Artificial Systems: An Introductory Analysis with Applications to Biology, Control, and Artificial Intelligence*, 1975.

[27] N. L. Cramer, "A representation for the adaptive generation of simple sequential programs," in *Proceedings of the 1st International Conference on Genetic Algorithms*, vol. 183, p. 187, 1985.

[28] J. R. Koza, *Genetic Programming: On the Programming of Computers by Means of Natural Selection*, The MIT Press, 1992.

[29] S. Luke, "Genetic programming produced competitive soccer softbot teams for robocup97," *Genetic Programming*, pp. 214–222, 1998.

[30] J. R. Koza, F. H. Bennett III, D. Andre, and M. A. Keane, "Automated WYWIWYG design of both the topology and component values of electrical circuits using genetic programming," in *Proceedings of the 1st Annual Conference on Genetic Programming*, pp. 123–131, MIT Press, 1996.

[31] R. Balzer, "A 15 year perspective on automatic programming," *IEEE Transactions on Software Engineering*, vol. 11, no. 11, pp. 1257–1268, 1985.

[32] L. Xu, H. H. Hoos, and K. Leyton-Brown, "Hydra: automatically configuring algorithms for portfolio-based selection," in *Proceedings of the 24th AAAI Conference on Artificial Intelligence*, 2010.

[33] G. E. Krasner and S. T. Pope, "A cookbook for using the model-view controller user interface paradigm in smalltalk-80," *Journal of Object-Oriented Programming*, vol. 1, no. 3, pp. 26–49, 1988.

[34] H. Garcia-Molina and K. Salem, "Main memory database systems: an overview," *IEEE Transactions on Knowledge and Data Engineering*, vol. 4, no. 6, pp. 509–516, 1992.

[35] A. Silberschatz, H. F. Korth, and S. Sudarshan, *Database System Concepts*, vol. 72, McGraw-Hill, New York, NY, USA, 2002.

[36] D. J. Montana, "Strongly typed genetic programming," *Evolutionary Computation*, vol. 3, no. 2, pp. 199–230, 1995.

[37] W. Banzhaf, *Genetic Programming: An Introduction on the Automatic Evolution of Computer Programs and Its Applications*, Morgan Kaufmann, 1998.

[38] M. Brameier and W. Banzhaf, *Linear Genetic Programming*, Springer, New York, NY, USA, 2007.

[39] P. P. S. Chen, "The entity-relationship model—toward a unified view of data," *ACM Transactions on Database Systems (TODS)*, vol. 1, no. 1, pp. 9–36, 1976.

8

A New Software Development Methodology for Clinical Trial Systems

Li-Min Liu

Department of Applied Mathematics, Chung Yuan Christian University, 200 Chung Pei Road, Chung Li 32023, Taiwan

Correspondence should be addressed to Li-Min Liu; lmliu@math.cycu.edu.tw

Academic Editor: Pekka Abrahamsson

Clinical trials are crucial to modern healthcare industries, and information technologies have been employed to improve the quality of data collected in trials and reduce the overall cost of data processing. While developing software for clinical trials, one needs to take into account the similar patterns shared by all clinical trial software. Such patterns exist because of the unique properties of clinical trials and the rigorous regulations imposed by the government for the reasons of subject safety. Among the existing software development methodologies, none, unfortunately, was built specifically upon these properties and patterns and therefore works sufficiently well. In this paper, the process of clinical trials is reviewed, and the unique properties of clinical trial system development are explained thoroughly. Based on the properties, a new software development methodology is then proposed specifically for developing electronic clinical trial systems. A case study shows that, by adopting the proposed methodology, high-quality software products can be delivered on schedule within budget. With such high-quality software, data collection, management, and analysis can be more efficient, accurate, and inexpensive, which in turn will improve the overall quality of clinical trials.

1. Introduction

Clinical trials (CTs) are measures to evaluate the safety and efficacy of a medical device or drug. CTs are crucial to modern healthcare industry and usually take substantial resources and time to complete with four major parties involved: the sponsor, the government agency, the participating hospitals (or sites), and the patients (or subjects) [1]. The clinical trial is usually supported financially by a sponsor that may be a pharmaceutical company, a medical device company, or even a government agency. Sponsors also define the scopes, procedures, protocols, and goal of their CTs. The definition of "protocol" in clinical trials is very different from the one commonly used in the computer engineering (please refer to the US Food and Drug Administration (FDA) for more information [2]). Data are collected on sites from subjects and recorded on well-defined forms, that is, case report forms (CRFs), to guarantee the quality of the collected data. For the safety of subjects, CTs should always follow predefined protocols and government regulations.

Today, almost all fields, including the healthcare industry, are benefited by high-speed computers and information technologies [3, 4]. High-speed internet accessibility is one of the prime examples. For computerizing CTs, several concepts were introduced over the past decade, including electronic health record (eHR) [5, 6], electronic data capture (eDC), and electronic CRF (eCRF). Although eDC and eCRF are sometimes used interchangeably [7], they can be formally defined as the following:

> "eDC: synonymously used with remote data entry; collecting data in (permanent) electronic form by systems... with or without a human interface..."

> "eCRF: data may be recorded either from source documents or the eCRF may be used as the primary source document..." [8].

More precisely, eCRFs are considered the replacement for paper-based CRFs while eDCs focus on two things: (1) data are captured remotely and (2) the whole lifecycle of data is always in electronic forms. It means that each site must have an eHR system to build eDC [9–13]. Unfortunately, study shows that only a small portion of the trial data (less than 40%) is available in hospitals' eHR [14]. Other tasks such as CT management, workflow control, and embedding controlled terminologies, standards and regulations (UMLS, SNOMED, CDISC, HL7, and 21 CFR Part 11) into software for CTs are also investigated [4, 15–22].

In this paper, a "Clinical Trial System" (CTS) is defined as a software system to handle trial data; therefore, a CTS includes data-related software, for example, eDC or eCRF, but excludes the rest, for example, CT management or workflow control. The three core components of a CTS are the data collection module, the data exportation module, and the backend database system. A CTS, eventually, exports data for statistical analysis by statisticians with professional statistics software, which is excluded in the current definition of CTS because it requires expertise completely different from software development. From the software developers' point of view, the main complexity of developing a CTS comes from the data collection system rather than data analysis system which requires skills from statisticians.

To deliver a quality software product as complicated as a CTS on time within budget, a predefined software development methodology (SDM, or so-called process model) should be followed. However, adopting existing purpose SDMs to develop a CTS requires the development team to disregard some fundamental guidelines of the SDM because all CTS share some unique properties (described in details in the following section).

The rest of the paper is organized as follows. Section 2 illustrates the CTS/SDMs, the process and properties of CTs and discusses the differences between using generic tools and domain-specific tools to develop CTS and reviews existing SDMs for CTS development. Section 3 describes the proposed SDM in details followed by the case study and discussions in Section 4. Finally, the conclusions are presented in Section 5.

2. Development of CTSs

2.1. Background. Modern CTS works not only as a vehicle at front end for collecting data but also as a complete system which can be as complex as any commercial software. To maintain data integrity, a CTS usually applies constraints such as simple value range check and complex cross-form value derivation. For reasons like data auditing, CRFs may also include nonnumerical fields like hand-drawn pictures (e.g., the position of ulcer), photographs (e.g., photographs before/after operations), or texts (e.g., doctor's comments). In addition, complicated flow branches can be defined in the protocol (e.g., subjects with different conditions/test results may require different flow path to fill additional/different CFRs).

Figure 1 shows an eCRF in the data collection module of a CTS implemented with functional buttons, selection boxes, a picture with hand-drawn marks, and several implemented constraints. With such complexity, most CTSs need to be custom made on a case-by-case basis and demand substantial resources from the sponsors.

Figure 2 shows three commonly used CTS architectures (dashed box indicates the data collection system with

databases). Figure 2(a) illustrates an architecture where the trial data are directly retrieved from hospital eHR by performing queries from the CTS front-end module and then saved into the backend databases. CTS front end and backend can be merged into one system as a single server if necessary. This architecture is convenient for CTs with a small number of sites with fully supported and identical eHR. Since data are not entered manually, this architecture provides the highest level of data integrity while eCRFs can serve as a data viewer. However, engineers need to develop a CTS front-end module for any site with a different eHR, which requires significant resources and cooperation from hospitals. This increases the risk of project failure. In addition, most hospitals do not have extra resources to work with every CT conducted in house.

Figure 2(b) indicates an architecture which requires a CTS user interface (UI) to collect trial data. In most cases, the CTS UI is implemented the same way as the CRFs developed in the protocol to ease the learning curve of the users. Data are manually entered from transcribed data or local eHR on sites. Since data are input manually, data integrity is lower than that in the previous architecture. On the other hand, this architecture has many advantages. For instance, the CTS UI can serve as the data viewer and be used at all sites. Today, most of the CTS UI is developed as a web-based application using a web browser for data input. A data management agency is an organization that facilitates computer hardware and software to maintain customers' data. Sponsors who do not have computer facilities may use the service provided by data management agency on a contract base. For trials with multiple sites and low eHR accessibility, this is the preferred architecture.

Figure 2(c) shows a CTS architecture similar to the one illustrated in Figure 2(b) with a local front-end database at each site. It, therefore, shares the same advantages/disadvantages discussed previously. In this design, the CTS front end has most of the complexities and is considered a completed CTS where the backend has only limited functionalities like data migration and synchronization. For CTs without a designated data management agency, this is the preferred architecture because the CTS at a particular site can serve as the data center. Detailed designs of CTS may vary from case to case.

A process model is defined as "*a distinct set of activities, actions, tasks, milestones, and work products that are required to engineer high-quality software*" [24]. In the past few decades, many SDMs have been proposed such as the waterfall model, the incremental model, the prototyping paradigm, the spiral model, the joint application development, agile methods, and the IBM Rational Unified Process (RUP) [25–33]. Figure 3 shows the "plan spectrum" of SDM where the unplanned/undisciplined hacking occupies the left extreme, while the inch-pebble planning occupies the other end of the spectrum [23]. Based on this model, all SDMs fall between these two extremes. Some SDMs work more effectively than others in some domain, but a panacea does not exist. As a matter of fact, CTS development shares the same patterns and properties (categorized into phases, described in details in the following subsection) which is

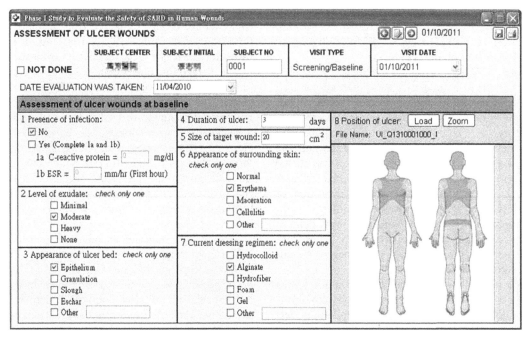

FIGURE 1: Example eCRF for "Assessment of Ulcer Wounds".

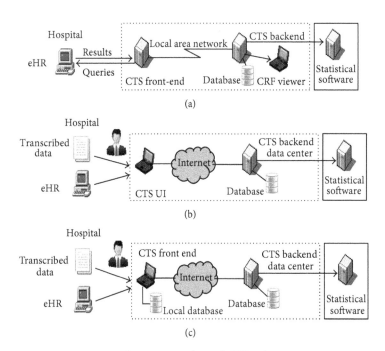

FIGURE 2: Three commonly used CTS architectures.

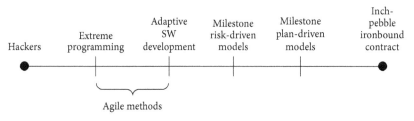

FIGURE 3: The planning spectrum of SDM [23].

more similar to the SDMs on the right-hand side of the spectrum.

2.2. Process and Properties of Clinical Trials. The properties that distinguish clinical trials from other application domains are described with the example (shown in Figure 4) of FDA clearance for class III medical devices in the US market using the activity diagram of the Unified Modeling Language (UML) [34, 35]. The pathway consists of three blocks (swimlanes): a government agency (FDA), the sponsor, and participating hospitals. Activities inside these blocks can be grouped into three categories: initial, core, and postactivities.

(1) *Initial Activities.* The sponsor is responsible for developing the CT protocol. Prior to that, initial activities such as the hypothesis study, feasibility study, risk assessment, and animal study may be required. For CT of a medical device, FDA also suggests that a quality management system be established by the sponsor as soon as possible following FDA regulations [36]. If a study fails to receive positive results from the initial activities, the process will be terminated and therefore a CTS will not be needed. Hence, starting the CTS development too early is not practical.

(2) *Core Activities.* One important CT property which needs to be considered in CTS development is protocol evolution, also the main activity in this category. Three major versions of CT protocols could be generated: the initial protocol, protocol in the first submitted IDE application, and FDA approved protocol. The core activities start with the CT protocol development. The initial protocol, which can be created by the sponsor without interference from hospitals, is sent to the institutional review boards (IRB) of each hospital for reviewing. CT subject enrollment can officially start only after the IRB approves the protocol plus an approved investigational device exemption (IDE) from the FDA. An IDE application is submitted to the FDA with the CT protocol and at least one hospitals' IRB approval. After reviewing an IDE application, the FDA replies with one of three status: *approval* (CT is allowed to proceed), *conditional approval* (CT is allowed to proceed but with conditions), or *disapproval* (CT is not allowed to proceed). A conditional approval requires the sponsor to answer FDA's questions or even rewrite the entire protocol. Any changes or amendments to the protocol need to be submitted to all hospitals' IRB for reviewing. The modified protocol may contain updated CRFs due to new data specification. The hospitals' IRB may also conditionally approve the study, and then the sponsor needs to provide amendments with explanations or updates. The amendments have to be submitted to the FDA and the IRB of all sites for reviewing. If the sponsor cannot provide meaningful responses to the FDA, the study would most likely be rejected and thus terminated (no need for CTS). If the sponsor fails to provide a satisfactory answer to any of IRB's questions, chances are the sponsor has to drop this hospital from the CT since the IRB will certainly reject the study.

(3) *Postactivities.* The main focus of postactivities is to apply for premarket approval (PMA). The PMA application should be supported by statistical analysis of the CT data. The first activity in this phase is, therefore, defined as "analyzing trial data" which is obviously irrelevant to CTS development.

This pathway is complicated with certain patterns. Due to the involvement of government agencies, the pathway is different from most processes of software development in other domains such as financial, industrial, or insurance. Based on the discussion above, a CTS has the following unique properties.

CTSP1. The development time is extremely short. CTS needs to be ready when IDE is approved and subject enrollment begins, which may be the next day of the IDE approval.

CTSP2. Every CT certainly has an approved protocol. Subject enrollment cannot start without a government-approved protocol. The CT protocol is considered the requirement specification of CTS because it contains detailed information about what or how the data will be collected.

CTSP3. The protocol is subject to change anytime during the CT. The CT protocol can be changed even when the system is online. The amended protocol is considered a new version of the CTS specification.

CTSP4. Not every protocol amendment affects CTS development. Protocol amendments may contain only explanations without extra data to be collected. The CTS development team does not have to react to such amendments.

CTSP5. Protocol development may take months to finish. For the safety of the subjects, a protocol will be carefully reviewed by FDA and IRB though the government is required to respond to IDE applications within a time limit but may not necessarily approve the protocol. Hence, it normally takes an extensive amount of time to receive IDE approval.

CTSP6. The CTS development team does not participate in protocol reviewing process. Protocols are reviewed by the government agency and hospitals' IRB, and CTS development engineers have no role in the reviewing process and are therefore excluded.

CTSP7. There is no need at all for CTS developers to be colocated with customers. According to CTSP2 and CTSP6, engineers are informed of the nonnegotiable protocol (the CTS requirement specification) passively. In most cases, CTS customers (users at sites) are given a nonnegotiable software system passively. In this sense, there is no need at all to maintain face-to-face or day-to-day communication between developers and customers.

CTSP8. There is no "rapid value" of the CTS. The concept of "rapid value" of a software system comes from a situation where customers can profit from a functional subsystem. We can hardly find such cases in CTs where subject data are

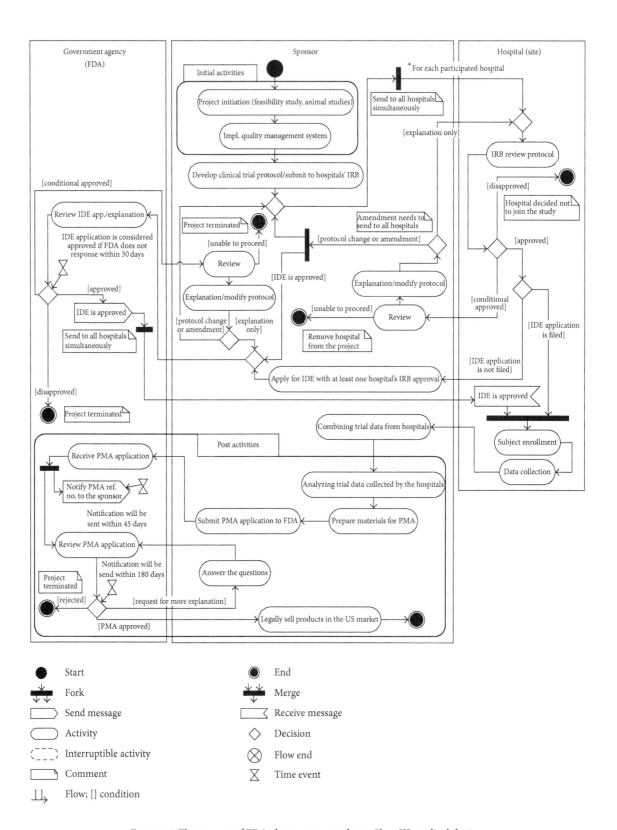

FIGURE 4: The process of FDA clearance to market a Class III medical device.

collected by CTS first and later by paper-based CRF just because the CTS development is not fully developed yet.

CTSP9. Every trial is unique. Each CT study has its own hypothesis, procedures, and endpoints. Every CT study has its own unique exit criteria. Data collection and data analysis differ from case to case. For pharmaceutical companies, which host a large amount of CTS development, software modules may possibility be reused, but, in general, it is not practical to construct a universal CT protocol.

CTSP10. There is no working legacy system. Usually a functional system exists to handle current jobs for most software development in other domains. This is not necessarily the case in a clinical trial. For example, the development of a new Class III medical device may not take advantage of any existing function system for other devices. In most cases, an entirely new CTS process needs to be developed for every new CT.

CTSP11. CTS architecture can be defined without protocol. The sponsor can define the CTS architecture without an approved protocol because CTS architecture, as shown in Figure 2, only describes how data will be collected rather than what to collect and how to analyze them.

CTSP12. Data collection portion can be online without exportation module. Data collection portion can be activated without the exportation module because the exportation module is functionally independent from the rest of the CTS. Engineers need to complete data collection module for subject enrollment, but not the exportation part which will be needed only when sufficient data have been collected, which may take months or even years.

CTSP13. There are unique factors to measure the level of success for CTS development. For example, according to CTSP1, it is highly possible that subjects are ready for enrollment before CTS is available. In such cases, one can either reject the subject or use the paper-based CRF first as an alternative and then transfer the data to the CTS later when it is ready. If a CTS is delivered on time, then the number of subjects whose data are collected by an alternative method should be zero. Such numbers can be used as a measure of the successfulness of CTS development, but it is beyond the scope of this research.

2.3. Tools for Developing CTS. CTS can be developed by generic software development tools or CTS-specific tools, for example, Oracle Clinical [37]. The former includes tools which are not specifically created for CTS development; the later represents the opposite general purpose development tools, for example, Java or .Net [38, 39]. Differences between these two approaches are summarized in Table 1.

The purchasing fee for general development tools is relatively lower than the cost of a specific tool. The cost for hiring engineers or project managers familiar with a specific tool like Oracle Clinical is high since such people

do have specific knowledge. In Figure 1, the user is allowed to draw on the picture at the lower right side, but for tools that do not support this kind of feature, adding this feature can cost a lot. In addition, Figure 1 shows a CTS form exactly the same as the paper-based CRF and end users with experience on paper-based CRF can easily learn how to use the CTS. On the contrary, for example, if the CTS is built by Oracle Remote Data Capture [37], then the end users must learn its user interface, which is different from what they were familiar with (paper-based CRF). If a sponsor already bought a software package, for example, a specific database management system, then it can be reused easily through generic tools, but not necessarily so for specific tools that may require modules from specific software vendor.

In general, developing a CTS with generic tools costs less than with CTS specific tools. Although free software is available, for example, EpiData [40], to generate an interface for data capturing, the stability, extensibility, and overall supports of such free software are relatively low, which not only raises the costs for adding features but also increases the risk of failure. End user of the CTS, nurses to input data or consultant to collect data on site, may need to spend more time to understand not only the CTS but other related systems of the specific tools. In practice, organizations, for example, pharmaceutical companies, host a large amount of CTS development with many experienced engineers, and project managers may prefer CTS-specific tools. Institutes with limited resources or individual researchers may prefer to use the relatively inexpensive generic tools. In the latter case, the process can be improved significantly by having an SDM built specifically for CTS development.

2.4. Reviews of Current Software Development Methodologies. This subsection reviews core concepts of the current SDMs in plan-driven methods, risk-driven methods, and agile methods as illustrated in Figure 3. Explanations of why these SDMs are not appropriate for CTS development will also be provided.

2.4.1. Plan-Driven and Risk-Driven Methods. Plan-driven methods include traditional SDMs like *the waterfall model, the incremental model, prototyping paradigm,* and *RUP.* All these SDMs define specific "phases". For example, the classic waterfall model contains five ordered linear phases: *requirement, analysis, design, constructions,* and *operations* [24]. The RUP contains four phases: *inception, elaboration, construction,* and *transition.* Documents and specifications will be generated at the end of each phase by engineers and customers [26]. However, all plan-driven SDMs require early finalization of system requirement, which clearly violates CTSP3. Delays in any of the early phases will compromise the development time and make CTSP1 even worse. Prototyping paradigm requires regular meeting between the developers and customers to clarify software requirement and system modules. But in CTS development, there is no need to clarify requirement since the CTS requirement is the FDA/hospital IRB approved protocol (CTSP2) which is developed and clarified by doctors and government agency without software

TABLE 1: Comparison of CTS development by generic and specific tools.

	Specific tools	Generic tools
Costs for acquiring tools	High	Low
Costs for qualified engineers	High	Low
Costs for adding special features	High if not supported	Low
End user learning curve	Relatively high	Low
Can CTS utilize software already acquired?	Depends	Yes
Any SDM to follow	Depends on vendors	No
Is the project manager required to know tools in depth?	Yes	No

engineers' involvement (CTSP6). Prototyping paradigm also requires constant face-to-face meeting with customers to verify their requirements or needs with a prototype. But with the FDA/hospital IRB approved protocol, there is no need for customers and developers to meet constantly. In addition, in CTS requirement, customers cannot profit from a CTS with only partial function (CTSP8). The RUP finalizes the architecture design at the second phase, while CTSP11 suggests it be done at the first phase. The RUP and other incremental models work well for developing a large-scale system that evolves as the process continues [24], but they may not be appropriate models in CTS development due to CTSP6 and CTSP8~10. Process models derived from the waterfall model, such as the incremental model [41, 42], have similar inherited disadvantages for developing CTSs.

The risk-driven spiral model is an evolutionary model with four regions: *determine objectives, evaluate, develop,* and *plan next phases* [24, 28, 43, 44]. Software is developed in a series of evolutionary releases (prototypes) from a successive loop. This model differs from other models mainly in that risk analysis is performed in each of the development cycle. The major risk of CTS development comes from its unique properties, and many of them cannot be resolved by risk analysis, for example, CTSP1. Spiral model inherits the core concept of prototyping paradigm and therefore shares the same disadvantages for CTS development. Process models derived from the spiral model, like WINWIN spiral model [45], exhibit the same problems for developing CTSs.

2.4.2. Agile Methods. Unlike the plan/risk-driven approaches, agile methods give up the concepts of "phases" and focus on the flexibility of the methods. Agile methods represent a group of light-weight methodologies including *scrum, extreme programming (XP), adaptive software development, feature-driven development,* and *agile unified process* (the light-weight version of RUP) while the XP is commonly known as the first agile method. In 2001, the *Manifesto for Agile Software Development* was published to define the approach now known as the agile software development [46]. The focal values of agile methods listed in this document are (1) *individuals and interactions* over processes and tools, (2) *working software* over comprehensive documentation, (3) *customer collaboration* over contract negotiation, and (4) *responding to change* over following a plan.

It is obvious that some of these focal values may not be proper for CTS development. For instance, for focal value (2),

CTSP8 shows that a partially working CTS can hardly provide benefits to the CT. For focal value (3), contracts between the developer and customer may not be necessary if they are in the same organization, for example, a pharmaceutical company. For other cases where the CTS is developed by a software consultant firm (with CTSP1~6), negotiating a contract agreed by both developers and customers is important. For focal values (4), since all CTS development follows the same process, as shown in Figure 4, defining an SDM that matches the process can significantly help to reduce the risk of failure.

Furthermore, some of the 12 principles of agile development are not suitable for CTS development by nature. For instance, the third principle "*deliver working software... from a couple of weeks to months...*" violates CTSP8. The fourth principle "*business people and developers must work together daily throughout the project*" goes against CTSP5~6. And the seventh principle "*working software is the primary measure of progress*" violates CTSP8 and CTSP10. The sixth and eighth principles emphasize frequent colocated face-to-face conversation, but according to CTSP2 and CTSP6~7, neither face-to-face meeting nor colocation is necessary. Agile methods work well for business software development but may not work well for CTS development, since over one-third of the 12 principles of agile development will be unnecessary, difficult, or impossible to carry out. For CTS development to be successful, it requires the project manager, engineers, and the customer to carefully disregard some of the basic agile principles. For project managers and engineers without experience on CTS development, adopting agile methods may increase the risks of the project due to possible complications caused by following all of the agile principles. In some CTS development projects, the project managers, to their rich experience and understanding of clinical trials, actually disregarded some basic agile principles; therefore, it is hardly justifiable to claim that the CTS was developed by agile methods.

Table 2 summarizes the CTS properties that are improper for the plan-, risk-driven, and agile method. In reality, it is almost impossible to follow guidelines and phases of traditional SDMs in CTS development. On the other side, if one adopts agile methods, some of the focal values and principles must be ignored. Then the successfulness of CTS development totally depends on experienced engineers and project managers to ensure the project is on the right track.

TABLE 2: SDMs and the CTS properties that make the SDM improper for CTS development.

SDMs	CTS properties that make the SDM improper for CTS development
Plan-driven	CTSP1, 3, and 6~11.
Risk-driven	CTSP1 (the risks of CTS development are different from risks discussed in risk-driven methods)
Agile methods	CTSP1~8, 10

For CTs initiated by institutes other than large pharmaceutical companies, adopting agile methods may increase risks of the project.

3. Proposed Software Development Methodology

Due to CTSP3~5, engineers may not obtain the CTS specification at an early stage of the project, which is a necessary condition for plan-oriented SDMs. On the other hand, agile methods focus on prototypes, rapid values, and constant meetings, and so forth, disregarding that engineers can take advantage of the fact that every CTS development shares the same patterns and properties. To design an SDM that fully covers the CTS properties and takes advantage of both plan-oriented and agile methods, one needs to carefully review the protocol evolution. Hence, the new SDM for CTS development naturally resides in the middle of the spectrum as shown in Figure 3, balancing the two end points of opposite views [47, 48]. Figure 5 shows the state transition diagram of the protocol evolution at hospital and sponsor site in UML. The state transition is relatively simple on the hospital side with only three states compared to those on the sponsor side. It is because the sponsor is responsible for protocol development. The three versions of protocol are shown in the comment blocks between state transitions on the sponsor side.

To handle the unique patterns and properties of CTS development, a new SDM is proposed, as shown in Figure 6, with four phases: *architecture design*, *system analysis and design*, *construction*, and *exportation*. Activities in all phases are iterative and incremental in nature. The phases are linked with intermediate objects like documents and software. Phases will be executed one after another, but, different from the traditional plan-driven SDM, the last three phases are triggered based on receiving messages. Objects not related to other phases are placed inside the shaded blocks.

3.1. Architecture Design Phase. The first phase, *the architecture design phase*, starts when the initial activities (as in Figure 4) obtain positive results and the sponsor decides to proceed. Major work products of this phase include *architecture description*, *standard operating procedure* (*SOP*), *auditing plan*, *prototypes* (for architecture demonstration), *risk assessment*, and *project plan*. *Risk assessment*, *prototypes*, and *project plan* (resources and personnel allocation plans) are also required at the first phase in other SDMs while the rest are unique to the proposed model.

Different from most current SDMs, the sponsor and engineers can design the system architecture, for example, Figure 2, without detailed specifications (protocol). In practice, once the overall system architecture is defined, changes are highly unlikely.

CTSs with different architectures may have totally different software components. For instance, if trial data can be retrieved from hospitals' eHR, then the CTS can be designed without an interface for manual data input. If data must be manually entered, a standard 2-tier database system should suffice for a CT without complex semantic checks. Otherwise, a 3-tier system is more appropriate for hosting those checks. Along with the *architecture description*, the sponsor and engineers are able to finalize *risk assessment*, *prototypes*, and *project plan*.

The *SOP* of how to collect data is defined based on the finalized CTS architecture in this phase. Two documents, *architecture description* and *SOP*, are prerequisites for the next phase and must be completed beforehand. Since the CTS architecture demands stability, iterations of activities of this phase should be limited to the minimum.

3.2. System Analysis and Design Phase. The second phase focuses on system analysis and design. Major work products include the *analysis model, system and database design model, test plan, test cases,* and *alternative plan*. This phase starts when the initial protocol is complete. The major activities in this phase are system analysis and design. Once the system design is complete, the work product *system and database design model* will be created. Based on this design model, engineers now have a clear picture of how many software components and database objects a CTS will include.

For cases in which the protocol is approved by the FDA and the participating hospitals before CTS is completed, the sponsor and engineers have two choices: (1) reject qualified subjects before CTS is completed or (2) allow subjects' registration and prepare an alternative plan to collect data before CTS is ready. The most popular alternative plan is to use traditional paper-based CRF to collect data. Alternative planning requires the latest amended protocol and the *SOP*. For cases in which the initial protocol is amended, engineers should decide whether a system architecture change is required. If this is the case, the entire development process should start all over again because changing CTS architecture, for example, from Figures 2(a) to 2(c), requires developing totally different software components. For cases where changes are required only in the data fields or adding forms, engineers can go through activities defined in this phase to update the system and database design model. For cases in which the protocol is not updated (only explanations are needed), the activity flow will simply end because software specification is unchanged.

For the analysis/design paradigm, either a function-oriented or an object-oriented approach can be adopted since both approaches are well established in the field of software engineering [49]. The database design, schema design, and normalization can be achieved by following the guidelines recommended in the database system [50].

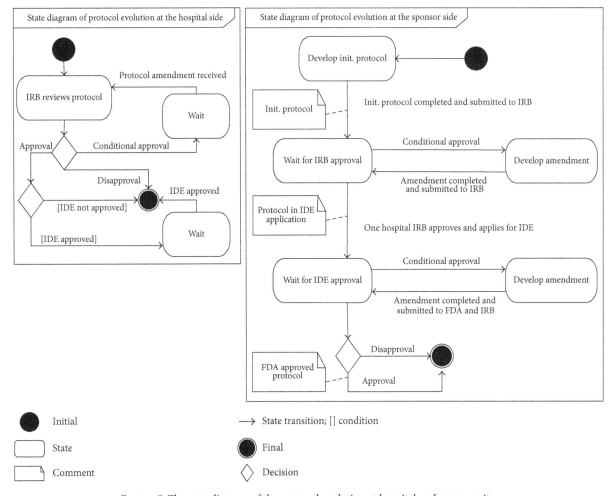

FIGURE 5: The state diagram of the protocol evolution at hospital and sponsor site.

3.3. Construction Phase. The third phase, the construction phase, focuses on developing a functional CTS data collection subsystem. Major work products are the *software components, integrated CTS data collection subsystem, user manual,* and *deployment procedure.* This phase starts after the IDE application is filed, which means the protocol has received at least one hospital approval. Based on the work products defined in the previous phases, engineers create backend database objects, design (in low level) and develop software components, integrate them into a functional subsystem, and meanwhile perform the unit/system test based on the test plans/cases.

To implement a single eCRF, as shown in Figure 1, engineers need to go through a series of activities, called *construction cycle,* including component level analysis, component construction/testing, CTS integration, and integration test. Ideally each construction cycle is independent from others if the eCRF does not contain any complicated rules associated with other forms. For CTS adopting architecture shown in Figure 2(a), a component can be considered a module used to retrieve data fields for a single CRF from hospital

eHR. In either case, construction cycles can be executed in parallel.

During implementation, engineers may receive conditional approval message "Data spec. changed" from FDA or IRB. In such cases, all activities must be interrupted (dashed rounded box in Figure 6). Amended protocol may "require architecture change" or "require system change". In both cases, messages will be sent and the activity flow will go back to previous phases as described in the previous subsection. Engineers may continue the construction cycles with no effects on a certain protocol amendment. Such design makes the proposed SDM maintain flexibility to handle specification changes (CTSP3~4).

If FDA approves the IDE after all construction cycles are completed, then the subject enrollment may begin with the integrated CTS data collection subsystem without any delay. Otherwise, the CTS *alternative plan* is invoked. The most important supporting documents are *deployment procedure* and *user manual.* Both of them will be updated in every construction cycle based on the integrated CTS data collection subsystem.

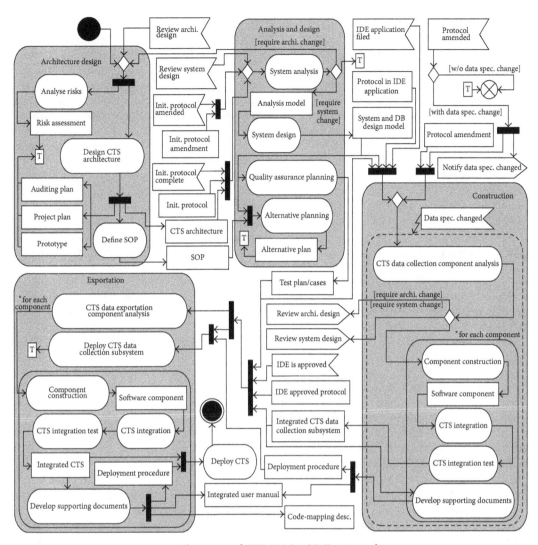

FIGURE 6: The proposed CTS SDM in UML activity diagram.

3.4. Exportation Phase. The last phase is the exportation phase because the CTS requires exporting data for statistical analysis. The development of data exportation subsystem needs not to be executed in the previous phase based on CTSP1 and CTSP12. Major work products are the *software components, integrated CTS, user manual, code-mapping descriptions,* and *deployment procedure.* This phase starts when the IDE is approved and subject enrollment is ready to begin. The first two activities, "deploy the CTS data collection subsystem" and "analysis of CTS data exportation subsystem", can be executed in parallel.

The construction cycle is similar between the third and fourth phases, but the fourth phase focuses on data exportation components. The construction cycle in both phases can be implemented in parallel if no complicated dependent rules exist. In the fourth phase, engineers work with statisticians on data exporting specifications and develop, test, and integrate software components into CTS. All supporting documents are supposed to be created at this time such as the *user manual* for data exportation and *code-mapping descriptions* for every exported data file. To generate quality analysis results, most

CTSs use professional statistical software. It is also possible that sponsors wishes to use statistical features provided by commercial database management systems rather than statistical software; then "data exportation components" represent "interfaces" of database management systems for statisticians (e.g., views of database tables).

3.5. Features of the Proposed SDM. There are two backward flows in the proposed SDM from the construction phase to the first and second phases in order to preserve the flexibilities. The development is parallel since the CTS constriction is based on components. Components which are not affected by a certain amendment can stay in the third phase. This approach enables the proposed SDM to have the advantage of incremental model with agile flexibilities. As illustrated in Figure 4, there are many activity loops, for example, getting approval from a hospital IRB or to get the IDE approved from the FDA. In the meanwhile, the development team must halt and wait for the activities to finish. During that "waiting time", based on other SDMS, the development team can do nothing but wait. The proposed SDM carefully places activities in that "waiting time" as illustrated in Figures 5 and 6.

In summary, the proposed SDM covers all thirteen CTS properties with the following features: (1) architecture design is performed at the first phase, CTSP12; (2) the development of CTS is split into two well-defined subsystems, CTSP1; (3) all phases are designed to be iterative and incremental, CTSP2~5; (4) engineers do not need to be involved in protocol development or colocated with sponsors, CTSP6~7; (5) there are two concrete milestones at the end of third and fourth phases (delivery of data collection subsystem and delivery of integrated CTS), CTSP8~10; (6) the limited time for development is optimally utilized, CTSP1; (7) experiments for engineers and PMs are not necessary conditions.

4. Case Study and Discussions

4.1. Case Study. The proposed SDM has been applied on three CTS developments and one of them (for the Phase-I study of a new silicon human dermis developed in Taiwan) is discussed in this section to demonstrate the feasibility and effectiveness. The government regulations for CTs in Taiwan are very similar to those in the USA with a similar pathway as shown in Figure 4 except that the Taiwanese government is not obligated to answer either IDE or PMA application within a certain period of time.

The study initially involved four participating hospitals without a common eHR; therefore, a 2-tier architecture similar to Figure 2(c) was adopted as the CTS architecture and one of the four sites was designated as the data center. A previously developed CTS was used as the demonstration prototype. The activities of the first phase were smoothly completed before the initial protocol was completed. These activities were executed only once, since the finalized architecture was never changed throughout the entire project. The object-oriented approach was used for system analysis and design in this study. The engineers finished all activities in the second phase before receiving the approval from the first hospitals' IRB. The construction phase is iterated three times due to protocol updates. In order to implement the CTS more efficiently, components without complicated constraints like "Screening Summary", "Death Report Form", and "Physician's Comments" were built first. Two new forms and several data fields were added later in response to government/IRB requests. The final CTS involves twelve visits from each subject with several dozens of constraints adopted and over one hundred forms. Figure 1 shows one of the forms. Since the data specification becomes stable after three conditional approvals (from three iterations), the engineers were told to proceed to the last phase to develop the data exportation subsystem. The whole CTS development was completed when the IDE was approved, and the CTS alternative plan was naturally not used in this case. In the end, the new proposed SDM was successfully applied to develop and deliver a large scale CTS with high quality on time, within budget, and without using any additional resources.

4.2. Discussions. For comparison of cost, all three CTS developments adopting the proposed SDM are considered against

the previous two CTS developments. The development cost was measured by accumulating all costs (for project manager, system designer, software developers, database developers, testers) divided by the number of eCRF. The average cost per form (as shown in Figure 1) was reduced over fifty percent. The later three CTS developments (with the proposed SDM) are more complex than the previous two with more forms and visits per subjects, and yet the number of meetings between sponsor and software consultant firm was reduced to one-third. Both previous CTS development failed to deliver on time. Data from some subjects were recorded on paper-based CRF without using the CTS at all. From these subjects' point of view, the CTS development totally failed.

One of the many advantages of this new SDM is that phases and work flows can be followed easily so that PMs can coordinate the CTS development effectively and efficiently. It is therefore not necessary to have members from the sponsor side to assume the role of PM; engineers or primary investigators can also be the PM, too. On the contrary, the CTS experiences of PM may become a major roadblock in a conventional SDM. As aforementioned, the risk of CTS development is high if it adopts agile methods and is supervised by an inexperienced PM. Similarly, the CTS experiences of engineers can reduce the risk of failure, but it is no longer a necessary condition because the activities are well defined and, as addressed earlier, the major risks of CTS development come from its unique properties rather than the experiences of its developers.

The results of the case study show that the proposed SDM outperforms conventional SDMs in many ways. First, the proposed SDM has the advantages of both the plan-oriented methods and agile methods. On one side, activities and phases in the proposed SDM are well planned, defined, and easily followed as in plan-oriented methods. On the other side, the proposed SDM maintains the flexibility to respond to specification changes as in a typical agile method. Second, the proposed SDM specifically discards the guidelines/principles suggested by both plan-oriented methods and agile methods which are unrelated to or violate CTS properties. Third, time is used as efficiently as possible in the new SDM to reduce the number of subjects needed to use the CTS alternative plan. Fourth, the flexibility of adopting a specific SDM for individual construction cycle is maintained. Engineers are allowed to adopt a familiar SDM, for example, the waterfall model, for a particular construction cycle for data collection and exportation to develop individual software components. Finally, the flexibility of a CT with multiple CTSs in different architecture is preserved. It is not necessary to have a CTS for all sites in the proposed SDM. Each CTS with different architecture can be implemented independently as long as the data exported to statistical software are considered acceptable by statisticians.

Based on the experiences of developing CTS with the proposed SDM, a few guidelines are proposed to reduce the risk of project failure. First, engineers should work closely with both the sponsors and the statisticians. Before the third phase is initialized, engineers must have a clear idea of what data will be collected and what data format will be used. At the exportation phase, engineers should provide data files in the formats the statisticians demand. For example, data in the same form with different visits can be exported differently (into one file or file per visit). Next, it is important to make sure that the engineers follow the proposed SDM and understand the unique properties of CTS beforehand. The sponsor cannot assume that the engineers who may have never participated in CTS development are familiar with the pathways as illustrated in Figure 4.

Handling late updates is always a challenge; that is, protocol changes after CTS is online. It may be rare but can happen. If the missing data are available in hospital records, the currently online CTS can still be used to enroll subjects. In the meantime, engineers should restart the activities in the second phase to retrieve necessary data. If the amended protocol requires data that are unavailable in hospital records, the data collected from enrolled subjects should be discarded and a new CTS development should start all over again.

5. Conclusion

Over half a century ago, software engineers recognized the importance of SDM and proposed several primitive and pioneering models like the code-and-fix and stage-wise model [51]. Since then, many SDMs were introduced, and the chance of successfully delivering quality software has been greatly improved by adopting a proper SDM. In this paper, the properties and patterns of developing a CTS are carefully examined. Based on these properties and patterns, a new SDM is proposed specifically for developing a CTS. The proposed SDM is verified in a large-scale real-world case. Results show that the advantages of plan/risk-driven and agile methods for CTS development are preserved by this new SDM. With the proposed SDM, project managers' and engineers' experience with CTS development is no longer a necessary condition. This SDM increases the successful rate of delivering quality software on time within budget and reduces the risk of the project. Moreover, it benefits both parties of software development because the sponsor/project managers can gain more control of software development and the developers can focus on software engineering. With a high quality software, data collection, management, and analysis can be more efficient, accurate, and less expensive. Consequently, the overall quality of a clinical trial can be significantly improved.

As for future works, more case studies of CTS developments can be performed with the proposed SDM. Research teams with recourses can apply the proposed SDM with an existing SDM on a same CTS development at the same time as the experiment group and control group, respectively, to compare the results.

References

[1] R. Tiruvoipati, S. P. Balasubramanian, G. Atturu, G. J. Peek, and D. Elbourne, "Improving the quality of reporting randomized controlled trials in cardiothoracic surgery: the way forward," *Journal of Thoracic and Cardiovascular Surgery*, vol. 132, no. 2, pp. 233–240, 2006.

[2] US FDA, "Final rule for good laboratory practice regulations," *Federal Register*, vol. 52, pp. 33768–33782, 1987.

[3] R. D. Kush, P. Bleicher, W. R. Kubick et al., *eClinical Trials: Planning and Implementation*, Thomson CenterWatch, Boston, Mass, USA, 2003.

[4] L. Clivio, A. Tinazzi, S. Mangano, and E. Santoro, "The contribution of information technology: towards a better clinical data management," *Drug Development Research*, vol. 67, no. 3, pp. 245–250, 2006.

[5] T. H. Payne and G. Graham, "Managing the life cycle of electronic clinical documents," *Journal of the American Medical Informatics Association*, vol. 13, no. 4, pp. 438–445, 2006.

[6] T. Schleyer, H. Spallek, and P. Hernández, "A qualitative investigation of the content of dental paper-based and computer-based patient record formats," *Journal of the American Medical Informatics Association*, vol. 14, no. 4, pp. 515–526, 2007.

[7] T. J. Kuhn, "The difference between eDC and eCRF," http://tjkuhn.wordpress.com/2008/03/14/the-difference-between-edc-and-ecrf.

[8] G. Nahler, *Dictionary of Pharmaceutical Medicine*, Springer, New York, NY, USA, 2009.

[9] B. Ene-Iordache, S. Carminati, L. Antiga et al., "Developing regulatory-compliant electronic case report forms for clinical trials: experience with the demand trial," *Journal of the American Medical Informatics Association*, vol. 16, no. 3, pp. 404–408, 2009.

[10] I. Pavlovic, T. Kern, and D. Miklavcic, "Comparison of paper-based and electronic data collection process in clinical trials: costs simulation study," *Contemporary Clinical Trials*, vol. 30, pp. 300–316, 2009.

[11] R. Kush, L. Alschuler, R. Ruggeri et al., "Implementing single source: the STARBRITE proof-of-concept study," *Journal of the American Medical Informatics Association*, vol. 14, no. 5, pp. 662–673, 2007.

[12] D. Kim, S. Labkoff, and S. H. Holliday, "Opportunities for electronic health record data to support business functions in the pharmaceutical industry–A case study from Pfizer, Inc.," *Journal of the American Medical Informatics Association*, vol. 15, no. 5, pp. 581–584, 2008.

[13] K Yamamoto, S. Matsumoto, H. Tada et al., "A data capture system for outcomes studies that integrates with electronic health records: development and potential uses," *Journal of Medical Systems*, vol. 32, no. 5, pp. 423–427, 2008.

[14] Integrating the Healthcare Enterprise International. IHE IT Infrastructure Technical Framework Supplement—RFD supplement, http://www.ihe.net/Technical_Framework/upload/IHE_ITI_TF_Suppl_RFD_TI_2006_09_25.pdf.

[15] J. R. Deitzer, P. R. Payne, and J. B. Starren, "Coverage of clinical trials tasks in existing ontologies," in *AMIA Annual Symposium Proceedings*, p. 903, 2006.

[16] R. H. Dolin, L. Alschuler, S. Boyer et al., "HL7 clinical document architecture, release 2," *Journal of the American Medical Informatics Association*, vol. 13, no. 1, pp. 30–39, 2006.

[17] R. L. Richesson, J. E. Andrews, and J. P. Krischer, "Use of SNOMED CT to represent clinical research data: a semantic characterization of data items on case report forms in vasculitis research," *Journal of the American Medical Informatics Association*, vol. 13, no. 5, pp. 536–546, 2006.

[18] J. E. Andrews, R. L. Richesson, and J. Krischer, "Variation of SNOMED CT coding of clinical research concepts among coding experts," *Journal of the American Medical Informatics Association*, vol. 14, no. 4, pp. 497–506, 2007.

[19] M. W. Haber, B. W. Kisler, M. Lenzen, and L. W. Wright, "Controlled terminology for clinical research: a collaboration between CDISC and NCI enterprise vocabulary services," *Drug Information Journal*, vol. 41, no. 3, pp. 405–412, 2007.

[20] CDISC, http://www.cdisc.org/.

[21] T. Strasser and G. Lotz, "An integrated system for workflow and data management in clinical trials," *Investigative Ophthalmology & Visual Science*, vol. 49, E-Abstract 5216, 2008.

[22] US FDA, "21 CFR Part 11: electronic records; electronic signatures; final rule," *Federal Register*, vol. 62, no. 54, p. 13429, 1997.

[23] B. Boehm, "Get ready for agile methods, with care," *Computer*, vol. 35, no. 1, pp. 64–69, 2002.

[24] R. S. Pressman, *Software Engineering: A Practitioner's Approach (7/e)*, McGraw-Hill Inc., New York, NY, USA, 2009.

[25] W. Royce, "Managing the development of large software systems: concepts and techniques," in *Proceedings of the WESCON*, 1970.

[26] H. Mills, "Top-down programming in large systems," in *Debugging Techniques in Large Systems*, R. Ruskin, Ed., Prentice Hall, Upper Saddle River, NJ, USA, 1971.

[27] L. Bally, J. Brittan, and K. H. Wagner, "A prototype approach to information system design and development," *Information and Management*, vol. 1, no. 1, pp. 21–26, 1977.

[28] B. W. Boehm, "Spiral model for software development and enhancement," *Computer*, vol. 21, no. 5, pp. 61–72, 1988.

[29] J. Wood and D. Silver, *Joint Application Development*, Wiley, New York, NY, USA, 1995.

[30] I. Jacobson, G. Booch, and J. Rumbaugh, *The Unified Software Development Process*, Addison-Wesley, Boston, Mass, USA, 1999.

[31] J. Highsmith, *Agile Software Development Ecosystems*, Addison-Wesley, Reading, Mass, USA, 2002.

[32] IBM Rational Unified Process (RUP), http://www-01.ibm.com/software/awdtools/rup/.

[33] I. Jacobson, G. Booch, and J. Rumbaugh, *The Unified Software DevelopmentProcess*, Addison-Wesley, Boston, Mass, USA, 1999.

[34] G. Booch, J. Rumbaugh, and I. Jacobson, *The Unified Modeling Language User Guide*, Addison-Wesley, Reading, Mass, USA, 2nd edition, 2005.

[35] US FDA, "Running Clinical Trials," http://www.fda.gov/ScienceResearch/SpecialTopics/RunningClinicalTrials/default.htm.

[36] US FDA, 21 CFR Part 820: Quality System Regulation; 2007.

[37] Oracle Clinical, http://www.oracle.com/us/industries/life-sciences/clinical/overview/index.html.

[38] Java Platform, http://www.oracle.com/technetwork/java/javase/overview/index.html.

[39] Microsoft.Net, http://www.microsoft.com/net/.

[40] S. Bennett, M. Myatt et al., "Data Management for Surveys and Trials: A Practical Primer Using Epidata," http://www.epidata.dk/downloads/dmepidata.pdf.

[41] H. Mills, "Top-down programming in large systems," in *Debugging Techniques in Large Systems*, R. Ruskin, Ed., Prentice Hall, Upper Saddle River, NJ, USA, 1971.

[42] J. Mcdermid and P. Rook, *Software Development Process Models. Software Engineer's Reference Book*, CRC Press, 1993.

[43] L. Maciaszek, *Practical Software Engineering: A Case-Study Approach (8/e)*, Addison-Wesley, Reading, Mass, USA, 2004.

[44] I. Sommerville, *Software Engineering (8/e)*, Addison-Wesley, Reading, Mass, USA, 2006.

[45] B. Boehm, A. Egyed, J. Kwan, D. Port, A. Shah, and R. Madachy, "Using the WinWin spiral model: a case study," *Computer*, vol. 31, no. 7, pp. 33–44, 1998.

[46] Agile Alliance. Manifesto for Agile Software Development, 2001.

[47] B. Boehm and R. Turner, "Using risk to balance agile and plan-driven methods," *Computer*, vol. 36, no. 6, pp. 57–66, 2003.

[48] B. Boehm, *Turner. Balancing Agility and Discipline—A Guide for the Perplexed*, Addison-Wesley, Reading, Mass, USA, 2004.

[49] S. R. Schach, *Object-Oriented and Classical Software Engineering (7/e)*, McGraw-Hill, Boston, Mass, USA, 2006.

[50] A. Silberschatz, H. Korth, and S. Sudarshan, *Database System Concepts (6/e)*, McGraw-Hill, Boston, Mass, USA, 2010.

[51] H. Benington, "Production of large computer programs," in *Proceedings of the Symposium on Advanced Programming Methods for Digital Computers*, pp. 15–27, 1956.

9

Clustering Methodologies for Software Engineering

Mark Shtern and Vassilios Tzerpos

Department of Computer Science and Engineering, York University, Toronto, ON, Canada M3J 1P3

Correspondence should be addressed to Mark Shtern, mark@cse.yorku.ca

Academic Editor: Letha Hughes Etzkorn

The size and complexity of industrial strength software systems are constantly increasing. This means that the task of managing a large software project is becoming even more challenging, especially in light of high turnover of experienced personnel. Software clustering approaches can help with the task of understanding large, complex software systems by automatically decomposing them into smaller, easier-to-manage subsystems. The main objective of this paper is to identify important research directions in the area of software clustering that require further attention in order to develop more effective and efficient clustering methodologies for software engineering. To that end, we first present the state of the art in software clustering research. We discuss the clustering methods that have received the most attention from the research community and outline their strengths and weaknesses. Our paper describes each phase of a clustering algorithm separately. We also present the most important approaches for evaluating the effectiveness of software clustering.

1. Introduction

Software clustering methodologies group entities of a software system, such as classes or source files, into meaningful subsystems in order to help with the process of understanding the high-level structure of a large and complex software system. A software clustering approach that is successful in accomplishing this task can have significant practical value for software engineers, particularly those working on legacy systems with obsolete or nonexistent documentation.

Research in software clustering has been actively carried out for more than twenty years. During this time, several software clustering algorithms have been published in the literature [1–8]. Most of these algorithms have been applied to particular software systems with considerable success.

There is consensus between software clustering researchers that a software clustering approach can never hope to cluster a software system as well as an expert who is knowledgeable about the system [9]. Therefore, it is important to understand how good a solution created by a software clustering algorithm is. The research community has developed several methods to assess the quality of software clustering algorithms [10–14].

In this paper, we present a review of the most important software clustering methodologies that have been presented in the literature. We also outline directions for further research in software clustering, such as the development of better software clustering algorithms or the improvement and evaluation of existing ones.

The structure of the paper is as follows. Section 2 presents three different applications of existing software clustering techniques in order to motivate the need for software clustering. An overview of the state of the art for software clustering algorithms is presented in Section 3. Section 4 classifies and presents the most prominent approaches for the evaluation of software clustering algorithms. Open research challenges related to software clustering are discussed in Section 5. Finally, Section 6 concludes the paper.

2. Software Clustering Applications

Before we present the technical aspects of software clustering in Section 3, we describe three distinct instances where existing software clustering techniques were used to solve important software engineering problems in the context of reflexion analysis, software evolution, and information recovery.

2.1. Reflexion Analysis.

The goal of reflexion analysis is to map components found in the source code onto the conceptual components defined in a hypothesized architecture. This mapping was originally established manually, which required a lot of work for large software systems [15]. Christl et al. [16] presented an approach, in which clustering techniques were applied to support the user in the mapping activity. They developed a semiautomated mapping technique that accommodates the automatic clustering of the source model with the user's hypothesized knowledge about the system's architecture. The role of software clustering was to identify concrete entities for which a mapping decision is "easy enough" to be made automatically. In addition, software clustering supports the user in manual mapping by detecting hypothesized entities that are likely to be the correct entity.

The authors have developed an application called HuGMe based on their concept. HuGMe has been applied successfully to extend partial maps of real-world software applications.

2.2. Software Evolution.

Software systems evolve through efforts to add new functionality, to correct existing faults, and to improve maintainability. Typically, software clustering tools attempt to improve the software structure (software restructuring) or to reduce the complexity of large modules (source code decoupling). Sometimes, software clustering can be used to help identify duplicate code [17]. In addition, software clustering is used to predict the fault proneness of software modules [18].

Software restructuring is a form of perfective maintenance that modifies the structure of a program's source code. Its goal is increased maintainability to better facilitate other maintenance activities, such as adding new functionality to or correcting previously undetected errors within a software system.

Lung et al. [19] presented a case study whose goal was to decouple two subsystems in order to reduce development time of new functionality. The goal of software clustering was to identify related components in the software system. The authors compared the produced software clustering output with the software design and detected a gap between the conceptual model and the actual design. After detailed investigation of the gap between both views, a problem with the conceptual model was identified. A new design was developed. The new design significantly improved the coupling of the software system.

The motivation of source code decoupling is to help reduce the complexity of complex modules or functions. The complexity of a module or a function is determined based on software metrics. Xu et al. [17] have presented a case study where software clustering is applied for source code decoupling at the procedure level. Software clustering attempts to group related statements together to produce a dependency rank between the groups. The authors suggest to divide a module or a function according to the result of software clustering. To help reverse engineers, the authors developed a user interface that displays the output of software clustering and the existing structure of the function being analyzed. This visualization tool allows easy identification of ill-structured and duplicated code.

2.3. Information Recovery.

The primary goal of reverse engineering is to recover components or to extract system abstractions. Several approaches and techniques, which are based on software clustering, have been proposed in the literature to support information recovery from a software system.

We present two case studies that focus on module and architecture recovery. We select module and architecture recovery because these methods focus on different abstraction levels. We consider module recovery a lower level of abstraction than architecture recovery.

Module recovery software clustering methods focus on discovering modules by analyzing dependencies extracted from the software system, such as function calls. A typical example of module recovery is Robert Schwanke's Arch tool that helps a software engineer to understand a software system by producing a decomposition of the system into subsystems [20]. Schwanke's clustering heuristic is based on the principle of maximizing the cohesion of procedures placed in the same module, while, at the same time, minimizing the coupling between procedures that reside in different modules.

The architecture recovery methods focus on discovering the system architecture by analyzing abstractions extracted from the source code, such as components (modules), subsystems, and design patterns. A typical example of architecture recovery is that presented by Bauer and Trifu [21]. They recover architecture based on clustering information about design patterns. Design patterns are used to identify architectural clues—small structural patterns that provide information to allow for a rating of the dependencies found between entities. These clues are used by software clustering to produce the final system decomposition.

As can be seen from the above examples of applying software clustering, it is an important technique that can be used to solve important problems.

3. Software Clustering

We now present the state of the art of software clustering research. We do so in the context of the more general framework of cluster analysis.

Cluster analysis is a group of multivariate techniques whose primary purpose is to group entities based on their attributes. Entities are classified according to predetermined selection criteria, so that similar objects are placed in the same cluster. The objective of any clustering algorithm is to sort entities into groups, so that the variation between clusters is maximized relative to variation within clusters.

The typical stages of cluster analysis techniques are as follows:

(1) fact extraction (Section 3.1),

(2) filtering (Section 3.2),

(3) similarity computation (Section 3.3),

(4) cluster creation (Section 3.4),

(5) results visualization (Section 3.5),

(6) user feedback collection (Section 3.6).

The process typically repeats until satisfactory results are obtained.

We discuss each stage in detail in the following.

3.1. Fact Extraction. Before applying clustering to a software system, the set of entities to cluster needs to be identified. Entity selection depends on the objective of the method. For example, for program restructuring at a fine-grained level, function call statements are chosen as entities [17]. When the software clustering method applies to design recovery problems [22–25], the entities are often software modules. Classes [21] or routines [26] can also be chosen as the entities.

After entities have been identified, the next phase is attribute selection. An attribute is usually a software artefact, such as a package, a file, a function, a line of code, a database query, a piece of documentation, or a test case. Attributes may also be high-level concepts that encompass software artefacts, such as a design pattern. An entity may have many attributes. Selecting an appropriate set of attributes for a given clustering task is crucial for its success.

Most often, software artefacts are extracted directly from the source code, but sometimes artefacts are derived based on other kinds of information, such as binary modules, software documentation. Most studies extract artefacts from various sources of input and store them in a language-independent model [27]. These models can then be examined and manipulated to study the architecture of the software being built. For instance, FAMIX [28] is used to reverse engineer object-oriented applications; its models include information about classes, methods, calls, and accesses. We often refer to these models as *factbases*.

The Tuple Attribute Language (TA) is a well-known format for recording, manipulating, and diagramming information that describes the structure of large systems. The TA information includes nodes and edges in the graph and attributes of these nodes and edges [29]. It is also capable of representing typed graphs (graphs that can have more than one type of edge). Therefore, the TA language is not limited to recording only the structure of large systems. It can also express facts that are gathered from other sources.

The Dagstuhl Middle metamodel [30], GXL [31], MDG [32], and RSF [33] are other examples of factbase formats.

The Knowledge Discovery Metamodel (KDM) [34] from the Object Management Group (OMG) can also be used for this purpose. KDM is a common intermediate representation for existing software systems and their operating environments, that defines common meta-data required for deep

semantic integration of Application Lifecycle Management tools. It can also be viewed as an ontology for describing the key aspects of knowledge related to the various facets of enterprise software.

In the following, we present the most common inputs for the artefact extraction process.

3.1.1. Source Code. Source code is the most popular input for fact extraction. Many researchers [21, 32, 35] are using the source code as the only trusted foundation for uncovering lost information about a software system.

There are two conceptual approaches to extracting facts from source code: syntactic and semantic. The syntactic (structure-based) approaches focus on the static relationships among entities. The exported facts include variable and class references, procedure calls, use of packages, association and inheritance relationships among classes.

Semantic approaches [36] include all aspects of a system's domain knowledge. The domain knowledge information present in the source code is extracted from comments, identifier names [37].

Syntactic approaches can be applied to any software system, whereas semantic approaches usually need to be customized to a specific software system due to domain specific assumptions, since two terms may be related in one domain knowledge and unrelated in another. For instance, stocks and options are related in a financial application and unrelated in a medical application. Knowledge spreading in the source code and absence of a robust semantic theory are other drawbacks of semantic approaches. However, the output from semantic approaches tends to be more meaningful than the one from syntactic approaches.

The software clustering community widely adopts structure-based approaches for large systems. In many cases the boundary between these approaches is not strict. Some clustering methodologies try to combine the strengths of both syntactic and semantic methods. The ACDC algorithm is one example of this mixed approach [9].

3.1.2. Binary Code. Some approaches work with the information available in binary modules. Depending on compilation and linkage parameters, the binary code may contain information, such as a symbol table that allows efficient fact extraction. This approach has three advantages.

(1) It is language independent.

(2) Binary modules are the most accurate and reliable information (source code may have been lost or mismatched to a product version of binary modules. Source mismatch situations occur because of human mistakes, patches, and intermediate/unreleased versions that are working in the production environment, etc.).

(3) Module dependency information is easy to extract from binary modules (linkage information contains module dependency relations).

The main drawbacks of this approach are that binary metadata information depends on building parameters and that the implementation of the approach is compiler/hardware dependent. Also, binary code analysis cannot always discover all relationships. In particular, the Java compiler erases type parameter information and resolvs references to final static fields of primitive types (constants) [38].

The binary code analysis method has been explored by the SWAG group [39]. SWAG has developed a fact extractor for Java called Javex. The output of the Java compiler is p-code. Javex is capable of extracting facts from the p-code and storing the facts using the TA format. Other researchers extracting information from bytecode are Lindig and Snelting [4] and Korn et al. [40]. An interesting concept of collecting information about a software system is presented by Huang et al. [41]. Their approach collects facts from components. Components developed for frameworks such as CORBA/CCM, J2EE/EJB, COM+. include interface information that can be easily extracted and explored.

Unfortunately, extraction tools based on source or binary code information cannot extract all facts about software systems. For instance, they cannot extract facts related to run-time characteristics of the software system. In addition, configuration information of component-based software systems, that are implemented and executed with the help of some common middleware (e.g., J2EE, COM+, ASP.NET), is unavailable because it is stored in middleware configuration files that are not part of the source or binary code of the software system. This configuration information is important because it includes declaration of required resources, security realm and roles, and component names for runtime binding. Therefore, while the source and binary code contains important information about a software system, it does not contain the complete information about the system.

3.1.3. Dynamic Information. Static information is often insufficient for recovering lost knowledge since it only provides limited insight into the runtime nature of the analyzed software; to understand behavioural system properties, dynamic information is more relevant [42]. Some information recovery approaches use dynamic information alone [43, 44], while others mix static and dynamic knowledge [8, 42, 45].

During the run-time of a software system, dynamic information is collected. The collected information may include the following.

(1) Object construction and destruction.

(2) Exceptions/errors.

(3) Method entry and exit.

(4) Component interface invocation.

(5) Dynamic type information.

(6) Dynamic component names.

(7) Performance counters and statistics:

    (a) number of threads,

    (b) size of buffers,

    (c) number of network connections,

    (d) CPU and memory usage,

    (e) number of component instances,

    (f) average, maximum, and minimum response time.

There are various ways of collecting dynamic information, such as instrumentation methods or third-party tools (debuggers, performance monitors). Instrumentation techniques are based on introducing new pieces of code in many places to detect and log all collected events. Such techniques are language dependent and not trivial to apply. The biggest concern with these techniques is ensuring that the newly generated software system has the same run-time behaviour as the original one. One option for implementing this approach is based on the Java Probekit [46]. Probekit is a framework on the Eclipse Platform that you can use to write and use probes. Probes are Java code fragments that can be inserted into a program to provide information about the program as it runs. These probes can be used to collect run-time events needed for dynamic analysis. An alternative way to collect run-time information is to use debugger-based solutions [43, 47, 48]. One advantage of using debuggers is that the source code remains untouched. Unfortunately, debugger information may not be sufficient to record the same aspects of the software system as instrumentation techniques. Also, some of the compilers cannot generate correct debug information when source code optimizations are enabled.

Today, managed runtime environments such as .NET and J2EE are popular paradigms. A virtual runtime environment allows gathering run-time information without modification of the source code. For instance, VTune analyzer [49] uses an industry standard interface in the JVM, the JVMPI (JVM Profiling Interface), for gathering Java-specific information. This interface communicates data regarding memory locations and method names of JIT (just-in-time) emitted code, calls between Java methods, symbol information, and so forth.

Performance monitors allow the collection of statistical information about software systems such as CPU, memory usage, and size of buffers. That information may uncover interesting behaviour relationships between software components.

Unfortunately, neither dynamic nor static information contains the whole picture of a software system. For instance, design information and historical information are not part of any input discussed so far.

3.1.4. Physical Organization. The physical organization of applications in terms of files, folders, packages, and so forth often represents valuable information for system understanding [50]. Physical organization is not limited to the software development structure. It may also include the deployment structure and build structure. The deployment structure often follows industrial standards. Therefore, the location of a specific module provides valuable information about its responsibilities.

It is important to consider the physical organization of the software system because it often reflects the main ideas of the system design.

3.1.5. Human Organization.
Human organization often reflects the structure of the system. Usually a developer is responsible for associated components. According to Conway, "Organizations which design systems are constrained to produce designs which are copies of the communication structures of these organizations" [51].

3.1.6. Historical Information.
Historical information explains the evolution of a software product. Recently, more research [52–54] using historical information to reveal software design has appeared. Historical information is collected from version management systems, bug tracking systems, release notes, emails, and so forth. Software evolution contains valuable information for the solution of the software understanding problem [55]. For example, release notes contain a lot of valuable knowledge about product features and product releases.

Unfortunately, it is usually difficult to automatically/ semiautomatically recover important system knowledge from historical sources due to the size and the lack of formatting of the extracted information.

3.1.7. Software Documentation.
Software documents contain a lot of helpful information about software systems. However, they cannot be entirely trusted since they are often outdated or unsynchronized [9, 56]. Facts extracted from software documents may not reflect the current state of the system. Therefore, the extracted facts should be validated with the current system. Hassan and Holt [57] present such an approach. The idea of the method is to collect information about a software system from existing documentation and domain knowledge. The gathered information is then verified against the current stage of the software implementation.

3.1.8. Persistent Storage.
Persistent repositories, such as databases, and output files, contain information that can be helpful for software understanding. Developers often attempt to understand a software system by analyzing the application repositories. Software clustering methods should be able to utilize this information to their advantage as well [58].

3.1.9. Human Expertise.
Humans may provide valuable facts based on their knowledge of requirement documents, high-level design, and other sources.

Every input source has different advantages and disadvantages. Even though the end result of the clustering process will likely improve if the input factbase contains information from different sources [59], the mixing of information from various sources is a challenging problem [23].

After the extraction process is finished, a filtering step may take place to ensure that irrelevant facts are removed, and the gathered facts are prepared for the clustering algorithm.

3.2. Filtering.
The filter phase is the final stage of preparing a factbase. The main goal of this stage is to discard unnecessary information, calculate facts that are a composition of existing facts, and apply a weighting scheme to the attributes.

For instance, all meaningless words extracted from source comments are discarded during the filter step [37]. In an ideal situation, the factbase should be small and consist of enough information to ensure meaningful clustering.

The information contained in the final factbase may be dependent on assumptions of a specific software clustering algorithm. Some algorithms expect that the factbase includes only relations between modules [25]; other algorithms do not make any assumptions about the facts [24].

The software research community most often applies the following filters:

(1) utility module processing,

(2) granularity projection.

These filters process the collected factbase and discard unnecessary information. The study presented in [60] shows that using a different methodology for the construction of the final factbase may affect results significantly.

This discovery emphasizes the importance of preparing the final factbase. Several tools have been developed that allow fact manipulation. For instance, Grok [29] is specifically developed for the manipulation of facts extracted from a software system. Other methods utilize SQL [61] or Prolog [21] for fact manipulations.

3.2.1. Utility Module Processing.
In many cases, modules containing utilities do not follow common design practices, such as high cohesion and low coupling. For example, utility modules may include drivers, commonly used methods. As a result, utilities may require special treatment. Some software clustering algorithms are not affected by utilities [24]; others, such as Bunch [62], may be affected [56]. Some authors have argued that removing utilities improves the overall results [1]. Others suggest considering utilities as a class that should be kept for further investigation, because it plays an important role in the implementation of the overall solution by allowing communication between other classes [56]. Therefore, the research community has not reached a conclusion about the best approach to dealing with utilities.

In cases where the software clustering method is affected by utilities, a utility filter should be applied. Such a filter identifies utilities based on the facts present in the factbase. There are different ways to do this. Hamou-Lhadj et al. [63] identified utilities as classes that have many direct client classes. Wen and Tzerpos [64] present a utility module detection method where a module is identified as a utility if it is connected to a large number of subsystems (clusters) rather than entities.

3.2.2. Granularity Projection.
A large number of software clustering algorithms attempt to cluster only course-grained software entities, such as modules or classes, rather than more fine-grained ones, such as functions or variables. However, facts extracted from software systems often contain

dependencies only between the fine-grained software entities.

The goal of a granularity projection filter is to use such low-level facts, such as function calls or variable references, in order to calculate dependencies between classes, and then remove the low-level facts from the factbase in order to retain facts only about the entities to be clustered. For instance, only classes and their dependencies might remain in the factbase after such a filter has been applied.

After the final factbase is constructed, the next step is to compute similarities.

3.3. Similarity Computation. Most software clustering methods initially transform a factbase to a data table, where each row describes one entity to be clustered. Each column contains the value for a specific attribute. Table 1 presents an example of a data table. It contains information about file-to-file relationships, where each entity and each attribute are files of the software system. The values of the attributes are calculated based on the dependencies between the files. In this example, file $f1.c$ depends on file $f3.c$ (possibly by calling a function in $f3.c$), while file $f3.c$ does not depend on $f1.c$.

In most cases, a different column corresponds to a different attribute. Sometimes, different columns contain information about related attributes. For example, categorical attributes (a categorical attribute is an attribute with a finite number of values (in practice, a *small* number of *discrete* values, such as developer names) and no inherent ranking) are often represented as a composition of multiple binary attributes [24]. Table 2 is an example of such a situation. It is an extension of Table 1 with a new categorical attribute representing developer names.

Categorical data can be represented in compact form as well. Table 3 is an example of compact form representation of the same data as in Table 2.

Clustering algorithms are based on a similarity function between entities [65]. However, some algorithms, such as hierarchical agglomerative ones, are applying the similarity function explicitly, while others, such as search-based algorithms, are using the similarity function only implicitly.

The most common type of similarity functions is resemblance coefficients. Other similarity functions include probabilistic measures and software-specific similarities.

3.3.1. Resemblance Coefficients. The input data matrix for a resemblance coefficient may contain different types of data, such as binary, numerical, categorical, or mixed. In the following, we discuss the most well-known resemblance coefficients developed for each one of these types of data.

Binary Resemblance. The intuition behind the calculation of resemblance coefficients is to measure the amount of relevant matches between two entities. In other words, the more relevant matches there are between two entities, the more similar the two entities are. There are different methods for counting relevant matches, and many formulas exist

TABLE 1: Data table example.

	$f1.c$	$f2.c$	$f3.c$
$f1.c$	1	1	1
$f2.c$	0	1	0
$f3.c$	0	0	1

TABLE 2: Categorical attribute presented as binary data.

	$f1.c$	$f2.c$	$f3.c$	Alice	Bob
$f1.c$	1	1	1	1	0
$f2.c$	0	1	0	0	1
$f3.c$	0	0	1	1	0

TABLE 3: Categorical attribute in compact form.

	$f1.c$	$f2.c$	$f3.c$	Developer
$f1.c$	1	1	1	Alice
$f2.c$	0	1	0	Bob
$f3.c$	0	0	1	Alice

TABLE 4: Examples of binary resemblance coefficients.

Similarity measure	Formula
Simple matching coefficient	$\dfrac{a+d}{a+b+c+d}$
Jaccard coefficient	$\dfrac{a}{a+b+c}$
Sorenson coefficient	$\dfrac{2a}{2a+b+c}$
Rogers and Tanimoto	$\dfrac{a+d}{a+2(b+c)+d}$
Russel and Rao	$\dfrac{a}{a+b+c+d}$

to calculate resemblance coefficients [66–68]. Some well-known examples are given in Table 4. In these formulas, a represents the number of attributes that are "1" in both entities, b and c represent the number of attributes that are "1" in one entity and "0" in the other, and d represents the number of attributes that are "0" in both entities.

A binary resemblance coefficient that is suitable for software clustering will ideally include the following two properties.

(1) 0-0 matches are ignored; that is, d is not part of the formula. The joint lack of attributes between two entities should not be counted toward their similarity [60].

(2) Heavier weight is assigned to more important factors [69].

A binary resemblance coefficient that fits these software clustering assumptions is the Sorenson coefficient [60]. Research [70] concludes that Jaccard and Sorenson have performed well, but the authors recommend using the Jaccard algorithm because it is more intuitive.

Categorical Resemblance. There are similarities between binary and categorical resemblance coefficients. The calculation of a categorical resemblance coefficient, similar to that of a binary resemblance coefficient, is based on the number of matches between two entities. When categorical attributes are represented as a set of binary attributes, then the calculation of the categorical coefficient is based on the calculation of the binary resemblance coefficient. When categorical attributes are represented in compact form, then the categorical coefficient is calculated based on the simple matching formula (See Table 4).

Numerical Resemblance. Numerical resemblance coefficients calculate distance between entities. Each entity is represented as a vector. For instance, entity $f1.c$ from Table 1 can be represented as vector $(1, 1, 1)$. Its distance to other vectors can be calculated using formulas such as

(1) Euclidean: $\sqrt{\sum_{i=1}^{n}((x_i - y_i)^2)}$,

(2) Maximum: $\max |x_i - y_i|$,

(3) Manhattan: $\sum_{i=1}^{n}(|x_i - y_i|)$.

Mixed Resemblance. An entity in the data table may be described by more than one type of attributes. At the same time, some values in the data table may be missing. For those cases, the widely used general similarity coefficient was developed by Gower [71]. Let x and y denote two entities and describe over d attributes. Then, the general similarity coefficient $S_{\text{Gower}}(x, y)$ is defined as

$$S_{\text{Gower}}(x, y) = \frac{1}{\sum_{k=1}^{d} w(x_k, y_k)} \sum_{k=1}^{d} w(x_k, y_k) s(x_k, y_k), \quad (1)$$

where $s(x_k, y_k)$ is a similarity component for the kth attribute and $w(x_k, y_k)$ is either one or zero, depending on whether or not a comparison is valid for the kth attribute of the entities.

3.3.2. Probabilistic Measures.

Probabilistic measures are based on the idea that agreement on rare matches contributes more to the similarity between two entities than agreement on more frequent ones [72]. The probabilistic coefficients require the distribution of the frequencies of the attributes present over the set of entities. When this distribution is known, a measure of information or entropy can be computed for each attribute. Entropy is a measure of disorder; the smaller the increase in entropy when two (sets of) entities are combined is, the more similar the two entities are. For a more detailed discussion on probabilistic coefficients, we refer to [73].

3.3.3. Software-Specific Similarity.

There are also similarity functions that have been developed specifically for the software clustering problem. Schwanke [74] introduced the notion of using design principles, such as low coupling and high cohesion. Koschke [75] has developed an extension of Schwanke's metric-based hierarchical clustering technique. The Koschke similarity functions include global declarations,

function calls. Also, the similarity method is considering name similarities between identifiers and filenames. Choi and Scacchi [2] also describe a similarity function based on maximizing the cohesiveness of clusters.

3.4. Cluster Creation.

At this point, all preparation steps are completed, and the clustering algorithm can start to execute. In this section, we discuss various software clustering algorithms. Wiggerts [72] suggests the following classification of software clustering algorithms:

(1) graph-theoretical algorithms,

(2) construction algorithms,

(3) optimization algorithms,

(4) hierarchical algorithms.

3.4.1. Graph-Theoretical Algorithms.

This class of algorithms is based on graph properties. The nodes of such graphs represent entities, and the edges represent relations. The main idea is to identify interesting subgraphs that will be used as basis for the clusters. Types of subgraphs that can be used for this purpose include connected components, cliques, and spanning trees. The two most common types of graph-theoretical clustering algorithms are aggregation algorithms and minimal spanning tree algorithms.

Aggregation algorithms reduce the number of nodes (representing entities) in a graph by merging them into aggregate nodes. The aggregates can be used as clusters or can be the input for a new iteration resulting in higher-level aggregates.

Common graph reduction techniques are the notion of the neighbourhood of a node [76], strongly connected components [77], and bicomponents [77].

Minimal spanning tree (MST) algorithms begin by finding an MST of the given graph. Next, they either interactively join the two closest nodes into a cluster or split the graph into clusters by removing "long" edges. The classic MST algorithm is not suited for software clustering due to the fact that the algorithm tends to create a few large clusters that contain many entities while several other entities remain separate [78]. Bauer and Trifu [21] suggest a two-pass modified MST algorithm. The first pass, which follows the classic MST concept, iteratively joins the two closest nodes into a cluster while the second pass assigns the remaining unclustered entities to the cluster they are the "closest" to.

3.4.2. Construction Algorithms.

The algorithms in this category assign the entities to clusters in one pass. The clusters may be predefined (supervised) or constructed as part of the assignment process (unsupervised). Examples of construction algorithms include the so-called geographic techniques and the density search techniques. A well-known geographic technique is the bisection algorithm, which at each step divides the plain in two and assigns each entity according to the side that it lies on.

An algorithm based on fuzzy sets was presented in [79]. An ordering is defined on entities determined by their grade of membership (defined by the characteristic function of the fuzzy set). Following this order, each entity is either assigned to the last initiated cluster or it is used to initiate a new cluster, depending on the distance to the entity which was used to initiate the last initiated cluster.

Mode analysis [80] is another example of a construction clustering algorithm. For each entity, it computes the number of neighbouring entities that are "closer" than a given radius. If this number is large enough, then the algorithm clusters the entities together.

3.4.3. Optimization Algorithms.

An optimization or improvement algorithm takes an initial solution and tries to improve this solution by iterative adaptations according to some heuristic. The optimization method has been used to produce both hierarchical [81] and nonhierarchical [82] clustering.

A typical nonhierarchical clustering optimization method starts with an initial partition derived based on some heuristic. Then, entities are moved to other clusters in order to improve the partition according to some criteria. This relocating goes on until no further improvement of this criterion takes place. Examples of clustering optimization methods are presented in [83, 84].

One of the famous representatives of the optimization class of algorithms is ISODATA [85]. Its effectiveness is based on the successful initial choice of values for seven parameters that control factors such as the number of expected clusters, the minimum number of objects in the cluster, and the maximum number of iterations. The algorithm then proceeds to iteratively improve on an initial partition by joining and splitting clusters, depending on how close to the chosen parameters the actual values for the current partition are.

Other optimization algorithms can be classified in four categories presented in detail below: genetic, hill-climbing, spectral, and clumping techniques.

Genetic clustering algorithms are randomized search and optimization techniques guided by the principles of evolution and natural genetics, having a large amount of implicit parallelism. Genetic algorithms are characterized by attributes, such as the objective function, the encoding of the input data, the genetic operators, such as crossover and mutation, and population size.

A typical genetic algorithm runs as follows.

(1) Select a random population of partitions.

(2) Generate a new population by selecting the best individuals according to the objective function and reproducing new ones by using the genetic operations.

(3) Repeat step (2) until a chosen stop criterion is satisfied.

Doval et al. [86] present a schema for mapping the software clustering problem to a genetic problem. The quality of a partition is determined by calculating a modularization quality function. There are several ways for the calculation of modularization quality. In general, the modularization quality measures the cohesion of clusters and their coupling.

The result of the algorithm is a set of clusters for which an optimal modularization quality was detected, in other words, clusters that feature an optimal tradeoff between coupling and cohesion. The Doval et al. genetic algorithm has been implemented as part of the Bunch software clustering tool [87].

Shokoufandeh et al. claim that the genetic Bunch algorithm is especially good at finding a solution quickly, but they found that the quality of the results produced by Bunch's hill-climbing algorithms is typically better [88].

Seng et al. proposed an improved software clustering genetic algorithm [89] based on Falkenauer's class of genetic algorithms [90]. According to the author, the algorithm is more stable than Bunch, and its objective function evaluates additional quality properties of the system's decomposition, such as individual subsystem size.

Hill-Climbing clustering algorithms perform the following steps.

(1) Generate a random solution.

(2) Explore the neighbourhood of the solution attempting to find a neighbour better than the solution. Once a neighbour is found, it becomes the solution.

(3) Repeat step (2) until there is no better neighbour.

Hill-climbing search methods have been successfully employed in various software clustering algorithms [83]. Mitchell's Ph.D. dissertation [32] shows promising results in terms of the quality and performance of hill-climbing search methods. His approach has been implemented as part of the Bunch software clustering tool [91, 92].

Bunch starts by generating a random partition of the module dependency graph. Then, entities from the partition are regrouped systematically by examining neighbouring partitions in order to find a better partition. When an improved partition is found, the process repeats; that is, the found partition is used as the basis for finding the next improved partition. The algorithm stops when it cannot find a better partition. The objective function is the modularization quality function used also in Bunch's genetic algorithm. Mahdavi et al. spresent an improvement to existing hill-climbing search approaches based on applying a hill-climbing algorithm multiple times. The proposed approach is called multiple hill climbing [22]. In this approach, an initial set of hill-climbing searches is performed. The created partitions are used to identify the common features of each solution. These common features form building blocks for a subsequent hill climb. The authors found that the multiple hill-climbing approach does indeed guide the search to higher peaks in subsequent executions.

Spectral clustering algorithms operate as follows.

(1) Build the Laplacian matrix corresponding to the system's dependency graph.

(2) Determine the dominant eigenvalues and eigenvectors of the Laplacian matrix.

(3) Use these to compute the clustering.

Some researchers have adapted spectral graph partitioning to the decomposition of software systems [88, 93]. This is based on a construction graph that represents relations between entities in the explored system. Spectral clustering algorithms are recursive. Each iteration splits the graph to two subgraphs and calculates the new value of the objective function. The recursion terminates as soon as the objective function stops improving.

First, the Laplacian matrix is calculated, and the smallest nonzero eigenvalue is found. This value will be used for the calculation of the characteristic vector (the characteristic vector is a n-dimensional vector $(x_1, \ldots, x_n)$ that defines two clusters. Entities whose x_i is 0 belong in the first cluster, entities whose x_i is 1 belong in the second cluster), which is used to partition the graph. The graph is divided into subgraphs based on the values of the characteristic vector. The algorithm uses the entries of the characteristic vector to split the entities so that the break-point maximizes the goal function. If the bisection improves the objective function, then the algorithm goes to the next iteration by splitting each sub-graph obtained in the previous step recursively. If splitting does not improve the solution, then the algorithm stops.

Xanthos [93] developed a spectral software clustering method that guarantees that the constructed partition is within a known factor of the optimal solution. The objective function used is the same as in the Bunch algorithms.

Finally, another form of algorithms that perform optimization is the so-called *clumping techniques* [72]. In each iteration, one cluster is identified. Repeated iterations discover different clusters (or clumps) which may overlap. A negative aspect of this method is that finding the same clump several times cannot be avoided completely.

3.4.4. Hierarchical Algorithms. There are two categories of hierarchical algorithms: agglomerative (bottom-up) and divisive (top-down).

Divisive algorithms start with one cluster that contains all entities and divide the cluster into a number (usually two) of separate clusters at each successive step. Agglomerative algorithms start at the bottom of the hierarchy by iteratively grouping similar entities into clusters. At each step, the two clusters that are most similar to each other are merged, and the number of clusters is reduced by one.

According to [94], divisive algorithms offer an advantage over agglomerative algorithms because most users are interested in the main structure of the data which consists of a few large clusters found in the first steps of divisive algorithms. Agglomerative algorithms start with individual entities and work their way up to large clusters which may be affected by unfortunate decisions in the first steps. Agglomerative hierarchical algorithms are most widely used however. This is because it is infeasible to consider all possible divisions of the first large clusters [72].

Agglomerative algorithms perform the following steps [95].

(1) Compute a similarity matrix.

(2) Find the two most similar clusters and join them.

(3) Calculate the similarity between the joined clusters and others obtaining a reduced matrix.

(4) Repeat from step (2) until two clusters are left.

The above process implies that there is a way to calculate the similarity between an already formed cluster and other clusters/entities. This is done via what is called the update rule function. Suppose that cluster i and cluster j are joined to form cluster ij. Typical update rule functions are

(1) single linkage: $\text{sim}(ij, k) = \min(\text{sim}(i, k), \text{sim}(j, k))$,

(2) complete linkage: $\text{sim}(ij, k) = \max(\text{sim}(i, k), \text{sim}(j, k))$,

(3) average linkage: $\text{sim}(ij, k) = (1/2)[\text{sim}(i, k) + \text{sim}(j, k)]$.

Maqbool and Babri [95] has concluded that for software clustering, the complete linkage update rule gives the most cohesive clusters. The same work introduced a new update rule called weighted combined linkage that provided better results than complete linkage. This result was achieved by applying the unbiased Ellenberg measure [95] and utilizing information regarding the number of entities in a cluster that accesses an artefact, thereby substantially reducing the number of arbitrary decisions made during the algorithm's clustering process.

UPGMA (Unweighted Pair Group Method with Arithmetic mean) [66] is an agglomerative hierarchical method used in bioinformatics for the creation of phylogenetic trees. Lung et al. [60] have shown applications of the UPGMA method in the software clustering context.

Andritsos and Tzerpos [24] presented the Scalable Information Bottleneck (LIMBO) algorithm, an agglomerative hierarchical algorithm that employs the Agglomerative Information Bottleneck algorithm (AIB) for clustering. LIMBO uses an information loss measure to calculate similarity between entities. At every step, the pair of entities that would result in the least information loss is chosen.

ACDC [96] is a hierarchical clustering algorithm that does not follow a standard schema. It cannot be assigned to the agglomerative or divisive category because the algorithm does not have an explicit iterative split or merge stage. ACDC uses patterns that have been shown to have good program comprehension properties to determine the system decomposition. ACDC systematically applies these subsystem patterns to the software structure. This results in most of the modules being placed into hierarchical categories (subsystems). Then, ACDC uses an orphan adoption algorithm [97] to assign the remaining modules to the appropriate subsystem.

We have discussed various algorithms and similarity techniques that have been adapted to the software clustering context.

An important observation is that there are two different conceptual approaches to developing a software clustering methodology. The first one attempts to develop a sophisticated structure discovery approach such as ACDC and Bunch. The second approach concentrates more on developing similarity functions [74, 75]. An important open research question is the following: which approach is the most promising for the future of software clustering?

3.5. Results Visualization. The output of the cluster discovery stage needs to be presented in a user friendly manner. The challenge is to present a large amount of data with its relations in such a way that a user can understand and easily work with the data. The presentation of software clustering results is an open research question that is related to scientific visualization (the computer modeling of raw data) and human-computer interaction.

The software reverse engineering community has developed various tools for the presentation of the output of software clustering. These often include the traditional software representation of a graph. Such tools include CodeCrawler [98], Rigi [33], and LSEdit [39]. Rigi and LSEdit allow manual modification of the clustering result.

A different research direction is to develop visualizations of software systems by using metaphors and associations. For instance, Code City [99] is a 3D visualization tool that uses the City metaphor to visualize software systems. It is an integrated environment for software analysis, in which software systems are visualized as interactive, navigable 3D cities. The classes are represented as buildings in the city, while the packages are depicted as the districts in which the buildings reside. The visible properties of the city artefacts depict a set of chosen software metrics.

A reverse engineer will understand the output produced by a software clustering method better if the visualization techniques improve. Once a user has understood the clustering results, they may be able to provide feedback that can be used to refine method parameters. Therefore, effective visualization of results opens the way for the development of interactive software clustering algorithms where a user can iteratively assess the current results and steer the software clustering process. This concept is described in the next section.

3.6. Feedback. During the clustering process, an expert user should be able to instruct the tool on how to improve the overall solution. Clustering algorithms that are able to process user feedback are called semiautomatic clustering algorithms. Christl et al. [16] present a semiautomatic algorithm that allows the mapping of hypothesized high-level entities to source code entities. Koschke [75] created a semiautomatic clustering framework based on modified versions of the fully automatic techniques he investigated. The goal of Koschke's framework is to enable a collaborative session between his clustering framework and the user. The clustering algorithm does the processing, and the user validates the results.

Semiautomatic cluster analysis algorithms are more complicated than the fully automatic ones. They produce results that are closer to the expectations of the user than those of fully automatic methods. This is both an advantage and a disadvantage. A software engineer may explore different aspects of the software system by validating clustering results and providing feedback to the semiclustering algorithm. On the other hand, the result of a semiautomatic clustering algorithm may not reflect the actual state of the software system, because in many cases the software engineer may have wrong or incomplete understanding of the current state of the system. This drawback may explain the fact that the reverse engineering research community is mostly developing automatic clustering algorithms.

4. Evaluation of Clustering Algorithms

Software clustering researchers have developed several evaluation methods for software clustering algorithms. This research is important because of these reasons.

(1) Most software clustering work is evaluated based on case studies. It is important that the evaluation technique is not subjective.

(2) Evaluation helps discover the strengths and weaknesses of the various software clustering algorithms. This enables the improvement of the algorithms by eliminating or alleviating the effect of the weaknesses.

(3) Evaluation can help indicate the types of system that are suitable for a particular algorithm. For instance, Mitchell and Mancoridis [12] think that Bunch [92] may not be suitable for event-driven systems.

The importance of evaluating software clustering algorithms was first stated in 1995 by Lakhotia and Gravley [100]. Since then, many approaches to this problem have been published in the literature. These can be divided in two categories depending on whether they rely on the existence of an *authoritative decomposition*, that is, a decomposition of the software system at hand into meaningful subsystems that has been constructed by an expert in this system, for example, the system architect or a senior developer. In contrast, we refer to decompositions created by software clustering algorithms as *automatic decompositions*.

Section 4.1 presents software clustering evaluation approaches that require an authoritative decomposition, while Section 4.2 discusses approaches that are independent of the existence of an authoritative decomposition.

4.1. Evaluation Based on Authoritative Decomposition. Before presenting the various approaches that have been presented in the literature to assess the similarity between automatic and authoritative decompositions, it is important to point out a crucial fact regarding such software clustering evaluation methods.

Different experts on the same software system may construct distinct software decompositions, since a software system may have several equally valid decompositions. In other words, an authoritative decomposition must be considered as one of many possible decompositions that can help understand a software system. As a result, clustering researchers should evaluate their approaches against all available authoritative decompositions. Furthermore, it is important to remember that evaluation results against a given authoritative decomposition are applicable only in the context of this particular authoritative decomposition, rather than being universally applicable.

With this caveat in mind, we present two orthogonal classifications of evaluation approaches that utilize authoritative decompositions.

The first classification depends on whether the approach considers only the two decompositions, that is, an automatic and an authoritative one or more aspects of the software system. Most evaluation methods do consider only the two decompositions.

However, some methods focus on the evaluation of a specific stage of the software clustering process. Such a method calculates the quality of a specific stage based on analysis of its inputs and outputs. For instance, an evaluation method that focuses on the evaluation of the analysis phase will take into account the input data model, compare the authoritative decomposition and the produced software clustering decomposition, and then calculate a number that reflects the quality of the produced decomposition. A typical example of such a method is EdgeSim [101].

The main reason for the development of both types of evaluation methods is that the quality of a produced decomposition depends on the

(1) selection of an appropriate clustering algorithm—a different clustering algorithm produces different outputs from the same factbase,

(2) selection of input parameters—a clustering algorithm might produce different outputs depending on selected input parameters, such as similarity function or input data model.

An orthogonal classification of software clustering evaluation methods depends on whether the decompositions compared are *nested* or not. Most evaluation approaches assume a *flat* decomposition, that is, one where no clusters are contained within other clusters. A small number of approaches deal with nested decompositions: the END framework [11] that allows for the reuse of flat evaluation approaches for nested decompositions without loss of information and the UpMoJo algorithm presented below.

The rest of this section presents the most prominent approaches for the comparison of an automatic decomposition to an authoritative one.

4.1.1. MoJo Family. Tzerpos and Holt developed a distance measure called MoJo [10]. It attempts to capture the distance between two decompositions as the minimum number of Move and Join operations that need to be performed in order to transform one decomposition into the other. A Move operation involves relocating a single entity from one cluster to another (or to a new cluster), while a Join operation takes two clusters and merges them into a single cluster. MoJo distance is nonsymmetric.

Wen and Tzerpos [102] presented an algorithm that calculates MoJo distance in polynomial time. They also introduced the MoJoFM effectiveness measure which is based on MoJo distance but produces a number in the range

0–100 which is independent of the size of the decompositions [103].

UpMoJo distance is an extension of MoJo distance so that it applies to nested decompositions [104]. An Up operation is added that allows entities to move to higher levels of the containment hierarchy, for example, from a cluster that is contained within other clusters to a top-level cluster.

4.1.2. Precision/Recall. Precision and Recall are standard metrics in Information Retrieval. They have been applied to the evaluation of software clustering by Anquetil and Lethbridge [13]. The method calculates similarity based on measuring intrapairs, which are pairs of entities that belong to the same cluster. The authors suggest to calculate precision and recall for a given partition as follows.

(i) *Precision.* Percentage of intrapairs proposed by the clustering method, which are also intrapairs in the authoritative decomposition.

(ii) *Recall.* Percentage of intra pairs in the authoritative decomposition, which are also intra pairs in the decomposition proposed by the clustering method.

Mitchell and Mancoridis [12] explain a drawback of the Precision/Recall metrics: "An undesirable aspect of Precision/Recall is that the value of this measurement is sensitive to the size and number of clusters."

4.1.3. Koschke and Eisenbarth. Koschke and Eisenbarth [14] have presented a way of quantitatively comparing automatic and authoritative partitions that establishes corresponding clusters (Good match), handles partially matching clusters (OK match), tolerates smaller divergences, and determines an overall recall rate. Their approach is as follows.

(1) Identify immediately corresponding clusters (Good match).

(2) Identify corresponding subclusters, that is, where part of a cluster of one partition corresponds to part of a cluster in the other partition (OK match).

(3) Measure accuracy of the correspondences between two partitions.

This metric has two drawbacks:

(1) it does not penalize the software clustering algorithm when an automatic decomposition is more detailed than the authoritative one,

(2) the recall rate does not distinguish between a Good match and an OK match.

The authors have also developed benchmark scenarios for the evaluation of software clustering and the calibration of software clustering parameters.

4.1.4. EdgeSim and MeCl. Mitchell and Mancoridis [101] developed the first method for the evaluation of a software clustering algorithm in conjunction with an input data model. They introduced a similarity (EdgeSim) and a distance (MeCl) measurement that considers relations between entities as an important factor for the comparison of software system decompositions. The EdgeSim similarity measurement normalizes the number of intra and intercluster edges that agree between two partitions. The MeCl similarity measurement determines the distance between a pair of partitions by first calculating the "clumps," which are the largest subset of modules from both partitions that agree with respect to their placement into clusters. Once the clumps are determined, a series of Merge operations are performed to convert the first partition into the second one. The actual MeCl distance is determined by normalizing the number of Merge operations.

Unfortunately, these two measures can be applied only when the input data model is a dependency graph. Another drawback of the method is the assumption that the authoritative decomposition is a direct reflection of the dependencies in the factbase. It is difficult to confirm that this assumption holds because the system expert that has constructed the authoritative decomposition has certainly used additional knowledge that may contradict this assumption. Wen and Tzerpos [105] explain the main drawback of EdgeSim and MeCl: "it only considers the misplacement of edges without considering the misplacement of the objects in the wrong clusters."

4.2. Evaluation Methods Not Based on an Authoritative Decomposition. The main drawback of methods that require an authoritative decomposition is that they assume that such a decomposition exists. To construct such a decomposition for a middle-size software system is a challenging task. Various research studies [14, 101, 106] deal with the construction of an authoritative decomposition. This work addresses two questions:

(1) what is the right process for the construction of an authoritative decomposition?

(2) why is the constructed decomposition authoritative?

Lakhotia and Gravley [100] said, "If we know the subsystem classification of a software system, then we do not need to recover it." Another aspect of the problem is that after a researcher constructs an authoritative decomposition, they may find out that the authoritative decomposition cannot be used for evaluation purposes. For instance, if the authoritative decomposition is flat then it is not suitable to evaluate algorithms that produce nested decompositions. Finally, a software system may have a number of different authoritative decompositions.

To overcome these problems several evaluation methods that evaluate a software clustering approach based solely on its output have been developed [13, 107]. Wu et al. [107] suggest comparing software clustering algorithms based on two criteria:

(1) stability,

(2) extremity of cluster distribution.

4.2.1. Stability. Stability reflects how sensitive is a clustering approach to perturbations of the input data. Raghavan [108] has shown the importance of developing such a metric. The intuition behind stability in software clustering is that similar clustering decompositions should be produced for similar versions of a software system. A stability function measures the percentage of changes between produced decompositions of successive versions of an evolving software system. Under conditions of small changes between consecutive versions, an algorithm should produce similar clustering [107].

Tzerpos and Holt [109] define a stability measure based on the ratio of the number of "good" decompositions to the total number of decompositions produced by a clustering algorithm. A decomposition, which is obtained from a slightly modified software system, is defined as "good" if and only if the MoJo distance between the decomposition and the decomposition obtained from the original software system is not greater than 1% of the total number of entities.

Wu et al. [107] argued that a drawback of the aforementioned stability measure is that 1% seems too optimistic in reality. In the same paper, the authors suggest a relative stability measure. This measure allows one to say that one algorithm is more stable than another with regard to a software system. To calculate the relative score of two clustering algorithms, the authors suggest constructing sequences of MoJo values calculated based on comparing two consecutive members of the sequence of decompositions obtained from a software system. Then, based on the two sequences of MoJo values, a number is calculated that represents a relative score of one algorithm over the other.

4.2.2. Extremity of Cluster Distribution. An interesting property of a clustering algorithm is the size of the clusters it produces. The cluster size distribution of a clustering algorithm should not exhibit extremity. In other words, a clustering algorithm should avoid the following situations.

(1) The majority of files are grouped into one or few huge clusters.

(2) The majority of clusters are singletons.

Wu et al. [107] presented a measure called NED (nonextreme distribution) that allows to evaluate the extremity of a cluster distribution. NED is defined as the ratio of the number of entities contained in nonextreme clusters to the total number of the entities.

Anquetil and Lethbridge [13] have investigated the causes of extreme cluster distribution. They found that poor input data model and unsuitable similarity metrics can cause such results. For instance, the majority of the clusters being singletons are a sign of a bad descriptive attribute. A reason that the majority of files are grouped into one or few huge clusters is a consequence of an ill-adapted algorithm or similarity metric.

The main drawback of both presented methods is that they can only identify "bad" software decompositions. It is easy to develop an algorithm that produces decompositions that are stable and nonextreme, while being entirely useless for program understanding purposes.

Mitchell and Mancoridis [12] developed a framework called CRAFT for the evaluation of software clustering algorithms without authoritative decomposition. The proposed evaluation process consists of two phases. The first phase is the construction of an authoritative decomposition. The CRAFT framework automatically creates an authoritative decomposition based on common patterns produced by various clustering algorithms. The initial step of the process is to cluster the target system many times using different clustering algorithms. For each clustering run, all the modules that appear in the same cluster are recorded. Using this information, CRAFT exposes common patterns in the results produced by different clustering algorithms, and it constructs an authoritative decomposition. The assumption of the approach is that agreement across a collection of clustering algorithms should reflect the underlying structure of the software system.

The second phase is to compare the created authoritative decomposition with the automatic decomposition by applying an evaluation method that requires an authoritative decomposition. The advantage of CRAFT is that it is applicable when an authoritative decomposition does not exist. The main drawback of the method is that the automatically produced authoritative decomposition may be unacceptable according to a software expert. It can only be as good as the algorithms it utilized.

We presented an overview of the important methods for the evaluation of software clustering algorithms. Most methods require an authoritative decomposition (either flat or nested). Methods that do not require an authoritative decomposition can be used to weed out bad clustering results, that is, to select appropriate parameters for the clustering algorithms.

5. Research Challenges

Having presented the state of the art of software clustering methods, we go on to discuss open research challenges in software clustering. We have selected research questions that are related to the following topics:

(1) attribute gathering,
(2) cluster discovery,
(3) visualization of results,
(4) user feedback,
(5) evaluation of clustering algorithms.

Before we present each topic in detail, we bring attention to the current situation with software clustering tools. The research community has shown many advantages to using software clustering methods in different software engineering areas. Unfortunately, software clustering methodologies are not widely accepted in the industrial environment. There is still a long way to go before software clustering methods become an effective and integral part of the IDE [58]. For that to happen, existing tools must become easier to install, more robust, and significantly more user-friendly in terms of the presentation and manual adjustment of clustering results.

5.1. Fact Extraction. We discussed various input sources for the attribute gathering process. Typically, a clustering method will utilize only one of these sources, such as source or binary code. However, it is possible to construct input metamodels that combine information from different sources [27]. The reason this does not happen more often in practice is the lack of an established methodology. Such a methodology has to answer various questions including the following.

(1) Is it important to mix various sources? How important is a good metamodel?

(2) Which source(s) contain(s) the most important information?

(3) What is an effective way to represent artefacts gathered from various input sources in the same format in one meta-model? In other words, we have to define a language that allows the expression of an artefact extracted from any input source.

(4) What is a reasonable weight scheme for artefacts combined from various sources? Does it vary based on factors such as the type of system or its development methodology?

(5) What are other input sources for extraction of artefacts that could be integrated into the input meta-model?

These are the key questions for the attribute gathering stage. The answers to those questions would allow the development of a good meta-model, which should result in better clustering results. In addition, these answers would allow the research community to merge their efforts to develop a common methodology for gathering attributes. Today, efforts are split on developing advanced methods for extracting data from specific input sources.

5.2. Cluster Discovery. The cluster discovery process encompasses both the similarity computing and cluster creation phases. It is a complicated process that has been discussed in many research studies. Still, several key questions remain unanswered. We present a list of as yet unsolved problems that pose interesting challenges to researchers in the area.

(1) The best direction towards improving this process needs to be determined. As mentioned earlier, the cluster discovery process can be improved by developing a new software clustering algorithm or developing a new resemblance coefficient technique. What is a better way to improve the cluster discovery process is an open question. Since this question is open, the research community is splitting its efforts by developing both software clustering algorithm and resemblance coefficient techniques instead of focusing on one or the other.

(2) Several software clustering algorithms and resemblance coefficient techniques have been developed. Therefore, selecting a software clustering algorithm and a suitable resemblance coefficient is a challenging

task. A comparative study tested on a number of systems is long overdue. It is possible that particular combinations of clustering algorithms with resemblance coefficients are better suited for a particular type of software system. A categorization of algorithms based on the types of software for which they work best would be beneficial to the software field.

(3) The decomposition of a software system into subsystems is a typical task of a reverse engineer. A software clustering method can produce a nested decomposition, typically, based on the output of a hierarchical algorithm. Currently, there is no optimization-based software clustering algorithm that can produce a nested decomposition. We know that optimization algorithms can efficiently construct flat decompositions of a software system. It would be worth investigating whether an optimization algorithm would be an efficient algorithm for extracting a nested decomposition from a software system as well.

(4) Since a particular software system may have various valid decompositions, the output of a software clustering algorithm is often not meaningful to a software engineer. To overcome this problem, some software clustering algorithms assign labels for each cluster. Label assignment is a challenging task, and it is undeveloped in the context of software clustering. The problem is that software clustering algorithms either do not assign labels or assign labels based on simplistic rules. The development of an advanced method for label assignment would be beneficial to the field.

5.3. Results Visualization. As presented earlier, the visualization of results is a challenging problem because often the results of software clustering methods are large decompositions. Therefore, it is complicated to develop a user interface, which is capable of presenting a software decomposition in a meaningful way to a software engineer. In addition, the user interface is supposed to allow navigation through software decomposition results and to link the decomposition to source files, documentation, and so forth. Software clustering methods would be more useful if the visualization of the results of the software clustering was improved.

5.4. User Feedback. The importance of developing semiautomatic clustering algorithms was discussed earlier in this paper. There are two main obstacles to developing advanced semiautomatic clustering algorithms. The first one is the lack of a user interface that allows the users to understand and evaluate the clustering results. The second and more important obstacle is that the results of the semiautomatic algorithm may not reflect the current state of the software system because it is driven by the user whose knowledge of the software system is often incomplete. We think that it is important to develop criteria that allow the algorithm to disregard wrong user feedback. When such criteria have been established, then the research community will be able

to pay more attention to semiautomatic software clustering algorithms.

5.5. Evaluation. Evaluation of software clustering algorithms has already been studied from various aspects, but still there are uncharted research areas including the following.

(1) Each clustering approach uses a different set of evaluation measures from the several measurements that have been presented in the literature. Consequently, we cannot compare evaluation results from different studies. To overcome this problem, the evaluation metrics have to be compared to each other. It is worth investigating whether certain metrics are correlated with each other for particular types of software systems.

(2) The research software community needs to define a standardized method of evaluating software clustering. This requires the collection of reference software systems. This collection has to contain many different types of software systems. The construction of such a collection is complicated because it is difficult to find good candidates. Most research studies propose using big open source software systems as reference systems. However typically, a big software system includes several types of software paradigms (event-based, web services, etc.). Another challenge is that new software types constantly appear. Until now, no study has developed a deep theoretic justification for the construction of a collection of reference systems. The reference collection would help to define a standard way of comparing software clustering systems. In addition, it would allow better exploration of properties of existing software clustering methods and development of new more advanced methods.

(3) Most of the research work presented in the literature is about the evaluation of the complete software clustering process. Until now, there is no dedicated study to establish a method for the evaluation of a specific phase of the software clustering process. Such a study would be an important tool for the research community. It would allow reverse engineers to select an appropriate algorithm for their task.

6. Conclusion

This paper presented the state of the art in the development and evaluation of software clustering methodologies. We also outlined the most important research challenges for this important area of research. It should be apparent that while important advances have already taken place, there are still many avenues for further research that will benefit software engineers everywhere.

References

[1] H. A. Muller, M. A. Orgun, S. R. Tilley, and J. S. Uhl, "A reverse engineering approach to subsystem structure identification," *Journal of Software Maintenance*, vol. 5, pp. 181–204, 1993.

[2] S. C. Choi and W. Scacchi, "Extracting and restructuring the design of large systems," *IEEE Software*, vol. 7, no. 1, pp. 66–71, 1990.

[3] N. Anquetil and T. Lethbridge, "File clustering using naming conventions for legacy systems," in *Proceedings of the Conference of the Center for Advanced Studies on Collaborative research (CASCON '97)*, pp. 184–195, November 1997.

[4] C. Lindig and G. Snelting, "Assessing modular structure of legacy code based on mathematical concept analysis," in *Proceedings of the IEEE 19th International Conference on Software Engineering*, pp. 349–359, May 1997.

[5] R. W. Schwanke, R. Altucher, and M. A. Platoff, "Discovering, visualizing, and controlling software structure," in *Proceedings of the International Workshop on Software Specification and Design (IWSSD '89)*, pp. 147–150, IEEE Computer Society Press, 1989.

[6] J. F. Cui and H. S. Chae, "Applying agglomerative hierarchical clustering algorithms to component identification for legacy systems," *Information and Software Technology*, vol. 53, no. 6, pp. 601–614, 2011.

[7] Y. Wang, P. Liu, H. Guo, H. Li, and X. Chen, "Improved hierarchical clustering algorithm for software architecture recovery," in *Proceedings of the International Conference on Intelligent Computing and Cognitive Informatics (ICICCI '10)*, pp. 247–250, Kuala Lumpur, Malaysia, June 2010.

[8] C. Patel, A. Hamou-Lhadj, and J. Rilling, "Software clustering using dynamic analysis and static dependencies," in *Proceedings of the Software Maintenance and Reengineering (CSMR '09)*, pp. 27–36, IEEE Computer Society, Kaiserslautern, Germany, March 2009.

[9] V. Tzerpos, *Comprehension-Driven Software Clustering*, Ph.D. thesis, University of Toronto, Toronto, Canada, 2001.

[10] V. Tzerpos and R. C. Holt, "MoJo: a distance metric for software clusterings," in *Proceedings of the 6th Working Conference on Reverse Engineering (WCRE '99)*, pp. 187–193, October 1999.

[11] M. Shtern and V. Tzerpos, "A framework for the comparison of nested software decompositions," in *Proceedings of the 11th Working Conference on Reverse Engineering (WCRE '04)*, pp. 284–292, Delft, The Netherlands, November 2004.

[12] B. S. Mitchell and S. Mancoridis, "Craft: a framework for evaluating software clustering results in the absence of benchmark decompositions," in *Proceedings of the 8th Working Conference on Reverse Engineering (WCRE 2001)*, pp. 93–102, Suttgart, Germany, October 2001.

[13] N. Anquetil and T. C. Lethbridge, "Experiments with clustering as a software remodularization method," in *Proceedings of the 6th Working Conference on Reverse Engineering (WCRE '99)*, pp. 235–255, Atlanta, Ga, USA, October 1999.

[14] R. Koschke and T. Eisenbarth, "A framework for experimental evaluation of clustering techniques," in *Proceedings of the International Workshop on Program Comprehension (IWPC '00)*, pp. 201–210, Limerick, Ireland, June 2000.

[15] G. C. Murphy, D. Notkin, and K. Sullivan, "Software reflexion models: bridging the gap between source and high-level models," in *Proceedings of the 1995 3rd ACM SIGSOFT Symposium on the Foundations of Software Engineering*, pp. 18–27, October 1995.

[16] A. Christl, R. Koschke, and M. A. Storey, "Automated clustering to support the reflexion method," *Information and Software Technology*, vol. 49, no. 3, pp. 255–274, 2007.

[17] X. Xu, C.-H. Lung, M. Zaman, and A. Srinivasan, "Program restructuring through clustering techniques," in *Proceedings of the IEEE International Working Conference on Source Code Analysis and Manipulation (SCAM '04)*, pp. 75–84, IEEE Computer Society, Ottawa, Canada, September 2004.

[18] S. Zhong, T. M. Khoshgoftaar, and N. Seliya, "Analyzing software measurement data with clustering techniques," *IEEE Intelligent Systems*, vol. 19, no. 2, pp. 20–27, 2004.

[19] C. H. Lung, M. Zaman, and A. Nandi, "Applications of clustering techniques to software partitioning, recovery and restructuring," *Journal of Systems and Software*, vol. 73, no. 2, pp. 227–244, 2004.

[20] R. W. Schwanke, "An intelligent tool for re-engineering software modularity," in *Proceedings of the 13th International Conference on Software Engineering*, pp. 83–92, May 1991.

[21] M. Bauer and M. Trifu, "Architecture-aware adaptive clustering of OO systems," in *Proceedings of the 8th European Conference on Software Maintainance and Reengineering (CSMR '04)*, pp. 3–14, Tampere, Finland, March 2004.

[22] K. Mahdavi, M. Harman, and R. M. Hierons, "A multiple hill climbing approach to software module clustering," in *Proceedings of the19th IEEE International Conference on Software Maintenance (ICSM '03)*, p. 315, IEEE Computer Society, Amsterdam, The Netherlands, September 2003.

[23] C. Xiao and V. Tzerpos, "Software clustering based on dynamic dependencies," in *Proceedings of the Software Maintenance and Reengineering (CSMR '05)*, pp. 124–133, IEEE Computer Society, Manchester, UK, March 2005.

[24] P. Andritsos and V. Tzerpos, "Information-theoretic software clustering," *IEEE Transactions on Software Engineering*, vol. 31, no. 2, pp. 150–165, 2005.

[25] A. Shokoufandeh, S. Mancoridis, and M. Maycock, "Applying spectral methods to software clustering," in *Proceedings of the Working Conference on Reverse Engineering (WCRE '02)*, p. 3, IEEE Computer Society, Richmond, VA, USA, November 2002.

[26] G. Canfora, J. Czeranski, and R. Koschke, "Revisiting the delta IC approach to component recovery," in *Proceedings of the 7th Working Conference on Reverse Engineering (WCRE '00)*, p. 140, IEEE Computer Society, Brisbane, Australia, 2000.

[27] D. Pollet, S. Ducasse, L. Poyet, I. Alloui, S. Cîmpan, and H. Verjus, "Towards a process-oriented software architecture reconstruction taxonomy," in *Proceedings of the 11th European Conference on Software Maintenance and Reengineering (CSMR '07)*, pp. 137–148, Amsterdam, Netherlands, March 2007.

[28] S. Demeyer, S. Tichekaar, and S. Ducasse, "FAMIX 2.1—the FAMOOS information exchange model," Tech. Rep., University of Bern, Bern, Switzerland, 2001.

[29] R. C. Holt, "Structural manipulations of software architecture using Tarski relational algebra," in *Proceedings of the 1998 5th Working Conference on Reverse Engineering*, pp. 210–219, October 1998.

[30] T. C. Lethbridge, S. Tichelaar, and E. Ploedereder, "The Dagstuhl Middle Metamodel: a schema for reverse engineering," *Electronic Notes in Theoretical Computer Science*, vol. 94, pp. 7–18, 2004.

[31] R. C. Holt, A. Schürr, S. E. Sim, and A. Winter, "GXL: a graph-based standard exchange format for reengineering,"

Science of Computer Programming, vol. 60, no. 2, pp. 149–170, 2006.

[32] B. S. Mitchell, *A Heuristic Search Approach to Solving the Software Clustering Problem*, Ph.D. thesis, Drexel University, Philadelphia, Pa, USA, 2002, Adviser-Spiros Mancoridis.

[33] H. A. Muller, S. R. Tilley, and K. Wong, "Understanding software systems using reverse engineering technology perspectives from the Rigi project," in *Proceedings of the Conference of the Center for Advanced Studies on Collaborative research (CASCON '93)*, pp. 217–226, IBM Press, Ontario, Canada, 1993.

[34] J. Bézivin, F. Jouault, and P. Valduriez, "On the need for megamodels," in *Proceedings of the Workshop on Best Practices for Model-Driven Software Development at ACM Conference on Object-Oriented Programming, Systems, Languages & Applications (OOPSLA '04)*, Vancouver, British Columbia, Canada, October 2004.

[35] L. Tahvildari, R. Gregory, and K. Kontogianni, "An approach for measuring software evolution using source code features," in *Proceedings of the Asia-Pacific Software Engineering Conference*, p. 10, 1999.

[36] S. Kawaguchi, P. K. Garg, M. Matsushita, and K. Inoue, "MUDABlue: an automatic categorization system for open source repositories," in *Proceedings of the 11th Asia-Pacific Software Engineering Conference (APSEC '04)*, pp. 184–193, Busan, Korea, December 2004.

[37] A. Kuhn, S. Ducasse, and T. Gîrba, "Enriching reverse engineering with semantic clustering," in *Proceedings of the 12th Working Conference on Reverse Engineering (WCRE '05)*, pp. 133–142, Pittsburgh, Pa, USA, November 2005.

[38] J. Dietrich, V. Yakovlev, C. McCartiny, G. Jenson, and M. Duchrow, "Cluster analysis of Java dependency graphs," in *Proceedings of the 4th ACM Symposium on Software Visualization (SOFTVIS '08)*, pp. 91–94, Munich, Germany, September 2008.

[39] http://www.swag.uwaterloo.ca.

[40] J. Korn, Y. F. Chen, and E. Koutsofios, "Chava: reverse engineering and tracking of Java applets," in *Proceedings of the 6th Working Conference on Reverse Engineering (WCRE '99)*, pp. 314–325, October 1999.

[41] G. Huang, H. Mei, and F. Q. Yang, "Runtime recovery and manipulation of software architecture of component-based systems," *Automated Software Engineering*, vol. 13, no. 2, pp. 257–281, 2006.

[42] E. Stroulia and T. Systa, "Dynamic analysis for reverse engineering and program understanding," *ACM SIGAPP Applied Computing Review*, vol. 10, no. 1, pp. 8–17, 2002.

[43] R. J. Walker, G. C. Murphy, B. N. Freeman-Benson, D. Wright, D. Swanson, and J. Isaak, "Visualizing dynamic software system information through high-level models," in *Proceedings of the ACM SIGPLAN Conference on Object-Oriented Programming Systems, Languages & Applications (OOPSLA '98)*, pp. 271–283, Vancouver, Canada, 1998.

[44] H. Yan, D. Garlan, B. Schmerl, J. Aldrich, and R. Kazman, "DiscoTect: a system for discovering architectures from running systems," in *Proceedings of the 26th International Conference on Software Engineering (ICSE '04)*, pp. 470–479, Scotland, UK, May 2004.

[45] Q. Zhang, Q. Qiu, and L. Sun, "Objectoriented software architecture recovery using a new hybrid clustering algorithm," in *Proceedings of the International Conference on Fuzzy Systems and Knowledge Discovery (FSKD '10)*, vol. 6, pp. 2546–2550, Shandong, china, August 2010.

[46] http://www.eclipse.org/tptp/platform/documents/probekit//probekit.html.

[47] D. B. Lange and Y. Nakamura, "Object-oriented program tracing and visualization," *Computer*, vol. 30, no. 5, pp. 63–70, 1997.

[48] T. Systa, *Static and Dynamic Reverse Engineering Techniques for Java Software Systems*, Ph.D. thesis, Tampere University, Tampere, Finland, 2000.

[49] M. Dmitriev, "Profiling Java applications using code hotswapping and dynamic call graph revelation," *ACM SIGSOFT Software Engineering Notes*, vol. 29, no. 1, pp. 139–150, 2004.

[50] M. Lungu, M. Lanza, and T. Gîrba, "Package patterns for visual architecture recovery," in *Proceedings of the 10th European Conference on Software Maintenance and Reengineering (CSMR '06)*, pp. 185–194, Bari, Italy, March 2006.

[51] M. Conway, "How do committees invent," *Datamation*, vol. 14, no. 4, pp. 28–31, 1968.

[52] R. Wuyts, *A Logic Meta-Programming Approach to Support the Co-Evolution of Object-Oriented Design and Implementation*, Ph.D. thesis, Vrije Universiteit Brussel, Amsterdam, Netherlands, 2001.

[53] G. Canfora and L. Cerulo, "Impact analysis by mining software and change request repositories," in *Proceedings of the 11th IEEE International Software Metrics Symposium (METRICS '05)*, pp. 261–269, Como, Italy, September 2005.

[54] M. Fischer, M. Pinzger, and H. Gall, "Populating a release history database from version control and bug tracking systems," in *Proceedings of the International Conference on Software Maintenance*, pp. 23–32, Amsterdam, The Netherlands, September 2003.

[55] A. Hassan and R. Holt, "Studying the evolution of software systems using evolutionary code extractors," in *Proceedings of the InternationalWorkshop on Principles of Software Evolution (IWPSE '04)*, pp. 76–81, Kyoto, Japan, September 2004.

[56] N. Medvidovic and V. Jakobac, "Using software evolution to focus architectural recovery," *Automated Software Engineering*, vol. 13, no. 2, pp. 225–256, 2006.

[57] A. E. Hassan and R. C. Holt, "Reference architecture for web servers," in *Proceedings of the 7th Conference on Reverse Engineering (WCRE '00)*, pp. 150–159, November 2000.

[58] H. A. Muller, J. H. Jahnke, D. B. Smith, M.-A. D. Storey, S. R. Tilley, and K. Wong, "Reverse engineering: a roadmap," in *Proceedings of the Proceedings of International Conference on Software Engineering (ICSE '00)*, pp. 47–60, Limerick, Ireland, June 2000.

[59] B. Andreopoulos, A. An, V. Tzerpos, and X. Wang, "Clustering large software systems at multiple layers," *Information and Software Technology*, vol. 49, no. 3, pp. 244–254, 2007.

[60] C. H. Lung, M. Zaman, and A. Nandi, "Applications of clustering techniques to software partitioning, recovery and restructuring," *Journal of Systems and Software*, vol. 73, no. 2, pp. 227–244, 2004.

[61] D. M. German, D. Cubranic, and M.-A. D. Storey, "A framework for describing and understanding mining tools in software development," in *Proceedings of the International Workshop on Mining Software Repositories (MSR '05), Proceedings of the International Workshop on Mining software repositories*, pp. 1–5, ACM, Saint Louis, Mo, USA, July 2005.

[62] S. Mancoridis, B. Mitchell, Y. Chen, and E. Gansner, "Bunch: a clustering tool for the recovery and maintenanceof software system structures," in *Proceedings of the International Conference on Software Maintenance (ICSM '99)*, IEEE Computer Society Press, Oxford, UK, August 1999.

[63] A. Hamou-Lhadj, E. Braun, D. Amyot, and T. Lethbridge, "Recovering behavioral design models from execution traces," in *Proceedings of the Ninth European Conference on Software Maintenance and Reengineering (CSMR '05)*, pp. 112–121, Manchester, UK, March 2005.

[64] Z. Wen and V. Tzerpos, "Software clustering based on omnipresent object detection," in *Proceedings of the 13th International Workshop on Program Comprehension (IWPC '05)*, pp. 269–278, St. Louis, Mo, USA, May 2005.

[65] A. K. Jain and R. C. Dubes, *Algorithms for Clustering Data*, Prentice-Hall, Upper Saddle River, NJ, USA, 1988.

[66] H. C. Romesburg, *Clustering Analysis for Researchers*, Krieger, Melbourne, Fla, USA, 1990.

[67] R. Naseem, O. Maqbool, and S. Muhammad, "Improved similarity measures for software clustering," in *Proceedings of the Software Maintenance and Reengineering (CSMR '11)*, pp. 45–54, march 2011.

[68] R. Naseem, O. Maqbool, and S. Muhammad, "An improved similarity measure for binary features in software clustering," in *Proceedings of the 2nd International Conference on Computational Intelligence, Modelling and Simulation (CIMSim '10)*, pp. 111–116, Islamabad, Pakistan, September 2010.

[69] H. Dhama, "Quantitative models of cohesion and coupling in software," in *Proceedings of the Annual Oregon Workshop on SoftwareMetrics (AOWSM '95)*, pp. 65–74, Elsevier Science, June 1995.

[70] J. Davey and E. Burd, "Evaluating the suitability of data clustering for software remodularisation," in *Proceedings of the 7th Conference on Reverse Engineering (WCRE '00)*, pp. 268–276, November 2000.

[71] T. M. Lim and H. W. Khoo, "Sampling properties of Gower's general coefficient of similarity," *Ecology*, vol. 66, no. 5, pp. 1682–1685, 1985.

[72] T. A. Wiggerts, "Using clustering algorithms in legacy systems remodularization," in *Proceedings of the 4th Working Conference on Reverse Engineering*, pp. 33–43, October 1997.

[73] P. H. A. Sneath and R. R. Sokal, *Numerical Taxonomy: The Principles and Practice of Numerical Classification*, Series of books in biology, W. H. Freeman, Gordonsville, VA, USA, 1973.

[74] R. W. Schwanke, "An intelligent tool for re-engineering software modularity," in *Proceedings of the 13th International Conference on Software Engineering*, pp. 83–92, May 1991.

[75] R. Koschke, *Atomic Architectural Component Recovery for Program Understanding and Evolution*, Ph.D. thesis, Stuttgart University, Stuttgart, Germany, 2000.

[76] G. von Laszewski, May 1993, A collection of graph partitioning algorithms:Simulated annealing, simulated tempering, kemighan lin, two optimal, graph reduction, bisection.

[77] R. A. Botafogo and B. Shneiderman, "Identifying aggregates in hypertext structures," in *Proceedings of the ACM Hypertext and Hypermedia*, pp. 63–74, ACM Press, NewYork, NY, USA, 1991.

[78] A. Trifu, *Using Cluster Analysis in the Architecture Recovery of Object-Oriented Systems*, M.S. thesis, University of Karlsruhe, Karlsruhe, Germany, 2001.

[79] I. Gitman and M. D. Levine, "An algorithm for detecting unimodal fuzzy sets and Its application as a clustering technique," *IEEE Transactions on Computers*, vol. C-19, no. 7, pp. 583–593, 1970.

[80] D. Wishart, "Mode Analysis: a generalization of nearest neighbour which reduces chaining effects," in *Numerical Taxonomy*, N. Taxonomy, Ed., pp. 282–311, Academic Press, New York, NY, USA, 1969.

[81] R. Lutz, "Evolving good hierarchical decompositions of complex systems," *Journal of Systems Architecture*, vol. 47, no. 6, pp. 613–634, 2001.

[82] A. S. Mamaghani and M. R. Meybodi, "Clustering of software systems using new hybrid algorithms," in *Proceedings of the IEEE 9th International Conference on Computer and Information Technology (CIT '09)*, pp. 20–25, Xiamen, China, October 2009.

[83] J. Clarke, J. J. Dolado, M. Harman et al., "Reformulating software engineering as a search problem," *IEE Proceedings*, vol. 150, no. 3, pp. 161–175, 2003.

[84] K. Praditwong, "Solving software module clustering problem by evolutionary algorithms," in *Proceedings of the 8th International Joint Conference on Computer Science and Software Engineering (JCSSE '11)*, pp. 154–159, Pathom, Thailand, May 2011.

[85] M. R. Anderberg, *Cluster Analysis for Applications*, Academic Press, New York, NY, USA, 1973.

[86] D. Doval, S. Mancoridis, and B. Mitchell, "Automatic clustering of software systems using a genetic algorithm," in *Proceedings of the Software Technology and Engineering Practice (STEP '99)*, pp. 73–81, Pittsburgh, PA , USA, August 1999.

[87] B. S. Mitchell and S. Mancoridis, "On the automatic modularization of software systems using the bunch tool," *IEEE Transactions on Software Engineering*, vol. 32, no. 3, pp. 193–208, 2006.

[88] A. Shokoufandeh, S. Mancoridis, T. Denton, and M. Maycock, "Spectral and meta-heuristic algorithms for software clustering," *Journal of Systems and Software*, vol. 77, no. 3, pp. 213–223, 2005.

[89] O. Seng, M. Bauer, M. Biehl, and G. Pache, "Searchbased improvement of subsystem decompositions," in *Proceedings of the Conference on Genetic and Evolutionary Computation (GECCO '05)*, pp. 1045–1051, ACM Press, Washington, DC, USA, June 2005.

[90] P. de Lit, E. Falkenauer, and A. Delchambre, "Grouping genetic algorithms: an efficient method to solve the cell formation problem," *Mathematics and Computers in Simulation*, vol. 51, no. 3-4, pp. 257–271, 2000.

[91] B. Mitchell and S. Mancoridis, "Using heuristic search techniques to extract design abstractions from source code," in *Proceedings of the Conference on Genetic and Evolutionary Computation (GECCO '02)*, New York, NY, USA, July 2002.

[92] S. Mancoridis, B. Mitchell, C. Rorres, Y. Chen, and E. Gansner, "Using automatic clustering to produce high-level system organizations of source code," in *Proceedings of the International Workshop on Program Comprehension (IWPC '98)*, IEEE Computer Society Press, Ischia , Italy, Junuary1998.

[93] S. Xanthos, 2006, Clustering Object-Oriented Software Systems using Spectral Graph Partitioning.

[94] L. Kaufman and P. J. Rousseeuw, *Finding Groups in Data: An Introduction to Cluster Analysis*, John Wiley, New York, NY, USA, 1990.

[95] O. Maqbool and H. A. Babri, "The weighted combined algorithm: a linkage algorithm for software clustering," in *Proceedings of the European Conference on Software Maintainance and Reengineering (CSMR '04)*, pp. 15–24, Tampere, Finland, March 2004.

[96] V. Tzerpos and R. C. Holt, "ACDC: an algorithm for comprehension-driven clustering," in *Proceedings of the 7th Conference on Reverse Engineering (WCRE '00)*, pp. 258–267, November 2000.

[97] V. Tzerpos and R. C. Holt, "Orphan adoption problem in architecture maintenance," in *Proceedings of the 4th Working Conference on Reverse Engineering*, pp. 76–82, October 1997.

[98] M. Lanza and S. Ducasse, "Polymetric views—a lightweight visual approach to reverse engineering," *IEEE Transactions on Software Engineering*, vol. 29, no. 9, pp. 782–795, 2003.

[99] R. Wettel and M. Lanza, "Program comprehension through software habitability," in *Proceedings of the International Conference on Program Comprehension (ICPC '07)*, pp. 231–240, Banff, Canada, June 2007.

[100] A. Lakhotia and J. M. Gravley, "Toward experimental evaluation of subsystem classification recovery techniques," in *Proceedings of the 2nd Working Conference on Reverse Engineering*, pp. 262–269, July 1995.

[101] B. S. Mitchell and S. Mancoridis, "Comparing the decompositions produced by software clustering algorithms using similarity measurements," in *Proceedings of the IEEE International Conference on Software Maintenance (ICSM '01)*, pp. 744–753, Florence, Italy, November 2001.

[102] Z. Wen and V. Tzerpos, "An optimal algorithm for MoJo distance," in *Proceedings of the International Workshop on Program Comprehension (IWPC '03)*, pp. 227–235, Portland, Ore, USA, May 2003.

[103] Z. Wen and V. Tzerpos, "An effectiveness measure for software clustering algorithms," in *Proceedings of the 12th International Workshop on Program Comprehension (IWPC '04)*, pp. 194–203, Bari, Italy, June 2004.

[104] M. Shtern and V. Tzerpos, "Lossless comparison of nested software decompositions," in *Proceedings of the 14th Working Conference on Reverse Engineering (WCRE '07)*, pp. 249–258, Vancouver, Canada, October 2007.

[105] Z. Wen and V. Tzerpos, "Evaluating similarity measures for software decompositions," in *Proceedings of the International Conference on Software Maintenance (ICSM '04)*, pp. 368–377, IEEE Computer Society, Chicago Ill, USA, September 2004.

[106] J. F. Girard and R. Koschke, "Comparison of abstract data types and objects recovery techniques," *Science of Computer Programming*, vol. 36, no. 2, pp. 149–181, 2000.

[107] J. Wu, A. E. Hassan, and R. C. Holt, "Comparison of clustering algorithms in the context of software evolution," in *Proceedings of the International Conference on SoftwareMaintenance (ICSM '05)*, pp. 525–535, IEEE Computer Society, Budapest, Hungary, September 2005.

[108] V. V. Raghavan, "Approaches for measuring the stability of clustering methods," *SIGIR Forum*, vol. 17, no. 1, pp. 6–20, 1982.

[109] V. Tzerpos and R. C. Holt, "On the stability of software clustering algorithms," in *Proceedings of the InternationalWorkshop on Program Comprehension (IWPC '00)*, pp. 211–218, Limerick, Ireland, June 2000.

10

Recovering Software Design from Interviews Using the NFR Approach: An Experience Report

Nary Subramanian,[1] **Steven Drager,**[2] **and William McKeever**[2]

[1] *Department of Computer Science, University of Texas at Tyler, Tyler, TX 75799, USA*
[2] *Information Directorate, Air Force Research Lab, Rome, NY 13441, USA*

Correspondence should be addressed to Nary Subramanian; nsubramanian@uttyler.edu

Academic Editor: Gerardo Canfora

In the US Air Force there exist several systems for which design documentation does not exist. Chief reasons for this lack of system documentation include software having been developed several decades ago, natural evolution of software, and software existing mostly in its binary versions. However, the systems are still being used and the US Air Force would like to know the actual designs for the systems so that they may be reengineered for future requirements. Any knowledge of such systems lies mostly with its users and managers. A project was commissioned to recover designs for such systems based on knowledge of systems obtained from stakeholders by interviewing them. In this paper we describe our application of the NFR Approach, where NFR stands for Nonfunctional Requirements, to recover software design of a middleware system used by the Air Force called the Phoenix system. In our project we interviewed stakeholders of the Phoenix system, applied the NFR Approach to recover design artifacts, and validated the artifacts with the design engineers of the Phoenix system. Our study indicated that there was a high correlation between the recovered design and the actual design of the Phoenix system.

1. Introduction

Design recovery in software systems involves obtaining design from artifacts such as code, system documentation, and execution environment, with the primary objectives being reduced maintenance costs, system enhancement, or system reengineering [1–3]. Design recovery is especially important for legacy systems where only a few software artifacts exist to aid their understanding: for example, there are systems that are decades old and will serve useful purposes if reengineered but whose only artifacts are limited documentation, a few stakeholders willing to share their experiences with the system, and the executable binary code [4].

Usual techniques for design recovery include code-based and domain knowledge-based techniques. Code-based techniques [4, 5] start with parsing the code and identifying elements and then obtain the design. In doing so an intermediate representation of the code is derived such as the hammock graphs, dependency graphs, or control flow graphs.

However, as mentioned in [4], knowledge about architecture, design decisions, and design constraints cannot be fully obtained from code analysis alone. Domain knowledge-based techniques are used for program comprehension [6] that uses knowledge representation such as graphs and trees and apply classical reasoning techniques to retrieve design patterns; they are mostly used to augment code-based techniques to capture higher level abstraction of designs; but this again does not fully capture the high level architecture for the system [7].

In our project, the objective was to obtain designs by interviewing stakeholders of a system. Stakeholders included users and managers. We were provided a rough idea of the environment in which the system operates but no access to system documentation. We were given time slots to interview system stakeholders and we were free to ask questions relevant to the system. From these interview notes we were to recover the design of the system. For the purpose of validation we were asked to recover design for the Phoenix system [8], which is a middleware system used by the US Air Force. The Phoenix system is a middleware system developed by the Air Force for use in tactical and enterprise systems. Phoenix belongs to the class of message-oriented middleware and provides transparent message transport facilities over multiple operating systems and network protocols. Applications can communicate with Phoenix using well-defined interfaces and exchange real time data. Phoenix operates using producer-consumer paradigm and uses store-and-forward technique for increased reliability of message transport over any unreliable communication links. The code base of Phoenix is over 100 K lines of code and consists of fifteen subsystems. Phoenix was a suitable candidate system for reverse engineering because of the ready availability of its user base as well as the access to its developers for validation. Additionally, Phoenix system's complexity is similar to those legacy systems of which Air Force is interested in recovering the designs.

Our process of reverse engineering from stakeholder interviews was guided by the NFR Approach [9–13], where NFR stands for nonfunctional requirements. The NFR Approach is knowledge driven, permits design trade-off analysis, provides a systematic process for recovering designs from domain knowledge, and rationalizes the process of design recovery from domain knowledge. It is a goal-based approach that has been used for forward engineering software systems where, starting with requirements for the system, the designs were developed [11, 13, 14]; however, since it can also capture information from documents [15], we find it suitable for design recovery from documentary evidence obtained from interviewing users.

During design recovery we obtain multiple views for the architecture [16–18] including component and connector view, detailed structural view, logical deployment view, physical deployment view, and use-case scenarios. In this NFR Approach-based process, we attempted to obtain several of these artifacts for the Phoenix system. The developers of Phoenix validated the resulting designs.

This paper is organized as follows: Section 2 discusses documentation of stakeholder interviews, Section 3 describes the NFR Approach briefly, Section 4 applies the NFR Approach to recover design for the Phoenix system, Section 5 discusses validation and lessons learnt, and Section 6 concludes the paper and provides directions for future work.

1.1. Related Work. Existing techniques for reverse engineering primarily rely on source code as a basis for design and requirement recovery [4, 7]. They can be categorized into static and dynamic approaches and into automatic and semiautomatic approaches. Static approaches reverse engineer from source code by creating an intermediate graphical representation of the code [5, 19–21] while dynamic approaches actually execute the code [22–24]. Automatic approaches [22, 25, 26] are completely tool-based that recover designs and requirements from source code, while semiautomatic techniques employ manual intervention in the process [22, 27, 28]. The NFR Approach has also been used in static source code-based reverse engineering case studies [20] with encouraging results.

There have been attempts to reverse engineer systems from domain information. An inductive learning approach

to recovering specifications has been described in [29] where the program behavior is studied. An approach that uses runtime use-case scenarios to extract requirements can be seen in [24]. An approach that uses financial information together with code details in C programming language is given in [28]. Also, design documentation and other system documentations for recovering ADA code are described in [1]. Design recovery by employing Unified Modeling Language to extract class diagrams has been shown in [21, 23], while the Unified Process has been used to recover design elements in [30] by employing use-case scenarios.

There have also been attempts to recover design information using metrics [31] such as weighted number of methods per class and coupling data to associate programs or subroutines to objects. They created a call graph structure to analyze data-intensive COBOL programs and classify them. A clustering technique that groups components realizing specific functions of a web application [32] has been proposed to develop UML diagrams for a web application.

The NFR Approach described in this paper appears to be unique in aiming to capture designs from stakeholder experiences and explicitly including the human feedback as a basis for design recovery. A high-level presentation of our approach was presented in [33]—this paper is a significantly more detailed description of our work.

2. Interviewing Stakeholders

In order to interview stakeholders we needed to first identify them. Phoenix development team had a list of users of Phoenix from which we shortlisted three major system development projects within the Air Force: Marti, Command and Control (C2), and E-Phoenix. Each of these projects develops a sophisticated system using Phoenix to provide communication linkages between system components. We were given contact information for users in each of these projects who were experienced in using the Phoenix system. Also the development team's manager was interviewed. Questions asked during interviews included the following.

(Q1) List problems faced before Phoenix was developed.

(Q2) Before Phoenix, how were the business processes it automated performed?

(Q3) List the main objectives for Phoenix system.

(Q4) List the business processes that Phoenix satisfies.

(Q5) List three problems with Phoenix system.

Each of these questions served a specific purpose. Q1 helped understand the problems that caused migration to Phoenix; Q2 was aimed at capturing the business domain knowledge; Q3 helped understand the expectations for the Phoenix system; Q4 helps understand how Phoenix was used for automating processes and obtain an understanding of the capability of Phoenix; Q5 lists problems that stakeholders now have with Phoenix itself which help understand unmet expectations. The interview was conducted in an informal but structured manner. The opinions of stakeholders were recorded and any misunderstandings were clarified

---

(1) *Why do you use Phoenix?*
Marti is a system of databases and messages to get images from aircraft to ground. The underlying infrastructure is Phoenix and it controls the dataflow. Data are typically images and CoT (cursor on target) messages; CoT messages are both text and XML. Phoenix usage is completely transparent; (user) did not know that Phoenix was being used until the code was reviewed.

(2) *Before Phoenix was available how did you accomplish these functions?*
Marti was never used without Phoenix

(3) *How do you use Phoenix? Can you list the steps?*
From a user perspective:
(a) On the Falcon View (a PC based mapping application) make a query for an image;
(b) Images are retrieved from Phoenix;
(c) Get the images.
(d) Click to see them on Falcon View
(e) View images or use RouteScout

From the Phoenix perspective:
(a) Add images or CoT messages to Postgres database
(b) No need to specific destination (ports are defined—it is a closed set)
(c) Images/messages sent to a fixed destination

(4) *List problems with Phoenix?*
No user documentation for Phoenix—a DFD of process to use Phoenix will be useful (especially if it includes data formats).
For Marti even the developer documentation is not there.
The Marti system is dependent on Postgres database—if Postgres fails then whole system fails.

Box 1: Answers obtained by interviewing a user of the Phoenix system.

by seeking subsequent feedback. This was an iterative and incremental process of knowledge gathering, where one set of interviews led to questions for other interviews.

An example response is given in Box 1 from one of the users. The interviews were conducted in an environment friendly to the interviewees, either in their office or in a conference room, for no more than thirty minutes each time. During interviews questions were asked to clarify responses. Clarifications were also asked by follow-up meetings or by e-mail. Responses during interviews were recorded by hand and subsequently transcribed using word processing software.

We then applied the NFR Approach to identify design alternatives for the Phoenix system from user responses. The use of the NFR Approach for this purpose is discussed in the next two sections.

3. The NFR Approach

The NFR Approach is a goal-oriented approach that can be applied to determine the extent to which objectives are achieved by a process or product. NFR stands for nonfunctional requirements, which represent properties of a system such as reliability, maintainability, and flexibility and could equally well represent functional objectives and constraints for a system. In this paper we applied the NFR Approach to reversely engineer a software system by evaluating whether a specific design element satisfied specific requirements for the system. The NFR Approach also allows functional requirements to be represented as hardgoals [34]. The NFR Approach uses a well-defined ontology for this purpose that includes NFR softgoals, hardgoals operationalizing softgoals, claim softgoals, contributions, labels, and propagation rules;

each of these elements is described briefly below (details may be seen in [9]). Furthermore, the NFR Approach uses the concept of satisficing, a term borrowed from economics, which indicates satisfaction within limits instead of absolute satisfaction, since absolute satisfaction of NFRs is usually difficult.

NFR softgoals represent NFRs and their decompositions. Elements that have physical equivalents (process or product elements) are represented by operationalizing softgoals and their decompositions. During decompositions (of either the NFR softgoals or the operationalizing softgoals), AND decomposition is used when each child softgoal of the decomposition has to be satisficed for the parent softgoal to be satisficed but the denial of even one child is sufficient to deny the parent, OR decomposition is used when satisficing of even one child satisfices the parent but all children need to be denied for the parent to be denied, and EQUAL decomposition has only one child for a parent and propagates the satisficing or the denial of the child to the parent.

Hardgoals represent functional requirements and their decompositions. Again hardgoals can be decomposed using AND, OR, or EQUAL decompositions. Contributions (MAKE, HELP, HURT, and BREAK) are made by operationalizing softgoals to the NFR softgoals and hardgoals. Reasons for contributions are captured by claim softgoals, and claim softgoals may form a chain of evidence where one claim satisfies another, which satisfies another, and so on. Each of the four types of contributions has a specific semantic significance: MAKE contribution refers to a strong positive degree of satisficing the objectives (represented by NFR softgoals) by artifacts (represented by operationalizing softgoals) under consideration, HELP contribution refers to a positive degree of satisficing, HURT contribution refers to a negative degree of satisficing, and BREAK contribution refers to a strong negative degree of satisficing.

Due to these contributions, some of the softgoals acquire labels that capture the extent to which a softgoal or hardgoal is satisficed: satisficed, weakly satisficed, weakly denied (or weakly not satisficed), denied (or not satisficed), or unknown (indicated by an absence of any label attribute). Labels are ranked in satisficing in the order: satisficed > weakly satisficed > unknown > weakly denied > denied. Moreover, high priority softgoals, hardgoals, decompositions, and contributions may be indicated using the criticality symbol.

Propagation rules propagate labels from child softgoal to the parent across decompositions, from operationalizing softgoals to NFR softgoals (or hardgoals) across contributions, and from claim softgoals to contributions; propagation rules aid in the rationalization process of the NFR Approach. Example propagation rules are as follows (details can be seen in [9]).

(R1) Determine labels for all operationalizing softgoals, claim softgoals, and contributions: each is either satisficed, denied, weakly satisficed, weakly denied, or unknown.

(R2) If a softgoal label is satisficed (denied) and it has a MAKE contribution to its parent, then the softgoal propagates its label to the parent.

(R3) If a softgoal label is satisficed (denied) and it has a BREAK contribution to its parent, then the softgoal propagates denied (satisficing) label to its parent.

(R4) If all labels propagated to a parent (either softgoal, hardgoal, or a contribution) are satisficed (denied), then that parent is satisficed (denied).

(R5) If there is a mix of labels propagated to a parent (either softgoal, hardgoal, or a contribution) and then if most of the labels are satisficed (denied), then the parent is weakly satisficed (weakly denied).

(R6) If the label of a softgoal is unknown, then if it is involved in an AND contribution, its label is assumed to be satisficed and if it is involved in an OR contribution, its label is denied.

(R7) In the case of AND-decomposed softgoals, if even one child softgoal has a denied label, then the parent is denied; otherwise the parent is satisficed.

(R8) In the case of OR-decomposed softgoals, if even one child softgoal has a satisficed label, then the parent is satisficed; otherwise the parent is denied.

(R9) If a contribution is denied, then a MAKE contribution becomes a BREAK contribution and vice versa; a weakly satisficed contribution becomes a weakly denied contribution and vice versa.

The propagation rule R1 states that a softgoal can have one of five labels—satisficed, weakly satisficed, weakly denied, denied, and unknown; this is true for hardgoals as well. Rules R2 and R3 state the label propagated by a softgoal to its parent via MAKE or BREAK contributions. Rules R4 and

R5 state the labels for parents based on contributions from their children. Rule R6 states what to do when a softgoal label is of unknown type—in this rule we have assumed an open policy approach wherein ignorance is considered favorably from a satisficing viewpoint: if a softgoal label is unknown, its impact on satisficing its parent is negligible— we let impact from softgoals whose satisficing is known to dominate the labels propagated to the parent. We discuss this further in a later section. Rules R7 and R8 state the labels propagated to the parent softgoal involved in an AND or OR decomposition with its children. Rule R9 states how unsatisficed contributions are treated: if a contribution is unsatisficed, then its type changes to the opposite type of satisficing.

These elements of the NFR Approach are captured in a graphical representation called the Softgoal Interdependency Graph (SIG). Each softgoal is named using the convention *Type* [*Topic*] where *Type* is the name of the softgoal and *Topic* is the context where the softgoal is used; *Topic* is optional for a softgoal and for a claim softgoal; the name may be the justification itself.

We applied the NFR Approach to analyze stakeholder experiences by transforming interview notes into SIGs for further analysis—this process is discussed in the next section. The partial ontology of the NFR Approach is shown in Figure 1.

3.1. Process for Applying the NFR Approach for Design Recovery. The steps for applying the NFR Approach for design recovery from interview notes are as follows.

(1) For each interview note develop the SIG including hardgoals, NFR softgoals, operationalizing softgoals, and claim softgoals.

(2) Apply satisficing labels and propagate labels up the SIG using the propagation rules.

(3) Identify those NFR softgoals that are satisficed by the Phoenix system.

(4) Use catalogs to identify those design alternatives that satisfice the NFR softgoals identified in step (3); these design alternatives are represented as operationalizing softgoals.

(5) Develop contributions to each operationalizing softgoal identified in step (4) from other SIGs obtained in step (1).

(6) Propagate labels from step (2) to each operationalizing softgoal in step (4). The design alternative (operationalizing softgoal) with the most satisficing label is the best candidate.

In the first step, develop the SIG that includes hardgoals and softgoals for each interview note. Then apply satisficing labels (satisficed, weakly satisficed, denied, and weakly denied) to all goals in a SIG and determine the satisficing of hardgoals and softgoals. Since design alternatives are compared along nonfunctional requirements when each alternative satisfies functional requirements [35], we identify those NFR softgoals that have been satisficed. We then

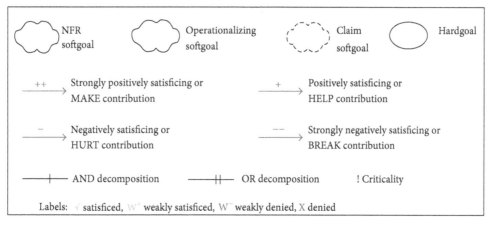

FIGURE 1: Partial ontology of the NFR Approach.

use catalogs to identify design alternatives that satisfice the identified NFR softgoals—these design alternatives become operationalizing softgoals in the SIG. We obtain corroboration from other SIGs for each of the design alternatives by identifying contributions between these SIGs and the design elements represented as operationalizing softgoals. We propagate labels to these operationalizing softgoals using the propagation rules of the NFR Approach. The design alternative with most highly ranked label is the best design candidate.

At this time we would like to contrast the NFR Approach with some of the other techniques in literature. The concept analysis technique [36] develops a tree of concepts and subconcepts that can be used to modularize the code for a system—concepts can represent functions for the system and serve as the basis for design recovery; however, the NFR Approach uses design catalogs that are justified by stakeholder claims using a rationalization process for design recovery. Also, the UML [37] while providing stereotypes for capturing design information does not have constructs for decompositions, contributions, labels, and propagation rules.

4. Application of the NFR Approach for Recovering Architecture of Phoenix System

The first step in applying NFR Approach is to generate the SIGs for each user interview document. The SIG obtained from the interview note of Box 1 is shown in Figure 2. At the bottom of the figure is the operationalizing softgoal, Phoenix user [Marti], which represents the fact that this user uses Phoenix for the Marti system developed by the Air Force. At the top are the hardgoals and softgoals extracted from the interview note. There are two NFR softgoals: Transparency [Users] and Reliability [Database], which refer to the fact that, respectively, users of Phoenix find it transparent and that the database is reliable. These two NFR softgoals arise from the two statements in the interview:

"Phoenix usage is completely transparent." and

"...system dependent on Postgres database (of Phoenix)—if Postgres fails then whole system fails."

There are also three hardgoals that represent the functional requirements of the system and arise from user statements: Controls Dataflow; Transports Images, Text, and XML Data; Uses Postgres Database.

The arrows between operationalizing softgoal and hardgoals/NFR softgoals are the contributions made by the operationalizing softgoal to the hardgoals and NFR softgoals. As per the user, the Phoenix system satisfices its hardgoals and so MAKE contributions exist to all hardgoals. Justifications for these MAKE contributions are given by the claim softgoals, which refer to the statement in the interview note that justifies the contributions. Likewise, Phoenix has a MAKE contribution to the NFR softgoal Transparency [Users] but has a BREAK contribution to the NFR softgoal Reliability [Database], and justifications for these are captured by the claim softgoals, which refer to the appropriate user statements.

We now apply the propagation rules to the SIG. All claim softgoals are satisficed since they are statements made by the user. Since all contributions between claim softgoals and the contributions they justify are MAKE contributions, by rule R2, all contributions between operationalizing softgoal Phoenix and hardgoals/NFR softgoals are all satisficed. Again by rule R2, all hardgoals are satisficed. Likewise, by rule R2 NFR softgoal Transparency [Users] is satisficed while by rule R3, the NFR softgoal Reliability [Database] is denied. This also means the SIG transcribes the interview note correctly since conclusions from the SIG match those on the note. This completes steps 1 and 2 of the process given in Section 3.1.

As can be seen from the SIG of Figure 2, the only satisficed NFR softgoal is Transparency [Users]. In the next step we turn to catalogs to identify architectural styles that will help achieve transparency for users: three techniques stand out—domain-specific (DS) middleware [38], service-oriented architecture (SOA) using web services [39], and proprietary SOA [40]. DS middleware is useful in a specific domain only; it will need significant reconfiguration for use in another domain. SOA is based on a structure of loosely coupled services interacting over a common bus; Web Services (a specific case of SOA) support brokering of loosely coupled services based on SOAP (Simple Object Access Protocol) protocol and UDDI (Universal Description,

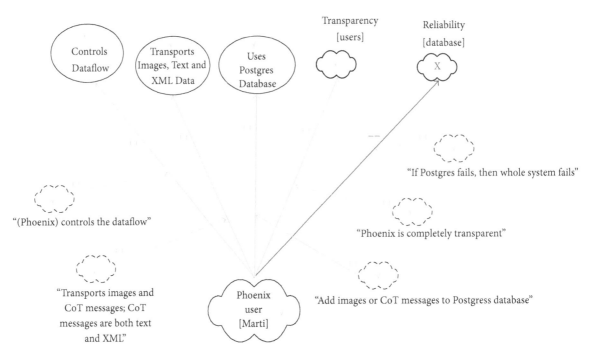

FIGURE 2: SIG representation of the interview note of Box 1.

Discovery, and Integration). Proprietary SOA uses its own protocols and underlying artifacts (including hardware communication channels) to seamlessly transport data.

The SIG of Figure 3 analyzes these architectural alternatives to identify the most suitable candidate for the Phoenix system. At the bottom of this figure is the SIG of Figure 2. In the middle are three operationalizing softgoals representing the three alternatives. At the top is the SIG from interviewing other users (from C2 and E-Phoenix projects)—only the relevant portions from these two SIGs are shown in Figure 3 and they are shown inverted for purposes of understanding. These corroborating users identified four hardgoals: services need channels, provides services, provides SOAP interaction, and provides REST services (REST standing for Representational State Transfer [41]). Of these hardgoals, only two are satisfied based on user statements; the remaining two were on the wish lists of users but not satisfied by Phoenix. The next step is to identify which of the alternatives satisfies all the functional requirements represented by hardgoals. For this purpose, contributions between hardgoals and these alternatives are drawn and claim softgoals capture justifications for these contributions. These justifications are shown in Table 1. There are also contributions between the three hardgoals in the lower SIG (it should be noted that Figure 3 is one SIG—however, for purposes of explanation we are dividing it into lower SIG that repeats Figure 2 and an upper SIG that captures corroborating statements from other users): Controls Dataflow; Transports Images, Text, and XML Data; Uses Postgres Database. Contributions from these hardgoals to the alternatives are all MAKE except for the one BREAK contribution from Uses Postgres Database hardgoal to the SOA [Web Services] operationalizing softgoal—to avoid clutter (and, more importantly, since they do not have

TABLE 1: Claims in Figure 4.

Claim softgoal	Justification
C1	Domain-specific middleware does not support multidomain services.
C2	SOA using web services does not provide channels (which are hardware dependent communication primitives).
C3	Proprietary SOA can be developed with required channels.
C4	Web services provide SOAP interaction.
C5	Proprietary SOA can be developed to provide multidomain services.
C6	Web services can provide REST services.
C7	Web services need not use Postgres database.

negative impact evaluation using propagation rules) only this BREAK contribution is shown in Figure 3.

We now apply propagation rules to find which alternative is most appropriate. Let us consider the labels received by each alternative—these are shown in Tables 2, 3, and 4. All claims C1 through C7 in Table 1 are satisfied and they have MAKE contributions to their parent contributions—therefore, by rule R2, all parent contributions in Figure 3 are satisficed, which means none of the contributions change their nature (i.e., rule R9 does not apply for any contribution).

The final label of the operationalizing softgoal DS middleware will be, by rule R5, weakly satisficed since most of the labels propagated to this softgoal are satisficed. This satisficing is indicated in Figure 3.

The final label of the operationalizing softgoal SOA [Web Services] will be, by rule R5, weakly denied since most of the

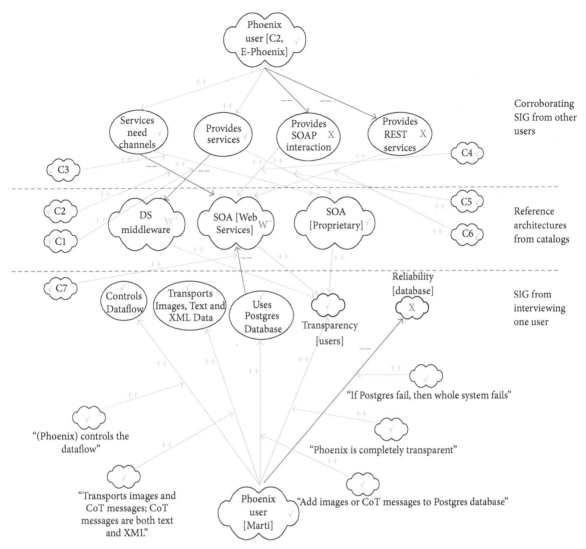

FIGURE 3: SIG for recovering architecture of Phoenix system.

TABLE 2: Labels propagated to the domain specific middleware alternative.

Source hardgoal	Hardgoal label	Hardgoal contribution	Label propagated	Rule applied
Provides Services	Satisficed	BREAK	Denied	R3
Controls Dataflow	Satisficed	MAKE (not shown in Figure 4)	Satisficed	R2
Transports Images, Text, and XML Data	Satisficed	MAKE (not shown in Figure 4)	Satisficed	R2
Uses Postgres Database	Satisficed	MAKE (not shown in Figure 4)	Satisficed	R2

labels propagated to this softgoal are denied. This satisficing is indicated in Figure 3.

The final label of the operationalizing softgoal SOA [Proprietary] will be, by rule R5, satisficed since all the labels propagated to this softgoal are satisficed. This satisficing is indicated in Figure 3.

Since SOA [Proprietary] is the satisficed operationalizing softgoal, the most appropriate architecture for Phoenix is a proprietary SOA architecture. Therefore, the initial architecture for the Phoenix system is shown in Figure 4.

In Figure 4, the SOA infrastructure component has the services interpretation module, execution module, message passing module, and the data storage module. The exposed services form the set of services that clients of the system can invoke. However, we need to flesh out details of this architecture. There are references to databases in interviews

TABLE 3: Labels propagated to the web services alternative.

Source hardgoal	Hardgoal label	Hardgoal contribution	Label propagated	Rule applied
Services need channels	Satisficed	BREAK	Denied	R3
Provides SOAP interaction	Denied	MAKE	Denied	R2
Provides REST services	Denied	MAKE	Denied	R2
Controls Dataflow	Satisficed	MAKE (not shown in Figure 4)	Satisficed	R2
Transports Images, Text, and XML Data	Satisficed	MAKE (not shown in Figure 4)	Satisficed	R2
Uses Postgres Database	Satisficed	BREAK	Denied	R3

TABLE 4: Labels propagated to the proprietary SOA alternative.

Source hardgoal	Hardgoal label	Hardgoal contribution	Label propagated	Rule applied
Services need channels	Satisficed	MAKE	Satisficed	R2
Provides services	Satisficed	MAKE	Satisficed	R2
Controls Dataflow	Satisficed	MAKE (not shown in Figure 4)	Satisficed	R2
Transports Images, Text, and XML Data	Satisficed	MAKE (not shown in Figure 4)	Satisficed	R2
Uses Postgres Database	Satisficed	MAKE (not shown in Figure 4)	Satisficed	R2

FIGURE 4: Initial architecture for the Phoenix system.

but these need not necessarily refer to databases inside of Phoenix. For the next level of design refinement, we will apply the NFR Approach to available public documentation of the Phoenix system.

4.1. Refining the Initial Architecture. There are two documents available for public view: the user manual (called the Final Technical Report or FTR) and a published paper [8]. Using information from these two documents we create a SIG for architecture refinement as shown in Figure 5. At the bottom of this figure is the SIG from documentation. The operationalizing softgoal Phoenix [Documentation] is AND-decomposed into softgoals FTR and Paper [Combs] referring to the two documentation sources. Some of the statements from this documentation are represented as hardgoals, and contributions are shown from the operationalizing softgoals to these hardgoals. All contributions are MAKE and justifications for these are the corresponding statements in the documents (these claim softgoals are not shown to avoid clutter). At the top of the SIG of Figure 5 are three hardgoals obtained from users of Marti and E-Phoenix systems and these hardgoals all receive MAKE contributions as well. In the middle are SOA elements from catalogs such as [39]. SOA needs mediation facility; a mediation facility stores

register information of publishers so that when consumers request, they are connected with appropriate publishers by the mediation facility. SOA provides services and based on the hardgoals the services are Query Service (QS) that responds to queries from Inquisitors (agents that query), Dissemination Service (DS) that provides information to consumers, Subscription Service (SS) that producers of information subscribe to, Service Brokering Service (SBS) that all services register with, and Repository Service (RS) that controls datastores. The proprietary SOA alternative has channels between services, a Registry that helps SBS register services, and Datastores based on Postgres for storing information. These elements of SOA are operationalizing softgoals. Also it can be seen that the operationalizing softgoal services are AND-decomposed into five child softgoals representing the five services discussed above. Moreover, we know that mediation facility in Phoenix seems to be provided by SBS (Service Brokering Service) since all services need to register with it—the MAKE contribution between hardgoal services register with SBS and operationalizing softgoal mediation facility captures this. Since SBS registers services, the Registry is associated with it (another MAKE contribution indicates this relationship). We know from interviewing one of the users that a channel needs to exist between each pair of services for communication—therefore MAKE contribution to operationalizing softgoal channels. We also know from FTR that Phoenix provides ten services and their names are known—these form the services provided by the SOA architecture. We also know that Inquisitor is connected to QS and DS, Consumer to DS, and Producer to SS. We also know that RS controls four types of repositories through

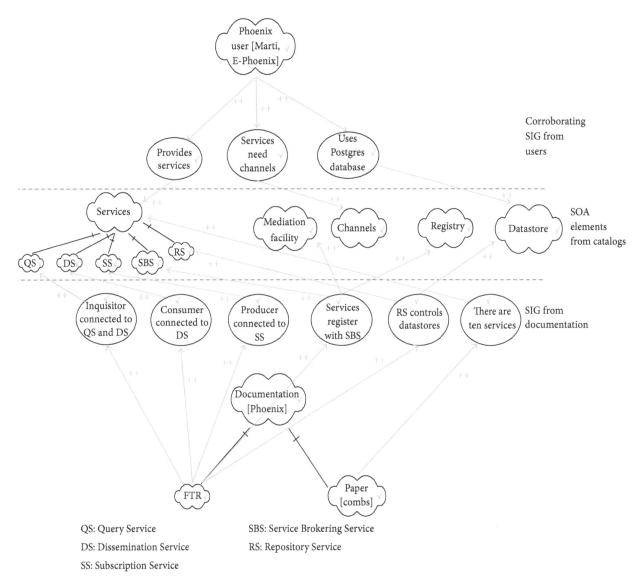

QS: Query Service   SBS: Service Brokering Service

DS: Dissemination Service   RS: Repository Service

SS: Subscription Service

FIGURE 5: Architecture refinement using the NFR Approach.

a repository interface (from FTR). By repeated application of propagation rule R2, all operationalizing softgoals representing SOA elements are satisficed. We then put all this information together to get the refined logical architecture of Figure 6.

The architecture of Figure 6 is the component and connector view of Phoenix system [18]. All components in circles indicate services, the rectangular block in the middle is the mediation facility (SBS), and all drum-shaped figures represent datastores and registry. All datastores are Postgres databases. Channels between services are represented by green arrows and normal arrows represent interfaces to databases.

4.2. Discussion of Design Documents Recovered. Using a similar approach of extracting information from documents, we recovered the following design elements for the Phoenix system:

(1) activity diagrams for different services;

(2) detailed component and connector views;

(3) deployment models.

Figures 7, 8, 9, and 10 show a few of the design views recovered for the Phoenix system. Figure 7 shows the activity diagram for a producer in the Phoenix system: initially all actors register their services with SBS (Service Brokering Service); when a producer has information to send, it establishes a channel with SS (Submission Service) and sends information to it. When a subscriber needs this information, it gets it from SS via the SBS and a copy is also stored in the RS (Repository Service).

The logical deployment diagram is shown in Figure 8 where there are seventeen services (the ten basic services and seven overhead services for Phoenix system such as the channel maintenance services) inside the deployed system. The physical deployment diagram of Figure 9 shows that the seventeen services are deployed as jar files inside the

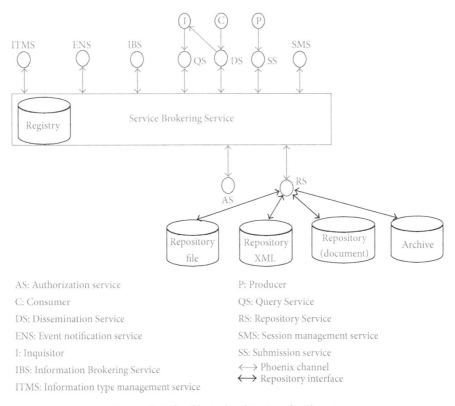

FIGURE 6: Refined logical architecture for Phoenix.

SpringSource Application Server [42], which resides on top of the Java Virtual Machine (JVM) which in turn runs on top of either Windows or Linux operating systems.

Figure 10 shows the detailed view of one service, the Submission Service (SS). The SS has four major components: Input Channel Manager, Information Validator, Policy Manager, and Forwarder. Inputs are received by the Input Channel Manager, which is processed by the Input Processor. Events (such as informing SBS) are fired by the Event Firer and messages are acknowledged by the Acknowledger. The Information Validator component has four subcomponents: ITMS Communicator, Cache Manager, Validator, and Transactions Logger. ITMS Communicator sends the input to the Information Type Management Service (ITMS) for confirming if the type of input is acceptable; the Cache Manager caches the input for later replay in case of errors; the Validator confirms that the format of the input is valid; the Transactions Logger logs the transactions for later audit. The Policy Manager component guides the functioning of the remaining three components by ensuring that established policies are followed in processing messages; the Forwarder component relays the processed message downstream.

5. Validation and Lessons Learnt

Recovered designs were validated by three of the original Phoenix development engineers. We presented the designs along with a questionnaire that required them to evaluate the artifacts by comparing them with the system documents for Phoenix (which we did not have access to) in the spirit of the Delphi technique [43]. The developers were provided activity diagrams, multiple views of architecture, and logical and physical deployment models. Based on the developers' responses the results are tabulated in Table 5.

As can be seen in Table 5, the component and connector view were 90% correct (in terms of the number and types of components and connections); however, there seems to be no central broker in the implementation of Phoenix and bidirectionality of links is an incorrect assumption (there are separate links for forward and reverse connections) and more data analysis in terms of further claim softgoal rationalizations can help uncover this information. The activity diagram for the scenario of producer submitting information to the dissemination service is 60% correct in terms of activities and 88% correct in terms of links but further iteration of information discovery process would have helped improve accuracy. Physical deployment model and detailed view were mostly correct though further iterations will help improve accuracy.

One of the lessons we learnt was the importance of domain knowledge for improving efficiency of design recovery—the number of iterations needed to get sufficient information from the stakeholders to capture design rationales depended on the complexity of the system. Domain knowledge could appear in the SIG as a claim softgoal or operationalizing softgoal. For example, the knowledge of what Marti system does will help us understand user's viewpoint much better.

In the SIG of Figure 3 we concluded the architecture type based on contributions to one NFR softgoal Transparency

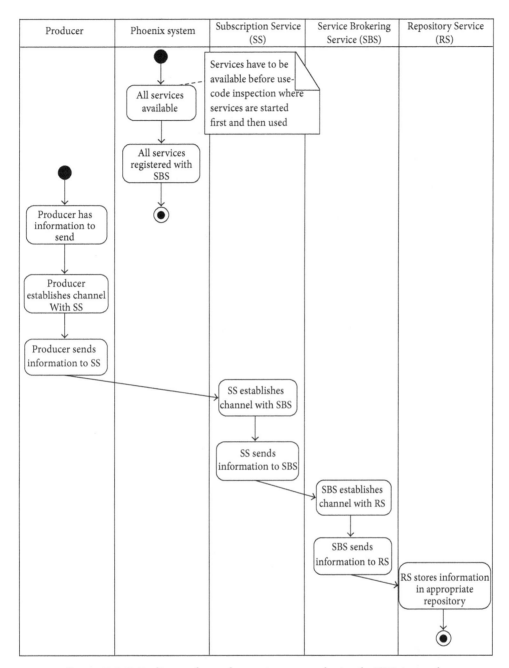

FIGURE 7: Activity diagram for producer actor recovered using the NFR Approach.

TABLE 5: Validation results.

Item	Positives	Scope for improvement
Component and connector view	90% correct	No central broker; Information Brokering Service (IBS) is more important than SBS; bidirectionality assumptions are incorrect.
Activity diagrams	60% activities correct; 88% links correct	Some of the links had wrong sources and/or destinations; some of the activities were in the wrong order.
Logical deployment model	100% correct	This has sparse information.
Physical deployment model	90% correct	We concluded SpringSource was used for application server—in fact, Java Services Container does this job.
Detailed views of services	93% correct	Forwarder should be Output Channel Manager.

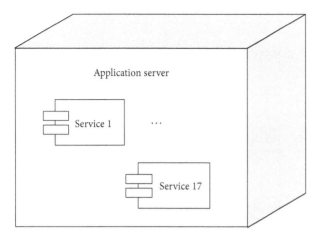

FIGURE 8: Logical deployment model for the Phoenix system.

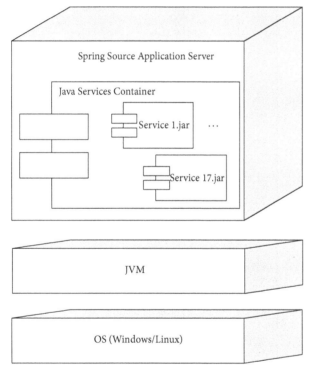

FIGURE 9: Physical deployment model for the Phoenix system.

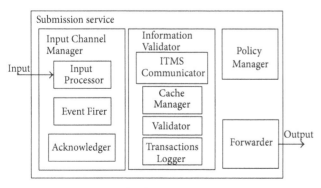

FIGURE 10: Detailed view for the Submission service of the Phoenix system.

[User]—what happens if more than one NFR softgoal is involved or if contributions are conflicting? In that case, the propagation rules of the NFR Approach can be used for trade-off analysis to determine the suitable candidate. In Figure 3, the current Phoenix architecture does not satisfice Reliability [Database] (conflicting NFRs)—therefore, the three architectural alternatives do not need to be reliable as far as their database is concerned; however, this also provides a design improvement opportunity for the next version of the system being recovered. If another NFR softgoal is involved in a synergistic manner (this is not the case in Figure 3), then architecture alternatives from catalogs will need to satisfice both NFRs to be considered a valid candidate.

A point that needs stressing is that frequent feedback from users will help converge faster for better designs since the feedback can be used to better guide the design recovery process especially when conflicting claims are made by stakeholders—in this case, it is quite possible that knowledge captured by a SIG is incomplete and more details will need to be discovered. Decisions reached during design recovery using the NFR Approach are traceable through the SIG since it helps maintain a historical record—therefore, if a recovered design aspect is found wrong, using SIG, we can trace the source of this fault and determine how to not only correct this fault but also evaluate the impact of this correction on the recovered design. In a sense, the process used by us is both bottom-up and top-down: bottom-up when knowledge from catalogs is employed to help in design recovery and top-down when the process is iterated to obtain finer details from previous iterations.

In our discussion in this paper we did not consider criticalities—if any component of the SIG (hardgoal, softgoal, decomposition, or contribution) is critical, then that component will have to be given special consideration during design recovery. For example, if one of the user requirements was high throughput and users considered this requirement favoring their use of Phoenix, then when selecting the appropriate architecture from catalogs, the one that uses store-and-forward mechanism may not be favored as much as an alternative that uses streaming messages since the latter usually has higher throughput. Likewise, in our discussion we assumed all contributions are satisfied (we did not have to use rule R9); however, in practice, some claims may become invalid as more knowledge is uncovered—in that case we can either deny the claim or deny the contribution or both. Therefore, the view captured by Figure 3 is our current knowledge—if things were to change, they can be easily captured in an updated SIG.

Another point to note is that the hardgoals are actually functional requirements for the Phoenix system; that is, in the process of applying the NFR Approach for recovering design we recover requirements as well-functional requirements in the form of hardgoals and nonfunctional requirements in the form of NFR softgoals. Finally, we used the StarUML tool with softgoal profile module [44] for drawing the SIGs—this tool helped us quickly create graphs and maintain versions of SIGs that served as historical records. This tool also keeps track of all SIG elements so that in spite of clutter this tool helps to quickly propagate labels up the SIG using propagation rules.

Therefore the process of design recovery from stakeholder interviews using the NFR Approach includes three steps. In the first step we identify and interview stakeholders associated with the target software system, collect and study software artifacts associated with the system, and study literature to acquire domain knowledge. In the second step, create SIGs from interviews, obtain candidate designs from catalogs, apply labels and propagation rules, and identify the most appropriate candidate based on user information. In the third step, develop SIGs to obtain design views for the architecture such as component and connector view, activity diagrams, detailed logical diagram, logical deployment diagram, and physical deployment diagram.

6. Conclusion and Future Work

Stakeholder views provide a unique viewpoint into a software system—their perception of the functionality of the software system can help verify whether the system is indeed achieving its objectives. Stakeholders for software systems in production (i.e., working or executing software systems) include users and managers. Moreover, for several legacy systems stakeholder views based on their experiences with the software system may be the only major source of information for the system since the original system documentation may no longer be available [4]. In this paper we discuss how we recovered the design for a software system called Phoenix [8] for the US Air Force from stakeholder interviews. Stakeholders were interviewed, catalogs of design information were created, and the NFR Approach [9–13] was applied to analyze interview notes and recover the designs. Activity diagrams, multiple views of architecture, and logical and physical deployment models were generated for the Phoenix system. We validated the recovered design artifacts by feedback from Phoenix's development engineers. The results are encouraging with many design views matching closely that of the developers' designs, which gives confidence that our process may be reused for other systems. The NFR Approach employed for analysis provides the ability to trade off conflicting stakeholder view points, helps record and resolve ambiguity inherent in knowledge acquisition from stakeholder experiences, helps trace recovered designs to the information sources, and maintains historical records in graphical representations called Softgoal Interdependency Graphs (SIGs).

In the future we plan to apply the NFR Approach to other systems at the Air Force to recover designs. We also plan to partially automate this process by incorporating natural language processing to identify elements of SIGs from interview notes, which should speed up the process considerably. Furthermore, integrating natural language processing with tools available for handling NFR Approach, for example, StarUML [44], will enable automating the processing of knowledge recovery from stakeholders. To increase convergence of designs we hope to include data from black-box tests, including performance tests, in the future. However, we believe that design recovery from stakeholder interviews using the NFR Approach is a promising technique for reverse engineering software systems.

Conflict of Interests

The authors certify that there is no actual or potential conflict of interests in relation to this paper. This paper was assigned the Case no. 88ABW-2014-0345 by the US Air Force and was cleared for publication on the 4th of February, 2014.

Acknowledgments

This research was sponsored by Air Force Research Laboratory/Information Directorate, Rome, NY, USA. In the summer of 2011 authors spent many months on this project and they thank several engineers at the lab for helping with their project including Mark Linderman, James Hanna, Vaughn Combs, James Milligan, Chris Schuck, Tim Blocher, Dawn Nelson, and Mark Mowers. They also thank the reviewers of the original version of this paper for their insightful comments that helped them significantly improve the paper.

References

[1] E. J. Byrne, "Software reverse engineering: a case study," *Software: Practice and Experience*, vol. 21, no. 12, pp. 1349–1364, 1991.

[2] E. J. Chikofsky and J. H. Cross, "Reverse engineering and design recovery: a taxonomy," *IEEE Software*, vol. 7, no. 1, pp. 13–17, 1990.

[3] D. E. Wilkening and K. Littlejohn, "Legacy software reengineering technology," in *Proceedings of the 15th AIAA/IEEE Digital Avionics Systems Conference*, pp. 25–30, October 1996.

[4] H. A. Muller, J. H. Jahnke, D. B. Smith, M. A. Storey, S. R. Tilley, and K. Wong, "Reverse engineering: a roadmap," in *Proceedings of the Conference on the Future of Software Engineering*, pp. 47–60, 2000.

[5] R. K. Keller, R. Schauer, S. Robitaille, and P. Page, "Pattern-based reverse-engineering of design components," in *Proceedings of the 21st International Conference on Software Engineering*, pp. 226–235, May 1999.

[6] T. J. Biggerstaff, "Design recovery for maintenance and reuse," *Computer*, vol. 22, no. 7, pp. 36–49, 1989.

[7] G. Canfora and M. Di Penta, "New frontiers of reverse engineering," in *Proceedings of the Future of Software Engineering Conference (FoSE '07)*, pp. 326–341, May 2007.

[8] V. T. Combs, R. G. Hillman, M. T. Muccio, and R. W. McKeel, "Joint battlespace infosphere: information management within a C2 enterprise," in *Proceedings of the 10th International Command and Control Research and Technology Symposium*, 2005.

[9] L. Chung, B. A. Nixon, E. Yu, and J. Mylopoulos, *Non-Functional Requirements in Software Engineering*, Kluwer Academic Publishers, Boston, Mass, USA, 2000.

[10] A. Vemulapalli and N. Subramanian, "Evaluating consistency between BPEL specifications and functional requirements of complex computing Systems using the NFR approach," in *Proceedings of the 4th International Systems Conference (SysCon '10)*, pp. 153–158, April 2010.

[11] L. Chung and N. Subramanian, "Adaptable architecture generation for embedded systems," *Journal of Systems and Software*, vol. 71, no. 3, pp. 271–295, 2004.

[12] L. Chung and N. Subramanian, "Process-oriented metrics for software architecture adaptability," in *Proceedings of the 5th IEEE International Symposium on Requirements Engineering*, pp. 310–311, August 2001.

[13] N. Subramanian and L. Chung, "Software architecture adaptability: an NFR approach," in *Proceedings of the 4th International Workshop on Principles of Software Evolution (IWPSE '01)*, pp. 52–61, September 2001.

[14] N. Subramanian, S. Drager, and W. McKeever, "Designing trustworthy software systems using the NFR approach," in *Emerging Trends in ICT Security*, B. Akhgar and H. Arabnia, Eds., pp. 203–225, Elsevier, 2014.

[15] N. Subramanian and L. Chung, "Representing and reasoning about agreements ... more agreeably," *Lus Gentium Journal*, vol. 12, pp. 205–258, 2006.

[16] M. Shaw and D. Garlan, *Software Architecture: Perspectives on an Emerging Discipline*, Prentice Hall, 1996.

[17] L. Bass, P. Clements, and R. Kazman, *Software Architecture in Practice*, Addison-Wesley, Boston, Mass, USA, 2003.

[18] P. Eeles and P. Cripps, *The Process of Software Architecting*, Addison-Wesley, New Jersey, NJ, USA, 2010.

[19] H. A. Muller, M. A. Orgun, S. R. Tilley, and J. S. Uhi, "A reverse engineering approach to subsystem structure identification," *Journal of Software Maintenance*, vol. 5, no. 4, pp. 181–204, 1993.

[20] Y. Yu, Y. Wang, J. Mylopoulos, S. Liaskos, A. Lapouchnian, and J. C. S. Do Prado Leite, "Reverse engineering goal models from legacy code," in *Proceedings of the 13th IEEE International Conference on Requirements Engineering (RE '05)*, pp. 363–372, September 2005.

[21] P. Tonella and A. Potrich, *Reverse Engineering of Object Oriented Code*, Springer, New York, NY, USA, 2005.

[22] M. Lanza and S. Ducasse, "Polymetric views: a lightweight visual approach to reverse engineering," *IEEE Transactions on Software Engineering*, vol. 29, no. 9, pp. 782–795, 2003.

[23] T. Systä, K. Koskimies, and H. Müller, "Shimba: an environment for reverse engineering Java software systems," *Software*, vol. 31, no. 4, pp. 371–394, 2001.

[24] M. Salah, S. Mancoridis, G. Antoniol, and M. Di Penta, "Towards employing use-cases and dynamic analysis to comprehend mozilla," in *Proceedings of the 21st IEEE International Conference on Software Maintenance (ICSM '05)*, pp. 639–642, September 2005.

[25] B. S. Mitchell and S. Mancoridis, "On the automatic modularization of software systems using the bunch tool," *IEEE Transactions on Software Engineering*, vol. 32, no. 3, pp. 193–208, 2006.

[26] G. Scanniello, A. D'Amico, C. D'Amico, and T. D'Amico, "Architectural layer recovery for software system understanding and evolution," *Software: Practice and Experience*, vol. 40, no. 10, pp. 897–916, 2010.

[27] R. Fiutem, P. Tonella, G. Antoniol, and E. Merlo, "Cliche-based environment to support architectural reverse engineering," in *Proceedings of the IEEE Conference on Software Maintenance (ICSM '96)*, pp. 319–328, November 1996.

[28] P. Tonella, G. Antoniol, R. Fiutem, and F. Calzolari, "Reverse engineering 4. 7 million lines of code," *Software*, vol. 30, no. 2, pp. 129–150, 2000.

[29] W. W. Cohen, "Recovering software specifications with inductive logic programming," in *Proceedings of the 12th National Conference on Artificial Intelligence*, pp. 142–148, August 1994.

[30] P. Dugerdil, "A reengineering process based on the unified process," in *Proceedings of the 22nd IEEE International Conference on Software Maintenance (ICSM '06)*, pp. 330–333, September 2006.

[31] A. Cimitile, A. De Lucia, G. A. Di Lucca, and A. R. Fasolino, "Identifying objects in legacy systems using design metrics," *Journal of Systems and Software*, vol. 44, no. 3, pp. 199–211, 1999.

[32] G. A. D. Lucca, A. R. Fasolino, F. Pace, P. Tramontana, and U. de Carlini, "WARE: a tool for the reverse engineering of web applications," in *Proceedings of the 6th European Conference on Software Maintenance and Reengineering*, pp. 241–250, 2002.

[33] N. Subramanian, S. Drager, and W. McKeever, "Engineering a trustworthy software system using the NFR approach," in *Proceedings of the Systems and Software Technology Conference*, Salt Lake City, Utah, April 2012.

[34] L. Chung, S. Supakkul, N. Subramanian et al., "Goal-oriented software architecting," in *Relating Software Requirements and Software Architectures*, pp. 91–110, Springer, 2011.

[35] D. Gross and E. Yu, "From non-functional requirements to design through patterns," *Requirements Engineering*, vol. 6, no. 1, pp. 18–36, 2001.

[36] M. Siff and T. Reps, "Identifying modules via concept analysis," *IEEE Transactions on Software Engineering*, vol. 25, no. 6, pp. 749–768, 1999.

[37] "Unified Modeling Language (UML)," http://www.uml.org/.

[38] D. C. Schmidt, "Middleware for real-time and embedded systems," *Communications of the ACM*, vol. 45, no. 6, pp. 43–48, 2002.

[39] T. Erl, *SOA Design Patterns*, Prentice Hall, New Jersey, NJ, USA, 2009.

[40] D. Sprott and L. Wilkes, "Understanding Service-Oriented Architecture," 2004, http://msdn.microsoft.com/en-us/library/aa480021.aspx.

[41] M. Elkstein, "Learn REST: A Tutorial," http://rest.elkstein.org/.

[42] "SpringSource," http://spring.io/.

[43] C. Hsu - and B. A. Sandford, "The Delphi technique: making sense of consensus," *Journal of Practical Assessment, Research, and Evaluation*, vol. 12, no. 10, 2007.

[44] "StarUML," http://staruml.sourceforge.net/en/modules.php.

11

Multiagent Systems Protection

Antonio Muñoz, Pablo Anton, and Antonio Maña

Escuela Técnica Superior de Ingeniería Informática, Universidad de Málaga, Spain

Correspondence should be addressed to Antonio Muñoz, amunoz@lcc.uma.es

Academic Editor: Kamel Barkaoui

Agent-systems can bring important benefits especially in applications scenarios where highly distributed, autonomous, intelligence, self-organizing, and robust systems are required. Furthermore, the high levels of autonomy and self-organizations of agent systems provide excellent support for developments of systems in which dependability is essential. Both Ubiquitous Computing and Ambient Intelligence scenarios belong in this category. Unfortunately, the lack of appropriate security mechanisms, both their enforcement and usability, is hindering the application of this paradigm in real-world applications. Security issues play an important role in the development of multiagent systems and are considered to be one of the main issues to solve before agent technology is ready to be widely used outside the research community. In this paper, we present a software based solution for the protection of multiagent systems concentrating on the cooperative agents model and the protected computing approach.

1. Introduction

In the area of information systems, security is one of the most interesting topics. Recently, with the huge growth in the number of distributed systems, the number of computing attacks has increased and therefore so has the number of protection systems. The first work done on software agents was in the mid 1970s by Hewitt and Baker [1]. Hewitt created an agent model (named Actor), which he defined as an autonomous object that interacts and executes concurrently with an internal state and communication capability. Since that initial conception, and due to the work developed in Distributed Artificial Intelligence (DAI), a new concept has arisen known as the Multi-Agent System. The main appeal of these systems is that they allow two or more entities to join forces to perform a common task, which is very difficult to complete individually. Nowadays a huge variation of software agents exists according to their features, abilities, or properties. Mobile agents are implementations of remote programs, that is, those programs developed in a computer and distributed in other computers to continue their execution [2]. The migration capability provokes different security risks and makes controlling the following aspects essential: the protection of hosts against agents and the protection of

agents against the host and authors to define the network protection.

The firsts MAS applications appeared in the middle of the 80s. These first systems covered a wide variety of environments (manufacturing systems, process control, air traffic control, information management). But most of them were built upon nonsecure infrastructures [3, 4]. Agent technology developers assumed that the underlying infrastructure was secure at that time, but evidently it is not now. Some other examples of agent-based applications that lacked a secure infrastructure are found in nuclear plants [5] and aircraft control [6] applications.

Regarding the infrastructures for agent-based systems development, the situation is quite similar. Some of the platforms for agents are Aglets http://aglets.sourceforge.net/, Cougaar http://www.cougaarsoftware.com/agents/agents-1 .htm, the flagship product of the Agent Oriented Software Group JACK http://www.agentsoftware.co.uk/ products/jack/index.html, the popular JADE (Java Agent DEvelopment Framework http://jade.tilab.com/, JAVACT http://www.javact.org/JavAct.html, and Jason for AgentSpeak(L) http://jason.sourceforge.net/Jason/Jason.html. All these tools and methodologies share a common negative point namely poor security against an attack on the platform in which the agency is running.

Some of the general software protection mechanisms can be applied to the *agent protection*. However, the specific characteristics of agents make mandatory the use of tailored solutions. First, agents are most frequently executed in potentially malicious pieces of software. Therefore, we cannot simplify the problem as is done in other scenarios by assuming that some elements of the system can be trusted. So the security of an agent system can be defined in terms of many different properties such as confidentiality, nonrepudiation, and so forth. but it always depends on ensuring the correct execution of the agent on agent servers (a.k.a agencies) within the context of the global environments provided by the servers.

The main approach presented in this paper is based on the "protected computing" technique, which is based on the partitioning of the software elements into two or more parts. The basic idea is to divide the application code into two or more mutually dependent parts. Some of these parts (which we will call private parts) are executed in a secure processor, while others (public parts) are executed in any processor even if it is not trusted. The main appeal of the solution presented in this paper is that users define the rules to make this division of code by means of an easy to use front end. Thus users can select those variables or those parts of code that are critical and must be protected. Additionally a batch protection tool is included that allows the protection of a portion of code or data.

We apply the protected computing model in order to protect agent societies in a multiagent setting, where several agents are sent to different (untrusted) agencies in order to perform some collaborative task. Because agents run in potentially malicious hosts, the goal in this scenario is to protect agents from the attacks of malicious hosts. The basic idea is to make agents collaborate, not only in the specific tasks they are designed to perform, but also in the protection of other agents. In this way, each agent acts as secure coprocessor for other agents.

Therefore, using the protected computing model, the code of each agent is divided into public and private parts. For the sake of simplicity, and without loss of generality, we will consider the simplest case where the code of each agent is divided in two parts: a public one and a protected one. From this description, it is easy to derive the possibilities of the division of the code into more parts. In particular, the inclusion of multiple private parts, which could even be designed to execute in different coprocessors, is especially relevant for the scenarios that we are considering. Usually, the private part, of each agent, has to be executed by another agent in another host. This scheme is suitable for protecting a set of several mutually dependent agents. Consequently, in this case, a conspiracy of all hosts is necessary in order to attack the system.

This paper focuses on multiagent systems and the security within them. More specifically, our work deals with static mutual security schemes [7] and is organized as follows: in Section 2 we review related publications and we introduce the MAS (multiagent system), mobile agents, JADE platform, and security schemes. Section 3 presents the application of the protected computing approach in the agent protection. Section 4 presents the main approach of this paper; the automatic generation of a MAS making use of the mutual static strategy. In Section 5, we describe the features and architecture of the tools developed, and finally we present our conclusion and future work.

2. Related Work

The purpose of this section is to provide a view on the main agent-based systems and agent-oriented tools, focusing on their security mechanisms. This paper covers a wide range of works from the first approaches to the more recent ones.

Several mechanisms for secure execution of agents have been proposed in the literature with the objective of providing security in the execution of agents. Most of these mechanisms are designed to provide some type of protection or some specific security property in a generic way. In this section, we will focus on solutions that are specifically tailored or especially well-suited for agent scenarios. Some protection mechanisms are oriented to the protection of the host system against malicious agents. Among these, SandBoxing is a popular technique that is based on the creation of a secure execution environment for nontrusted software. In the agent world, a sandbox is a container that limits, or reduces, the level of access its agents have and provides mechanisms to control the interaction between them.

Another technique, called proof-carrying code, is a general mechanism for verifying that the agent code can be executed in the host system in a secure way [8]. For this purpose, every code fragment includes a detailed proof that can be used to determine whether the security policy of the host is satisfied by the agent. Therefore, hosts just need to verify that the proof is correct (i.e., it corresponds to the code) and that it is compatible with the local security policy. This technique shares some similarities with the constraint programming technique; they are based on explicitly declaring what operations the software can or cannot perform. One of the most important issues of these techniques is the difficulty of identifying which operations (or sequences of them) can be permitted without compromising the local security policy.

Other mechanisms are oriented towards protecting agents against malicious servers. Sanctuaries [9] are execution environments where a mobile agent can be securely executed. Most of these proposals are built with the assumption that the platform where the sanctuary is implemented is secure. Unfortunately, this assumption is not applicable in our scenario. Several techniques can be applied to an agent in order to verify self-integrity in order to avoid the code or the data of the agent being inadvertently manipulated. Antitamper techniques, such as encryption, checksumming, antidebugging, antiemulation among others [10, 11] share the same goal, but they are also orientated towards the prevention of the analysis of the function that the agent implements. Additionally, some protection schemes are based on self-modifying code, and code obfuscation [12].

In agent systems, these techniques exploit the reduced execution time of the agent in each platform.

Software watermarking techniques [13] are also interesting. In this case, the purpose of protection is not to avoid the analysis or modification but to enable the detection of such modification. The relationship between all these techniques is strong. In fact, it has been demonstrated that neither perfect obfuscation nor perfect watermarking exists [9]. All of these techniques share the fact that they only provide short-term protection.

Many proposals are based on checks. In these systems, the software includes software and hardware-based "checks" to test whether certain conditions are met. However, because the validation function is included in the software, it can be discovered using reverse engineering and other techniques. This is particularly relevant in the case of agents. Theoretic approaches to the problem have demonstrated that self-protection of the software is unfeasible [14]. In some scenarios, the protection required is limited to some parts of the software (code or data). In this way, the function performed by the software, or the data processed, must be hidden from the host where the software is running. Some of these techniques require an external offline processing step in order to obtain the desired results. Among these schemes, function hiding techniques allow the evaluation of encrypted functions [15]. This technique focuses on protecting the data processed and the function performed, thus it is an appropriate technique for protecting agents. However, it can only be applied to the protection of polynomial functions.

The case of online collaboration schemes is also interesting. In these schemes, part of the functionality of the software is executed in one or more external computer. The security of this approach depends on the impossibility for a part to identify the function performed by the others. This approach is very appropriate for distributed computing architectures such as agent-based systems or grid computing, but has the important disadvantage of the impossibility of its application to off-line environments.

Additionally, there are techniques that create a two-way protection. Some of these are hardware-based, such as the Trusted Computing Platform. With the recent appearance of ubiquitous computing, the need for a secure platform has become more evident. Therefore, this approach adds a trusted component to the computing platform, usually built-in hardware used to create a foundation of trust for software processes [16].

The protected computing concept [17] at the core of the strategy presented in this paper. This approach is based on the idea of dividing the code in two or more mutually dependent parts that will be executed in a trusted processor, while remaining parts can be executed in any other processor, whether trusted or not. In the application of this strategy for the security of multiagent systems, we have achieved a model in which each agent collaborates with one or more remote agents that are executed in different agencies, trusted or not. The approach presented in this paper is based on the collaboration feature of multiagent systems. However contrary to the online collaboration schemes in which the selection of those parts of the functionality of the software to execute in external computers, in our approach the difficult task of selecting those parts is carried out by the developer of the multiagent system that although is not a security expert can decide which are the most critical parts of his software.

Thus a unique successful attack requires the cooperation of every agency in the system, which, in practice, does not make sense. In mutual protection, we can differentiate between two schemes.

(i) Static mutual protection: This solution is the simplest and is fully implemented and described in this paper, which is fundamentally for restricted systems in which the number of agents in the system is previously fixed.

(ii) Dynamic mutual protection: this approach consists of an evolved solution from the static mutual approach, which is more flexible. This approach is applicable for any real multiagent system.

3. Protected Computing Approach Applied to Agent Protection

The Protected Computing approach is based on the division of code in two or more parts. Some of these parts will be executed in a trusted processor, but the others will be executed in a regular processor. These divisions are performed in such a way that the execution of the application is not possible without the collaboration of the trusted processor. One of the most important aspects of this technique is the way in which the code is divided. This might be carried out in mutually dependent parts, but it is essential that

(i) the public part of code will not be able to be used to get information from the private one;

(ii) a communication trace is not possible between each part to get information from the private part.

The Protected Computing scheme can be applied in order to protect a society of collaborating agents by making every agent collaborate with one or more remote agents running in different hosts. These agents act as secure coprocessors for the first one. We call *Mutual Protection* to the application of Protected Computing to MAS.

In Figure 1, we show how every agent interacts with one or more remote agent, and these are executed in different agencies. Then the agents protect each other one by one. A possible attack of this scheme would need the collaboration of every agency to hack the system, but this case is beyond the scope of this paper due to its irrelevance in real applications.

Mutual Protection strategy presents two different schemes according to the requirements of the system. In the first scheme, called *Static Mutual Protection*, the collaboration among agents is predefined. This means that each agent has the private code of at least one agent in the collaboration. Secondly, *Dynamic Mutual Protection* offers the possibility that every agent in the system pretends to be a trusted processor for the remaining agents. In which case, the interaction among agents is not predefined.

To split the code into parts, the developer has to use the Automatic Tool for Code Partitioning (CPT). Since the

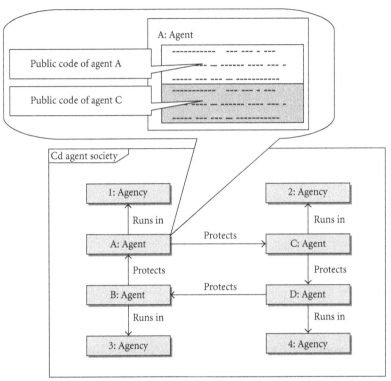

FIGURE 1: An agent society with mutual protection.

code partition is a difficult task, and specialised expertise is required to carry it out, this tool makes code partitioning easier (creating the public and private parts) according to a set of rules that we call *Protection Profile*. The result of the operation of this tool is a set of public parts and a set of private parts. These parts will be used in a different way depending on the Mutual Protection scheme applied (static or dynamic). Figure 2 shows two different protection schemes as two different ways. A detailed description of these approaches can be found in the subsequent subsections.

3.1. Static Mutual Protection. The Static Mutual Protection strategy can be successfully applied to many different scenarios. However, there will be scenarios where it will not possible to predict the possible interactions between the agents, where the agents will be generated by different parts, when that will involve very dynamic multihop agents. In these cases, the Static Mutual Protection strategy will be difficult or impossible to apply. Therefore, we propose a new strategy named Dynamic Protection where each agent will be able to execute arbitrary code sections on behalf of other agents in the society. The work presented in this paper is based on this static scheme. In this case, private parts of the agent must be included in the agent or in the protector's agents before the execution starts.

The main appeal of this scheme is the increased performance of the system since a split of code between private and public parts is done. Code parts are distributed before system start replacing those parts of private code by their associated call.

Therefore, the efficiency of the system is hardly influenced. Nevertheless, the system is very restricted and the previous setting of the system is mandatory, and agents are protected before their execution.

An example of the possible applications of this scheme is that of a competitive bidding. In this scenario, a client requests bids from several contractors to provide goods services. It is important that the bidding takes place simultaneously, so that none of the contractors can access the offer from the others, because this would give them an advantage over the others. The client can use several single-hop agents to collect the offers from the contractors. Each agent will be protected, using the Static Protection strategy, by other agents. This is possible since the client generates the set of agents, which is static and known a priori. We can also safely assume that a coalition of all contractors will not happen. In fact, no technological solution can prevent all contractors to reach an external agreement. Because each agent is protected by other agents running in the hosts of the competitors, and because the protected computing model ensures that it is neither possible to discover nor to alter the function that the agents perform and it is also impossible to impersonate the agents, we know that all agents will be able to safely collect the bids, guaranteeing the fairness of the process.

A different example is given by a monitoring system based on agents of a power plant control software. In this system, each agent controls a parameter and the fact that the value of this is in a specific range beyond which is risky. Evidently the number of agents in this system is deterministic but the global system requires a high level of security. Static mutual protection strategy fits in the requirements of this scenario.

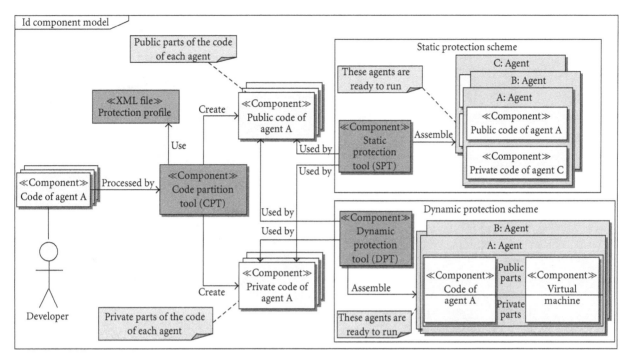

FIGURE 2: Mutual protection of agents process.

3.2. Dynamic Mutual Protection. The Static Mutual Protection strategy can be successfully applied to different scenarios. However, there are many real-world scenarios where it is not possible to foresee the potential interactions between the agents due to the agents being generated by different parts, or it involves very dynamic multihop agents. In these cases, the Static Mutual Protection strategy is not suitable. The Dynamic Protection Strategy is able to execute arbitrary code sections on behalf of other agents in the society. As shown at the top of Figure 3, each agent includes a public part, an encrypted private part and a specific virtual machine similar to the one described in [18]. This virtual machine allows agents to execute on-the-fly code sections (corresponding to the private parts) received from other agents.

The Dynamic Protection Strategy process is illustrated in Figure 3. In the first exchange, ag1 acts as the protected agent, while ag2 acts as the protecting agent (secure coprocessor) for the first one. In the exchange, ag1 sends a private code section to the virtual machine of ag2. This virtual machine processes the private section and returns some results (results1). Subsequent exchanges illustrate ag3 acting as protecting agent for ag2 (in this case the protected agent), and finally ag1 protecting ag3. The scalability of this scheme is very good since only a few agents (one in most cases) are involved in the protection of any other agent.

4. Paper Contribution

The general aim of the work presented here is to allow the system developers to create secure agent-based systems, namely, a developer should be able to protect his MAS using the mutual static libraries producing an equivalent version of the system. Despite the fact that code distribution tasks imply the selection and protection of different parts iteratively it is not difficult, but it is tedious and certainly not efficient if it is performed manually. We consider the possibility of changing the security setting, studying results and deciding the most appropriate settings for our specific MAS to be useful points. For this reason, Secure Agent Generator tool is focused on automating the whole process increasing the efficiency.

Results of this contribution are fully integrated in the JADE platform providing solutions that allow the development and execution of securely multiagent systems based on the mutual static strategy. Figure 4 shows an overview of the protection process.

Secure Agent Generator tool has as feedback the insecure MAS, that is, a set of nested agents developed to achieve certain goals. This solution is composed of a set of agents defined by Java classes (.class files). Evidently, the output of this tool is an equivalent MAS in functionality. However, the new version of the system is secure according to the strategy used and the parameters set in the protection profile. Secure Agent Generator tool is made up of several sequential tasks: read, analyse, modify and create .class files. A ".class" file has a quite complex and hard to manage internal structure. A huge number of references and the low level code made it a hard and tedious task to analyse and create. Different approaches to handle these files exist, among them we highlight BCEL [19], Javassist [20], or ASM [21]. We bowed to use BCEL due to several reasons; it is the most popular in the community, well documented, fully developed in Java and deployed in Apache software foundations, which provides an easier integration.

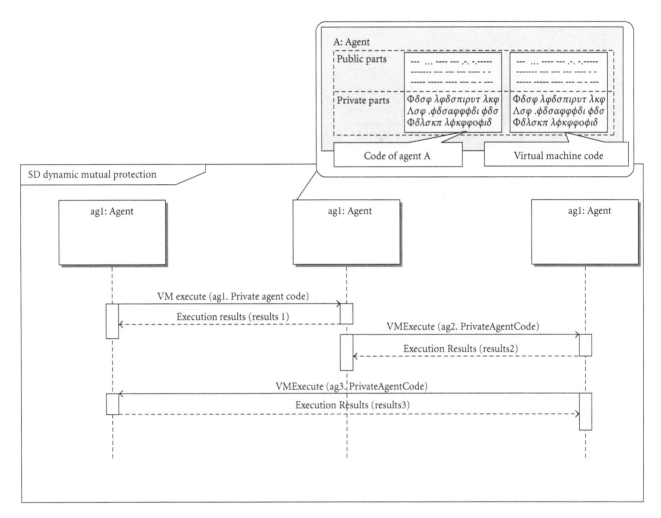

FIGURE 3: Structure of an agent with dynamic mutual protection.

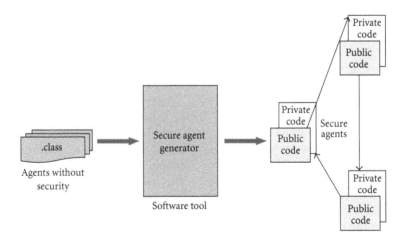

FIGURE 4: Secure agent generator tool.

This paper presents a methodology to protect agent-based systems using the protected computing approach. This methodology is split to two different strategies. The first approach, namely, the Static Mutual Protection, is based on the restriction that the number of agents in the system is fixed and the protection is performed at compiling time. This approach provides good results in practice because the efficiency is not really affected. The second approach, the Dynamic Mutual Protection is based on protection at runtime. This strategy is more flexible but the efficiency can be affected considerably. Static Mutual Protection strategy is fully implemented and a set of assisting tools are created to facilitate the protection task. Meanwhile the Dynamic strategy is fully designed and actually being implementated.

5. Architecture

In this section we provide an in-depth description of the most important features and characteristics of the functionalities provided by our tool. It is important to highlight the fact that we are focused on the development of a tool for the automatic generation of secure MAS, implementing the mutual static strategy that as input has a set of agents that compound the nonsecure MAS.

It is important to note that the feedback files, the set of nonsecure agents, must fulfil a set of restrictions (preconditions) as described; every file must be precompiled and stay in ".class" format; every file must represent a class inherited from jade core Agent. And internal anonymous classes are not allowed in these files.

Similarly, there are some output conditions to take into consideration; each of these new agents will have a protector agent preassigned, which cannot be changed at runtime. However, our aim is that the output MAS is equivalent to the input MAS, meaning the behaviour of the new MAS with the security incorporated will be exactly the same as that of the input MAS. Another aspect to mention is the fact that the main architecture of the system follows the model view controller pattern. However, the view is a simple graphic user interface to facilitate the use of the assistant tool.

This process has three clearly differentiated phases: the loading of original agents, security settings that meet requirements and the final creation of secure agents. Each of these phases was implemented with a set of classes in charge of providing a correct execution.

Despite the description, we think that the most appropriate way to illustrate the whole process is by means of a practical example, thus showing the role of every phase in the process. The code of a nonsecure JADE agent inherits from Agent class and its execution code is inside the setup() method. As we have previously stated, it is necessary that each agent has a protector agent associated, thus the minimum number of agents for a secure MAS is two. Let us also suppose that this example contains an empty agent (no instructions nor data) with the role of protector. The class that illustrates Figure 5 shows the code of a nonprotected agent, which is inherited from the Agent class.

Following, every phase of the process is described by means of a concrete example.

```
public class Example extends Agent {

    // Fields definition
    ...
    protected void setup(){

      // Code not to be protected
      System.out.println("Not to be..");

      // Code to be protected
      System.out.println("To be...");

    }
}
```

Figure 5: Example code.

```
System.out.println("Example");

GETSTATIC java/lang/System.out: Ljava/io/PrintStream
LDC "Example"
INVOKEVIRTUAL java/io/PrintStream.println(Ljava/lang/String;)V
```

Figure 6: Matching.

5.1. Phase I: Loading. This is the first phase in the generation of the secure agents process. The goal of this step is to load a .class files and analyse their content. To this end, we have selected the set of nonsecure agents, and then we have identified and analysed all its elements, that is, methods, fields, instructions, internal classes, and so forth.

In this class files analysis stage, we have used the static component of the BCEL libraries. This part of the API provides the methods to load a class file and the automatic generation of the structure of a class file [22]. This process is repeated until, for each of the elements from the file class (methods, fields, internal classes, instructions, etc.), a modelling object is created and is used to handle it.

Each element generated with BCEL component is a read only one. However, it is important to save information from each of these elements by means of annotations. In order to do this, we created classes that inherit directly from the BCEL classes. In these new classes, we introduce all the useful information for the next phases. In this analysis process, we clearly saw the special case of the instructions, this is a more complex case than the rest of the elements. Inside these class files, there is a section dedicated to class methods. Among other elements inside these methods, we found bytecode instructions. These instructions are useless if they are executed separately because normally they depend on the previous one to them and the next one. A relationship is stated between a java instruction and the set of instructions in bytecode. For this reason, we decided to group them in sets corresponding to a java instruction finalised in ";".

Once all agents are loaded in the system, we progress to the setting phase. This phase is very important because we indicate the degree of security and describe the protection links in it. The information of this phase is very relevant due to the fact it selects the elements to be protected.

5.2. Phase II: Setting. The setting phase is the simplest of the three and the easiest to implement. This stage controls the specification of security parameters for the creation of the new secure agents. Among the compounding parts of a JADE agent, there are two elements to be protected instructions and data (Class fields.). The information needed to determine the security degree is indicated in the percentage of instructions and data to protect. All this information is modelled with a class called SecureAgentConfiguration. With regards to how to indicate the security parameters, we have implemented two separate ways. The first method is needed in order to specify for each of the loaded agents (first phase) the security parameters in the system. This fact implies the selection of every agent and the insertion of the percentage of instructions and selection of fields to protect. This method is a bit more tedious due to the number of agents loaded and the number of testing proofs to perform. For this reason, we have implemented an option that allows us to apply a security template to all agents by means of an XML file. We have developed three basic templates and the possibility to build a customised template.

This example shows the percentage of instructions and data, 50 is the value in this case, to protect. We must take into consideration that there are two different cases in which the percentage value is different for instructions and data. Sometimes the static data or the brunch instructions are clear examples of that. Before progressing to the third phase, we have to select the protection links, meaning to indicate what the protection is like among the agents. It is not necessary to carry out the action manually since there is an option to automate it in the graphic tool. In example, we only have two agents, so one protects the other and vice versa.

5.3. Phase III: Creating Secure Agents.

Finally, we have the secure agent creation phase. Thanks to the previous stages, in this stage we collected all the information needed for this creation.

For each of the original already gathered, at least two new classes may be created, one related to the new secure agent with its public code (data and instructions) and the other with the private code. In addition to these classes, we will have as many agents containing the original agent as the number of new classes created.

To create these new precompiled classes, we make use of the dynamic component of BCEL. This part of the BCEL API will facilitate the creation of the skeleton of class files and, depending on the security parameters set in the previous phase, the original code is inserted in one part or the other. In Figure 7, we can see the content of the public part of the new secure agent based in the example in Figure 8. Nevertheless, the class code has been modified as indicated in Figure 7

The new class is an inheritance of the SecureAgent class providing a complete integration in the JADE framework. An initialization section is added in the setup method to mark the protector and the protected agent. Any additional code to perform the protection is needed to be inserted. There will be as many internal agents containing the original agent as the number of new classes are created.

For the protected code, a new class is created that implements the PrivateCode interface, but in this new class it is essential to insert: protected fields (in our example they do not exist); The "execute()" method that contains the protected code divided by sections. The information to know which section to execute is in the method arguments. In the

```
public class SecEj extends SecureAgent{

    protected void setup()  {

        // Init
        ...

        // Not protected instruction
        System.out.println("Not to be..");

        // Call to remote code
        ACLMessage msg = new ACLMessage(.);
        msg.setContent("execute-my-..");
        myArgs = argument;
        msg.addReceiver(this.protectedBy);
        send(msg);
    }
}
```

FIGURE 7: Secure agent.

```
public class Prv implements PrivateCode{
    public Object execute(Object o){

        // Protected code
        System.out.println("To be...");
        return null;
    }
}
```

FIGURE 8: Private code.

example, the code to protect has only one section then this is directly in the execute() method.

5.4. Phase IV: Validating Secure Agent System.

An important aspect of this approach is the validation of the secure system, that is, that we can ensure that the generated system is secure. According to the model proposed by the static mutual protection strategy a correct execution of the system implies that every agent complete its goals. If any error occurs during the execution of the multi-agent system the whole system halts. Obviously this error can be produced by an attack or simply a misunderstanding error in the communication (i.e., an inconsistency of data due to any fail in the communicating channel).

6. Conclusion and Ongoing Work

A full methodology to protect multiagents in multi-agent systems based on the protected computing approach is the main contribution of this paper. In previous sections, we have shown some assisting tools to implement the mutual protection strategy using a friendly interface. A new field is concerned with performing some analytical and statistical studies on the kind of protection to implement, according to the set of requirements of each system.

Methodology proposed in this paper is based on the partitioning of the code of every agent of a system and a distribution of these parts. For the sake of efficiency, the part of code inserted in other agents (private part of code) are not too long, according to each specific example. This distribution of code could decrease in efficiency especially in those systems composed of a high number of agents but a balance between security and usability is a traditional issue to solve in any real world system.

We have highlighted some of the problems (interoperability, limit to free competition, lack of owner control, lack of assurance, etc.) of the Trusted Computing approach, which make it unacceptable as it is now. Our view is that none of these problems is without solution. We strongly believe that the cooperation of the scientific community can help in solving these problems in the right way.

Obviously the static mutual protection scheme is a deterministic system, that is, a fixed number of agents at entry. However, this approach provides excellent results for those systems in which it fits as shown in the examples in the paper. In order to improve the dynamism of this methodology, we are working on the development of tools to implement the dynamic strategy.

Once we have implemented automatic tools for assisting the deployment of the static mutual protection scheme, next step is the development of assisting tools for the implementation of the dynamic mutual protection scheme. This approach is more complex due to the needed implementation of a restricted specific virtual machine to execute remotely parts of code of agents. Currently, this work is ongoing and it is in its final development stages.

Finally, this paper has demonstrated the existence of alternatives and add ons to current approaches that the scientific community should explore in order to guarantee the best possible solution for the agent protection problem.

References

[1] C. Hewitt and H. Baker, "Actors and continuous functionals," 1977.

[2] H. S. Nwana, "Software agents: an overview," *The Knowledge Engineering Review*, vol. 11, no. 3, pp. 205–244, 1996.

[3] N. R. Jennings and K. Sycara, "A roadmap of agent research and development," 1998.

[4] B. Chaib-draa, "Industrial applications of distributed AI," *Communications of the ACM*, vol. 38, no. 11, p. 4, 1995.

[5] H. Wang and C. Wang, "Intelligent agents in the nuclear industry," *Computer*, vol. 30, no. 11, pp. 28–34, 1997.

[6] U. M. Schwuttke and A. G. Quan, "Enhancing performance of cooperating agents in real-time diagnostic systems," in *Proceedings of the 13th international Joint Conference on Artifical intelligence (IJCAI '93)*, pp. 332–337, Chambery, France, 1993.

[7] A. Maña, A. Muñoz, and D. Serrano, "Towards secure agent computing for ubiquitous computing and ambient intelligence," in *Ubiquitous Intelligence and Computing*, vol. 4611 of *Lecture Notes in Computer Science*, pp. 1201–1212, Springer, New York, NY, USA, 2007.

[8] G. C. Necula, "Proof-carrying code," in *Proceedings of the 24th ACM SIGPLAN-SIGACT Symposium on Principles of Programming Languages (POPL '97)*, pp. 106–119, ACM, New York, NY, USA, 1997.

[9] B. S. Yee, "Secure Internet programming," in *A Sanctuary for Mobile Agents*, pp. 261–273, Springer, London, UK, 1999.

[10] J. P. Stern, G. Hachez, F. Koeune, and J.-J. Quisquater, "Robust object watermarking: application to code," in *Proceedings of the 3rd International Workshop on Information Hiding (IH '99)*, pp. 368–378, Springer, 2000.

[11] G. Hachez, *A comparative study of software protection tools suited for E-commerce with contributions to software watermarking and smart cards*, Ph.D. thesis, Universite Catholique de Louvain, March 2003.

[12] C. S. Collberg and C. Thomborson, "Watermarking, tamper-proofing, and obfuscation—tools for software protection," *IEEE Transactions on Software Engineering*, vol. 28, no. 8, pp. 735–746, 2002.

[13] S. Katzenbeisser and F. A. Petitcolas, Eds., *Information Hiding Techniques for Steganography and Digital Watermarking*, Artech House, Norwood, Mass, USA, 1st edition, 2000.

[14] O. Goldreich, "Towards a theory of software protection and simulation by oblivious rams," in *Proceedings of the 9th Annual ACM Symposium on Theory of Computing (STOC '87)*, pp. 182–194, ACM, 1987.

[15] T. Sander and C. F. Tschudin, "On software protection via function hiding," in *Information Hiding*, D. Aucsmith, Ed., vol. 1525 of *Lecture Notes in Computer Science*, pp. 111–123, Springer, 1998.

[16] S. Pearson, *Trusted Computing Platforms: TCPA Technology in Context*, Prentice Hall PTR, Upper Saddle River, NJ, USA, 2002.

[17] A. Maña and A. Muñoz, "Mutual protection for multiagent systems," in *Proceedings of the 3rd International Workshop on Safety and Security in Multiagent Systems*, p. 37, Citeseer, Hakodate, Japan, 2007.

[18] A. Maña, J. Lopez, J. J. Ortega, E. Pimentel, and J. M. Troya, "A framework for secure execution of software," *International Journal of Information Security*, vol. 3, no. 2, pp. 99–112, 2004.

[19] Apache Software Foundation, *BCEL (Byte Code Engineering Library)*, 2006.

[20] S. Chiba, *Javassist (Java Programming Assistant)*, Sun Microsystems, 2009.

[21] OW2 Consortium. ASM.

[22] T. Lindholm and F. Yellin, *The JavaTM Virtual Machine Specification*, Sun Microsystem, 1999.

12

Bug Localization in Test-Driven Development

Massimo Ficco,[1, 2] Roberto Pietrantuono,[3] and Stefano Russo[2, 3]

[1] Dipartimento di Ingegneria dell'Informazione, Seconda Università di Napoli Via Roma, 81031 Aversa (CE), Italy
[2] Laboratorio ITeM "C. Savy", Consorzio CINI, Via Cinthia-Edificio 1, 80126 Napoli, Italy
[3] Dipartimento di Informatica e Sistemistica, Università di Napoli Federico II, Via Claudio 21, 80125 Napoli, Italy

Correspondence should be addressed to Roberto Pietrantuono, roberto.pietrantuono@unina.it

Academic Editor: Hossein Saiedian

Software development teams that use agile methodologies are increasingly adopting the test-driven development practice (TDD). TDD allows to produce software by iterative and incremental work cycle, and with a strict control over the process, favouring an early detection of bugs. However, when applied to large and complex systems, TDD benefits are not so obvious; manually locating and fixing bugs introduced during the iterative development steps is a nontrivial task. In such systems, the propagation chains following the bugs activation can be unacceptably long and intricate, and the size of the code to be analyzed is often too large. In this paper, a bug localization technique specifically tailored to TDD is presented. The technique is embedded in the TDD cycle, and it aims to improve developers' ability to locate bugs as soon as possible. It is implemented in a tool and experimentally evaluated on newly developed Java programs.

1. Introduction

Test driven development (TDD) is a technique to incrementally develop software, that was sporadically used for decades, and that re-emerged in the last years as development paradigm in the context of the so-called *agile methodologies*.

The increasing adoption of extreme programming (XP) in various industrial projects as well as the identification of TDD as a key strategy in agile software development have captured in recent years an increasing attention also by academic research. As stated by Janzen and Saiedian [1], the TDD is an example of how the academic research sometimes follows the most spread and accepted software practice, rather than leading it. The XP methodology is conceived to reduce the time-to-market of software systems, and the use of TDD practice in XP allows developing more robust programs. Several studies showed this trend, claiming the attention of various researchers, which started to study the ability of TDD to detect software faults earlier in the development process [2–5].

In TDD, the developer writes unit tests from a set of user requirements/functionalities, before writing the code itself. Then s/he implements the code needed to pass the tests, until he succeeds. When a bug is detected, it is promptly fixed. Once the tests are passed, the developer performs the refactoring of the code to acceptable standards; then s/he proceeds to define a new set of test cases for other functionalities and implements a new piece of code to pass them.

In this cycle, even when the tests are successful, the code for new functionalities can easily compromise the previously implemented ones, introducing what are called *regression bugs*. This is not an unusual event in the TDD, since whenever the developer writes the code for some functionalities, s/he does not have a complete view of the whole system in detailed design documents (differently from traditional development cycles) and thus can affect the behavior of the code already implemented.

In order to identify potential regression bugs, the developer, once implemented a group of functionalities, executes regression tests [6], before proceeding to implement new functionalities. To obtain robust programs in low development times, it is essential for developers to be able to correct these bugs promptly.

The described process is particularly suited for relatively small systems. However, when the size and complexity of the system significantly increase, locating regression bugs manually becomes a very challenging task. When regression tests reveal a failure, the debugger should track the bug propagation chain by repeatedly running the tests step by step, until s/he identifies the bug source. If the system is large and complex, with many interacting units and intricate interdependencies, the effort to locate a bug can become unacceptable. In this phase, a tool to improve the debugging process would allow the TDD practice to yield high productivity also in large projects.

In this paper, we propose a technique to speed up the bug localization activity in the TDD process. It is based on an anomaly detection approach that is iteratively applied to each TDD cycle. The basic idea is to compare at each cycle the behaviour of the application observed during regression testing with a reference "correct" behavioral model as intended by the developer, that is, a model describing how the application should behave. In particular, when a failure occurs, the technique identifies any deviation from the reference model and then highlights the ones most likely related to the bug.

For this aim, we implemented a tool that collects deviations from the expected behavior and assigns them a weight measuring their likelihood of representing the bug. Evaluation metrics are defined and implemented in order to assign such weights and rate the identified anomalies. Based on this ranking, the debugger inspects directly those points that are most likely related to the bug.

The implemented metrics are evaluated by applying the tool to a known open-source Java library, namely *JFreeChart* (JFreeChart (version 1.0.9) is a free Java chart library to develop professional quality charts. It is available at: http://www.jfree.org/jfreechart/), using a fault injection technique to reproduce the presence of bugs in the code, and considering the goodness of the final deviations ranking.

The overall approach and the implemented tool are also evaluated by running a set of experiments in which several groups of students developed a new application from scratch (from the same set of requirements) by using the TDD approach. In these experiments, the debugging times, measured during the development without the support of the proposed technique, are compared with the tool-supported debugging times, in which developers employed the tool at each TDD cycle. Results show a significant improvement of debugging times across TDD cycles.

The rest of this paper is organized as follows: Section 2 outlines the background about the TDD practice; Section 3 describes the proposed solution and provides some implementation details. Section 4 shows the experimental evaluation and discusses the obtained results. Finally, Section 5 is devoted to related work, and Section concludes the paper.

2. TDD

TDD consists of few basic steps iteratively repeated over time, with the aim of translating user requirements into test cases, that guide the developer in the code implementation process. It does not replace traditional testing, instead it defines a proven way to ensure effective unit testing and provides a working specification for the code. Figure 1 shows the main steps of a TDD process. They may be summarized as follows.

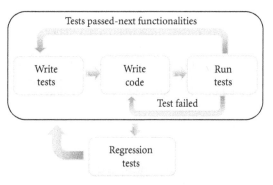

FIGURE 1: TDD process.

(1) The developer writes an automated test case that defines a new functionality to be implemented.

(2) Then he writes the code necessary to pass the defined test.

(3) The developer runs the test. If the test gives negative outcome, he refactors the new code and skips to the next functionality. Otherwise, he refines its code until the test is passed.

(4) The developer periodically reruns all the written test cases, to be sure that the new code does not cause failures in the previous code (the previously implemented functionality). This phase is called *regression tests*.

In the literature, the features of TDD have been shown to bring benefits not only by reducing the development time, but also by producing more robust code [5]. Several empirical studies have been conducted on the effectiveness of TDD practice, both by industry and by academia. Williams et al. [7] have shown how TDD produced, in their experiments, higher-quality code. In the same year, George and Williams [8] reported reduction in defects density up to 40% compared to an ad hoc testing approach, while in [6] and [3], the authors reported, respectively, quality improvements of 18% and 50%, with an impact on the development time of 15–20% (i.e., they showed that sometimes TDD adoption took longer) with respect to a traditional development. Another study [9] confirmed these results, reporting an even higher reduction in faults density. However, results in [4] show that TDD helps in reducing overall development effort and in improving developer's productivity, but the authors observed that the code quality seems to be affected by the actual testing efforts applied during a development style. There are other studies, like the one conducted by Geras et al. [10], or two other academic ones [11, 12], that observed no significant differences in the developer's productivity, even if they involved programmers who had little or no previous experience with TDD. The authors highlighted the need to improve testing skills of the developers for effectively adopting test-first approaches.

2.1. Regression Tests. An important role in the TDD is played by regression tests. Unlike traditional development cycle, in the TDD, regression bugs are very likely to be introduced during the work cycles, since when a developer implements a functionality, s/he does not have a complete view of the system to develop in its detailed design (e.g., due to the lack of a design documentation, or because the user requirements are not yet fully defined). The developer does not clearly know how the successive functionalities will affect the current one. Hence, changes in a code area may inadvertently cause a software bug in another area, and a function that worked correctly in a previous step may stop working.

The detection of regression bugs is therefore a crucial step in TDD, which occurs "inside" the development, not after. For instance, let us suppose that we are developing a simple software application (e.g., an online bookshop) made up of 7 functionalities, and that we have already developed the first two functionalities (see Algorithm 1).

For simplicity, suppose that the functionality F2 is responsible for shipping an order; it will include a method *ship (ISBN)* that needs the current number of available items with the given ISBN, denoted with *currentN*. The management of the current availability of books is devoted to another functionality, F6, not yet implemented. F6 will be in charge of verifying the current availability (by the method *verifyAvail*) and of updating it (the method *updateAvail*).

During the implementation of F2, test cases give negative outcome; hence, the developer skips to develop the third functionality. F2 test cases assume that the *currentN* value comes from F6 methods (i.e., they use a *driver*, since F6 is still not implemented). Based on the number of ordered items and on the *currentN* value, it ships the order (and updates the availability, temporarily through a *stub*) or returns an error.

The developer then proceeds in the development up to the sixth functionality, responsible for managing the items availability. During the F6 implementation, the developer realizes that the *updateAvail* method needs to distinguish between a *sale* order, by a client, or a *purchase* order by the bookshop manager to increase the current availability. Then s/he introduces a boolean variable (*SalePurchase*) to discriminate the two cases. As a consequence of this unforeseen requirement, s/he has to modify F2 code. The modified code is reported in part 3 of Algorithm 1 . As may be noted, the developer makes a mistake during the F2 modification, introducing a bug: a wrong logical condition in the first *if* statement is specified (an AND operator instead of an OR). Test cases for F6 give negative outcom; hence, the developer skips to the seventh functionality. The problem comes up only when the developer executes regression tests. When the developer implemented the *ship* method in F2, s/he did not have a clear view of F6 and did not handle the case causing the failure.

An example of more subtle bugs is in the F6 code; during the F6 implementation, the developer makes a mistake in the computation of the variable *currentN* (used by F2) in the function *updateAvailability*. In particular, s/he omits a check on the maximum capacity of items that can be stored. Test cases for F6 give negative outcome, since they have only to check that the availability is correctly updated. Hence, the developer skips to the next functionality; however, the variable *currentN* can assume a wrong value (greater than

the maximum capacity), which can bring to erroneous behaviours of the F2 functionality. Again, the problem comes up only when the developer executes regression tests, when s/he can realize that the variable *currentN* may be in an inconsistent state.

In a complex system, the situation is typically worse than the exemplified ones, since from the bug activation to the failure manifestation, there may be a very long and intricate chain (e.g., the variable *currentN* of the example could have been used by other functionalities without causing failures up to F2); tracking back from the failure to the bug is not trivial. The present work aims to ease the identification of this kind of bugs that are not detected by unit tests, and that typically are the main cause of development time wasting in the TDD cycle.

3. Anomaly Detection Approach

The use of a debug-aiding technique in the TDD process allows guiding the debugger through the identification of potential root causes of failures introduced during the development, as the one reported in Algorithm 1.

In the following, we refer to a failure occurrence as a consequence of a chain *fault-error-failure*, in which a software fault, once activated, becomes an error, propagating through the system up to the interface. As bugs in the code are software faults, just for the purpose of this work, we use the term *software fault* or simply *fault* interchangeably with the term *bug*. During the fault propagation, the system exhibits some behaviors different from the expected ones. We call such deviating behaviors *anomalies* or *violations*. In the described example, the omitted control in the *updateAvail* method represents the bug, which, once activated (i.e., the control flows through the method), propagates up to the *ship* method and becomes a failure when an order is shipped with a wrong *currentN* value (greater than the number of books actually available). In that case, a *violation* may be a value of the *currentN* variable at the exit point of the *getCurrentN* method different from expected (e.g., outside an expected range).

From the bug activation to the failure manifestation, there is, in general, a chain of one or more violations. Highlighting such violations may be very important for debugging purposes, since they point out where the bug is propagating. However, identifying a violation requires (i) a clear description of the system expected behavior and (ii) the definition of what a deviation from this behavior means. Moreover, since there can be a high number of violations and very complex violation chains, we need a way to distinguish the most relevant violations (i.e., the most related to the failure-causing bug). Thus, a tool should support the tasks of (i) building an accurate model of the expected behavior of the system, (ii) identifying violations with respect to the built model, and (iii) discriminating the most relevant violations (according to their proximity to the bug). This support would lead the debugger to inspect directly the points closest to the bug, thus reducing debugging (and development) time.

```
(1) Functionality F2::shipOrder
orderData getOrderData() { ··· }
void ship(sellOrderData) {
if(orderData.Number < 0 || !(checkISBN(orderData.ISBN))
    {// return error}
N = F6::getCurrentN(orderData.ISBN);
if((N - orderData.Number) < 0) {
    //return error
    ...
}
else {
    //ship order
    ...
    F6::updateAvail(sellOrderData)
    ...
}
}
//other methods to support the shipment
...

(2) Functionality F6::ManageAvailability
Boolean verifyAvail() { ··· }
updateAvail (orderData, SalePurchase) {
if (SalePurchase == ''Sale'') {
  if ((currentN - orderData.Number) < 0) {
      //return error
      ...
  }
else {
    //execute update
    currentN = currentN - orderData.Number
    ...
  }
}
else if (SalePurchase == ''Purchase'') {
    currentN = currentN + orderData.Number
//!! ---check on Maximum Capacity missed---- !!
    ...
  }
}
else { ··· //error }
...
}
// other methods
...

(3) Functionality F2::shipOrder, modified after F6 Implementation
string SalePurchase = ''sale'';
orderData getOrderData() { ··· }
void ship(sellOrderData) {
if(orderData.Number < 0 || !(checkISBN(orderData.ISBN))
        && !(stringIsValid(SalePurchase))
    // return error
//!---wrong logical condition ----!
...
N = F6::getCurrentN(orderData.ISBN);
if((N - orderData.Number) < 0) { //return error }
else { //ship order
    F6::updateAvail(sellOrderData, SalePurchase) }
...
} //other methods to support the shipment
```

ALGORITHM 1: Regression bugs in an online bookstore.

In this work, the description of the expected system behavior relies on a dynamic analysis technique that derives behavioral models from execution traces. The behavioral model is described by a set of execution traces reporting the interactions among methods. The interactions are described in terms of *invariants* and *call sequences*. An invariant is a relation describing a property that should be always preserved. In particular, we consider input/output (I/O) invariants, which can be inferred from tests execution by observing the exchanged argument values. For instance, an invariant involving a single variable x may require it to be comprised in the range $[a, b]$; an invariant involving two variables may require they to respect the relation $x < y$. A behavioral model is therefore made up of a set of I/O invariants and a sequence of function calls (reported in a trace file). For building such models, we consider the technique presented in [13], which produces a trace file representing the behavioral model that reports the sequence of calls and invariants on I/O method's arguments, built (and updated) at each entry/exit point of methods. Note that the iterative nature of TDD process favors the adoption of techniques based on invariants construction, since it allows building more and more accurate behavioral models as development proceeds across TDD cycles. *A **violation** to this*

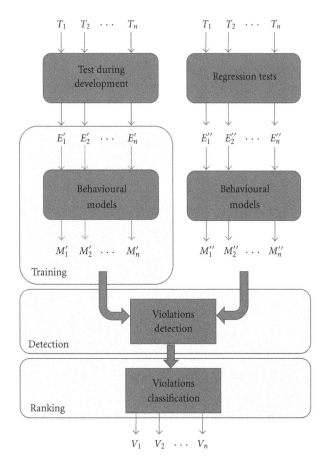

FIGURE 2: The proposed approach. T_i are test cases, E_i are execution traces resulting from tests execution, and M_i are the inferred models. V_i are the final list of violations.

model is caused either by a deviation from the built invariants (i.e., an argument value that violates the property described by the invariant) and/or by a sequence of calls different from the expected ones. For instance, for an I/O invariant over a variable x such that $a < x < b$, a violation is caused by a value of x outside the range $]a, b[$.

As shown in Figure 2, the solution we propose is based on an anomaly detection approach that acts in three phases: *training, detection,* and *ranking,* which are applied to each TDD cycle. In the *training* phase, the behavioral model of the application representing the expected "correct" behavior is built. In the *detection* phase, an anomaly detection method is adopted to highlight the deviating behaviors (i.e., *violations*) with respect to the correct behavior. Then, in the *ranking* phase, all inferred violations are rated, in order to identify the violations closest to the bug.

Training. TDD steps include writing tests for a given group of functionalities, and then writing code to pass the them. Tests are executed until success, before skipping to the next functionalities. Training takes place during the (successful) execution of these tests, that represent the desired behavior for those functionalities. In particular, while executing these tests $(T_1, \ldots, T_n)$, traces $(E'_1, \ldots, E'_n)$ are gathered and

a series of behavioral models $(M'_1, \ldots, M'_n)$ are built. The models, obtained from the test executions (only from passed tests), represent the behaviors that are expected for the functionality being tested, that is, the desired and hence "correct" behavior.

Detection. After that, a group of functionalities is implemented; in the last step of a TDD cycle, regression tests are executed (with the already available test suites). During this step, execution traces are gathered again and compared to the built models to detect violations. In practice, the call sequences and the argument values are observed and compared with the call sequences and the I/O invariants of the correct behavioral models. Thus, if some code fragment, written to implement a new functionality, has altered the behavior of a previously implemented one, or if a bug introduced in a functionality (and not correctly fixed) causes a behavior different from the expected one, the technique will capture these *violations.*

Ranking. During the detection phase, different violations are inferred. We call "*bug-related*" violations all those violations directly related to a bug (i.e., that are consequence of bug activation). The remaining violations that are not related to a bug represent *false positives.* In order to discriminate false positives, as well as to reduce the time required to analyze the volume of bug-related violations, we propose a weight-based solution for ranking. In particular, the detected violations are rated according to their likelihood of being the closest violation to the bug that caused the failure.

3.1. Ranking. As previously stated, the adopted anomaly detection approach does not directly detect the bug, but it identifies violations that appear along the fault-failure chain. However, such an approach may generate a large volume of violations, and no diagnosis is provided in order to help the debugger to identify whether a violation is a true positive (i.e., bug related) or a false positive (i.e, behaviours not related to the bug). Moreover, in the case of true positives, no information is provided to determine which violation is closest to the bug activation. The goal of the ranking phase is to rate *bug-related* violations according to their closeness to the bug activation. In this process, more distant bug-related violations have to be rated in the lower part of the ranking; *fals positives*, which are not related to the bug, should be rated even lower, in the last positions. For this aim, we defined a metric that assigns a value to violations representing their likelihood of being the closest one to the bug.

In particular, we consider three criteria to determine the final probability values:

(1) we consider that during the execution of regression tests, if a bug is present, it may cause more than one test case execution to fail. Hence, we will have a set of execution traces corresponding to the failed tests. In this case, those violations that are common to more executions with failing outcome are deemed more likely to be related to the failure-causing bug. Essentially, if a violation (e.g., an argument value out

of the expected range) is always present when the system fails, then it will be more likely related to the bug;

(2) given a violation v_i, we consider, as additional criteria to determine the final probability value of v_i, the number of violations present in the failed execution traces containing v_i;

(3) the occurrence position of v_i in such traces.

Trying to translate these qualitative considerations into a metric, we define, given a violation v_i, the following parameters:

(1) the number of failed executions in which v_i is present (Nf) over the number of executions in which v_i is present (N). The violation v_i is as much likely to be a *bug-related* violation as the ratio Nf/N is close to 1. In the case that the ratio amounts to 1, this means that each execution containing v_i failed;

(2) for each failed execution, we consider the ratio $1/nP$, where nP is the number of violations in that execution. If v_i was the only violation in that execution, it would be very likely related to the bug causing the failure. The less the number of violations, the more likely a violation is deemed responsible for (i.e., directly related to) the failure;

(3) for each failed execution, we consider the position of v_i in the execution trace with respect to the other detected violations. Also in this case, we consider the ratio $1/pos$, where pos is the position (starting from 1 to n, with n being the number of violations in the considered execution). If v_i is the first violation in the considered failed execution, it will be not a consequence of other violations (thus, it is considered more likely related to the bug). On the other hand, when the position of v_i is closer to n, it is more likely a consequence of other violations (thus, it is less likely the closest one to the bug activation).

Taking the extreme case, v_i has probability 1 to be related to the bug if the following conditions contemporarily stand:

(1) $Nf = N$, that is, each time v_i is present in an execution, that execution fails;

(2)

$$\sum_{\text{executions}} \left[pF * \left(\frac{1}{nP} * \frac{1}{\text{pos}} \right) \right] = Nf \text{ with}$$

$pF = 1$ if the execution containing v_i failed,

$pF = 0$ otherwise.   (1)

Equation (1) means that for each failed execution ($pF = 1$), which contains v_i, v_i is the only present violation, which implies it in the first position (i.e., $nP = 1$ and pos = 1).

In these conditions, the contributions 1 and 2 will be both equal to N. Therefore, the metric can be formalized, with respect to the extreme case, as follows:

$$p_i = P(v_i \text{ is bug-related})$$

$$= \frac{Nf + \sum_{\text{executions}} \left[pF * \left((1/nP)^\alpha * (1/\text{pos})^\beta \right) \right]}{2N}, \quad (2)$$

that is 1 in the described extreme conditions. The factors α and β (both comprised between 0 and 1) are needed to weigh the importance of the parameters 2 and 3, respectively (i.e., the number of violations and the relative position).

Referring to the example presented in Section 2.1 (Algorithm 1), suppose that the bug introduced in the F6 functionality produces a value of the *currentN* variable, that violates an I/O invariant built on the method *getCurrentN* of F2 (i.e., a value out of the range observed during the model construction phase). Assume that this violation appears in three different executions during the regression tests, and that two of these executions fail (i.e., $Nf = 2$ and $N = 3$). Now, assuming that the violation appears in the two failed executions in the positions pos = 10 and pos = 5, respectively, and that for these executions $nP = 120$ and $nP = 50$. In such a case, the probability value assigned to the violation wo-uld be

$$P(v_i \text{ is bug-related})$$

$$= \frac{2 + \left[(1/120)^{0.3} * (1/10)^{0.5} \right] + \left[(1/50)^{0.3} * (1/5)^{0.5} \right]}{6}$$

$$= 0.369.$$

$$(3)$$

In this example, the main contribution is given by the number of failed executions in which v_i is present (two out of three) that is 0.333. Instead, the high number of violations in both failed executions causes a very little contribution (0.035). At the extreme, if v_i was the only present violation in the two failed executions, the value would be 0.666, which is the maximum value assignable with two failed executions over three. The conditions (1) and (2), that correspond, respectively, to the first and the second terms of (2) numerator, both contribute to the final probability with a value between 0 and 0.5. In this case, with two failed executions containing v_i, their contribution is at most 0.333 for both. Thus, the value Nf, other than determining the first contribution, also limits the second contribution, since the latter considers only failed executions. An improvement to this metric can be brought by considering that it does not take into account potential relationship among violations referring to the same method. More violations referring to the same method could indicate a high likelihood that the fault is located in that method. Thus, a further refinement is possible; all the violations referring to the same method (even with different I/O violations on the exchanged parameters) are grouped together, and for each method M in the execution trace, the following value is assigned:

$$M\text{-value} = \frac{\sum_i p_i}{\sum_j p_j}, \qquad (4)$$

where p_i is the probability value assigned to the violation v_i. The index i belongs to the set of all violations referring to the method M, and j refers to all the violations. In this way, a ranking with respect to the likelihood for the method to exhibit the violation closest to the bug is done, rather than on the single closest violations. This second version of the metric has shown significant improvements, as described in the experimental section.

With this schema, other refinements are possible. For instance, in order to further penalize those violations with lower probability, a third version is obtained by considering each probability p_i divided by the relative position of v_i (considering just the ranking relative to the method M). For instance, consider two methods A and B. Suppose that method A is responsible for the bug, and the second version of the metric reported one violation rated in the first position of method A's ranking (e.g., v_A^1 with probability $p_1 = 0.9$), and method B has two violations (e.g., v_B^1 and v_B^2 with probabilities $p_1 = 0.7$ and $p_2 = 0.3$, resp.), in the first and second position of method B's ranking. The M_value numerator assigned to A with the second metric would be 0.9, and the M_value numerator for B would be $0.7 + 0.3 = 1$. Instead, by considering the relative position (third version of the metric), the numerator for A will still be 0.9, but the numerator value assigned to B will be $0.7 + 0.3/2 = 0.85$, penalizing the second violation in B; this would correctly identify method A as the most probable related to the bug.

More drastic refinements could be considered, by further penalizing the violations that are in the lowest part of the ranking, but they would not always yield the right result. At the extreme, the risk is to cancel the positive effect introduced by the second version. Thus, in the experimentation, we took into account only the three described versions of the implemented metric, referring to them as first, second, and third metrics.

3.2. Implementation. A prototype tool embedded in the TDD cycle has been implemented to evaluate the performance of the described technique. Figure 3 represents the tool high level architecture. We named the tool **ReTest**.

The first block is the *model builder*. It is responsible for instrumenting the application, monitoring it, and building, from the execution traces, the behavioral models. For each execution trace, it builds and stores a model. In particular, the *Model builder* block uses the tool *Daikon* [13]. *Daikon* is a dynamic analysis tool that derives invariants from execution traces. It infers a set of invariants by observing the exchanged parameter values and by statistically comparing them with a set of 160 predefined templates. It starts with a set of syntactic constraints for the considered variables and incrementally considers the input values. At each step, it eliminates the constraints violated by the value to obtain a set of constraints satisfied by all inputs. Statistical considerations allow Daikon

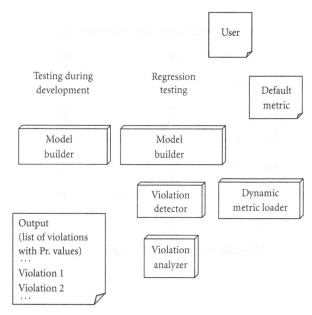

FIGURE 3: The tool architecture.

to identify constraints that are verified incidentally. The output of *Daikon* is a list of I/O invariants for each of the instrumented points.

The behavioral model is therefore described by a set of execution traces reporting the sequence of calls and invariants built (and updated) at each entry/exit point of methods, and stored in a file. Figure 4 shows a simple example developed by Daikon's author [14] describing invariants built on a Java class `StackAr` that implements a stack with a fixed maximum size. The class has two fields, namely, `Object[]theArray` and `int topOfStack`, representing, respectively, the array that contains the stack elements and the index of the top element (with -1 meaning stack empty). Among the class methods, Figure 4 shows invariants produced for the `isFull` method.

The output for each invariant is described below:
`this.theArray != null`: the reference `theArray` was never observed to be null after it was set in the constructor.
`this.theArray.getClass() ==`
`java.lang.Object[].class`: the runtime class of `theArray` is `Object[]`.
`this.topOfStack >= -1`,
`this.topOfStack <= this.theArray.length - 1`: `topOfStack` is between -1 and the maximum array index, inclusively.
`this.theArray[0..this.topOfStack] elements !=`
`null`:
all of the stack elements are nonnull, that is, the test suite never pushed null on the stack.
`this.theArray[this.topOfStack+1..]elements ==`
`null`:
all of the elements in the array that are not currently in the stack are null.
Likely invariants are also found at each method entry and exit. These correspond to the pre- and postconditions for

the method. There is one precondition for the `StackAr` constructor: `capacity >= 0`: `StackAr` was never created with a negative capacity.

The postconditions for the StackAr constructor are `orig(capacity) == this.theArray.length`: the size of the array that will contain the stack is equal to the specified capacity.

`this.topOfStack == -1`,

`this.theArray[] elements == null`: initially, the stack is empty, and all of its elements are null. There are no preconditions for the `isFull` method other than the object invariants. The postconditions are as follows

`this.topOfStack == orig(this.topOfStack)`,

`this.theArray == orig(this.theArray)`,

`this.theArray[] == orig(this.theArray[])`: neither the `topOfStack` index, nor the reference to the `theArray` array, nor the contents of the array are modified by the method.

`(return == true) <==>`

`(this.topOfStack == this.theArray.length -`
`1)`:

when `isFull` returns true, `topOfStack` indexes the last element of `theArray`.

`(return == false) <==>`

`(this.topOfStack < this.theArray.length -`
`1)`:

when `isFull` returns false, `topOfStack` indexes an element prior to the last element of `theArray`.

Models are traces containing such kind of invariants in sequence for each instrumented method call and that are iteratively updated.

The second block is the *violation detector*, which is responsible for detecting differences between the models obtained in the training phase and the models obtained in the detection phase. The *violation detector* block is based on a tool related to the *Daikon* suite, that is *InvariantDiff*, whose goal is to detect violations to a set of I/O invariants. This block detects both I/O invariant violations, supported by *InvariantDiff*, and violations to the sequence of calls that have been recorded.

Violations are stored and then analyzed by the *Violation Analyzer* block. This block rates violations to determine their likelihood of being related to a bug. The block implementing the three described metrics is the *Default Metric* block. Finally, the tool design also includes a *Metric Loader* block to allow the user to define and adopt its own metric. The output is a list of violations reporting the involved methods and variables and the corresponding probability values assigned by the metric.

Figure 5 shows a screenshot of the tool, during experiments, displaying the output file that reports the final list of violations. Information reported in this output file is the name of the violation detected, the name of the involved package, class and method, and the values of each parameter used by the metric (i.e., Nf, N, the positions of violation in the failed execution traces, the number of violations in failed executions, the values for α and β, and the final probability value assigned to that violation). In the example, the reported violation had a probability of 0.351 to be the closest one to

the bug activation (i.e., it is the one most likely related to the bug). Debugger would start its debugging process from the first violation reported in this output file.

The implemented tool uses Java as development language, Eclipse as development environment, and JUnit to run test cases. Hence, it can be executed during development in conjunction with JUnit framework and seamlessly added as a plugin to the Eclipse IDE. This aspect favors the usability of the tool, since both Java and JUnit are widely used and well known in both industry and academia. In our experiments, students confirm these considerations; however, the tool is a prototype and has been used only by students; hence, any systematic evaluation of usability would still be premature.

As for portability, being based on JUnit and on a *Daikon* Java front end (i.e., *Chicory*), the implemented tool currently works only with Java programs. However, future extension is straightforward, since it is sufficient to use the *xUnit* family tools and the other Daikon front ends to support other languages too (such as C/C++).

4. Experimentation

The proposed ranking metrics are evaluated by emulating both the development of additional functionalities to an existing application (i.e., an extension to an existing application) and the presence of various types of faults (by a faults injection campaign). These experiments allowed us to evaluate the three metrics by considering the goodness of the ranking, that is, the closeness of the first rated *bug-related* violation to the actual bug. A comparison with a well-known algorithm for debugging, namely SOBER [15], is also provided. Once evaluated the ranking ability of the proposed metrics, the technique is also experimented on an application developed from scratch by using the TDD approach.

4.1. Metric Evaluation. To evaluate metrics performance, *ReTest* is applied to a well-known open-source Java library, namely *JFreeChart* (JFreeChart (version 1.0.9) is a free Java chart library to develop professional quality charts. It is available at: http://www.jfree.org/jfreechart/), being available both the source code and the unit test cases. JFreeChart source code consists, in the chosen version, of a set of about 560 classes and 7500 functions, amounting to nearly 200 K Lines-of-Code (LoC). *ReTest* is applied to a subset of this code in the packages `org.jfree.chart.util` and `org.jfree.chart.renderer`, corresponding to 2618 LoC.

4.1.1. The Procedure. In order to evaluate the effectiveness of the three metrics in a TDD process, we emulated the development by executing the four steps of TDD and by emulating the presence of faults via *fault injection*.

The first two steps of TDD (i.e., "Write Tests" and "Write Code") do not require relevant efforts, since both the tests and the source code are available. The third and fourth steps (i.e., "Run Tests" and "Regression Tests") are carried out by using the *JUint* framework. In the regression test phase, *ReTool* evaluates the violations caused by injected bugs and

```
Object invariants for StackAr

this.theArray != null
this.theArray.getClass() == java.lang.Object[].class
this.topOfStack >= -1
this.topOfStack <= this.theArray.length - 1
this.theArray[0..this.topOfStack] elements != null
this.theArray[this.topOfStack+1..]elements == null
Preconditions for the StackAr constructor

capacity >= 0
Postconditions for the StackAr constructor

orig(capacity) == this.theArray.length
this.topOfStack == -1
Postconditions for the isFull method

this.theArray == orig(this.theArray)
this.theArray [] == orig(this.theArray[])
this.topOfStack == orig(this.topOfStack)
(return == false) <==>
 (this.topOfStack < this.theArray.length - 1)
(return == true) <==>
 (this.topOfStack == this.theArray.length - 1)
```

FIGURE 4: An excerpt of invariants of the StackAr program.

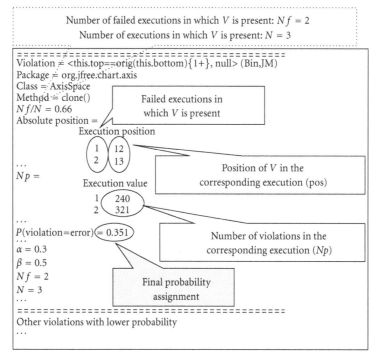

FIGURE 5: The output file reporting the violations list.

rates them according to the defined criteria. In particular, the experiments are performed as follows:

(i) as a first step, we choose a group of functionalities (and the corresponding unit test cases to be run) that represent the functionalities to be developed;

(ii) then we manually inject a fault in the code, by paying attention to not inject faults detectable by unit test cases (because in this case, the fault is supposed

to be removed before completing the functionality implementation, and thus prior to the regression tests). If injected faults are detected by unit test cases, the experiment is repeated by changing the injection;

(iii) once injected the fault, the unit test cases corresponding to the chosen functionalities are run (with the instrumentation of our tool), in order to verify if the code passes the tests. During unit tests execution, the behavioral models are built;

(iv) when unit tests do not detect any faults, development of that functionality is supposed to end. Then, regression tests are performed over all the functionalities developed till then, since the injected bug can cause anomalies in previously developed functionalities, as argued above. During regression tests, the tool automatically collects violations, computes metric values, and classifies them according to their likelihood of being related to the injected bug.

Thus, the output of the last step is a list of violations, which can be either *false positives* or *bug-related* violations. The debugger starts in such a bug report from the violation rated in the first position by the tool. If it is a *bug-related* violation (i.e., a consequence of the bug), s/he locates the bug by inspecting the code starting from that violation. If it is a *false positive*, s/he is not able to locate the bug and, after some time, skips to the second violation, until s/he meets a *bug-related* violation. Hence, it is possible to consider two evaluation measures:

(1) the first one is the position of the first *bug-related* violation in the ranking carried out by the tool. The higher this position, the higher the debugging time;

(2) we consider the *violation chain*, $VC = \{v_1, v_2, \ldots, v_n\}$, as the sequence of violations in the execution trace that occurred from the bug activation to the failure. Let V denote the bug-related violation reported by the tool in the first position of the bug report, as the closest one to the bug according to its ranking. To evaluate how much this ranking is correct and useful, the second measure is the *length* of the violations chain between the bug and V, we call it *VC length*. Since debugger would start from V to localize the bug, the higher *VC length*, the more time the debugger will employ to locate the bug (more code needs to be inspected).

The latter measure turned out to be much more important than the position of the first *bug-related* violation, since in almost all the performed experiments, the tool rated in the first position a *bug-related* violation (i.e., false positives are almost always rated in the lowest positions). Actually, if the tool rates in the first position a false positive, the tool performance has to be considered not acceptable (as showed in the next section), since the debugger would be misled and would spend too much time before skipping to the second violation. When the first violation is a *bug-related* one (in almost all the cases), the relevant evaluation measure is therefore the VC length in the execution trace.

4.1.2. Fault Injection. Fault injection is a common approach to evaluate debugging techniques (e.g., [15–21]). There are several approaches to emulate software faults. Faults can be reproduced either by modifying the source code of the target application, that is, by injecting the actual fault (software mutation, SM), or by injecting errors. Software mutation has been shown to be the most accurate way to emulate

TABLE 1: Kind of injected faults.

ODC type	Description
Function	Affects significant capability (such as end-user interfaces or global data structure) and requires design change
Assignment	Affects a few lines of code (such as initialization of control blocks or data structure)
Checking	Addresses program logic that has failed to validate data and values
Algorithm	Includes efficiency or correctness problems that affect the task and requires reimplementation

software faults [22]. It can be applied when the source code is available, and it allows to emulate all the software faults encompassed by a well-known classification scheme, that is, the orthogonal defect classification (ODC, [23]).

For these reasons, we preferred SM to error injection techniques, such as SWIFI, and to binary mutation also known as G-SWFIT [24]. Indeed, SWIFI does not allow to reproduce software faults that require large modifications to the code, or that are due to design deficiencies, such as *function faults* (see [23]). By G-SWFIT, it is tricky to assure that injection locations actually reflect the high-level constructs where faults are prone to appear. Moreover, it cannot assure that binary mutations are the same as generated by source code mutations. Hence, we inject faults directly into the source code (according to the ODC classification). Table 1 indicates the ODC types that have been injected and their meaning.

4.1.3. Results. We applied the outlined procedure for an experimental set of 20 different faulty versions and evaluated the performances of the three implemented metrics. Experiments produced the results reported in Table 2, for the three implemented metric versions. In particular, Table 2 shows, for each experiment, the *VC length* between the bug activation and V, (i.e., the *bug-related* violation reported in the first position by the tool), and the number of violations detected during each experiment. Note that more violations may refer to the same method called several times. Experiments marked with a "$*$" character are the ones in which the tool rated as first violation a false positive (in which cases the tool performances are considered as not acceptable). In all the other cases, the first rated violation is a *bug-related* violation.

Results show that best performances are obtained by the third metric. In 75% (15 over 20) of the experiments has the *VC length* is less than six. Compared to the first metric, the latter shown the same results for just 6 experiments (30%), while the second metric for 14 over 20 experiments (70%). In the remaining cases (resp., 25%, 70%, and 30%), the *VC lenght* is always greater than ten, thus significantly compromising the ability of the technique to locate bugs in acceptable time (also in these cases, the third metric shows better results).

TABLE 2: Results showing the *VC length* in the execution trace from the bug activation to the *bug-related* violation *V* and the number of total violations in each test.

Test	VC length/Tot. violations by metric 1	VC length/Tot. violations by metric 2	VC length/Tot. violations by metric 3
1	73/596	1/596	1/596
2	1/77	2/77	1/77
3	39/293	3/293	3/293
4	142/168	133/168	126/168
5	49/301	1/301	1/301
6	211/291	13/291	13/291
7	109/172	3/172	3/172
8	87/231	5/231	5/231
9	1/46	22/46	22/46
10	1/31	1/31	1/31
11	16/56	4/56	4/56
12	21/133	6/133	6/133
13	23/129	5/129	5/129
14	276/312*	211/312*	19/312*
15	37/93	2/93	2/93
16	1/43	2/43	1/43
17	2/77	1/77	1/77
18	123/149*	61/149*	33/149*
19	16/211	103/211	3/211
20	1/37	1/37	1/37

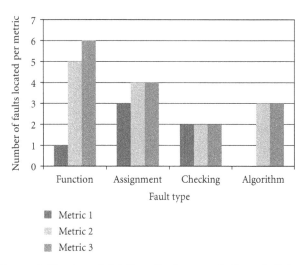

FIGURE 6: Number of violations (in the range 1–6) per fault type and per metric.

4.1.4. Considerations. Results show that the introduction of the second criterion (i.e., violations grouped according to the method they refer to) has been successful. A further improvement has been obtained by giving less importance to the violations rated at the lowest part of the ranking (i.e., the third metric), bringing the most of the *VC length* values under six. In the experimentation phase, described in the next section, we adopted the third metric, which provided the best results.

From the analysis of the injected faults, it has been also possible to observe the metrics behaviors with respect to different fault types. The diagram in Figure 6 represents the number of violations whose VC length is in the range 1–6 (i.e., the best results), classified per injected fault type and per used metric.

The three metric versions behave almost in the same way for *assignment* and *checking* fault type. This means that grouping violations by methods is quite irrelevant for these types of fault. The second and third metrics introduce improvements in the *function* and *algorithm* category. The changes introduced by these metrics affect the ability to localize faults related to the "logic" of the code (e.g., "Algorithm"). The most relevant improvement introduced by the third metric is about the *function faults*. This type of faults affects the design, requiring design changes and large modifications to the code. Grouping by methods and giving more importance to the first violations led to better localization of these more complex faults. This can be

explained by considering that faults requiring significant design changes very likely cause more violations for the method where they are injected.

4.1.5. Comparison with SOBER. Performances of the ranking algorithm are compared with a known debugging algorithm, called SOBER [15]. Sober is a statistical approach to localize bugs that models evaluation patterns of predicates in both correct and incorrect runs. It regards a predicate as bug relevant if its evaluation pattern in incorrect runs differs significantly from that in correct ones. In particular, given a set of instrumented predicates, SOBER computes for each predicate *P* a score indicating its bug relevance, based on values taken by *P* in both correct and failing executions. Observing the values of *P*, its *evaluation bias*, representing the probability that *P* is observed as *true* in each evaluation, is computed as follows: $\pi(P) = n_t/(n_t + n_f)$, where n_t is the number of times *P* is evaluated to true in one execution, and n_f is the number of times *P* is evaluated to false.

Considering multiple executions, SOBER computes the probability density function (*pdf*) of $\pi(P)$ in all correct executions, and the *pdf* of $\pi(P)$ in failing executions: the bigger the "dissimilarity" between the two *pdf*s (according to a given similarity function; see [15] for details), the higher the bug relevance score of the predicate *P*.

Our approach, even using different information, shares with SOBER the principle of distinguishing correct and incorrect runs, and of evaluating the difference between them to assign a score to violations.

We applied SOBER in our case-study, comparing results with the ones obtained with *ReTool*. We instrumented test cases execution during regression tests, that is, in the step four of the procedure outlined in Section 4.1.1. The instrumented predicates have been then classified by the SOBER algorithm. Then, we proceeded with debugging considering the top 5 most suspicious predicates in the ranking, adhering to the choice made in [15] (i.e., *k* = 5, *k* being the number of predicates taken into account in the bug report).

TABLE 3: Results showing the percentage of code inspected before finding the bug with *ReTool* and SOBER.

Test	Inspected code (%) metric 1	Inspected code (%) metric 2	Inspected code (%) metric 3	Inspected code (%) SOBER
1	48.1	0.4	0.4	3.2
2	0.3	0.9	0.3	0.2
3	38.0	3.1	3.1	6.4
4	67.8	70.6	75.2	18.5
5	41.3	0.2	0.2	11.9
6	92.6	15.1	15.1	4.8
7	54.4	1.4	1.4	7.2
8	49.5	2.6	2.6	1.0
9	0.2	18.3	18.3	46.3
10	0.8	0.8	0.8	2.6
11	17.8	5.9	5.9	8.0
12	19.5	7.4	7.4	32.1
13	20.7	4.6	4.6	65.4
14	96.2	91.3	55.0	14.1
15	32.2	1.5	1.5	9.9
16	0.4	0.6	0.4	3.2
17	1.3	1.0	1.0	0.2
18	87.6	74.5	53.0	67.9
19	13.6	62.3	2.1	3.4
20	0.5	0.5	0.5	22.8
Mean	34.14	18.15	12.44	16.46

Table 3 shows obtained results in terms of (approximated) percentage of inspected statements to reach the bug. With respect to the three metrics of *ReTool*, we observe that SOBER has, in the average (i.e., last row of Table 3), better performances than the first metric of *ReTool* and similar performance to the second metric. The third metric of *ReTool* outperforms SOBER, even though with a little margin (it requires about 4% less code to be inspected with respect to SOBER), confirming that the choice of penalizing violations with lower bug relevance probability is valid. Note that experiments number 14 and 18 required a great percentage of code to be examined with *ReTool*, since the first violation was not bug related (i.e., it was a false positive). Hence, future effort should be devoted to eliminate the occurrence of false-positives. It should be also noted that SOBER and the third metric of *ReTool* exhibit a more regular behavior, that is, with low variations among experiments (with regard to this aspect, SOBER is slightly better than the third metric, since variance of SOBER results is about 10% less than variance of metric 3).

Figure 7 reports the same data grouped by the percentage of code inspected, that is, the number of bugs that have been found when a certain percentage of code is inspected. In this histogram, it is important to observe the number of bugs found with the lowest percentages of inspected code; indeed, bug reports requiring high percentages of code to be inspected may be not very useful.

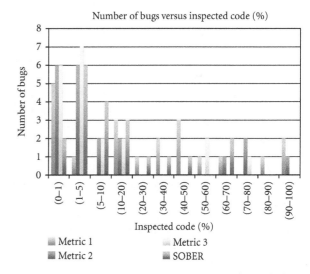

FIGURE 7: Number of violations (in the range 1–6) per fault type and per metric.

By inspecting less than 1% of the code, *ReTool* allowed finding more bugs than SOBER. Considering the inspection of at least 5% of the code (i.e., [0-1] and [1–5] intervals), SOBER outperforms metrics 1, but not metric 2 and 3; when the percentage goes up to 20% of inspected code, SOBER performance reaches metrics 2 and 3 (15, 16, and 17 bugs are found, resp., for SOBER, metrics 2 and 3, whereas metric 1 finds 9 bugs). The other bugs are clearly found when more than 20% of the code is inspected. It should be noted that metrics 2 and 3 do not have intermediate values: either they allow revealing a bug within 20% of code, or with more than 50% of code inspected.

Experimental results should be interpreted with care. As threats to validity, it should be noted that:

(i) we selected for SOBER $k = 5$, as suggested by authors in [15]. Choosing a different value for k may change SOBER performances in these experiments. On the other hand, it makes no much sense trying different k values and then starting the debug; it would require too much time;

(ii) experimentation is carried out on one program; this, of course, limits the generalization of results (for instance, also performances of SOBER are different and are better with respect to experiments described in [15]). Certainly, the case study application affects experimental results;

(iii) the program structure may influence performance of *ReTool*. Indeed, violations indicate the method containing the bug, and also the variable(s), passed as argument, which violated the invariant. The inspection points are actually the set/get points regarding that variable(s) in that method. Thus, the average number of LoC of methods affect performance of *ReTool*: in our case, *JFreeChart* is well designed, since it has about 25 lines of code per method, hence actually reducing the inspection to few points per method, but this could not be always the case.

Considering that SOBER acts with a different source of information (i.e., predicates), neglecting information at method level, the latter point suggests that combining SOBER and *ReTool* is certainly a valuable way to be pursued in the future.

4.2. Case Study. Performances of the proposed technique (in terms of obtainable saving of time in the bug localization process) have been also experimentally evaluated on an application for multimedia library management, implemented by several student teams according to the TDD approach. Differently from the previous case, thus application is a newly developed application. The involved groups of students started from the same requirements, consisting in a set of 16 use cases describing the functionalities to be developed. The experimentation was carried out in two steps.

In the first step, the application development has conducted according to the TDD cycle. Each time a group of functionalities was developed, the team executed the corresponding regression tests, obtaining a certain number of failures. At the end of each of these cycles, the "faulty" version of the current implemented software was stored. Then the team started the debugging process and proceeded with the development of new functionalities.

In this first step, a manual debugging was carried out in order to locate and fix the bugs, during which information about the debugging process was collected. In particular, at each debugging session, developers recorded the number of fixed faults, the time needed to remove each fault, and information to identify a fault (i.e., the method where it was located and the code line number). At the end of the development of all functionalities, developers reported the list of manual debugging times for each located fault. Such results are shown in the third column of Table 4.

In the second step, the debugging times with the support of the tool are compared with manual debugging times previously measured. In particular, by using *ReTest*, the teams performed the debug on stored intermediate software faulty versions. To avoid mutual influences, each team worked on the program faulty versions developed by another team. Each time a failure was experienced, the tool reported violations rated according to their likelihood of being related to the bug, and debugging started from the first violation (the tool-supported debugging time is shown in the fourth column of Table 4).

Table 4 summarizes the results for three of the developer groups. In these experiments, violations were rated according to the best version of the implemented metric, that is, the third one. The table reports the manual debugging times (column 3), as well as the tool-supported debugging times (column 4). The first column represents the program version stored at the end of each implementation session. Since the groups developed the code independently, the number of times they decided to run regression tests (thus the number of implementation sessions) is also, in general, different from one group to another. Of course, the same stands for the number of committed faults (second column). The last row of each subtable reports the first-order statistics (mean and variance) for the manual debugging time (third column) versus the tool-supported debugging time (fourth column).

The fifth column values indicate if the tool rated in the first position a *bug-related* violation or a *false positive*. In particular, it reports the position of the first *bug-related* violation in the ranking carried out by the tool (a value per each fault). In the considered experiments, only one case presents a false positive in the first position (the last version of the second group).

The sixth column reports the length of the *violation chain*. As discussed, this parameter is more important than the fifth column parameter, since in all the cases, except one, the tool rated in the first position a *bug-related* violation. At the bottom of the table, mean and variance for the overall experiments, as well as the total debugging times, are reported.

Results show that performances of the tool allowed developers to gain, in the average, 2′52″ per fault (i.e., 40.75%) in the program developed by the first group, 3′48″ (i.e., 30.40%) in the one developed by the second group, and 4′41″ (i.e., 48.61%) in the third group's program. By averaging the whole set of experiments (last row), the mean saving time amounted to 3′54″ per fault (i.e., 40.91%). Variances of tool-supported debugging times also turned out to be lower in all the three experimented cases, being 5720″ (i.e., 15.02%) less than the manual debugging time in the first group program, 4380″ (i.e., 3.96%) in the second, and 3224″ (i.e., 3.80%) in the third (7222″, i.e., 8.80% in total).

A lower variance in results indicates that the use of a semiautomatic tool allows reducing the differences among faults in terms of difficulty to be found, hence balancing the effort required to find different kinds of faults.

Results are also supported by the *t*-student hypothesis test, which indicates that the difference between tool-supported debugging time and manual debugging time is significant at a confidence level greater than 98% (*P* value = .014774).

4.2.1. Considerations. As shown in the last columns of Table 4, when the first *bug-related* violation is not in the first position of the ranking (i.e., the tool rated a *false positive* as first violation), performances significantly reduce (see the last row of the second group), since the debugger spends too much time in the inspection of the code starting from a violation that is not related to the bug. Moreover, we experienced that in the other cases, in which the first rated violation is a *bug-related* violation, the tool-supported times are significantly lower than the manual times. In two cases, namely, the third row of the first group and the second row of the third group, the tool-supported time is higher than the manual time (in particular, when the violations chain is longer than eight). This happens because the debugger has to inspect too many code lines before locating the bug, due to the distance (in terms of number of violations) between the first-rated *bug-related* violation and the actual bug. The threshold of eight is of course limited to the experimented case study. In general, there will be for a given application a limit of the violation chain length over which the application of the tool is worse than the manual debugging. In the average, the usage of the tool allowed us to obtain significant time savings.

TABLE 4: Debugging times with manual versus tool-supported experiments. The 5th column indicates the position in the ranking of the first *bug-related* violation (BR) (a value per fault). The 6th column is the *VC length* in the execution trace from the bug activation to the bug-related violation V.

Group 1					
Version	No. faults	Manual time	Tool time	Position of the 1st BR	VC length
N1	1	11′10″	2′00″	1	1
N2	3	16′20″	9′30″	1,1,1	3,4,1
N3	1	7′40″	9′20″	1	9
		Manual time mean (and variance) per fault: 7′02″ (38070″)			
		Tool time mean (and variance) per fault: 4′10″ (32350″)			
Group 2					
Version	No. faults	Manual time	Tool time	Position of the 1st BR	VC length
N1	0	0	0	—	—
N2	2	23′40″	8′10″	1,1	3,1
N3	1	19′00″	12′50″	1	5
N4	1	7′20″	13′50″	2	1
		Manual time mean (and variance) per fault: 12′30″ (110470″)			
		Tool time mean (and variance) per fault: 8′42″ (106090″)			
Group 3					
Version	No. faults	Manual time	Tool time	Position of the 1st BR	VC length
N1	3	35′00″	9′30″	1,1,1	3,1,4
N2	1	8′10″	15′20″	1	14
N3	3	24′20″	9′50″	1,1,1	2,2,1
		Manual time mean (and variance) per fault: 9′38″ (84681″)			
		Tool time mean (and variance) per fault: 4′57″ (81457″)			
Summary					
		Manual time mean (and variance) per fault: 9′32″ (82087″)			
		Tool time mean (and variance) per fault: 5′38″ (74865″)			

4.2.2. Scalability. One more relevant point is the scalability of the proposed tool. The cost of our tool is caused by (i) instrumentation and (ii) ranking algorithm. As for the first point, the cost regarding instrumentation (i.e., *model builder* and *violation detector*) is dependent on Daikon tool suite, since it is the tool used to build invariants and detect violations. This aspect is treated in detail in [13]. To summarize the main points, this cost is (i) linear in the number of potential invariants at a program point; actually, since most invariants are soon discarded, time is linear in the number of true invariants, which is a small constant in practice; (ii) it is linear in the number of times a program point is executed (i.e., linear to test suite size), and (iii) linear in the number of instrumented program points (that is proportional to the size of the program). Some actions that can be taken to reduce instrumentation and invariants computation cost are as follows: (i) reducing the number of instrumented points to few critical points, (ii) reducing the number of executions, (iii) reducing the number of variables (see "the Daikon Invariant Detector", http://groups.csail.mit.edu/pag/daikon/).

The scalability of the ranking algorithm depends on the number of executions and the number of violations in each execution. Indeed, in order to assign probabilities to violations, for each violation v_i, the algorithm has to scan both correct and incorrect executions (let us denote them with N_f and N_c, resp.), to see if v_i is present in those executions, and to determine its position of occurrence (cf. with (2)). The time complexity per each violation is therefore $O((N_f + N_c) * AverageV)$, being $AverageV$ the average number of violations in each execution. Then, probability values assigned to violations have to be ordered. Thus, the total complexity is $O((N_f + N_c) * AverageV) + V * \log * V)$, where V is the final list of violations.

As for the second metric, the complexity is unchanged, since probability values for each method, which have to be summed to generate M values (cf. with (4)), are stored in a data structure and summed while the algorithm scrolls and scores violations.

As for the third metric, a further operation proportional to the number of the final list of violations V is required, in order to divide p_i values for the relative position of the violation, hence getting to $O((N_f + N_c) * AverageV) + V * \log * V + V)$.

Comparing with SOBER, we note that (i) the first and the second metrics have the same complexity, being SOBER complexity equal to $O((N_f + N_c) * k) + k * \log * k)$ where k is the number of predicates; (ii) the third metric has higher complexity than SOBER, due to the additional factor V; and (iii) the number of violations V is typically lower than the number of predicates, since it refers to methods.

5. Related Work

In the past, much work dealt with bug localization by either static analysis or dynamic analysis techniques. Static analysis approaches rely on source code knowledge and are used to verify program correctness against one or more properties (e.g., relevant examples are software model checking [25, 26], or static slicing, by Weiser [27, 28]).

Dynamic analysis, as opposed to static analysis, aims to give information about the system by observing its execution traces. It attempts to overcome the static analysis limitations, such as the difficulty to cope with large-size applications, with changes of evolving systems, and with the increasing use of off-the-shelf (OTS) items, where the source code is not always available. Most of approaches today are classifiable as dynamic analysis; examples are (i) dynamic slicing, (ii) techniques based on behavioral models, (iii) and statistical debug. Our approach also falls into dynamic analysis category, being based on runtime execution traces analysis.

Dynamic slicing approaches monitor the system during an execution and trace the program elements covered. Only the statements covered at runtime are considered to build the slices; this lead to smaller slices with respect to those generated by static slicing approaches. It was first introduced by Korel and Laski [29]. A recent approach based on dynamic slicing is proposed in [30], which through a *callstack-sensitive* slicing and slices intersection reduces the slice sizes by leveraging the series of calls active when a program fails. Similar approaches considering the sequence of *active* function calls to improve slicing were previously proposed in [31, 32].

Several dynamic analysis approaches and tools based on behavioral models appeared in the literature (e.g., [13, 33–36]). Among these, one of the most successful ones is *Daikon* [13]. It is a tool that automatically discovers likely invariants from executions of instrumented programs, by building a wide spectrum of invariants using definite invariant templates. The authors in [33, 37] extend *Daikon*, proposing a tool (BCT) that allows to infer invariants on both the observation of call sequences among monitored objects (i.e., interaction invariants), and on the exchanged parameter values (i.e., the I/O invariants). It uses the *Daikon* inference engine for discovering I/O invariants, and an incremental algorithm, named *Kbehavior*, to build a finite state automata (FSA) representing the call sequences among objects.

The DIDUCE project tool [36] tests a more restricted set of predicates within the target program and relaxes them in a similar manner to *Daikon* at runtime. When the set of predicates becomes stable, it relates further violations as indications of potential bugs.

Also our approach relies on the use of behavioral models builder tools to describe the behavior of the system under development, and in particular it is based on *Daikon*. However, differently from the mentioned tools and techniques, the presented tool adds the ability to distinguish those behaviors most likely related to the bug, through a ranking process of detected violations by the implemented proximity metrics.

There are several approaches that use statistical considerations to assign a score to events of interest. One technique falling into this category is SOBER [15], presented in Section 4.1.5. Even if SOBER describes the application behavior differently from our approach (it uses predicates), our tool takes some concepts from it to define the metric for violations ranking (such as the distinction between correct and incorrect executions to judge a violation).

Other statistical techniques have been proposed in the program analysis and bug detection [16, 17, 38]. Among these, authors in [17] present a statistical debugging algorithm that aims at separating the effects of different bugs and identifies predictors that are associated with individual bugs, with the goal of making it easier to prioritize debugging efforts. Statistical debugging is recently improved by an adaptive monitoring strategy [39] that starts by monitoring a small portion of the program, and then automatically refines instrumentation over time. Based on analysis of feedback in a given stage, the technique automatically chooses new behaviors that could cause failures and monitors them during the successive stage, thus reducing the overhead. This approach can be complementary to ours, since it is able to improve performances in terms of instrumentation overhead.

Similarly, the HOLMES project [18] also contributed to statistical debugging by introducing a strategy based on paths profiling (it counts the number of times each path is taken in an acyclic region) to pinpoint likely causes of failures. The tool also uses an iterative profiling for an adaptive instrumentation, by exploiting partial feedback data to select and instrument predicates in successive iterations.

The authors in [19] propose a context-aware approach also based on control flow paths, which considers predicate correlations and control flow paths that connect the bug predictors for better diagnosis of bugs. One more statistical debugging algorithm is presented in [20], which aims at identifying predictors that are associated with individual bugs, separating the effects of different bugs. The algorithm, differently from previous ones (and from our approach), does not consider exact values of predicate counts but considers whether a predicate was true at least once, making no further distinctions among nonzero counts. This makes instrumentation lighter and more scalable. However, unlike in [39], the instrumentation is nonadaptive.

Another relevant tool falling in this category is Tarantula [21]. Tarantula algorithm assigns scores to statements and ranks the statements from most suspicious to least suspicious. It utilizes a concept similar to ours, in that it considers pass/fail information about test cases (along with the entities that were executed by each test case, such as statements, branches, methods, and the source code), and the concept that entities executed by failed test cases are more likely to be faulty than those executed by passed test cases. Performances of this tool are also evaluated in [40].

An important debugging technique is the delta debugging [41, 42]. It was introduced in 1999 by Zeller in a seminal paper in this area [43] and used in several contexts (e.g., in diagnosis [44]). Delta debugging aims at simplifying or isolating failure causes by systematically narrowing down failure-inducing circumstances until a minimal set remains.

The algorithm aims at identifying the smallest set of changes that caused a regression in a program. It requires the following information: a test that fails because of a regression, a previous correct version of the program, and the set of changes performed by programmers. The delta debugging algorithm works in this way: it iteratively applies different subsets of the changes to the original program to create different versions of the program and identify the failing ones. The minimal set of changes that permit to reproduce the failure is reported.

Our approach lies in between "*Daikon-like*" techniques, that is, based on behavioral models and statistical debug techniques, since it uses the former approach to describe the application behavior (in terms of invariants) and to detect violations (in the training and detection phases), and some criteria of the latter to rate those anomalous behaviors possibly related to bugs (in the ranking phase).

Moreover, a key difference is that the presented technique is specifically tailored for the TDD process; the continuous iterations of TDD allowed us to embed a semiautomatic debug step from the earliest stages of the development cycle, where a greater effectiveness in bug detection is actually required. Indeed, debugging applications during their development help greatly reducing maintenance costs.

The structure of the TDD approach also justifies the adoption of techniques based on behavioral models in the training phase, since repeated iterations allow for building more and more accurate behavioral models.

Finally, it is worth reporting some different approaches to debugging, such as those taken in [45] and in [46]. In the former, authors present a technique for supporting in-house debugging of field failures, based on a three-step procedure: field failing executions recording, execution traces minimization, and replaying of the minimized execution to help debugging (within a debugger). In the latter ([46]), a spectra-based technique is presented; here, the concept of execution time is considered as an indicator of anomalous behaviors, and hence of potential bugs: time spectra are collected from passing and failing runs, observed behavior models are created using the time spectra of passing runs, and deviations from these models in failing runs are identified and scored as potential causes of failures.

The tool presented in [47], named *Whyline*, combines more program analysis techniques, such as static and dynamic slicing, precise call graph, in order to allow user to choose a set of *why* or *why didn't* question about program output derived from program's code and execution, and then to generate an answer to the questions. Such questions represent the user's will to understand the program's behaviour starting from the output.

There are several other, more narrowed, approaches that focus on some specific aspects of bug localization problem. Examples are the techniques presented in [48, 49], where the problem of memory leak detection is faced, and in [50], whose focus is on faults in concurrent programs.

6. Conclusion and Future Work

In this work, we presented a technique to help developers localize bugs, embedded in the test-driven development cycle. The technique has been implemented in a tool, written in Java, that during the unit tests execution allows to build a model of the expected behavior of the software under development and then compares the behavior observed in the regression test phase with the built model in order to detect anomalies.

These anomalies are rated according to the defined metrics and assigned a probability to be related to the failure-causing bug. The developer uses the ranking to inspect the code and localize the bug. The proposed metrics have been evaluated through an existing open-source application, in which a fault injection campaign has been carried out and the goodness of the ranking process carried out by the tool has been analyzed. The technique performances have been verified by evaluating the tool's ability to reduce debugging time with respect to manual debugging on a new application developed by groups of students according to the TDD cycle. Results encourage further investigation of the tool on other software applications and potential integration with existing approaches.

In particular, as for future work, we are attempting to improve the accuracy of the implemented metrics in the identification of bug location, by considering the combination of features of other statistical-based algorithms with our technique. The goal is to improve the bug proximity information inside the method that most likely contains the bug, by combining violations of invariants on methods and on object values with approaches based on predicates, which currently do not consider information related to methods.

Moreover, we are evaluating the introduction of static information derived from software specifications (such as constraints on some critical exchanged values or mandatory sequences of calls) in order to ease the distinction among *false positives* and erroneous behaviors.

Finally, we are investigating the factors that mainly impact the value of α and β, in order to reduce the start-up time spent to tune them; preliminary analyses show that the coupling degree among modules has a significant impact, but further investigations are needed.

References

[1] D. Janzen and H. Saiedian, "Test-driven development: concepts, taxonomy, and future direction," *Computer*, vol. 38, no. 9, pp. 43–50, 2005.

[2] R. Kaufmann and D. Janzen, "Implications of test-driven development: a pilot study," in *Proceedings of the 18th ACM*

SIGPLAN Conference on Object-Oriented Programming Systems, Languages, and Applications (OOPSLA '03), pp. 298–299, Anaheim, Calif, USA, 2003.

[3] E. M. Maximilien and L. Williams, "Assessing test-driven development at IBM," in *Proceedings of the 25th IEEE International Conference on Software Engineering (ICSE '03)*, pp. 564–569, IEEE CS Press, May 2003.

[4] A. Gupta and P. Jalote, "An experimental evaluation of the effectiveness and efficiency of the test driven development," in *Proceedings of the 1st International Symposium on Empirical Software Engineering and Measurement (ESEM '07)*, pp. 285–294, September 2007.

[5] R. C. Martin, "Professionalism and test-driven development," *IEEE Software*, vol. 24, no. 3, pp. 32–36, 2007.

[6] B. George and L. Williams, "A structured experiment of test-driven development," *Information and Software Technology*, vol. 46, no. 5, pp. 337–342, 2004.

[7] L. Williams, E. M. Maximilien, and M. Vouk, "Test-driven development as a defect-reduction practice," in *Proceedings of the 14th IEEE International Symposium on Software Reliability Engineering (ISSRE '03)*, p. 34, IEEE Computer Society, 2003.

[8] B. George and L. Williams, "An initial investigation of test driven development in industry," in *Proceedings of the ACM Symposium on Applied Computing (SAC '03)*, pp. 1135–1139, ACM Press, 2003.

[9] T. Bhat and N. Nagappan, "Evaluating the efficacy of test-driven development: industrial case studies," in *Proceedings of the 5th ACM/IEEE International Symposium on Empirical Software Engineering (ISESE '06)*, pp. 356–363, ACM Press, 2006.

[10] A. Geras, M. Smith, and J. Miller, "A prototype empirical evaluation of test driven development," in *Proceedings of the 10th International Symposium on Software Metrics (METRICS '04)*, pp. 405–416, IEEE Computer Society, 2004.

[11] M. M. Müller and O. Hagner, "Experiment about test-first programming," in *Proceedings of the International Conference of Software Engineering (ICSE '02)*, vol. 149, no. 5, pp. 131–136, 2002.

[12] M. Pancur, M. Ciglaric, M. Trampus, and T. Vidmar, " Towards empirical evaluation of test-driven development in a university environment," in *Proceedings of the International Conference on Computer as a Tool (EUROCON '03)*, vol. 2, pp. 83–86, 2003.

[13] M. D. Ernst, J. Cockrell, W. G. Griswold, and D. Notkin, "Dynamically discovering likely program invariants to support program evolution," *IEEE Transactions on Software Engineering*, vol. 27, no. 2, pp. 99–123, 2001.

[14] M. D. Ernst, J. H. Perkins, P. J. Guo et al., "The Daikon system for dynamic detection of likely invariants," *Science of Computer Programming*, vol. 69, no. 1–3, pp. 35–45, 2007.

[15] C. Liu, X. Yan, L. Fei, J. Han, and S. P. Midkiff, "SOBER: statistical model-based bug localization," in *Proceedings of the 10th European Software Engineering Conference (ESEC/FSE '05)*, pp. 286–295, 2005.

[16] W. Dickinson, D. Leon, and A. Podgurski, "Finding failures by cluster analysis of execution profiles," in *Proceedings of the 23rd International Conference on Software Engineering (ICSE '01)*, pp. 339–348, 2001.

[17] B. Liblit, M. Naik, A. X. Zheng, A. Aiken, and M. I. Jordan, "Scalable statistical bug isolation," in *Proceedings of the ACM SIGPLAN Conference on Programming Language Design and Implementation (PLDI '05)*, pp. 15–26, 2005.

[18] T. M. Chilimbi, B. Liblit, K. K. Mehra, A. V. Nori, and K. Vaswani, "HOLMES: effective statistical debugging via efficient path profiling," in *Proceedings of the 31st IEEE International Conference on Software Engineering (ICSE '09)*, pp. 34–44, IEEE Computer Society, 2009.

[19] L. Jiang and Z. Su, "Context-aware statistical debugging: from bug predictors to faulty control flow paths," in *Proceedings of the 22nd IEEE/ACM International Conference on Automated Software Engineering (ASE '07)*, R. E. K. Stirewalt, A. Egyed, and B. Fischer, Eds., pp. 184–193, ACM Press, 2007.

[20] B. Liblit, M. Naik, A. X. Zheng, A. Aiken, and M. I. Jordan, "Scalable statistical bug isolation," in *Proceedings of the ACM SIGPLAN Conference on Programming Language Design and Implementation (PLDI '05)*, V. Sarkar and M. W. Hall, Eds., pp. 15–26, ACM Press, 2005.

[21] J. A. Jones and M. J. Harrold, "Empirical evaluation of the tarantula automatic fault-localization technique," in *Proceedings of the 20th IEEE/ACM International Conference on Automated Software Engineering (ASE '05)*, D. F. Redmiles, T. Ellman, and A. Zisman, Eds., pp. 273–282, ACM Press, 2005.

[22] M. Hiller, J. Christmansson, and M. Rimèn, "An experimental comparison of fault and error injection," in *Proceedings of the IEEE International Symposium on Software Reliability Engineering (ISSRE '98)*, pp. 369–378, 1998.

[23] R. Chillarege, I. S. Bhandari, J. K. Chaar et al., "Orthogonal defect classification—a concept for in-process measurements," *IEEE Transactions on Software Engineering*, vol. 18, no. 11, pp. 943–956, 1992.

[24] J. Durães and H. Madeira, "Emulation of software faults: a field data study and a practical approach," *IEEE Transactions on Software Engineering*, vol. 32, no. 11, pp. 849–867, 2006.

[25] E. Clarke, O. Grumberg, and D. Peled, *Model Checking*, MIT Press, 1999.

[26] T. Ball, M. Naik, and S. K. Rajamani, "From symptom to cause: localizing errors in counterexample traces," in *Proceedings of the 30th ACM SIGPLAN-SIGACT Symposium on Principles of Programming Languages (POPL '03)*, pp. 97–105, 2003.

[27] M. Weiser, "Program slicing," *IEEE Transactions on Software Engineering*, vol. 10, no. 4, pp. 352–357, 1984.

[28] M. Weiser, "Programmers use slicing when debugging," *Communications of the ACM*, vol. 25, no. 7, pp. 446–452, 1982.

[29] B. Korel and J. Laski, "Dynamic program slicing," *Information Processing Letters*, vol. 29, no. 3, pp. 155–163, 1988.

[30] S. Horwitz, B. Liblit, and M. Polishchuk, "Better debugging via output tracing and callstack-sensitive slicing," *IEEE Transactions on Software Engineering*, vol. 36, no. 1, pp. 7–19, 2010.

[31] D. Binkley, "Semantics guided regression test cost reduction," *IEEE Transactions on Software Engineering*, vol. 23, no. 8, pp. 498–516, 1997.

[32] J. Krinke, "Context-sensitivity matters, but context does not," in *Proceedings of the IEEE International Workshop on Source Code Analysis and Manipulation (SCAM '04)*, pp. 29–35, 2004.

[33] L. Mariani and M. Pezzè, "Behavior capture and test: automated analysis of component integration," in *Proceedings of the 10th IEEE International Conference on Engineering of Complex Computer Systems (ICECCS '05)*, pp. 292–301, 2005.

[34] V. Dallmeier, C. Lindig, A. Wasylkowski, and A. Zeller, "Mining object behavior with ADABU," in *Proceedings of the International Conference on Software Engineering (ICSE '06)*, pp. 17–24, 2006.

[35] B. Schmerl, D. Garlan, and H. Yan, "Dinamically discovering architectures with DiscoTect," in *Proceedings of the European Conference on Software Engineering (ESEC/FSE '05)*, pp. 103–106, 2005.

[36] S. Hangal and M. S. Lam, "Tracking down software bugs using automatic anomaly detection," in *Proceedings of the 24th International Conference on Software Engineering (ICSE '02)*, pp. 291–301, 2002.

[37] D. Lorenzoli, L. Mariani, and M. Pezzè, "Automatic generation of software behavioral models," in *Proceedings of the 30th International Conference on Software Engineering (ICSE '08)*, pp. 501–510, ACM Press, New York, NY, USA, 2008.

[38] A. Podgurski, D. Leon, P. Francis et al., "Automated support for classifying software failure reports," in *Proceedings of the 25th International Conference on Software Engineering (ICSE '03)*, pp. 465–475, 2003.

[39] M. B. Dwyer, A. Kinneer, and S. G. Elbaum, "Adaptive online program analysis," in *Proceedings of the 29th IEEE International Conference on Software Engineering (ICSE '07)*, pp. 220–229, IEEE Computer Society, 2007.

[40] R. Santelices, J. A. Jones, Y. Yu, and M. J. Harrold, "Lightweight fault-localization using multiple coverage types," in *Proceedings of the 31st IEEE International Conference on Software Engineering (ICSE '09)*, pp. 56–66, IEEE Computer Society, 2009.

[41] A. Zeller and R. Hildebrandt, "Simplifying and isolating failure-inducing input," *IEEE Transactions on Software Engineering*, vol. 28, no. 2, pp. 183–200, 2002.

[42] H. Cleve and A. Zeller, "Locating causes of program failures," in *Proceedings of the 27th International Conference on Software Engineering (ICSE '05)*, pp. 342–351, ACM Press, New York, NY, USA, 2005.

[43] A. Zeller, "Yesterday, my program worked. Today, it does not. Why?" in *Proceedings of the 7th European Software Engineering Conference Held Jointly with the 7th ACM SIGSOFT International Symposium on Foundations of Software Engineering (ESEC/FSE '07)*, pp. 253–267, Springer, London, UK, 2007.

[44] J. Tucek, S. Lu, C. Huang, S. Xanthos, and Y. Zhou, "Triage: diagnosing production run failures at the user's site," in *Proceedings of the 21st ACM SIGOPS Symposium on Operating Systems Principles (SOSP '07)*, pp. 131–144, ACM Press, 2007.

[45] J. Clause and A. Orso, "A technique for enabling and supporting debugging of field failures," in *Proceedings of the 29th International Conference on Software Engineering (ICSE '07)*, pp. 261–270, IEEE Computer Society, 2007.

[46] C. Yilmaz, A. M. Paradkar, and C. Williams, "Time will tell: fault localization using time spectra," in *Proceedings of the 30th International Conference on Software Engineering (ICSE '08)*, W. Schafer, M. B. Dwyer, and V. Gruhn, Eds., pp. 81–90, ACM Press, 2008.

[47] A. J. Ko and B. A. Myers, "Debugging reinvented: asking and answering why and why not questions about program behavior," in *Proceedings of the 30th International Conference on Software Engineering (ICSE '08)*, pp. 301–310, ACM Press, New York, NY, USA, 2008.

[48] G. Xu and A. Rountev, "Precise memory leak detection for java software using container profiling," in *Proceedings of the 30th International Conference on Software Engineering (ICSE '08)*, pp. 151–160, ACM Press, New York, NY, USA, 2008.

[49] J. Clause and A. Orso, "LEAKPOINT: pinpointing the causes of memory leaks," in *Proceedings of the 32nd ACM/IEEE International Conference on Software Engineering (ICSE '10)*, vol. 1, pp. 515–552, ACM Press, New York, NY, USA, 2010.

[50] S. Park, R. W. Vuduc, and M. J. Harrold, "Falcon: fault localization in concurrent programs," in *Proceedings of the 32nd ACM/IEEE International Conference on Software Engineering (ICSE '10)*, vol. 1, pp. 245–254, ACM Press, New York, NY, USA, 2010.

13

Evaluation of Tools and Slicing Techniques for Efficient Verification of UML/OCL Class Diagrams

Asadullah Shaikh,[1,2] **Uffe Kock Wiil,**[1] **and Nasrullah Memon**[1,3]

[1] *The Maersk Mc-Kinney Moller Institute, University of Southern Denmark, 5230 Odense, Denmark*
[2] *Universitat Oberta de Catalunya, Barcelona 08018, Spain*
[3] *Mehran University of Engineering & Technology, Jamshoro 76062, Pakistan*

Correspondence should be addressed to Asadullah Shaikh, shaikhasad@hotmail.com

Academic Editor: Andrea De Lucia

UML/OCL class diagrams provide high-level descriptions of software systems. Currently, UML/OCL class diagrams are highly used for code generation through several transformations in order to save time and effort of software developers. Therefore, verification of these class diagrams is essential in order to generate accurate transformations. Verification of UML/OCL class diagrams is a quite challenging task when the input is large (i.e., a complex UML/OCL class diagram). In this paper, we present (1) a benchmark for UML/OCL verification and validation tools, (2) an evaluation and analysis of tools available for verification and validation of UML/OCL class diagrams including the range of UML support for each tool, (3) the problems with efficiency of the verification process for UML/OCL class diagrams, and (4) solution for efficient verification of complex class diagrams.

1. Introduction

UML/OCL models are designed in order to provide a high-level description of a software system which can be used as a piece of documentation or as an intermediate step in the software development process. In the context of model-driven development (MDD) and model-driven architecture (MDA), a correct specification is required because the entire technology is based on model transformation. Therefore, if the original model is wrong, this clearly causes a failure of the final software system. Regrettably, verification of a software product is a complex and time-consuming task [1] and that also applies to the analysis of the software models. With increasing model size and complexity, the need for efficient verification methods able to cope with the growing difficulties is ever present, and the importance of UML models has increased significantly [2].

There are formal verification tools for automatically checking correctness properties on models [3–6], but the lack of scalability is usually a drawback. We have considered the static structure diagram that describes the structure of a system, modeled as a UML class diagram. Complex integrity

constraints will be expressed in OCL. In this context, the fundamental correctness property of a model is *satisfiability*.

We focus our discussion on the verification of a specific property: satisfiability—"is it possible to create objects without violating any constraints.?" The property is relevant in the sense that many interesting properties; for example, redundancy of an integrity constraint can be expressed in terms of satisfiability [7]. Two different notions of satisfiability can be checked, either weak satisfiability or strong satisfiability. A class diagram is weakly satisfiable if it is possible to create a legal instance/object of a class diagram which is non mpty; that is, it contains at least one object from some class. Alternatively, strong satisfiability is a more restrictive condition requiring that the legal instance has at least one object from each class and a link from each association [4].

Reasoning on UML class diagrams without OCL integrity constraints is an EXPTIME-complete problem [8]. The UML class diagram analysis is a complex problem. However, the addition of OCL constraint makes the problem undecidable in general. In order to avoid this undecidability, the automatic verification procedure is required. Furthermore, the addition of unrestricted (Some approaches restrict the set of supported OCL constructs, e.g., to make the verification decidable. In this paper, we consider general OCL constraints with no limitations on their expressivity.) OCL constraints makes the problem undecidable. The unrestricted form of OCL constraints is not limited in expressiveness to equality, size, and attribute operations.

Current solutions for checking satisfiability employ formalisms such as description logics [9], higher-order logics [10], database deduction systems [11], linear programming [12], SAT [13], or constraint satisfaction problems [4, 8]. However, all the approaches which support general OCL constraints share a common drawback, a high worst-case computational complexity. Their execution time may depend exponentially on the size of the model, understanding size as the number of classes/attributes/associations in the model, and/or the number of OCL constraints [14–16].

Hitherto, the existing tools are only capable of verifying model properties; such tools verify the model properties much quicker when the input is a small UML/OCL class diagram. In case of a large UML/OCL class diagram as input, these tools become so inefficient that verification becomes impractical. Therefore, there is a need for efficient verification tool or technique to cope with this complexity problem. As the complexity of a model can be exponential in terms of model size (i.e., the number of classes, associations, and inheritance hierarchies), reducing the size of a model can cause a drastic speedup in the verification process. One possible approach is *slicing*, which is partitioning the class diagram and OCL constraints into smaller fragments according to certain criteria. This partition should preserve the property under verification in the sense that it should be possible to assess the property in the original model from the analysis of the partitions. A careful definition of the partition process is needed to ensure this.

In this paper, we propose a survey and a benchmark based on analysis of current formal verification tools. The survey is based on

(i) identification of verification and validation tools,

(ii) evaluation of current verification and validation tools,

(iii) the UML support for each verification and validation tool.

Furthermore, we have identified some issues related to the efficiency of verification of UML/OCL class diagrams. Therefore, our focus is to address those issues along with an appropriate solution. The solution is named as UML/OCL slicing technique (UOST). The technique includes a set of heuristics that are used to partition a model when determining its satisfiability. That is, given a model "m", the technique partitions m into $m_1, m_2, m_3, \ldots, m_n$ submodels, where m is satisfiable if all $m_1, m_2, m_3, \ldots, m_n$ submodels are satisfiable. We provide an experimental evaluation of this technique using a verification tool for UML to CSP which is called UMLtoCSP [4] and Alloy [6]. We examine both small and large UML/OCL class diagrams with 2, 15, 17, 50, 100, 500, and 1000 classes and several OCL

invariants to measure the efficiency of the verification process through our proposed UOST. It also provides extensive results achieved by adding the slicing technique to an external tool (Alloy). The primary reason for showing the results in both Alloy and UMLtoCSP is to demonstrate that the developed slicing technique is neither tool dependent nor formalism dependent. It can be applied into any formal verification tool for UML/OCL models.

The remainder of the paper is structured as follows. Section 2 provides a description and evaluation of selected UML/OCL tools. It also presents an efficiency analysis based on two of the tools. In Section 3, a solution to the identified efficiency problem is presented while Section 4 is comprised of nondisjoint solution. Section 5 presents the experimental results based on the proposed solution. In Section 6, related work is presented. Finally, Section 7 provides the conclusions and identifies directions for future work.

2. Evaluation of Existing UML/OCL Tools

This section presents a description of UML/OCL tools and methods that are widely used for the purpose of verification and validation of UML class diagrams. After evaluation of existing UML/OCL tools, we have discovered certain limitations in most of the verification and validation tools.

2.1. Analysis of UML/OCL Tools. The analysis is based upon a close view of each UML/OCL tool including the range of support for UML by each tool. The purpose of UML/OCL tools is to check the model properties that need to be verified. We have analyzed six UML/OCL tools in all. The first four subsections 2.1.1–2.1.4 discuss the verification tools: (1) HOL-OCL, (2) UMLtoCSP, (3) Alloy, (4) UML2Alloy. The last two subsections 2.1.5 and 2.1.6 discuss the validation tools: (5) USE and (6) MOVA. Each tool focuses on a different formalism and verification procedure. Therefore, the verification time is entirely based on a specific formalism. There are several environments that provide verification capability for UML/OCL class diagrams. Each environment has several advantages and disadvantages summarized in this section.

2.1.1. HOL-OCL. Higher-order logic and object constraint language (HOL-OCL) is a theorem-proving environment that is incorporated in the model driven engineering (MDE) framework [17]. It is based on the UML [18] and OCL [19] specification annotated into Isabelle/HOL [10]. In principle the HOL-OCL is based in su4sml [17] and Isabelle/HOL, which is UML/OCL repository. Also the interface consists of SML of Isabelle/HOL. Through HOL-OCL, satisfiability of class invariants can be proved.

The purpose of HOL-OCL is to support the subsets of "UML core" related to UML class diagrams. The limitations of HOL-OCL are that it does not support qualifiers for association ends, enumeration and association classes, but it supports the association relations and represents those relations by association's ends.

HOL-OCL supports only the standard OCL data types, that is, Integer, Real, String, and Boolean, but these data types are considered different than UML standard data types, that is, Integer, UnlimitedInteger, String, and Enumeration.

HOL-OCL is a theorem prover that needs user assistance because it does not support automations. This is a limitation of HOL-OCL. Moreover there are some data types that cannot be modeled explicitly into HOL-OCL-like OclVoid, OclModelElementType, and OclType [3].

2.1.2. UMLtoCSP. UMLtoCSP is a tool for formal verification of UML/OCL class diagrams [4], which is based on constraint solver as the verification engine. It is designed as a verification tool, which is limited to take ArgoUML-generated XMI [20] class diagrams as an input along with OCL text files and generate the results automatically in the form of "Yes" and "No." UMLtoCSP checks the correctness of model properties, such as strong and weak satisfiability of a model or the lack of redundant constraints. This tool translates the model into a constraint satisfaction problem (CSP), and then it relies on the constraint solver ECLiPSe [21] to verify if the solution exists in CSP or not. The whole process is fully automated and does not require any manual interaction during the verification process.

The development of the tool is in Java along with ECLiPSe constraint libraries with combined libraries of Dresden toolkit [22] that are used for parsing in UMLtoCSP. MDR is used for the import/export of XMI.

In terms of UML support, this tool is limited to class diagrams. It accepts the model with associations and generalization but it lacks dependencies, aggregations, and stereotypes. In terms of OCL it only supports writing invariants with pre- and postconditions, while query operations are not supported at all.

2.1.3. Alloy. Alloy is a language [6] which is used to describe structural properties. It uses first-order logic (FOL) for modeling design and is regarded as a lightweight design tool which permits devise designs properly and checks its correctness using the alloy analyzer. The designer formulates a design in the Alloy language, which is FOL dependent on relations, and checks the property correctness using alloy analyzer. The analyzer translates the alloy formula into Boolean Formula in conjunctive normal form (CNF) and resolute it with SAT solver.

Alloy does not take a UML class diagram as input. The model in Alloy must be written textually using the Alloy graphical user interface. Alloy syntax is compatible with UML; the assessment is quite complicated because the model does not contain any textual syntax; therefore, every model requires a set of constraints in order to perform verification. The prototype of Alloy is made in Java solver "SAT4J" in order to run on every platform.

2.1.4. UML2Alloy. UML2Alloy is research tool which is used to verify UML using Alloy in the technology of model-driven development (MDD) [23]. UML2Alloy is playing an important role to create a bridge between UML and Alloy. Users can take advantage of UML2Alloy by applying the benefits of the Alloy analyzer to UML class diagrams.

The tool takes an ArgoUML-generated XMI file in order to transform the UML model into Alloy code. It transforms the input into assertions, simulations, or invariants. The tool translates the classes into signatures and subclasses in subsignatures. If the class is abstract, then it is considered as an abstract signature. It translates the class attributes into signature fields.

Furthermore, as far as the OCL is concerned, it does not support shorthand OCL notations. The class invariants are normally converted to Alloy facts. Invariants can also be translated into assertions. Initially invariants are translated to a predicate and then a fact statement.

2.1.5. USE. UML-based specification environment (USE) is a tool used for the validation of UML and OCL Models [24]. The formalism behind USE is A snapshot sequence language (ASSL). The construction of an ASSL script is manual, as the user needs to define the order in which objects will be created. At this point, the reader may not see that ASSL scripts normally describe sets of snapshots (system states); that is, ASSL scripts determine search spaces which have to be searched by the ASSL generator. This feature is enabled through the ASSL "try" statements which try different system state constellations out, inducing backtracking if the considered constellation does not lead to a valid snapshot. As a consequence, the order of object creations does not need to be manually determined.

The validation in USE is based on manual insertion; it allows the analysis of specification in order to validate the UML class diagram and its OCL constraints to avoid the defects in early stages of the development process. USE has a wide range of UML support; it fully provides validation syntax of class diagrams, sequence diagrams, and activity diagrams, while none of the above tools supports that much. In terms of OCL, it fully supports writing invariants using pre- and postconditions.

2.1.6. MOVA. MOVA is a tool [25], which is based on UML modeling. It is designed as a validation tool, which allows writing OCL constraints for UML class diagrams, drawing the instances of class diagram and validating OCL constraints over the instances of a class diagram. The tool has a user interface which permits the user to draw UML classes and object diagrams. It allows writing and verifying invariants and writing and assessing queries.

MOVA was developed initially in Java for the ITP/OCL tool [26]. It is a validation tool along with text input UML modeling. The tool provides a set of commands for building classes and object diagrams. It is written in Maude [27] which is a rewriting-based programming language that implements membership equation logic. The process of the MOVA graphical user interface is altered in ITP/OCL text-input commands and executed in Maude.

Mova has limited support for OCL and UML. In terms of UML, it supports drawing of classes, objects, associations, and generalizations while in terms of OCL it allows writing invariants, instances of UML classes without any support of pre- and postconditions at all.

TABLE 1: Comparison of tools based on formalism, verification, and translation.

Tool	Formalism	Verification	Translation	Limitations
HOL-OCL	Higher-Order logic	User-assisted	Automatic	Undecidability
UMLtoCSP	CSP	Automatic	Automatic	Accepts ArgoUML class diagram only and bounded verification
Alloy	Relational Logics	Automatic	Manual	No operation support involving integers
UML2Alloy	Alloy analyzer simulation	Automatic	Automatic	Accepts ArgoUML class diagram only
USE	ASSL	Automatic	Manual	Validation only
Mova	Maude	Automatic	Manual	Validation only

TABLE 2: Comparison of UML support for each verification and validation tool.

Relationship name	HOL-OCL	UMLtoCSP	Alloy	UML2Alloy	USE	MOVA
Abstraction	No	No	No	No	No	No
Aggregation	Yes	No	No	Yes	Yes	No
Association	Yes	Yes	Yes	Yes	Yes	Yes
Association classes	Yes	Yes	Yes	Yes	Yes	No
Binding	No	No	No	No	No	No
Composition association	Yes	No	No	No	No	No
Dependency	No	No	No	No	No	No
Generalization	Yes	Yes	Yes	Yes	Yes	Yes
Interface realization	No	No	No	No	No	No
Instantiation	No	No	No	No	No	No
Realization	No	No	No	No	No	No
Usage	No	No	No	No	No	No
N-ary	No	No	No	No	Yes	No

2.2. Comparison and Support of UML/OCL Tools. This section is based on the comparison and benchmark of UML/OCL tools discussed in Section 2.1. Generally, the comparison of UML/OCL tools is a challenging task whenever different formalisms are involved. Each verification method has different specification, and, therefore, the process of verification is also dissimilar. Currently, several challenges are being faced by researchers/developers just because of not having coordination among these tools. Table 1 shows a simple comparison between tools, used formalisms, verification, translation, and limitations.

We have developed several UML/OCL class diagrams which were verified by various verification and validation tools such as HOL-OCL, UMLtoCSP, Alloy, UML2Alloy, USE, and Mova. To the best of our knowledge, these tools are widely used for verification and validation purpose. Therefore, for each UML/OCL tool, we have provided a different range of UML supporting features. With the help of this support, a researcher can readily identify the tool support pertinent to the supported examples, while ignoring those instances where this support is not recorded. This would result in considerable saving of time and effort for the designers. Table 2 briefly compares the UML class relationship for different verification and validation tools, and Table 3 briefly compares the support of different stereotypes.

A class diagram defines different relationships between different objects of classes and all the possible relationships that appear in a class diagram such as associations, generalizations, and dependencies. In UML a stereotype is one way to extend the core semantics of the modeling language to express new things.

2.3. Efficiency Analysis of UML/OCL Tools. For the sake of brevity and without loss of generality, in this section we have examined the verification time in UMLtoCSP and Alloy. We have chosen UMLtoCSP and Alloy for our experimental results because these tools are widely used for verification, while Mova and USE are validation tools. UML2Alloy supports transformation of UML/OCL class diagram into Alloy specification; therefore, the experimental results are same as in Alloy. HOL-OCL is an interactive proof environment for OCL which we will consider for our future experiments. For each example, we have used the following parameters for the experiment: each class may have at most 4 instances, associations may have at most 1010 links, and attributes may range from 0 to 1022 for UMLtoCSP. Table 4 describes the set of benchmarks used for our comparison: the number of classes, associations, invariants, and attributes. The column "Verification Time" highlights the time taken by the tool to generate valid instances of a class diagram. The benchmarks

TABLE 3: Comparison of UML stereotypes by each tool.

Stereotype	HOL-OCL	MOVA	UMLtoCSP	Alloy	UML2Alloy	USE
Auxiliary	No	No	No	Yes	No	No
Enumeration	Yes	Yes	No	Yes	Yes	Yes
Type	No	No	No	No	No	No

TABLE 4: Description of UML/OCL benchmarks and verification time (UMLtoCSP).

Example	Classes	Associations	Attributes	Invariants	Verification Time
Paper-Researcher	2	2	6	1	0.04 s
Coach	15	12	2	2	5008.76 s
DBLP	17	27	38	26	Time-out
Tracking System	50	60	72	5	3605.35 s
Script 1	100	110	122	2	Time-out
Script 2	500	510	522	5	Time-out
Script 3	1000	1010	1022	5	Time-out

"Script" were programmatically generated in order to test large input class diagrams. The models "Paper-Researcher" and "Coach" serve as worst-case scenarios (models with many interdependent constraints) for verification time. Each experiment is conducted using a Intel Core 2 Duo Processor 2.1 Ghz with 2 Gb of RAM. All times are measured in seconds, and a time-out limit has been set at 2 hours (7200 seconds).

Similarly, we have programmed the Digital Bibliography and Library Project (DBLP) structural schema in the Alloy specification. The schema of the DBLP system is modeled as a UML class diagram [28]. The class diagram has 17 classes and 26 integrity constraints. Table 5 summarizes the verification time (TVT) obtained using the Alloy analyzer where Column (TT) is the translation time, Column (ST) is the solving time, and the summation of the TT and ST is the total verification time (TVT).

The above experiments show that verification is a time-consuming process for complex UML/OCL class diagrams.

2.4. Findings. Table 6 shows the findings related to the efficiency of the verification process. The verification time is largely depending on the UML/OCL model size and its complexity. Based on our analysis, we believe that this is a common problem for all such UML/OCL verification tools and methods and that these tools are unable to verify complex UML/OCL class diagrams. Therefore, an efficient method/technique that addresses is required the problem by reducing the verification time.

3. UML/OCL Model Slicing

The input of our method is a UML class diagram annotated with OCL invariants. Figure 1 introduces a class diagram that will be used as an example; the diagram models the information system of a bus company. Several integrity constraints are defined as OCL invariants.

TABLE 5: Description of experimental results (Alloy).

Scope	TT	ST	TT + ST = TVT
2	0.125 s	0.047 s	0.172 s
3	0.187 s	0.078 s	0.265 s
4	0.281 s	0.172 s	0.453 s
5	0.473 s	0.190 s	0.663 s
6	0.671 s	0.344 s	1.015 s
7	0.969 s	0.484 s	1.453 s
⋮	⋮	⋮	⋮
1000	Time-out	Time-out	Time-out

TT: Translation Time. ST: Solving Time. TVT: Total Verification Time.

TABLE 6: Efficiency analysis for UMLtoCSP and Alloy.

	UMLtoCSP		Alloy
Classes	Efficiency	Scope	Efficiency
2	0.04 s	2	0.172 s
15	5008.76 s	3	0.265 s
50	3605.35 s	4	0.453 s
100	Time-out	5	0.663 s
500	Time-out	6	1.015 s
1000	Time-out	7	1.453 s
⋮	⋮	⋮	⋮
1050	Time-out	1000	Time-out

Two different notions of satisfiability will be considered for verification: *strong* satisfiability and *weak* satisfiability. A class diagram is weakly satisfiable if it is possible to create at least one instance of at least one class out of all classes in the class diagram. Alternatively, in the case of strong satisfiability, it is an obligation that at least one object of all classes must be instantiated [4]. For example, it is possible that objects of

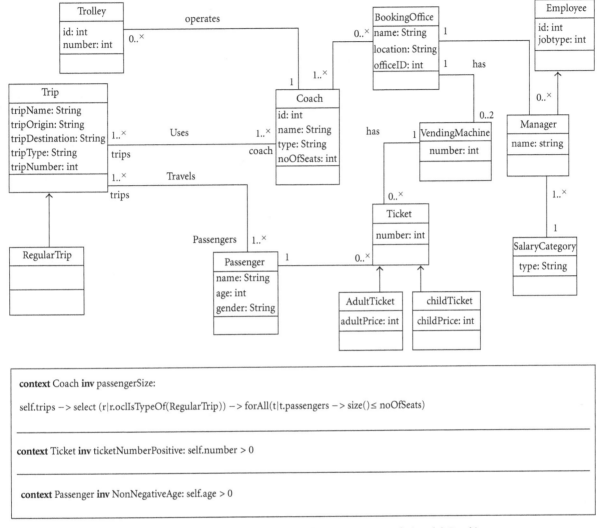

context Coach **inv** passengerSize:

self.trips $->$ select (r|r.oclIsTypeOf(RegularTrip)) $->$ forAll(t|t.passengers $->$ size()$\leq$ noOfSeats)

context Ticket **inv** ticketNumberPositive: self.number > 0

context Passenger **inv** NonNegativeAge: self.age > 0

FIGURE 1: UML/OCL class diagram used as running example (model Coach).

all classes are not instantiated due to multiple inheritance, composition, and aggregation. In this case, the model will be considered as unsatisfiable in the case of strong satisfiability. Consequently, strong satisfiability requires the existence of an object for each concrete subclass of an abstract class.

The proposed approach instantiates objects for verification purposes based on a given class diagram and OCL constraints of the system. A successful verification result ensures that the model complies with the system specifications imposed at the start of the development phase, and, therefore, the developers may continue with transforming the model into software code.

The algorithm takes a UML/OCL model as an input, breaks it into several submodels with respect to invariants, and verifies the properties of each constraint to determine whether the input class diagram has legal instances which satisfy all integrity constraints of class attributes. The slicing algorithm can be applied over a large model to reduce the size and complexity of the UML/OCL model, so that it can be verified more efficiently. Slicing of UML class

diagrams is dependent on the OCL constraints. Thus, if there are 3 constraints in the model, slicing might result in three submodels.

A *slice S* of a UML class diagram *D* is another valid UML class diagram where any element (class, association, inheritance, aggregation, etc.) appearing in *S* also appears in *D*, but the reverse does not necessarily hold.

In the context of satisfiability, saying that "a class *X* depends on a class *Y*" means that creating an object of class *Y* creates an obligation that must be satisfied by class *X*, for example, the existence of *n* corresponding objects in class *X*. Relationships like associations, aggregations, and inheritance hierarchies can create these types of dependencies. For instance, in associations the dependency is typically bidirectional, as the multiplicity of each association end imposes a dependency on the other class.

3.1. The UOST Process. The method introduced for computing UML/OCL slicing is shown in Figure 2. The process begins in step 1 by identifying the classes, associations,

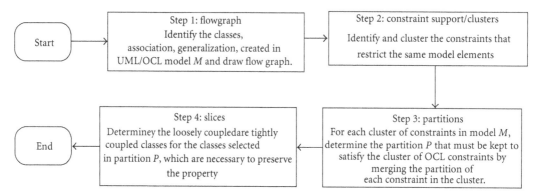

FIGURE 2: UOST process steps.

and generalizations created in model M and subsequently drawing a flowgraph. In step 2, we identify OCL invariants and group them if they restrict the same model elements. We call this "clustering of constraints" (constraint support). The constraint support defines the scope of a constraint. The support information can be used to partition a set of OCL invariants into a set of independent *clusters* of constraints, where each cluster can be verified separately. The following procedure is used to compute the clusters:

(i) compute the constraint support of each invariant;

(ii) keep each constraint in a different cluster;

(iii) select two constraints x and y with nondisjoint constraint supports and located in different clusters and merge those clusters;

(iv) repeat the previous step until all pairs of constraints with nondisjoint constraint supports belong to the same cluster.

In step 3, for each cluster of constraints in model M, the partition P is determined that holds all those classes and relationships restricted by the constraints in the cluster. In this step, we can capture the possible number of slices with the consideration of OCL invariants. Each partition will be a subset of the original model.

In step 4, tightly coupled classes are added to each partition in accordance with the lower bound ≥ 1 association. It means that if the constraint is restricted from class X, it is necessary to check the lower bound ≥ 1 associated classes with X. In this step, all the associated classes are added to a partition, which results in a model slice.

3.2. Flowgraph Creation: Step 1. In this section and the next, we illustrate the UOST slicing Algorithm 2 through an example. Consider the "model Coach" scenario whose UML class diagram and OCL constraints are shown in Figure 1. There are three constraints that restrict the classes, and out of them two are local invariants and one is global. An invariant is called local to a class C if it can be evaluated by examining only the values of the attributes in one object of class C. However, expressions that do not fit into this category, because they need to examine multiple objects of the same class or some objects from another class, are called global.

By applying step 1 (Figure 2), we build a flowgraph based on the identification of classes, associations, and generalizations as shown in Figure 3. We use the concept of a flowgraph to capture the dependencies among model elements. This concept is also used by other slicing approaches [29–31]. A flowgraph is a set of vertices and directed arcs where the vertices represent classes from a class diagram and the arcs model relationships between these classes. In our approach, a flowgraph contains vertices and arcs for each pair of classes connected by associations, generalizations, aggregations, or compositions. We consider two types of relationships among classes: tightly associated and loosely associated classes. These relationships attempt to capture the necessity of creating instances of one class when an instance of the other exists. Loosely coupled classes have an association with a lower bound of 0 (e.g., $0 \cdots 3$); this means if an object of class A is instantiated, then it is not necessary that an object of class B must be instantiated. Tightly coupled classes are the inverse of loosely coupled classes; that is, they have an association with a lower bound greater than 1 (e.g., $1 \cdots *$).

In the case of aggregation, composition, and generalized classes, we count them as tightly coupled classes. To differentiate aggregation, composition, and generalized classes from associations in the flowgraph, we use a solid undirected edge (——) as a shortcut for two directed arcs between the two classes. A tightly coupled association between two classes is shown as a solid arc ($\longrightarrow$), while a loosely coupled association is shown as a dashed arc ($--\rightarrow$). Table 7 briefly summarizes the criteria to assign loosely coupled and tightly coupled relationships, and Algorithm 1 shows the steps that compute a flowgraph for a given class diagram.

3.3. Applying UOST: Step 2, 3, and 4. In this section, we compute constraint support, partitions, and build the final slices for verifiability.

Considering the model Coach where *Model M (Coach, Trolley, Booking Office, Passenger, Ticket, Trip, RegularTrip, VendingMachine, Manager, Employee, SalaryCategory, Adult-Ticket, and ChildTicket)* and *Constraints C (passengerSize, ticketNumberPositive, and NonNegativeAge)*. We are supposed to find the legal instances of three invariants, that is, passengerSize, ticketNumberPositive, and NonNegativeAge.

Input: A model M
Output: A labeled directed graph $G = \langle V, E \rangle$

(1) {Start with the empty graph}
(2) Let $V \leftarrow \emptyset$ and $E \leftarrow \emptyset$
(3) {Add all classes of the model to the flowgraph}
(4) **for** class c in model M **do**
(5) $V \leftarrow V \cup \{c\}$
(6) **end for**
(7) {Create incoming and outgoing arcs in the flowgraph}
(8) **for** each association end A in model M **do**
(9) $E \leftarrow (x, y)$ where x is the type of the association end and y is the type of the other class in the association
(10)   **if** the lower bound of the multiplicity of A is ≥ 1 **then**
(11)   Label the arc (x, y) as tightly coupled
(12)   **else if** the lower bound of the multiplicity of $A = 0$ **then**
(13)   Label the arc (x, y) as loosely coupled
(14)   **end if**
(15) **end for**
(16) **for** each generalization, aggregation and composition G between classes x and y **do**
(17) $E \leftarrow E \cup \{(x, y)\} \cup \{(y, x)\}$
(18)   Label the arcs (x, y) and (y, x) as tightly coupled
(19) **end for**

ALGORITHM 1: Flowgraph creation.

Input: Property being verified
Output: A partition P of the model M into non-necessarily disjoint submodels

(1) $G \leftarrow BuildFlowGraph(M)$ {Creating the flowgraph}
(2) {Cluster the OCL constraints}
(3) **for** each pair of constraints $c1, c2$ in M **do**
(4)   **if** $ConstraintSupport(M, c1) \cap ConstraintSupport(M, c2) \neq \emptyset$ **then**
(5) $MergeInSameCluster(c1, c2)$
(6)   **end if**
(7) **end for**
(8) {Work on each cluster of constraints separately}
(9) **for** each cluster of constraints Cl **do**
(10)   subModel $\leftarrow$ empty model {Initialize the subModel to be empty}
(11)   {Initialize worklist}
(12)   workList $\leftarrow$ Union of the ConstraintSupport of all constraints in the cluster
(13)   **while** workList not empty **do**
(14) $node \leftarrow$ first(workList) {Take first element from workList and remove it}
(15)   workList $\leftarrow$ workList \ $node$
(16)   **for** each subclass or superclass c of $node$ **do**
(17)   subModel $\leftarrow$ subModel $\cup \{c\}$
(18)   **if** c was not before in the subModel **then**
(19)   workList $\leftarrow$ workList $\cup \{c\}$
(20)   **end if**
(21)   **end for**
(22)   **for** each class c tightly coupled to $node$ **do**
(23)   **if** $Property$ = weak SAT **then**
(24)   subModel $\leftarrow$ subModel $\cup \{c\}$
(25)   **else if** $Property$ = strong SAT **then**
(26)   workList $\leftarrow$ workList $\cup \{c\}$
(27)   **end if**
(28)   **end for**
(29)   **end while**
(30) **end for**

ALGORITHM 2: Slicing algorithm.

TABLE 7: Loosely and tightly coupled classes.

UML relationship	Loosely/tightly coupled	Arc/Edge
Association: lower bound ≥ 1 (e.g., $1 \cdots *$)	Tightly coupled	$\longrightarrow$
Association: lower bound $= 0$ (e.g., $0 \cdots 3$)	Loosely coupled	$\dashrightarrow$
Generalization, aggregation, and composition	Tightly coupled	$\longrightarrow$

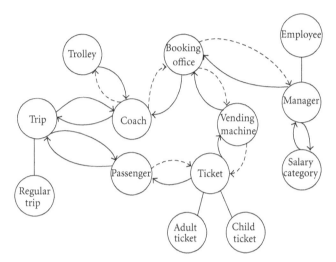

FIGURE 3: Flowgraph of the model Coach.

Applying step 2, we identify and cluster the OCL constraints. It is necessary to cluster the invariants beforehand, as the set of model elements constrained by each invariant may have an interaction. Considering Figure 1, there are three invariants that restrict class Coach, Ticket, and Passenger. In this case, constraint *NonNegativeAge* will be merged with *passengerSize* because the properties of these constraints can be satisfied from similar model elements. Meanwhile, the properties of *ticketNumberPositive* can be satisfied from different model elements.

In step 3, for each constraint and group of constraints in model M, the partition P that holds all those classes and multiplicities from which the cluster of invariants are constrained will be determined. In this step, we can capture the possible number of slices with the consideration of OCL invariants. Each partition will be a subset of the original model.

In step 4, all the tightly coupled classes are added into formed partitions in order to preserve the property of an invariant because it is necessary that the object of each class must be instantiated in case there is strong satisfiability; otherwise, the property will not be satisfied. For the cluster of passengerSize and NonNegativeAge, we need classes *Coach, Trip, RegularTrip,* and *Passenger* while classes *Ticket, BookingOffice, Trolley, VendingMachine, Manager, Employee, SalaryCategory, AdultTicket,* and *ChildTicket* can safely be removed from the slice (i.e., s1).

Similarly, to satisfy the properties of ticketNumberPositive, we require classes *BookingOffice, Coach, Trip, RegularTrip, Passenger, VendingMachine, Ticket, AdultTicket,* and *ChildTicket,* while classes *Trolley, Manager, Employee,* and

SalaryCategory can be deleted from the slice (i.e., s2). Figures 4(a) and 4(b) highlight the final slices passed to the verification tool for strong satisfiability. The members of a slice are hence defined as follows:

(i) the classes and relationships in the cluster of constraint supports are part of the slice;

(ii) any class with a tightly coupled relationship to a class in the slice is also a part of the slice, as is the relationship.

4. Nondisjoint Solution

In this section, we present the solution that still preserves the satisfiability in case of nondisjoint submodels. Nondisjoint submodels may occur if a common class is used in several constraints. In the worst case, the clustering technique in Section 3 may result in the whole UML model and consequently no improvements in verification time. The nondisjoint solution can be selected by the designer in the tool (UMLtoCSP) if the model is constrained by several invariants in a way which makes clustering ineffective. The nondisjoint solution differs from the UOST process (see Figure 2) in that it works without clustering the model elements, hence making it still possible to improve verification time.

The nondisjoint solution is defined as follow.

Let C be a set of classes, and let $A = \bigcup_{c \in C} A_c$ be the set of attributes. $M = C$ is the model consisting of these classes. Let R be the set of binary associations among two classes. Each association R is defined as a tuple $(C_1, C_2, m_1, M_1, m_2, M_2)$, where

(i) $C_1 \in C$ is a class

(ii) $C_2 \in C$ is a class

(iii) m_1 and m_2 are nonnegative integers $\in Z^+$, where m_1 and m_2 correspond to the lower bound of the multiplicity of each association end for C_1 and C_2, respectively

(iv) M_1 and M_2 are nonnegative integers or infinity ($M_1 \in (Z^+ \bigcup \{\infty\})$), where M_1 and M_2 correspond to the upper bound of the multiplicity of each association end for C_1 and C_2, respectively, and $M_i \geq m_i$.

A model M can be defined as a tuple: (C, A, R). A submodel S of model $M = (C, A, R)$ is another model (C', A', R') such that

(i) $C' \in C$,

(ii) $R' \in R$,

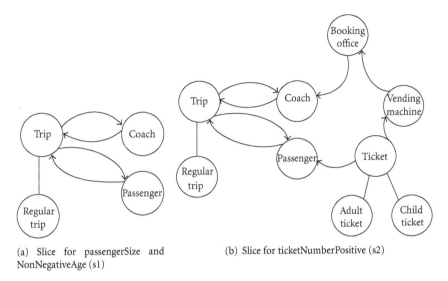

(a) Slice for passengerSize and NonNegativeAge (s1)

(b) Slice for ticketNumberPositive (s2)

FIGURE 4: Slices s1 and s2 of model Coach.

(iii) $A' \in A$,

(iv) $c \in C' \rightarrow A_c \subseteq A'$,

(v) $(C_1, C_2, m_1, M_1, m_2, M_2) \in R' \rightarrow C_1, C_2 \in C'$.

An OCL expression specifies the model entity for which the OCL expression is defined. CL represents the OCL invariants while CL_c are the clusters of constraints. The work list is defined as W_L which is the union of the constraint support of all constraints in the cluster.

   (i) *Satisfiability (Strong/Weak)* If the objects of a given class C in a submodel S are instantiated as per given expression in the cluster of OCL constraints CL_c, then submodel S is satisfiable.

   (ii) *Unsatisfiability* If there are two or more constraints whose interaction is unsatisfiable, then submodel S is also unsatisfiable. It indicates that some expression in the OCL invariant is violated and that the objects of the classes cannot be instantiated according to the given OCL expression.

A class diagram can be unsatisfiable due to several reasons. First, it is possible that the model provides inconsistent conditions on the number of objects of a given type. Inheritance hierarchies, multiplicities of association/aggregation ends, and textual integrity constraints (e.g., Type::allInstances() → size() = 7) can restrict the possible number of objects of a class. Second, it is possible that there are no valid values for one or more attributes of an object in the diagram. Within a model, textual constraints provide the only source of restrictions on the values of an attribute, for example, self.x = 7. Finally, it is possible that the unsatisfiability arises from a combination of both factors; for example, the values of some attributes require a certain number of objects to be created, which contradicts other restrictions.

To sum up, an unsatisfiable model either contains an unsatisfiable textual or graphical constraint or an unsatisfiable interaction between one or more textual or graphical constraints; that is, the constraints can be satisfied on their own but not simultaneously.

In a class diagram, there could be a possibility to have one or more relationships between two classes; that is, a class may have a relationship with itself and there may be multiple relationships between two classes. Multiple links between two classes or a link from one class to itself is called a "cycle." For example, a cycle exists between "Researcher" and "Paper" in Figure 5. The "maximum label" is the highest upper-bound multiplicity of the associations in a cycle. For example, the maximum label is 1 for constraints restricting papers and 3 for constraints restricting researchers.

Any cycle in the class diagram where the maximum label is 1 is inherently satisfiable, and it will be called *safe*. However, cycles where the maximum label ≥2 can be unsatisfiable. Such cycles will be called *unsafe*. By "safe" we mean any cycle where the maximum label is 1 and imposing a single constraint is inherently satisfiable where the OCL expression is `self.attrib op expression` where *attrib* is an attribute of a basic type (Boolean, Integer, Float, String) not constrained by any other constraint, *op* is a relational operator $(=, \neq, <, >, \leq, \geq,)$ and *expression* is a "safe" OCL expression which does not include any reference to *attrib*. The safe expression is a side-effect-free expression which cannot evaluate to the undefined value in OCL (`OclUndefined`). This means that we do not allow divisions that can cause a division-by-zero or collection operations which are undefined on empty collections like first().

We present the nondisjoint solution if slicing is applied over a UML model without clustering the constraints (i.e., without step 2 in the UOST process).

There are three major steps that need to be considered as a solution:

   (i) find the common class in all slices of the model (M);

   (ii) for each constraint, find the maximum of the lower-bound (m_1) multiplicities relevant to the constraint from all associations of the common class. Set this

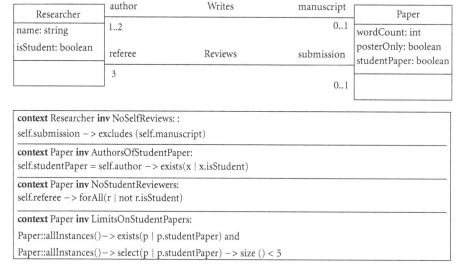

FIGURE 5: UML/OCL class diagram of "Paper-Researcher" [32].

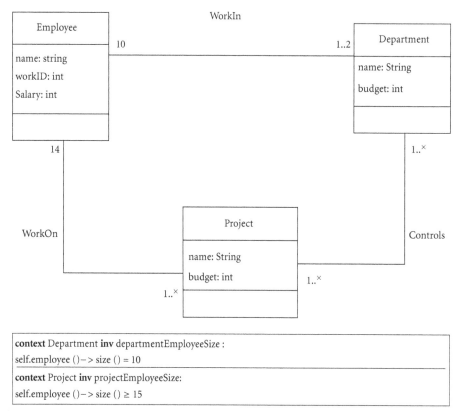

FIGURE 6: UML/OCL class diagram used as nondisjoint solution (Company model).

maximum as the base value. $Base_c = \max(m_1)$, where $(c, C_2, m_1, M_1, m_2, M_2) \in R$;

(iii) compare the base value using the expression given in each constraint.

The OCL constraints can be either textual OCL invariants or graphical restrictions like multiplicities of association ends. This property is important not only because it can

point out inconsistent models, but also because it can be used to check other interesting properties like the redundancy of an integrity constraint. For example, there could be a case where the invariants are constrained from the same class of the model. Figure 6 introduces a class diagram of "Company model" used to exemplify our nondisjoint solution. There are two constraints, *departmentEmployeeSize*, and *projectEmployeeSize* whose properties need to be checked. Invariant *departmentEmployeeSize* is satisfiable; however, invariant *projectEmployeeSize* is unsatisfiable due to a violation of multiplicity. After applying the slicing technique without clustering the invariants, we will receive two submodels, that is, two nondisjoint slices. Slice 1 will consist of class "Department" and class "Employee" for constraint *departmentEmployeeSize*. Similarly, class "Project" and class "Employee" for invariant *projectEmployeeSize* will be part of slice 2.

In this case, slice 1 is satisfiable; however, slice 2 is unsatisfiable. The definition of the slicing procedure ensures that the property under verification is unsatisfiable after partitioning because the overall interaction of the model is unsatisfiable.

Initially, our nondisjoint approach finds the common class in all slices of model (M), that is, class "Employee." Secondly, the method finds the maximum of minimum (max_min) multiplicities from the common class (Employee) for each constraint considering its navigation. For example, the navigation of invariant "departmentEmployeeSize" is class "Department" navigating to class "Employee". Therefore, the approach considers the multiplicity between the navigation of class department and class employee, that is, "10" and "1···2". As the constraint restricts class employee, "10" is the base value for the "departmentEmployeeSize" invariant. Similarly, "14" is the base value for the navigation of class "Project" and class "Employee."

Finally, the method compares the base value (i.e., 10) for invariant "departmentEmployeeSize" using the expression given in a constraint self.employee() → size() = 10 whose interaction is satisfiable. However, invariant "projectEmployeeSize" is violating the condition, that is, using the expression self.employee() → size() ≥15, where 14 is not ≥15. Hence, the overall interaction of the model is unsatisfiable.

5. Empirical Study

This section presents the speedup achieved by slicing in two of the tools, that is, UMLtoCSP [4] and Alloy [6]. We have developed prototype implementations of the slicing procedure in UMLtoCSP and Alloy to conduct these experiments. The goal of the empirical study is to show the achieved speedup in the verification process before and after slicing. Therefore, the general question addressed here is

"How can we improve the efficiency of the verification process for complex UML/OCL class diagrams?"

5.1. UOST Implementation in UMLtoCSP. We have implemented our proposed slicing technique (UOST) in UMLtoCSP [4] in order to show the improvement of the efficiency in the verification process. After developing UOST, we renamed the tool to UMLtoCSP (UOST). The execution time of verification of an original UMLtoCSP depends mainly on the number of classes/attributes and the parameters offered during the transformation to the constraint satisfaction problem (CSP). In case of small models, UMLtoCSP provides quick results while for larger ones, the tool takes a huge of amount of time. In order to evaluate the efficiency

TABLE 8: Description of the examples.

Example	Classes	Associations	Attributes	Invariants
Paper-Researcher	2	2	6	1
Coach	15	12	2	2
DBLP	17	27	38	26
Tracking System	50	60	72	5
Script 1	100	110	122	2
Script 2	500	510	522	5
Script 3	1000	1010	1022	5

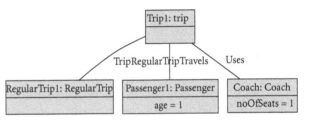

FIGURE 7: Submodel 1 (s1) object diagram for strong satisfiability.

of our developed UOST approach in UMLtoCSP, several models have been used (Table 8). UMLtoCSP takes a lot of time to verify the instances of large examples; therefore, we set a time out to 2 hours which is equal to 7200 seconds. If UMLtoCSP does not verify the model in the prescribed time, we will count this situation as *Time out*.

Table 9 summarizes the experimental results obtained by UMLtoCSP and UMLtoCSP (UOST) running on an Intel Core 2 Duo 2.10 Ghz with 2 Gb of RAM, where the column OVT is the original verification time of UMLtoCSP, column TVT is the total verification time of all slices of UMLtoCSP (UOST), and column speedup shows the efficiency obtained after the implementation of the slicing approach. We have used the following parameters for the experiments: each class may have at most 4 instances, associations may have at most 1010 links, and attributes may range from 0 to 1022. The speedup is calculated using the equation below:

$$\left\{1 - \left(\frac{\text{TVT}}{\text{OVT}}\right)\right\} * 100. \tag{1}$$

Figure 7 shows the object diagram for s1 in the case of strong satisfiability, and Figure 8 represents the object diagram for s2 in the case of weak satisfiability, where there is no need to instantiate unused subclasses (i.e., AdultTicket and ChildTicket). The object diagrams are generated using UMLtoCSP (UOST).

As a conclusion, the process of slicing is fast even for large and complex models having hundreds of classes. However, this effectiveness depends primarily on the specific type of models being considered. As such, small models and models where UMLtoCSP already performed well gain little from slicing. Similarly, models with no unconstrained attributes and all classes and constraints being interdependent gain little advantage under this technique. In the worst case, the verification time with slicing is the same as that without

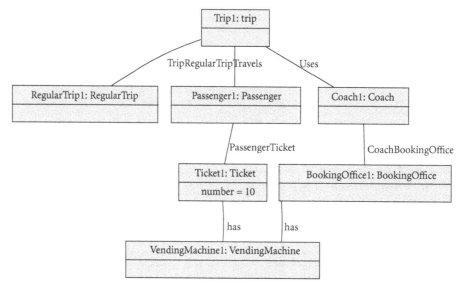

FIGURE 8: Submodel 2 (s2) for weak satisfiability.

TABLE 9: Description of experimental results (UMLtoCSP).

	Before slicing (UMLtoCSP)		After slicing (UMLtoCSP UOST)				
Classes	Attributes	OVT	Attributes	ST	SVT	TVT	Speedup %
2	6	0.04 s	3	0.00 s	0.040 s	0.040 s	0%
15	2	5008.76 s	0	0.00 s	0.178 s	0.178 s	99.99%
17	38	Time out	6	0.020 s	0.432 s	0.452 s	N/A
50	72	3605.35 s	55	0.016 s	0.031 s	0.047 s	99.99%
100	122	Time out	117	0.016 s	0.032 s	0.048 s	N/A
500	522	Time out	502	0.062 s	0.028 s	0.090 s	N/A
1000	1022	Time out	1012	0.282 s	0.339 s	0.621 s	N/A

OVT: Original Verification Time. ST: Slicing Time. SVT: Sliced Verification Time. TVT: Total Verification Time.

slicing. In contrast, dramatic improvements in speed-up by the order of several magnitudes are observed where slicing manages to partition the model and abstract attributes. The tiny overhead introduced by slicing and the tool-independent nature of this approach are additional reasons in favor of adding slicing to existing formal verification toolkits.

5.1.1. DBLP Conceptual Schema in UMLtoCSP. In this section, we have applied our slicing technique to the digital bibliography and library project (DBLP) structural schema modeled as a UML class diagram [33]. It is a computer science bibliographical website and has existed since the 1980s. The DBLP structural schema deals with people and their publications, which can be edited books and authored publications. The class diagram has 17 classes and 27 integrity constraints. This case study is interesting for our problem since it has complex invariants and is a real-world case study. Therefore, we intend to apply our slicing approach to this DBLP case study in order to show that our methods work upon external case studies and can improve the efficiency of the verification process. After applying the technique, two submodels are received: submodel 1

consists of 10 classes annotated with 8 OCL constraints and submodel 2 comprises of 2 classes annotated with 2 OCL constraints. UMLtoCSP did not verify the DBLP UML/OCL class diagram even in two hours of time due to the scope of invariants. However, with the slicing technique, the same model is now verifiable in just 0.452 seconds. Table 9 summarizes the experimental results for DBLP conceptual schema. We have achieved a 99% speedup for the verification of the "DBLP" class diagram.

5.2. Limitations. Our proposed technique is limited in scope and cannot partition the UML/OCL class diagram and abstract the attributes if the constraints are restricted to all classes using all attributes of the class diagram. In this case, the technique will consider a UML/OCL class diagram as a single model, and, therefore, there will be no difference between UMLtoCSP and UMLtoCSP (UOST). Table 10 describes the worst case examples that cannot be sliced using UOST. The example *Paper-Researcher* is a real-world example which contains 2 classes, 6 attributes, 2 associations, and 4 invariants while example *Company* is script generated and has 100 classes, 100 attributes, 100 associations, and 100 invariants. In these examples, partitioning cannot be done

TABLE 10: Worst-case examples.

Tool and example	Classes	Associations	Attr	Inv	NOS	OVT
UMLtoCSP (Paper-Researcher)	2	2	6	4	0	0.040 s
UMLtoCSP (UOST) (Paper-Researcher)	2	2	6	4	0	0.040 s
UMLtoCSP (Company)	5	7	3	5	0	0.070 s
UMLtoCSP (UOST) (Company)	5	7	3	5	0	0.070 s
UMLtoCSP (Script)	100	110	122	100	0	Time out
UMLtoCSP (UOST) (Script)	100	110	122	100	0	Time out

Attr: Associations. Inv: Invariants. NOS: Number of Slices. OVT: Original Verification Time.

TABLE 11: Description of the examples.

Example	Classes	Associations	Attributes	Invariants
Paper-Researcher	2	2	6	1
Coach	15	12	2	2
DBLP	17	27	38	26
Tracking System	50	60	72	5
Script 1	100	110	122	2
Script 2	500	510	522	5
Script 3	1000	1010	1022	5

by the proposed UOST technique because each instance of a class is constrained by an invariant.

5.3. UOST Implementation in Alloy. In this section, we present several examples in the Alloy specification in order to prove that our developed slicing technique is neither tool dependent nor formalism dependent. We compare the verification time of several UML/OCL class diagrams using the Alloy analyzer with and without the UOST technique. Table 11 describes the set of benchmarks used for our comparison: the number of classes, associations, invariants, and attributes. The benchmarks "Script" was programmatically generated, in order to test large-input models. Of these models, we consider the "Script" models to be the best possible scenarios for slicing (large models with many attributes and very few constraints).

Tables 12, 13, 14, 15, 16, and 17 summarize the experimental results obtained using the Alloy analyzer before and after slicing, running on an Intel Core 2 Duo Processor 2.1 Ghz with 2 Gb of RAM. Each table represents the results as described in the benchmark (Table 11). The execution time is largely dependent on the defined scope; therefore, in order to analyze the efficiency of verification, the scope is limited to 7. The Alloy analyzer will examine all the examples with up to 7 objects and try to find one that violates the property. For example, scope 7 means that the Alloy analyzer will check models whose top level signatures have up to 7 instances.

All times are measured in seconds (s). For each scope (before slicing), the translation time (TT), solving time (ST), and the summation of the TT and ST, which is the total execution time, are described. Similarly, for each scope (after

slicing) we measure the sliced translation time (STT), sliced solving time (SST), and the summation of STT and SST. Similarly, the column speedup shows the efficiency obtained after the implementation of the slicing approach.

Previously with no slicing, it took 0.820 s (scope 7) for the execution of the "Tracking System" and 282.161 s (scope 7) for "Script 3." Using the UOST approach, it takes only 0.058 s (scope 7) for "Tracking System" and 0.052 s (scope 7) for "Script 3." It is an improvement of 93% and 99.98%, respectively. In addition, the improvement can also be achieved for larger scopes as well. For instance, results for up to scope 50 can be achieved for the "Tracking System" and scope 35 for "Script."

5.3.1. DBLP Conceptual Schema in Alloy. We have programmed DBLP in Alloy in order to show the results in an external tool with a more real-world example. The specification of the class diagram is the same as above. The execution time in Alloy is largely dependent on the defined scope. We already explored the results with smaller scopes; however, in this section we present experimental results (with slicing and without slicing) with larger scopes, that is, 15–19. After applying the technique, two submodels are received: submodel 1 consists of 10 classes annotated with 8 OCL constraints and submodel 2 comprises of 2 classes annotated with 2 OCL constraints. Table 18 summarizes the experimental results for DBLP conceptual schema where we have achieved maximum 57% improvement for a real-world case study. The percentage is calculated using the following equation:

$$\left\{ 1 - \left(\frac{TT + ST}{STT + SST} \right) \right\} * 100. \tag{2}$$

5.4. Statistical Comparison. In this section, we present some statistical comparisons of the various experiments comparing the verification time before and after slicing using UMLtoCSP (Table 9) and Alloy (Tables 12–18). We have included the mean verification time and the standard deviation for both "before slicing" and "after slicing" cases. Table 19 briefly summarizes the results.

6. Related Work

In this section, we discuss existing work on model partitioning or slicing. Most of the work in this area is done

TABLE 12: Slicing results in Alloy for Paper-Researcher example.

	Before slicing			After slicing			
Scope	TT	ST	TT + ST	STT	SST	STT + SST	Speedup %
2	0.003 s	0.009 s	0.012 s	0.003 s	0.005 s	0.008 s	34%
3	0.007 s	0.008 s	0.015 s	0.003 s	0.006 s	0.009 s	40%
4	0.012 s	0.008 s	0.020 s	0.004 s	0.006 s	0.010 s	50%
5	0.017 s	0.010 s	0.027 s	0.004 s	0.009 s	0.013 s	52%
6	0.016 s	0.015 ms	0.031 s	0.005 s	0.009 s	0.014 s	55%
7	0.019 s	0.015 ms	0.034 s	0.006 s	0.009 s	0.015 s	56%

TT: Translation Time. ST: Solving Time. STT: Sliced Translation Time. SST: Sliced Solving Time.

TABLE 13: Slicing results in Alloy for Coach example.

	Before slicing			After slicing			
Scope	TT	ST	TT + ST	STT	SST	STT + SST	Speedup %
2	0.007 s	0.010 s	0.017 s	0.003 s	0.005 s	0.008 s	53%
3	0.014 s	0.019 s	0.033 s	0.005 s	0.008 s	0.013 s	61%
4	0.028 s	0.020 s	0.048 s	0.007 s	0.010 s	0.017 s	62%
5	0.036 s	0.031 s	0.067 s	0.012 s	0.015 s	0.027 s	65%
6	0.045 s	0.050 s	0.095 s	0.017 s	0.015 s	0.032 s	67%
7	0.081 s	0.077 s	0.158 s	0.034 s	0.017 s	0.051 s	68%

TT: Translation Time. ST: Solving Time. STT: Sliced Translation Time. SST: Sliced Solving Time.

for UML architectural models, model slicing, and program slicing which is limited to slicing only. Their goal of slicing is to break larger programs or models into small submodels to reuse the required segments. However, research work on partitioning of UML/OCL class diagrams in terms of verifiability is not found in the literature. Previously, we proposed a slicing technique for models considering a UML class diagrams annotated with unrestricted OCL constraints and a specific property for verification [15, 16]. The slicing approach was based on disjoint slicing, clustering, and the removal of trivially satisfiable constraints. An implementation of the slicing technique has been developed in a UMLtoCSP tool. Experimental results demonstrate that slicing can verify complex UML/OCL models and speed up the verification time.

In contrast, this paper presents an improved slicing technique which can still preserve the property under verification for nondisjoint set of submodels. We have also demonstrated results in an external tool, "Alloy," in order to prove that the proposed slicing technique is not limited to a single tool (i.e., UMLtoCSP) but can also be used for other formal verification tools. The slicing procedure breaks the original model into submodels (slices) which can be verified independently and where irrelevant information has been abstracted. The definition of the slicing procedure ensures that the property under verification is preserved after partitioning.

6.1. UML Model Slicing. The theory of *model slicing* to support and maintain large UML models is mostly discussed in the literature. Current approaches of model verification have an exponential worst-case runtime. Context-free slicing of the model summarizes static and structural characteristics

of a UML model. The term context points towards the location of a particular object. It takes into account static and structural aspects of a UML model and excludes the enclosure of interaction information [34]. Similarly, to compute a slice of a class hierarchy of a program, it is necessary to eliminate those slices that are unnecessary thereby ensuring that the behavior of the programs would not be affected. This approach represents the criteria of model abstraction [35].

One possible approach to manage the complexity of the UML metamodel is to divide the metamodel into a set of small metamodels for each discussed UML diagram type [36]. The proposed method defines a metamodel of a directed multigraph for a UML Metamodel Slicer. The slicer builds sub-metamodels for a diagram with model elements. Another slicing technique for static and dynamic UML models presents the transformation of a UML architectural model into a model dependency graph (MDG). It also merges a different sequence of diagrams with relevant information available in a class diagram [37].

6.2. Architectural Slicing. The concept of *architectural slicing* is used to remove irrelevant components and connectors, so that the behavior of the slice is preserved [38]. This research introduces a new way of slicing. Architectural slicing is used to slice a specific part of a system's architecture. The sliced part is used to view high-level specifications. Similar to this approach, a dependency analysis technique is developed which is based on the slicing criteria of an architectural specification as a set of component parts [28]. The technique is named chaining. It supports the development of software architecture by eliminating unnecessary parts of the system.

TABLE 14: Slicing results in Alloy for Tracking System.

Scope	Before slicing			After slicing			
	TT	ST	TT + ST	STT	SST	STT + SST	Speedup %
2	0.020 s	0.046 s	0.066 s	0.005 s	0.008 s	0.013 s	81%
3	0.083 s	0.091 s	0.174 s	0.009 s	0.011 s	0.020 s	89%
4	0.096 s	0.185 s	0.254 s	0.013 s	0.011 s	0.024 s	90%
5	0.158 s	0.173 s	0.332 s	0.020 s	0.012 s	0.032 s	90%
6	0.233 s	0.367 s	0.600 s	0.025 s	0.023 s	0.048 s	92%
7	0.325 s	0.495 s	0.820 s	0.030 s	0.028 s	0.058 s	93%

TT: Translation Time. ST: Solving Time. STT: Sliced Translation Time. SST: Sliced Solving Time.

TABLE 15: Slicing results in Alloy for Script 1.

Scope	Before slicing			After slicing			
	TT	ST	TT + ST	STT	SST	STT + SST	Speedup %
2	0.110 s	0.133 s	0.243 s	0.007 s	0.009 s	0.016 s	93%
3	0.161 s	0.290 s	0.451 s	0.009 s	0.009 s	0.018 s	96%
4	0.224 s	0.591 s	0.815 s	0.014 s	0.012 s	0.026 s	97%
5	0.349 s	0.606 s	0.955 s	0.017 s	0.016 s	0.033 s	97%
6	0.589 s	1.077 s	1.666 s	0.027 s	0.025 s	0.052 s	97%
7	0.799 s	1.392 s	2.191 s	0.038 s	0.025 s	0.063 s	97%

TT: Translation Time. ST: Solving Time. STT: Sliced Translation Time. SST: Sliced Solving Time.

TABLE 16: Slicing results in Alloy for Script 2.

Scope	Before slicing			After slicing			
	TT	ST	TT + ST	STT	SST	STT + SST	Speedup %
2	1.839 s	3.021 s	4.860 s	0.006 s	0.007 s	0.013 s	99.7%
3	2.567 s	7.489 s	10.056 s	0.011 s	0.008 s	0.019 s	99.8%
4	3.374 s	8.320 s	11.694 s	0.014 s	0.009 s	0.023 s	99.8%
5	4.326 s	21.837 s	26.163 s	0.018 s	0.014 s	0.032 s	99.8%
6	5.231 s	32.939 s	38.170 s	0.025 s	0.014 s	0.039 s	99.8%
7	6.477 s	59.704 s	66.181 s	0.035 s	0.016 s	0.051 s	99.9%

TT: Translation Time. ST: Solving Time. STT: Sliced Translation Time. SST: Sliced Solving Time.

TABLE 17: Slicing results in Alloy for Script 3.

Scope	Before slicing			After slicing			
	TT	ST	TT + ST	STT	SST	STT + SST	Speedup %
2	9.548 s	12.941 s	22.489 s	0.006 s	0.008 s	0.014 s	99.93%
3	9.734 s	30.041 s	39.775 s	0.013 s	0.010 s	0.023 s	99.94%
4	12.496 s	66.861 s	79.357 s	0.019 s	0.010 s	0.029 s	99.96%
5	15.702 s	85.001 s	100.703 s	0.022 s	0.013 s	0.035 s	99.96%
6	19.496 s	185.118 s	204.614 s	0.029 s	0.016 s	0.045 s	99.97%
7	23.089 s	259.072 s	282.161 s	0.035 s	0.017 s	0.052 s	99.98%

TT: Translation Time. ST: Solving Time. STT: Sliced Translation Time. SST: Sliced Solving Time.

TABLE 18: Slicing results in Alloy for DBLP conceptual schema.

Scope	Before slicing			After slicing			
	TT	ST	TT + ST	STT	SST	STT + SST	Speedup %
15	10.373 s	3.649 s	14.022 s	5.801 s	0.946 s	6.747 s	52%
17	15.462 s	8.838 s	24.300 s	9.568 s	1.394 s	10.962 s	55%
19	23.170 s	3.958 s	27.128 s	10.656 s	0.872 s	11.528 s	57%

TT: Translation Time. ST: Solving Time. STT: Sliced Translation Time. SST: Sliced Solving Time.

TABLE 19: Some statistical comparisons on empirical observations.

Type of empirical study	Mean values (in seconds)		Standard deviation	
	OVT	TVT	OVT	TVT
UMLtoCSP Verification Time (Table 9)	N/A	0.405	N/A	0.484
Alloy for Paper-Researcher (Table 12)	0.026	0.012	0.027	0.013
Alloy for Coach example (Table 13)	0.087	0.030	0.100	0.034
Alloy for Tracking System (Table 14)	0.469	0.038	0.547	0.042
Alloy for Script 1 (Table 15)	1.304	0.041	1.495	0.045
Alloy for Script 2 (Table 16)	33.695	0.034	40.977	0.037
Alloy for Script 3 (Table 17)	151.112	0.038	185.205	0.040
Alloy for DBLP Conceptual Schema (Table 18)	22.331	9.933	22.165	9.620

OVT: Original Verification Time (before slicing). TVT: Total Verification Time (after slicing).

Furthermore, the notion of dynamic software architecture slicing (DSAS) supports software architecture analysis. This work is useful when a huge amount of components is available. DSAS extracts the useful components of the software architecture [39].

6.3. Program Slicing. Program slicing [1, 31] techniques work on the code level, decomposing source code automatically. In this research, a dataflow algorithm is presented for program slices. A recursive program written in the Pascal language is used to compute the slices. A comparable algorithm is developed to slice the hierarchies of C++ programs. It takes C++ class and inheritance relations as an input and eliminates all those data members, member functions, classes, and relationships that are irrelevant ensuring that the program behavior is maintained. This work inspired us to reduce and eliminate those classes and relationships which do not have any relation to the UML/OCL class diagram [1].

However, to the best of our knowledge, none of the previous approaches consider OCL constrains and none is oriented towards verification of UML/OCL class diagrams. All the related work presented so far is not similar to our approach because it is based on the slicing of UML models while our proposed slicing techniques also cover verifiability of UML/OCL models. In contrast, we compute a slice that includes only those classes which are necessary to preserve in order to satisfy the OCL constraints that restrict the classes.

7. Conclusion and Future Work

This paper presents an evaluation of UML/OCL tools along with benefits and limitations. There is a common problem with the efficiency of the verification process in the UML/OCL tools. Therefore, we have further examined the problem with efficiency analysis, that is, worst-case runtime. We have proposed a slicing technique (UOST) to reduce the verification time in order to improve the efficiency of the verification process. The approach accepts a UML/OCL model as input and automatically breaks it into submodels where the overall model is satisfiable if all submodels are satisfiable. We propose to (1) discard from the model those classes that do not restrict any constraints and are not tightly

coupled and (2) eliminate all attributes irrelevant for the analysis being performed. The presented approach of model slicing can ease model analysis by automatically identifying the parts of the model that are useful to satisfy the properties in the model. During the verification process, complex models require many resources (such as memory consumption and CPU time), making verification unbearable with existing tools. UOST can help reduce the verification time. We have implemented this approach in UMLtoCSP and in an external tool Alloy to provide a proof of concept.

As our future work, we plan to integrate the slicing technique in the HOL-OCL tool and in USE. So far, we have applied the slicing in verification tools, and our next step is to work on validation tools such as USE and Mova.

References

[1] G. Georg, J. Bieman, and R. B. France, "Using alloy and uml/ocl to specify run-time configuration management: a case study," in *Proceedings of UML Workshop on the Practical UML-Based Rigorous Development Methods*, Lecture Notes in Informatics, 2001.

[2] J. Cabot and R. Clarisó, "UML/OCL verification in practice," in *MoDELS'08*, Workshop on Challenges in MDE, 2008.

[3] A. D. Brucker and B. Wolff, "The hol-ocl book," 2010, http://www.brucker.ch/bibliography/download/2006/brucker.ea-hol-ocl-book-2006.pdf.

[4] J. Cabot, R. Clarisó, and D. Riera, "UMLtoCSP: a tool for the formal verification of UML/OCL models using constraint programming," in *Proceedings of the 22nd International Conference on Automated Software Engineering (ASE '07)*, pp. 547–548, ACM, 2007.

[5] M. Gogolla, J. Bohling, and M. Richters, "Validation of uml and ocl models by automatic snapshot generation," in *Proceedings of the 6th International Conference Unified Modeling Language*, pp. 265–279, Springer, 2003.

[6] D. Jackson, "Alloy: a lightweight object modelling notation," *ACM Transactions on Software Engineering and Methodology*, vol. 11, no. 2, pp. 266–290, 2002.

[7] J. Cabot, R. Clarisó, and D. Riera, "Verification of uml/ocl class diagrams using constraint programming," in *Proceedings of the IEEE International Conference on Software Testing Verification and Validation Workshop (ICSTW '08)*, pp. 73–80, IEEE Computer Society, 2008.

[8] D. Berardi, D. Calvanese, and G. De Giacomo, "Reasoning on UML class diagrams," *Artificial Intelligence*, vol. 168, no. 1-2, pp. 70–118, 2005.

[9] M. Balaban and A. Maraee, "A UML-based method for deciding finite satisfiability in description logics," in *DL'2008*, vol. 353 of *CEUR Workshop Proceedings*, 2008.

[10] A. D. Brucker and B. Wolff, "The HOL-OCL book," Tech. Rep. 525, ETH Zurich, 2006.

[11] A. Queralt and E. Teniente, "Reasoning on UML class diagrams with OCL constraints," in *ER'2006*, vol. 4215 of *LNCS*, pp. 497–512, Springer, 2006.

[12] A. Maraee and M. Balaban, "Eficient reasoning about finite satisfiability of UML class diagrams with constrained generalization sets," in *ECMDA-FA'2007*, vol. 4530 of *LNCS*, pp. 17–31, Springer, 2007.

[13] D. Jackson, *Software Abstractions: Logic, Language and Analysis*, MIT Press, 2006.

[14] J. Cabot, R. Clariso, E. Guerra, and J. de Lara, "Verification and validation of declarative model-to-model transformations through invariants," *Journal of Systems and Software*, vol. 83, no. 2, pp. 283–302, 2010.

[15] A. Shaikh, R. Clarisó, U. K. Wiil, and N. Memon, "Verification-driven slicing of uml/ocl models," in *Proceedings of the 25th IEEE/ACM International Conference on Automated Software Engineering (ASE '10)*, ACM, 2010.

[16] A. Shaikh, U. K. Wiil, and N. Memon, "Uost: Uml/ocl aggressive slicing technique for eficient verification of models," in *SAM*, pp. 173–192, 2010.

[17] A. D. Brucker and B. Wolff, "Hol-ocl: a formal proof environment for uml/ocl," in *Proceedings of the Fundamental Approaches to Software Engineering Conference (FASE '08)*, pp. 97–100, 2008.

[18] Object Management Group, "Unified modeling language," 2010, http://www.uml.org.

[19] Object Management Group, "Object constraint 6 language," 2010, http://www.omg.org/spec/OCL/2.0/.

[20] ArgoUML, Argouml, 2010, http://argouml.tigris.org.

[21] K. R. Apt and M. G. Wallace, *Constraint Logic Programming using ECL^{i}PS^e*, Cambridge University Press, 2007.

[22] B. Demuth, "The Dresden OCL toolkit and its role in Information Systems development," in *Proceedings of the 13th International Conference on Information Systems Development (ISD '04)*, Vilnius, Lithuania, 2004.

[23] "Uml2alloy," http://www.cs.bham.ac.uk/~bxb/UML2Alloy/.

[24] M. Gogolla, J. Bohling, and M. Richters, "Validating UML and OCL models in USE by automatic snapshot generation," *Software and Systems Modeling*, vol. 4, no. 4, pp. 386–398, 2005.

[25] MOVA, Mova, 2010, http://maude.sip.ucm.es/mova.

[26] M. Clavel, M. Egea, and V. T. D. Silva, "Mova: a tool for modeling, measuring and validating uml class diagrams," 2007.

[27] M. Clave, F. Durán, S. Eker et al., "Maude: specification and programming in rewriting logic," *Theoretical Computer Science*, vol. 285, no. 2, pp. 187–243, 2002.

[28] D. J. R. J. A. Stafford and A. L. Wolf, "Chaining: a software architecture depen- dence analysis technique," Tech. Rep., University of Colorado Department of Computer Science, 1997.

[29] F. Lanubile and G. Visaggio, "Extracting reusable functions by flow graph-based program slicing," *IEEE Transactions on Software Engineering*, vol. 23, no. 4, pp. 246–259, 1997.

[30] Q. Lu, F. Zhang, and J. Qian, "Program slicing: its improved algorithm and application in verification," *Journal of Computer Science and Technology*, vol. 3, no. 1, pp. 29–39, 1988.

[31] M. Weiser, "Program slicing," *IEEE Transactions on Software Engineering*, vol. SE-10, no. 4, pp. 352–357, 1984.

[32] J. Cabot, R. Clariso, and D. Riera, "Papers and researchers: an example of an unsatisfiable uml/ocl model," http://gres.uoc.edu/UMLtoCSP/examples/Papers-Researchers.pdf.

[33] DBLP, Digital bibliography andy library project, http://guifre.lsi.upc.edu/DBLP.pdf.

[34] H. H. Kagdi, J. I. Maletic, and A. Sutton, "Context-free slicing of UML class models," in *Proceedings of the IEEE ICSM International Conference on Software Maintenance (ICSM '05)*, pp. 635–638, IEEE Computer Society, 2005.

[35] J.-D. Choi, J. H. Field, G. Ramalingam, and F. Tip, "Method and apparatus for slicing class hierarchies," http://www.patentstorm.us/patents/6179491.html.

[36] J. H. Bae, K. Lee, and H. S. Chae, "Modularization of the UML metamodel using model slicing," in *ITNG*, pp. 1253–1254, IEEE Computer Society, 2008.

[37] J. T. Lallchandani and R. Mall, "Slicing UML architectural models," in *ACM/SIGSOFT SEN*, vol. 33, pp. 1–9, 2008.

[38] J. Zhao, "Applying slicing technique to software architectures," CoRR, cs.SE/0105008, 2001.

[39] T. Kim, Y.-T. Song, L. Chung, and D. T. Huynh, "Dynamic software architecture slicing," in *Proceedings of the 23rd International Computer Software and Applications Conference (COMPSAC '99)*, pp. 61–66, IEEE Computer Society, 1999.

Permissions

The contributors of this book come from diverse backgrounds, making this book a truly international effort. This book will bring forth new frontiers with its revolutionizing research information and detailed analysis of the nascent developments around the world.

We would like to thank all the contributing authors for lending their expertise to make the book truly unique. They have played a crucial role in the development of this book. Without their invaluable contributions this book wouldn't have been possible. They have made vital efforts to compile up to date information on the varied aspects of this subject to make this book a valuable addition to the collection of many professionals and students.

This book was conceptualized with the vision of imparting up-to-date information and advanced data in this field. To ensure the same, a matchless editorial board was set up. Every individual on the board went through rigorous rounds of assessment to prove their worth. After which they invested a large part of their time researching and compiling the most relevant data for our readers. Conferences and sessions were held from time to time between the editorial board and the contributing authors to present the data in the most comprehensible form. The editorial team has worked tirelessly to provide valuable and valid information to help people across the globe.

Every chapter published in this book has been scrutinized by our experts. Their significance has been extensively debated. The topics covered herein carry significant findings which will fuel the growth of the discipline. They may even be implemented as practical applications or may be referred to as a beginning point for another development. Chapters in this book were first published by Hindawi Publishing Corporation; hereby published with permission under the Creative Commons Attribution License or equivalent.

The editorial board has been involved in producing this book since its inception. They have spent rigorous hours researching and exploring the diverse topics which have resulted in the successful publishing of this book. They have passed on their knowledge of decades through this book. To expedite this challenging task, the publisher supported the team at every step. A small team of assistant editors was also appointed to further simplify the editing procedure and attain best results for the readers.

Our editorial team has been hand-picked from every corner of the world. Their multi-ethnicity adds dynamic inputs to the discussions which result in innovative outcomes. These outcomes are then further discussed with the researchers and contributors who give their valuable feedback and opinion regarding the same. The feedback is then collaborated with the researches and they are edited in a comprehensive manner to aid the understanding of the subject.

Apart from the editorial board, the designing team has also invested a significant amount of their time in understanding the subject and creating the most relevant covers. They scrutinized every image to scout for the most suitable representation of the subject and create an appropriate cover for the book.

The publishing team has been involved in this book since its early stages. They were actively engaged in every process, be it collecting the data, connecting with the contributors or procuring relevant information. The team has been an ardent support to the editorial, designing and production team. Their endless efforts to recruit the best for this project, has resulted in the accomplishment of this book. They are a veteran in the field of academics and their pool of knowledge is as vast as their experience in printing. Their expertise and guidance has proved useful at every step. Their uncompromising quality standards have made this book an exceptional effort. Their encouragement from time to time has been an inspiration for everyone.

The publisher and the editorial board hope that this book will prove to be a valuable piece of knowledge for researchers, students, practitioners and scholars across the globe.

List of Contributors

Takashi Yamanoue, Kentaro Oda and Koichi Shimozono
Computing and Communications Center, Kagoshima University, Korimoto, Kagoshima 890-0065, Japan

Keisuke Hotta, Yui Sasaki, Yukiko Sano, Yoshiki Higo and Shinji Kusumoto
Graduate School of Information Science and Technology, Osaka University, Osaka 565-0871, Japan

Pablo Becker and Luis Olsina
GIDIS Web, Engineering School, Universidad Nacional de La Pampa, General Pico, Argentina

Philip Lew
School of Software, Beihang University, Beijing, China

Mourad Badri and Fadel Toure
Software Engineering Research Laboratory, Department of Mathematics and Computer Science, University of Quebec at Trois-Rivieres, Trois-Rivieres, QC, Canada G9A 5H7

Marc Zeller and Christian Prehofer
Fraunhofer Institute for Communication Systems ESK, Hansastraße 32, 80686 Munich, Germany

Osamu Mizuno and Michi Nakai
Kyoto Institute of Technology, Matsugasaki Goshokaido-cho, Sakyo-ku, Kyoto 606-8585, Japan

Gabriel A. Archanjo and Fernando J. Von Zuben
Laboratory of Bioinformatics and Bioinspired Computing, School of Electrical and Computer Engineering, University of Campinas (Unicamp), 13083-970 Campinas, SP, Brazil

Li-Min Liu
Department of Applied Mathematics, Chung Yuan Christian University, 200 Chung Pei Road, Chung Li 32023, Taiwan

Mark Shtern and Vassilios Tzerpos
Department of Computer Science and Engineering, York University, Toronto, ON, Canada M3J 1P3

Nary Subramanian
Department of Computer Science, University of Texas at Tyler, Tyler, TX 75799, USA

Steven Drager and William McKeever
Information Directorate, Air Force Research Lab, Rome, NY 13441, USA

Antonio Munoz, Pablo Anton and Antonio Mana
Escuela Tecnica Superior de Ingeniería Informatica, Universidad de Malaga, Spain

Massimo Ficco
Dipartimento di Ingegneria dell'Informazione, Seconda Universita di Napoli Via Roma, 81031 Aversa (CE), Italy
Laboratorio ITeM "C. Savy", Consorzio CINI, Via Cinthia-Edificio 1, 80126 Napoli, Italy

Roberto Pietrantuono
Dipartimento di Informatica e Sistemistica, Universita di Napoli Federico II, Via Claudio 21, 80125 Napoli, Italy

Stefano Russo
Laboratorio ITeM "C. Savy", Consorzio CINI, Via Cinthia-Edificio 1, 80126 Napoli, Italy
Dipartimento di Informatica e Sistemistica, Universita di Napoli Federico II, Via Claudio 21, 80125 Napoli, Italy

Asadullah Shaikh
The Maersk Mc-Kinney Moller Institute, University of Southern Denmark, 5230 Odense, Denmark
Universitat Oberta de Catalunya, Barcelona 08018, Spain

Uffe Kock Wiil
The Maersk Mc-Kinney Moller Institute, University of Southern Denmark, 5230 Odense, Denmark

Nasrullah Memon
The Maersk Mc-Kinney Moller Institute, University of Southern Denmark, 5230 Odense, Denmark
Mehran University of Engineering & Technology, Jamshoro 76062, Pakistan

Printed in the USA
CPSIA information can be obtained
at www.ICGtesting.com
JSHW051441221024
72173JS00006B/1542

9 781632 402943